"The exerciser's Old Testament."—*Time*
"The Bible of the fitness movement."—*Newsweek*
"The pioneer."—*Fortune*

THE AEROBICS WAY is a vital program to help improve health, increase longevity, and prevent heart attacks—a program that can be tailored to the needs of any individual, of any age, a program that has already changed the lives of millions.

THE AEROBICS WAY brings together for the first time:

—A complete compendium of all the information you want and need to begin an Aerobics program: why it is good for you, what it will do, how to start, how to keep going.
—A totally new Chart Pack for men and women of all ages that leads you gradually, week by week, to good health through any number of possible exercises, including jogging, walking, swimming, cycling, racquetball, and many, many more.
—A new, up-to-date, accurate set of point c⋯⋯⋯⋯⋯⋯⋯⋯⋯bics points e⋯⋯⋯
—⋯⋯⋯⋯⋯⋯⋯⋯⋯t with the ⋯⋯⋯⋯⋯⋯⋯⋯ed at the ⋯

Bantam Books by Kenneth H. Cooper, M.D.
Ask your bookseller for the books you have missed

AEROBICS
AEROBICS FOR WOMEN (with Mildred Cooper)
THE AEROBICS WAY
THE NEW AEROBICS
THE AEROBICS PROGRAM FOR TOTAL WELL-BEING
RUNNING WITHOUT FEAR

Dr. Kenneth H. Cooper's Preventive Medicine Program
CONTROLLING CHOLESTEROL

# the aerobics way

New Data on the World's Most
Popular Exercise Program

by

Kenneth H. Cooper, M.D., M.PH.

BANTAM BOOKS
TORONTO • NEW YORK • LONDON • SYDNEY • AUCKLAND

*This edition contains the complete text
of the original hardcover edition.*
NOT ONE WORD HAS BEEN OMITTED.

THE AEROBICS WAY
*A Bantam Book / published by arrangement with
M. Evans and Company, Inc.*

*PRINTING HISTORY*
*M. Evans edition published November 1977*
*2nd printing* . . . . . . . . . . . . . . *November 1977*
*3rd printing* . . . . . . . . . . . . . . *November 1977*
*Playboy Book Club edition March 1978*
*Sports Illustrated Book Club edition February 1978*
*Good Health Club edition March 1978*
*Bantam edition / September 1978
12 printings through January 1989*

*Cover photograph by Bob Kornegay/Freelance
Photographers Guild*

*All rights reserved.
Copyright © 1977 by Kenneth H. Cooper.
No part of this book may be reproduced or transmitted
in any form or by any means, electronic or mechanical,
including photocopying, recording, or by any information
storage and retrieval system, without permission in writing
from the publisher.
For information address: M. Evans and Company, Inc.,
216 E. 49th Street, New York, New York 10017.*

ISBN 0-554-26083-9

*Published simultaneously in the United States and Canada*

Bantam Books are published by Bantam Books, a division of Bantam Doubleday Dell
Publishing Group, Inc. Its trademark, consisting of the words "Bantam Books" and
the portrayal of a rooster, is Registered in U.S. Patent and Trademark Office and in
other countries. Marca Registrada. Bantam Books, 666 Fifth Avenue, New York,
New York 10103.

PRINTED IN THE UNITED STATES OF AMERICA

KR   21   20   19   18   17   16   15   14   13   12

To my son Tyler, who at six years of age has shown great patience and understanding in accepting the long hours of work required in the preparation of this book when he would much rather have had Daddy spending that time with him

# Acknowledgments

I want to express my appreciation of and acknowledge the contribution of Robert Hardesty in the preliminary development of this manuscript and the wisdom and guidance of Charles Veley in finalizing it. The staff of the Aerobics Center has been most supportive and nearly all the new charts and data came from the Institute for Aerobics Research. Our research librarian Mary Fay Marks was of special assistance in preparation of the bibliography. Yet, without question, my most helpful and constructive critic continues to be my loving wife, Millie, who has that unique ability to communicate in both the spoken and written word.

# Contents

# Preface

In 1968 *Aerobics* was published in an effort to make the American people more aware of their need for exercise and to encourage them to use exercise in the practice of preventive medicine. *Aerobics* resulted from years of research, working with relatively young United States Air Force personnel. The program was therefore designed primarily for men under thirty years of age.

Yet, much to my surprise, the majority of the people who purchased *Aerobics* were over forty, and many were women. This necessitated the publication of *The New Aerobics* in 1970. There we deemphasized initial field testing (the twelve-minute test), particularly for people over thirty-five years of age, and encouraged a six-week starter program followed by age-adjusted progressive programs. Greater emphasis was placed on the initial-screening physical examination. In later editions of *The New Aerobics* the point system was changed to incorporate the concept of endurance points, awarding more points for longer-endurance-type activities. The emphasis in *The New Aerobics* was on exercising safely.

Still, neither of the first two books was written for women. Realizing that women have special needs and problems, my wife, Millie, and I collaborated on *Aerobics for Women*, published in 1972. This book was written specifically for women, with answers to the questions and needs that many had brought to our attention.

Now, in the last five years, knowledge in the area of exercise as it applies to the practice of preventive and rehabilitative medicine has increased tremendously. Some of this information has come from research being conducted at our own Aerobics Center here in Dallas, Texas. Since 1971 we have had the ideal organization to study the medical value of exercise: a medical clinic where over 10,000 patients have been extensively evaluated (the Cooper Clinic); a medically prescribed and supervised exercise program with over 1300 active members (the Aerobics Activity Center); and a research institute whose responsibility is conducting research and collecting, storing, and analyzing data from the other two divisions (the Institute for Aerobics Research). As a result of the studies being conducted at the Aerobics Center and the research of countless others, we have probably learned more in the past five years than we did in the previous twenty.

That new information plus the consolidation of all the programs is the basis for this volume. Readers of the previous books will find some repetition of concepts and ideas first introduced in the original books, but they will also find considerable new information further substantiating the need for exercise in the maintenance of good health. I hope my new readers will find this a book that is complete, concise, and motivating. Regardless of whether you are young, old, overweight, athletic, or suffering from heart disease, you will find programs that can be utilized safely and effectively. Consult with your physician, read the book in its entirety, and then embark on a program that can add a new dimension to your life. Millions of people all over the world have discovered the satisfaction, pride, and sense of well-being that accompany the disciplined, physically active, and healthy life. I hope you will join these swelling ranks and begin to appreciate the statement that "it is easier to maintain good health than it is to regain it, once it is lost."

Get fit . . . keep fit . . . and may you enjoy life to its fullest!

KENNETH H. COOPER, M.D.

*Dallas, 1977*

# 1

# Aerobics: Its Need and Social Acceptance

Any book or exercise program concentrating on the maintenance of good health must immediately consider the number one health problem in the Western hemisphere: heart and blood vessel disease. Nearly one million people die annually in the United States from diseases of the cardiovascular system—accounting for 55 percent of all deaths.

Concepts in the treatment and prevention of disease of the heart and blood vessels have changed dramatically over the years. In the 1950s, when I was in medical school, the accepted way to treat heart disease was bedrest, restricted activity, medications, and, in selected cases, surgery. The major emphasis was on treatment and very little attention was placed on prevention. Consequently the problem continued to increase almost to epidemic proportions, and not only among older patients. Between the years 1950 and 1970 the greatest increase in deaths from heart attacks was in young men 25 to 44 years of age. In men 45 to 64 years of age there was only a minimal increase.

Tremendous expenditures of public and private funds were made in an effort almost exclusively to treat this problem. During this twenty-year period the annual cost of health care in this country increased dramatically from $12 billion to $70 billion. After 1970 the health care cost rose at an even greater rate, and in 1975 the cost approached $120 billion. Since for the first time health care spending approached defense spending, a move was made to control these spiraling costs.

It was obvious that the way to reduce the cost of medical

care was not through more hospitals, more physicians, more sophisticated and expensive equipment, but through prevention and teaching people preventive care. It was not so much that people were dying; they were killing themselves! Specialists in preventive medicine have proclaimed for years that with proper weight, proper diet, proper exercise, controlling blood pressure, and eliminating the use of tobacco, heart disease can be controlled, and this is the major reason this book is being written: to provide updated guidelines that will help you in the implementation of these fundamental principles of preventive medicine, particularly preventive cardiology. There are age-adjusted, sex-adjusted systematized exercise programs, dietary recommendations, suggestions regarding weight and blood pressure control, and tips on how to quit smoking—all necessary if you want to assure yourself of maximal protection from one of the self-inflicted diseases in the Western hemisphere.

It was in this spirit of preventive medicine that the aerobics program was developed in the early 1960s and the first book published in 1968. Today we are immensely gratified that the response exceeds all our previous expectations. The basic tools of aerobics—the 12-minute field test, the treadmill tests used to diagnose heart disease and to determine levels of fitness, the point system to measure the amount of exercise, the progressive programs to furnish a weekly prescription for exercise—are now in use today by millions of people all over the world. Come with me now on a whirlwind tour around the world and let's see what is happening.

Our first stop is the beautiful islands of Hawaii, not really "abroad," but it seems that way. Without question, Hawaii—particularly Honolulu—is the jogging capital of the world. Throughout the day and night, people jog all over the islands, encouraged by the mild climate and light Pacific breezes. Kapiolani Park in Honolulu is the most popular place, especially in the late afternoon and on weekends. Each Sunday morning Dr. Jack Scaff, a leading cardiologist, conducts a marathon clinic, open to all.

It is not uncommon to have over one thousand people attend one of the Sunday morning sessions—including the lieutenant governor, the Honorable Nelson K. Doi. Among those thousand, Dr. Scaff has a very active group of runners who are running marathons even though all have had one or more heart attacks! He and his postcoronary patients are dramatically changing some of our concepts about the treatment of patients following heart attacks.

From Hawaii we travel to the thriving, industrialized islands of Japan, where heart disease was infrequent until the post–World War II era. In conjunction with a thriving economy and an acceptance of Western eating and smoking habits has occurred an epidemic of obesity and an alarming increase in the incidence of heart disease. Foreseeing a problem, the government began to sponsor preventive medicine programs and, overnight, the jogging boom hit Japan. Recently, while I was visiting in Tokyo, my Japanese host said, "Dr. Cooper, I will be willing to make a wager that any time of the day or night we drive around the Imperial Palace, we will find at least one person jogging."

"In the heart of downtown Tokyo?" I asked.

"Yes, and you will see both sexes and all ages!"

I'm happy I didn't accept his wager; there were almost as many joggers in Tokyo as there were in Honolulu.

Aerobics, exercise, and preventive medicine have no language, ethnic, or cultural barriers. I am convinced that people everywhere are interested in better health and physical fitness. For, you see, "how we live so often determines how we die."

Throughout the Orient, whether it was Korea, Hong Kong, Singapore, or Indonesia, people were exercising in search of that better life. I can recall the tropical island of Bali in eastern Indonesia where I lectured to a group of young physical educators in the midst of a tropical rainstorm. Every ear tuned in to the lecture entitled "How exercise can be used as a means of achieving optimum health."

It has now been almost ten years since the first *Aerobics* publications were released, and during that time it has been a continual source of inspiration to meet people, all over the world, who are "aerobically" involved. The books have been translated into many foreign languages including German, Portuguese, Spanish, Swedish, Japanese, Hebrew, Russian, and Dutch.

During the summer of 1975 I was invited to visit West Germany to personally observe one of the government-supported cardiac clinics. The largest of the twenty-five clinics is Höhenreid, located sixty kilometers from Munich. There are 550 beds in this ultramodern hospital, 330 of which are set aside for preventive programs. If an employee has several coronary risk factors (such as a lack of physical fitness, high blood pressure, stress, and obesity) he or she is encouraged to spend four weeks at one of their centers in a closely supervised dietary, exercise, and educational program. The remaining 220 beds are for patients who have already had heart attacks, and their rehabilitation program lasts six weeks. Do you know what it costs each patient for such personalized attention? Nothing! The cost is paid by insurance companies, the government, and industry. Long ago it was discovered in Germany that it was cheaper to keep people healthy than to get them healthy, and cheaper to rehabilitate than to replace! We have been a little slow in this country to accept these basic principles of preventive and rehabilitative medicine.

Would you believe that a heart association would sponsor the establishment of measured courses where people can determine their aerobic fitness by means of a jogging test? I wouldn't have believed it, either, but in Holland it's happened. Over one hundred "Cooperbahn" courses, 1,000 meters in length, have been established all over the Netherlands so the Dutch people can take the "Coopertest." Physical activity, including walking, cycling, skating, and running, is an accepted way of life in Holland—and, in cooperation with the Dutch Sports Federation, the Dutch Heart Association is encouraging this movement.

What country has over 80 million people involved in its competitive sports movement, four large institutes for physical culture, and a sports program heavily supported by its government? Recall which country usually wins the greatest number of medals in the Summer Olympics. Yes, Russia. For many years there has been a large sports program in Russia, but only recently has jogging "hit the public hard." In Moscow, jogging is rapidly growing in popularity and the local polyclinics give advice and instructions. All new housing projects must have athletic facilities, ranging from swimming pools and soccer fields to ministadiums and tracks. There is no ruble-pinching in Russia when it comes to the sports movement. Russians believe that when they invest in sports, they are investing in good health.

To wind up this worldwide tour, let's visit a country that without doubt is the aerobics capital of the world. The only problem is that "aerobics" doesn't translate well into Portuguese and they have nicknamed the program "Cooper." In fact, in Brazil when people ask, "Have you done your Cooper?" they are asking, "Have you done your jogging?" In 1969–70 the Brazilian *futebol* team (soccer to us) used the aerobics program for off-season conditioning in preparation for the World Cup play in Mexico City in July 1970. The players responded well to their program and were highly conditioned by the time of the World Cup play. As a result, they overwhelmed their opponents in the second half of play, won six consecutive matches, and retired the World Cup, since this was their third win.

The aerobics program was popular immediately throughout South America, but particularly Brazil. COOPER signs were set up marking off jogging courses so people could take the "Coopertest." What a thrill it is to go to Rio de Janeiro, jog along Copacabana beach with hundreds of Brazilian men, women, and children, and every 400 meters pass a permanent COOPER sign marking off the course. The Reverend Billy Graham knew of this interest in Brazil and also knew of my Christian commitment when he asked me to accompany him to Rio to participate in his evangelistic crusade. One of the highlights of my life was that Sunday afternoon, October 6, 1974, when I gave a brief testimony on the interrelationship between physical and spiritual fitness to an audience of nearly 240,000 people assembled in Maracanã Stadium.

Throughout the world, aerobics is joining the preventive medicine boom—just as it should, according to the words of Marc Lalonde, Canadian Minister of National Health and Welfare:

Good health is the bedrock on which social progress is built. A nation of healthy people can do those things that make life worthwhile, and as the level of health increases, so does the potential for happiness.

In the United States, it's also been most gratifying to see the upsurge in fitness interest. There are now estimated to be 8–10 million *regular* joggers in America today. Here in Dallas, nearly 800 people run daily at our Aerobics Center, logging more than 1,500 miles. Many of these runners are top corporate officials.

In fact, each October business leaders from all over the United States come to the Aerobics Center to run in the Tyler Cup, a corporate track meet named in honor of the Dallas-based corporation that sponsors it. To qualify an executive must be over thirty-five years of age, must rank in the top ten of his corporation, and must be able to run two miles. In 1976 Tyler Cup V attracted 160 participants, representing sixty corporations from fifteen states. All were board chairmen, chief executive officers, presidents, or in other top corporate positions.

Why do they come from so far away to run around a track? "The main idea is to promote fitness among business leaders, their employees and families," says Tyler Corporation president Joseph McKinney. "These men have gotten the message about fitness. We hope they take it back to the 700,000 employees they represent."

Of course, running is only the visible tip of the iceberg. Tennis, raquetball, cycling, skiing, swimming, soccer— these aerobic sports are also at a record high. A national survey conducted by the President's Council on Fitness estimated that in 1974 nearly 60 million Americans were engaged in some type of regular physical activity.

Already the statistics are beginning to show a change. Since the late 1960s there has been almost a 14 percent decrease in death from heart disease, along with a slight increase in the average American's life span from 70.9 years in 1970 to 72.0 in 1974. Why the good news? Noted cardiovascular specialist Weldon J. Walker gives credit to more preventive action, controlling risk factors associated with cardiovascular disease and strokes. And famous heart surgeon Michael DeBakey recently said that prevention is the "only approach" to controlling heart disease that offers hope for the future.

We have truly begun to attack the problem of heart disease, but we have far to go. Every year American industry now loses $19.4 *billion* in production time because of premature coronary death and pays $15 billion just for employee sick leave.

General Motors spends more for employee health care than it does for the purchase of steel.

Today, according to 1976 findings published in the *American Heart Journal,* one man in three will have symptomatic arterial disease *before* age sixty. And early death from acute myocardial infarction will be the first and only "symptom" in about 40 percent of these cases. If you're an American, the odds are very strong, no matter who you are, that your heart needs help—with a systematized preventive program.

But let's consider the alternatives—the treatment options currently available if your heart hasn't had preventive care and does begin to show symptoms. We have medications for treatment of some cases. There are the well-publicized heart transplants and pacemakers, and there is also the widely used coronary bypass operation, in which occluded coronary arteries are bypassed with other blood vessels.

How effective is coronary bypass surgery? There have been a number of questions raised recently on this subject that are certainly worth consideration, since each of these operations cost an average $10,000 to $15,000. In 1974 alone, Americans paid $800 million just for this one operation, for which the average hospital mortality rate varies from 0.8 to 4 percent. One study published in the *New England Journal of Medicine* concludes that treatment with medications gave results comparable to surgery for patients in the "high risk" category of coronary insufficiency, who would normally be candidates for bypass surgery. Another study on almost 900 men who had had this surgical procedure showed that, within a median time of fourteen months following surgery, 11 percent of those under age fifty-five and 26 percent of those older had retired from their jobs. In addition, 30 percent of all the other patients had changed their occupational status following the operation. Only one fifth of those who were retired before surgery went back to work. If active rehabilitation is not practiced after the operation, the same problem will probably recur.

What about medication, transplants, pacemakers? Again, consider the expense, and consider the odds—which are no more encouraging than those for coronary bypass surgery. Also, consider that if you do require medical or surgical treatment, you must still follow many of the preventive or rehabilitative medical practices outlined in this book.

But if your first symptom is sudden death, as it is for approximately 40 percent of all heart attack victims, our advanced treatment techniques, our coronary care units, our defibrillators, and our cardiac rehabilitation programs will have come too late. That's the strongest possible reason why your heart needs help now, and the strongest possible reason for following the programs this book outlines.

In these chapters you will also find an evaluation of current anti-exercise and mini-exercise theories, including those of the *Type A Behavior and Your Heart*, "Jogging Can Kill You," and *Total Fitness in 30 Minutes a Week* theorists. We will discuss and evaluate some highly publicized weight reduction plans, including the Atkins and Stillman diets, and provide the information you need to begin a diet that is medically sound. We will discuss the effect that fitness has on emotional stress and mental performance, and on other areas of your own health.

Finally, this book will answer many of the special questions I regularly hear about exercise, and about the special concerns of men, women, children, teen-agers, senior citizens, and athletes.

I hope you will go over the data thoroughly with your physician. Chances are he has kept up with the trend toward preventive medicine and that he will already be familiar with the research you will read about here. But if he's not, I hope you will take time to point out how you are interested in a preventive program, rather than in simply recovering from whatever difficulties your heart, and you, may encounter.

So whether you're healthy now, or are coronary-prone, or have just undergone bypass surgery, my objective is the same. I want you to begin the regular system of aerobic exercise and preventive medical maintenance that this book outlines in detail.

I want you to stay away from confusing fads and claims, from remedies that are of minimal benefit, and from those that may mask more serious problems and so do more harm than good.

I want you to enjoy feeling better than you have felt for many years—and I want you to continue feeling that way for many years to come.

# 2

# Where Do I Start?
# A Thorough Evaluation
# of Your Heart

With heart disease still at epidemic proportions, you would think that the details of a cardiac examination would be as familiar to Americans as, say, flu immunization shots. Yet I can assure you that this is not the case. In fact, the vast majority of the nearly 2 million men and women who will become coronary statistics this year will never have had a complete examination of their heart, including a maximal performance stress electrocardiogram. Many of them will *never* have had even a resting electrocardiogram. And this is also true for most American men and women ages 35–54, for whom heart attacks rank either number one or number two as the leading cause of death.

Why do we in the United States have such a dismal record of using this or other proven diagnostic techniques now available? We could speculate on a number of reasons, many based on the reluctance of most of us to visit the doctor or the dentist for any kind of checkup unless there's something wrong with us. Also, physicians, as we've said, bear their share of the responsibility for not placing more emphasis on prevention and practicing it themselves. Insurance companies, for their failure to offset costs of preventive examinations with health insurance benefits, have likewise been found at fault.

Yet, regardless of who's to blame, the issue is meaningless for you unless you make the effort and take the exam yourself. And it will take some effort, believe me.

"Wait a minute," I can hear you saying, "I already

had my physical checkup this year. It wasn't much of an effort, even when I had the blood sample taken. What's so different about a preventive medical examination?"

In a word, exercise. A complete cardiac examination not only consists of the blood tests, the medical history, listening to the chest, and blood pressure determination that nearly everyone is familiar with; it also requires that your heart be monitored during rest and exercise with an electrocardiograph. This monitoring is called a maximal or near-maximal performance exercise electrocardiogram or, in shorter terms, a stress ECG.

Don't confuse the stress ECG with a resting ECG. If your physician monitors your heart's performance while you recline on the examining table, that's a resting electrocardiogram. Metal electrodes are taped to several points on your chest and torso, and wires running from those electrodes carry the electrical signals that travel throughout the cells of your heart during every beat to the electrocardiograph, which records those signals on paper. Heart tissue that is functioning normally conducts this electricity according to a certain recognizable pattern. If part of the heart tissue is not functioning normally, the flow of electricity is diverted, changing the pattern that appears on the electrocardiograph accordingly.

Several electrodes are used to get a "look" at the heart, electrically speaking, from several different points of view. The signal sent by one area of your heart may indicate a normal function in that area, where at the same time another area, better "seen" electrically by an electrode taped to a different spot on your torso, may be sending signals that indicate a problem. By switching the electrocardiograph machine to record signals from each of these electrode "cameras" one at a time, your physician can get an electronic look at each separate area of your heart. The more electrodes used, the more specifically the physician can pinpoint the location of any given problem your heart's having as you lie there, at rest, on the examination table.

# The Stress ECG

Yet the resting ECG is not an adequate test for heart abnormality. The reason for this inadequacy is not at all difficult to understand: it's as basic as the need for a highway test if you're about to buy a used car. You wouldn't switch on the ignition, let the engine idle there in the parking lot, and then buy the car, would you? Of course not. If you wanted to test that car for problems, you'd get it out on the highway. You'd accelerate to a high speed. You'd see how that car performed under stress. And out on the highway you might find problems showing up that you'd never have noticed if you'd just stayed in the parking lot and listened to the engine idle.

The same principle holds true for your heart. In order to determine if it has problem areas that need attention, we have to see how it performs under stress. When it's functioning at a high rate of speed, it may have difficulties that simply don't show up while you're resting. And since your heart needs to function at high speeds on various occasions during your daily routine, we ought to know about those difficulties so we can take action.

# Maximal Heart Rate

How high should your heart rate be elevated in order to give your heart's performance an adequate test? Well, depending on your age and condition, there is a limit to how fast your heart *should* go, no matter how long or how hard you exercise. This limit is termed the maximal heart rate. It's the level at which the heart is being worked to its utmost capacity. Based on the results of thousands of exercise stress tests on men and women of all ages, we have established norms to predict the maximal heart rate for you before you take your test. The predicted maximal rates decrease as you get older—as you can see from this chart. (A more complete chart appears in the appendix.)

If you study this chart carefully, you will see that in response to physical conditioning, younger people notice a slight decrease in maximal heart rate, whereas older people show a marked increase. This seems somewhat paradoxical unless you understand the physiology behind it. The conditioned heart seems to function most efficiently at a maximal rate between 175 and 190. During exercise, the unconditioned heart tends to beat faster in younger people, and slower in older people. As the heart responds to physical training, the amount of work the heart is capable of performing increases and the volume of blood pumped with each beat (stroke volume) also increases, allowing for this crossover effect. Certainly the maximal heart rate decreases with age, but much more slowly in physically fit people as compared to those who are totally inactive.

### PREDICTED MAXIMAL HEART RATES
(Beats per minute)
### INSTITUTE FOR AEROBICS RESEARCH

| AGE | VERY POOR & POOR CONDITION | FAIR CONDITION | GOOD OR ABOVE |
|---|---|---|---|
| 20 | 201 | 201 | 196 |
| 30 | 190 | 193 | 191 |
| 40 | 179 | 186 | 186 |
| 50 | 168 | 179 | 180 |
| 60 | 158 | 172 | 175 |
| 70 | 147 | 165 | 170 |

The predicted maximal heart rate will be the general target that your physician uses to determine an end point for your exercise stress test. To put it another way, he (or she) will encourage you to keep exercising until your heart is beating at approximately its maximal rate—unless, of course, any irregularity begins to appear on the electrocardiograph monitor. Should any such irregularity appear, the exercise is always terminated immediately. The heartbeat is monitored by the electrocardiograph during the recovery period also—the time during which you've stopped exercising and are sitting or lying down, getting your wind back. I might add that it's monitored very closely during recovery, since a number of irregularities do not show up until this point of the examination is reached.

All right, then, you can expect to exercise during this examination. What kind of exercise? There are three varieties presently in use for these tests, though only one of the three meets our requirements for an adequate test.

The oldest of the stress tests requires you to exercise by stepping up and down on an elevation of some sort: a small footstool, a stepstool, or one or two stair steps, for example. With electrodes taped to your torso, you step up and down repeatedly and rapidly for a given amount of time, elevating your heart rate. Then you sit or lie down and rest, and the electrocardiograph is switched on and the reading taken. It's necessary to wait until after you've finished the up-and-down motion to take the reading, since the vigorous jolting would interfere with the electrical signals.

The difficulty with this type of test is that it does not provide an exercise electrocardiogram at all—only a recovery electrocardiogram. Further, it lacks the precision of a treadmill test, because there is no way to ensure that you are stepping along at a precise rate. Your physician can encourage you to keep up with a metronome or some other pacing device, of course, but there's nothing to keep you from slowing down or speeding up—or both. With the step test, the sensitivity for detecting early heart disease is less than it is with the other techniques.

The second variety of stress test uses a stationary bicycle. You pump the pedals, working against a certain amount of resistance in the mechanism. Your speed against this resistance can be measured and, taken with the amount of time you're pedaling away, provides a total amount of "work" that you've done—which is why this is often called a bicycle "ergometer" test. It's widely used in Europe, as are bicycles.

The bicycle ergometer has two distinct advantages over the step test. First, it lets us monitor your heart and blood pressure with ease while you exercise. And second, it provides an indication of how much exercise you're capable of doing—an indication that, as we shall see, is very important. Yet the bicycle has its disadvantages, too. First, the legs of many Americans are simply not conditioned to bicycles: they tire while the rest of the body has not yet reached its maximal point, and may thus prevent the heart from reaching its maximal rate. Also, as I said in *Aerobics*, it's difficult to keep someone from just coasting along at a lower speed with a stationary bicycle; whether or not people push themselves to capacity depends too much on their motivation.

That's why we prefer the treadmill. With a motorized treadmill, we can control precisely how much exercise a person does, yet we can also monitor the heartbeat and the blood pressure during the exercise period. The smooth, steady walking motion you perform on the treadmill does not disrupt the ECG signals; and to take your blood pressure, your physician or the attendant simply straps on the sphygmomanometer cuff and the diaphragm of the stethoscope before you begin the test. Then, every few minutes as you're walking, he pumps up the cuff, listens to your pulse through the stethoscope, and so obtains the reading. (This determination is reasonably accurate). We know how fast you're walking since we control the speed of the treadmill: 3.3 miles per hour, according to the procedure we use. That's a rate slow enough to give your heart a workout when we combine that speed with a progressive, gradual increase in elevation.

At the Cooper Clinic we use the Balke treadmill test, which consists of walking on a flat-surface treadmill at 3.3 miles per hour (90 meters/min.) during the first minute. You get the "feel" of the treadmill during this time, as you warm up. After the first minute the incline of the treadmill is raised 2 percent, so that you're walking just slightly uphill. Each minute thereafter, the angle is increased by another 1 percent, so that gradually the amount of work you have to do to keep up with the 3.3 mph pace is increased. After 25 minutes, the incline stays the same (25%) and the speed is increased 0.2 mph per minute. This *gradual* increase in the effort required of you is a good safety factor (as you'll read in the chapter on safety when we discuss the warmup period). As you keep on working progressively harder, we continue to monitor your heartbeat and blood pressure. And by the time the angle's been raised uphill to an incline of, say, 15 or 20 percent, you'll know you've been exercising. Your heart's likely to be quite close to its maximal rate. In other words, we've really taken you out on the highway, so to speak, to see what you can do.

## The Evidence

"Okay, a nice theory," I can hear you saying. "This comparison you're making between people and automobiles makes sense on the surface. But does it really hold up? How likely is it that you'll find something by making me sweat like this that you wouldn't uncover just by giving me a resting ECG?"

The odds are better than 1 out of every 10. Evaluating the tests on 3,345 men, mean age 44.5 years, done here at the Cooper Clinic, we found that 10.7 percent showed normal on the resting ECG yet showed a cardiac problem of one kind or another during the stress ECG. Most of these 358 men were surprised to learn that they had a heart condition—but glad to learn about it in time to start corrective action.

Studies done elsewhere corroborate this finding. For example, a report published in the *British Heart Journal* found 12.3 percent of a population of 510 men (ages 40–65) showed abnormal exercise ECGs yet had no indication of any problem when their resting ECG was taken. None of these 63 men had noticed any of the other signs of heart disease, either: no angina, valvular disease, or previous myocardial infarction. Had they not taken the exercise ECG, none of them would have known that their hearts needed help.

We should emphasize, too, that this exercise ECG should be continued to the point where voluntary fatigue, or the predicted maximal heart rate for the individual patient, has been reached. In other words, you need to really push yourself to capacity in order for the test to be a valid and accurate diagnostic tool. This point is also substantiated in the medical literature. In the study I just mentioned, for example, *half* of the abnormal responses would have been missed if the subject had stopped exercising when his heart was beating at only 85 percent of his predicted maximal heart rate. Another researcher, Jack H. Wilmore, at the University of California, Davis, writes after studying 650 male volunteers: "On the basis of its diagnostic value, the submaximal test must be seriously questioned. The individual who demonstrates a negative submaximal test, but who has identifiable coronary disease at the higher workloads, is given a clean bill of health and a false sense of security if he is stopped short of volitional fatigue."

A false sense of security: needless to say, that's the one thing we must be extremely careful to avoid giving a patient. There are too many stories, and too many of them true, about a man who has his complete physical examination, is given a clean bill of health, and then drops dead shortly afterward of a massive heart attack. Well, that hasn't happened with any of our patients, and one of the reasons why is that we utilize maximal treadmill stress testing with multilead monitoring as a diagnostic tool.

## False Positive and False Negative

There are very few tests of human function or performance that are 100 percent reliable. The treadmill test is in this category, but, utilizing the latest technology, the false negative responses can be kept to a minimum. With a false negative test, the ECG is normal but in reality the patient has one or more coronary arteries that are partially blocked, as shown by X ray of the heart (coronary arteriography). In these cases, usually the obstruction is minimal or there is adequate collateral circulation around the obstruction. This type of coronary disease is of less clinical significance than disease that causes classic changes.

A false positive test is also occasionally seen. In such cases the stress ECG is abnormal but a subsequent coronary arteriogram is normal. False positive tests are more commonly seen in women. Certain medications can cause this type of response, and there also exists the possibility of an obstruction in a small vessel—too small to be seen on the coronary arteriogram. I tend to consider that a false positive test indicates at least some abnormality of function, even though it can't be seen by X ray. Following these patients longitudinally is the only way the significance of both false positive and false negative tests ultimately will be determined.

## Fitness Classification

Yet there is another reason to take the stress ECG test up to the maximal heart rate and voluntary fatigue. Not only does this test give an indication of cardiac abnormality (or the lack of it), but it also is an accurate measure of your level of fitness. And the fitness level, we're finding, is another important diagnostic tool when it comes to making a prognosis regarding the health of your heart.

What is your fitness level? Simply put, it's your endurance or aerobic capacity—determined by the amount of time you can stay on the treadmill, maintaining that 3.3 mph speed while the incline gets progressively steeper. To measure only your fitness level, we wouldn't need the ECG machine at all—only the treadmill and a stopwatch. Yet we wouldn't consider giving you the test without the ECG, because for our cardiac diagnosis, and for obvious safety reasons, we want to monitor your heart's performance *while* you're showing how much endurance you have.

The results of your test may be a surprise, as a twenty-eight-year-old "body building" champion demonstrated at the Cooper Clinic recently. He had just won a state contest, and he looked it. His chest was huge; his waist was slim. His biceps bulged, and when he posed, muscle groups would literally stretch the skin to its maximum. You could understand why the judges had selected him as the champion. Yet after a relatively poor performance on the treadmill test, his heart rate was 193 and he was totally exhausted and nauseated. He had great musculoskeletal strength, but poor cardiovascular reserves. He had restricted his exercise only to muscle building.

Our muscular friend didn't feel any better, either, when one of our technicians told him that his performance barely exceeded that of a sixty-four-year-old grandmother we had tested earlier—and that she had had a heart attack two years before her examination!

Based on the amount of time you stay on the treadmill, you'll be classified into one of six fitness categories, as shown on the charts on the following pages.

As you'll notice, the criteria for fitness classification differ according to sex and age. This differentiation is based on the natural decrease in maximal working capacity as a person grows older, as well as on a statistically demonstrable difference in physiological variables between men and women (heart and lung size, for example).

With your fitness level determined, your physician has two important advantages that would be lacking if you hadn't taken the maximal stress test. First, he can now be precise about where to start you off in your exercise program. Since he knows what you can do today, he's in a better position to judge what kind of workouts you should be doing tomorrow and in the weeks to come. He can prescribe activity that will produce a "training effect" (which we'll describe in detail in the next chapter) yet without placing undue stress and hardship on your system.

Second, as you'll read in the next chapter, your fitness level is one of the coronary risk factors that can be numerically weighed, according to your age and sex, to give an overall statistical evaluation of your cardiac health. With the results of your blood tests, your medical history, and your lean body mass (a measurement of your body's fat percentage, determined by either calipers or underwater displacement and weighing techniques), your physician can arrive at an overall coronary risk profile for you that takes each of these coronary risks into account. And having determined your level of coronary risk more precisely, your physician can make a more authoritative

# FITNESS CATEGORIES ADOPTED 2/1/77

## Men

### LIMITS (MIN)

| FITNESS CATEGORY (Percentage in each category) * | AGE |  |  |  |  |  |
|---|---|---|---|---|---|---|
|  | <30† | 30-39 | 40-49 | 50-59 | 60+ |  |
| Very Poor (13.8%) | <12:50 | <12:00 | <11:00 | <9:00 | <5:30 |  |
| Poor (19.8%) | 12:50-15:29 | 12:00-14:59 | 11:00-13:29 | 9:00-11:29 | 5:30- 8:49 |  |
| Fair (29.6%) | 15:30-18:59 | 15:00-17:59 | 13:30-16:59 | 11:30-14:59 | 8:50-12:29 |  |
| Good (19.7%) | 19:00-21:59 | 18:00-20:59 | 17:00-19:59 | 15:00-17:59 | 12:30-15:44 |  |
| Excellent (11.9%) | 22:00-24:59 | 21:00-23:59 | 20:00-22:59 | 18:00-21:14 | 15:45-20:37 |  |
| Superior (5.1%) | >25:00 | >24:00 | >23:00 | >21:15 | >20:38 |  |

* Based on testing 5,267 men using the Balke treadmill technique. (A more complete fitness classification chart can be found in the appendix.)

† < Means "less than"; > means "more than."

22

# FITNESS CATEGORIES ADOPTED 2/1/77

## Women

### LIMITS (MIN)

AGE

| FITNESS CATEGORY (Percentage in each category) * | <30† | 30–39 | 40–49 | 50–59 | 60 + |
|---|---|---|---|---|---|
| Very Poor (13.0%) | <7:46 | <7:15 | <6:00 | <5:38 | <4:00 |
| Poor (18.3%) | 7:46–10:09 | 7:15– 9:29 | 6:00– 7:59 | 5:38– 6:59 | 4:00– 5:32 |
| Fair (31.2%) | 10:10–12:59 | 9:30–11:59 | 8:00–10:59 | 7:00– 9:29 | 5:33– 7:59 |
| Good (20.3%) | 13:00–15:59 | 12:00–14:59 | 11:00–12:59 | 9:30–11:59 | 8:00–10:59 |
| Excellent (11.3%) | 16:00–17:59 | 15:00–16:59 | 13:00–15:59 | 12:00–14:59 | 11:00–11:59 |
| Superior (5.8%) | >18:00 | >17:00 | >16:00 | >15:00 | >12:00 |

* Based on testing 929 women using the Balke treadmill technique. (A more complete fitness classification chart can be found in the appendix.)

† < Means "less than"; > means "more than."

23

recommendation regarding your need to change your weight, your diet, your exercise habits, or your intake of tobacco, alcohol, or medication.

I still remember when it was time to give advice to Bob Johnston after his stress ECG four years ago. Bob was thirty-six then, overweight, inactive, a heavy smoker, and he had a lot of stress at work. After only ten minutes, he staggered off the treadmill, totally exhausted. "Bob," I told him, "your physical condition is so bad that you need to walk another two minutes just to fail!"

Bob laughs about that now. His smoking, obesity, and inactivity have long since disappeared. He is a competitive marathoner, and last checkup he stayed on the treadmill 27½ minutes, which classified him in the top 1 percent of all people we have stress tested!

## A Word about Safety

Even though most people are quick to understand the value of a complete cardiac examination, some are hesitant about the idea of increasing their heart rate up to a maximal level during a stress test. "Isn't it dangerous to overdo exercise?" they ask. Or, "I *know* I'm not in good condition. Isn't it risky to elevate my heart rate above the resting level?"

I respond to these natural concerns for safety by giving the safety statistics we have compiled during our years of maximal stress testing here at the Cooper Clinic. Since 1971, 16,500 maximal treadmill stress tests have been administered here to men and women 10 to 84 years of age and their results entered into our computer. Nearly 10 percent had known coronary heart disease, and 20 percent had hypertension. During each of these tests an attendant and physician monitored the electrocardiogram and stopped the test at signs of any abnormality. Defibrillation and oxygen equipment were on hand for emergencies.

Out of these 16,500 tests, only 4 significant problems have occurred, none resulting in a fatality.

Four emergencies, zero fatalities, out of 16,500 tests.

With proper screening, supervision, and monitoring, maximal stress testing is a valuable diagnostic procedure of proven safety. We consider it an essential first step in a cardiac examination, or in any complete preventive medical checkup for someone over age thirty-five.

To make it easier for you to take that first step, you'll find in the appendix to this book a partial list of preventive medical centers where stress ECG examinations are given. There may, of course, be other facilities even closer to where you live, but if your physician isn't familiar with them this list will at least get you started.

And once you've found out the location of the stress testing facility nearest you, I have one prescription. Go. Regularly. Once a year.

But the first time, if you've been inactive in the past, my suggestion is that you walk, don't run.

# 3

# Is My Heart in Shape?
# Your Personal Coronary
# Risk Profile

Nearly all of the patients who come to the Cooper Clinic ask about the condition of their heart. They've heard of the frightening statistics about heart disease, and many of them know the one statistic that is perhaps most frightening of all: approximately 40 percent of the individuals who have heart attacks die without warning. Suddenly. Without chance of benefiting from one of our fine coronary care units, and without hope of bypass surgery.

How can we give patients warning, before this first and final symptom strikes them down, so that they can take preventive action?

At the Cooper Clinic we have developed predictability charts based on the data collected on thousands of patients. Each chart includes a list of primary and secondary "risk factors" that the American Heart Association has associated with coronary heart disease. Some of these factors, such as cigarette smoking, high blood pressure, or cholesterol, may be *causal* agents that have a direct chemical or physiological effect on the heart. Others, such as family history or abnormal ECG patterns, are "risk factors" in the sense that they help to *predict* heart function problems. In this chapter I'm going to look at these factors, which were identified primarily from a study of 5,000 men and women that began in Framingham, Massachusetts, in 1949.* Then I'm going to discuss predict-ability results with another more recently used diagnostic tool: the treadmill stress test.

After that, I'm going to show you how to use our clinic's coronary risk profile for your age and sex, so that with your physician you can predict your own level of coronary risk. And, finally, I'm going to show how the coronary risk profile score can be improved using a pre-ventive medicine program that includes aerobic exercise.

Thousands of our patients, hundreds of them with heart problems, have improved their scores and therefore lowered their risk level. I hope you'll make use of the same pro-gram that's worked for them.

## The Primary Risk Factors

These are the ten "primary" risk factors listed by the American Heart Association:

*1. Family History.* If you have a blood relative who had a heart attack before age fifty, the odds are greater that you may have heart problems than if your family's been free from heart disease, other factors being equal. That's according to our own statistics here at the Cooper Clinic. Other researchers use the age of sixty as a cutoff point, while still others list only blood relatives who died of heart disease as a risk factor. Recent theories suggest that a tendency to develop mutating artery-wall cells, which grow into atherosclerotic plaques, may be genetically in-herited. But as yet there's no certainty as to why coronary disease appears to run in families—only the statistical evidence that it often does.

*2. Stress and Stress-producing Personality Behavior Patterns.* Tension, stress, and aggressive behavior patterns

---

* The Framingham study was an effort by the National Insti-tute of Health (NIH) to determine the role that various risk factors play in causing heart disease. Nearly the entire com-munity of Framingham, Massachusetts, was involved in the study, and the results published by Dr. Kannel and his asso-ciates have provided much of our current knowledge about what seems to cause coronary heart disease.

place a strain on the heart that has long been recognized as potentially lethal. In a stress situation, the body's hormonal systems act as they've been programmed to do since the Stone Age: they speed up the heart rate and increase the blood pressure to prepare the body for "flight or fight." If the body does flee, or fight, these adrenal hormones are metabolized: in common terms, the "tension" is "burned up." But if the body does neither, or if a personality pattern continually interprets the world as a challenge or a threat—a stress situation—the hormones remain in the bloodstream. The body can't relax. The heart and blood vessels are under constant, low-grade pressure, and the wear and tear may show up as heart disease.

Stress, of course, may come from outside the body—an automobile accident or a hostile supervisor at the shop or the office. An exciting athletic event may prove too much for a deconditioned heart.

A classic example of this phenomenon occurred in 1941 when the Green Bay Packers played the Chicago Bears in a championship game at Wrigley Field. It was an exciting game won in the final few seconds by the Green Bay Packers by a score of 16 to 14. According to the *Chicago Tribune,* "when the stands had cleared that day, they counted 7 heart attacks and 2 deaths that occurred" —among the spectators, not the participants.

This episode reminds me of a definition I heard recently of a professional football game: 22 men on the field desperately in need of rest, and 65,000 people in the stands desperately in need of exercise! Yet this externally induced stress can usually be avoided. When stress comes from within the mind, however—from a drive to excel, or from some other form of nervous tension— the heart can't escape. It is this secondary form of stress that Drs. Meyer Friedman and Ray Rosenman describe in their book *Type A Behavior and Your Heart.* The "Type A" individual is the person who continuously stresses himself—who plans today for tomorrow; who reads trade journals in the bathroom; who shaves or dictates while he's driving to work; who can't bear to wait in line at a restaurant; who is constantly on the phone while on vacation; who, to sum it up, sometimes acts as if he's trying to be the wealthiest person in the cemetery. This is the man whose behavior correlates with an increased frequency of heart attacks.

Though the *Type A* book attempted to make the case that this behavior alone, without any of the other risk factors, was enough to bring on a heart attack, the medical community has generally viewed such a conclusion as overstated. Still, I agree with the idea that the Type A personality needs to make a change—not only in his personality, but in his diet, rest, exercise, smoking, and weight-control habits. Exercise, as we've just noted, tends to burn up the tensions of the day so that the body and the heart can relax. Also, as you'll see in a later chapter, exercise tends to have a positive effect on one's mental outlook, reducing what Friedman calls "free-floating hostility."

If you recognize yourself as a Type A personality, or if external events in your life are placing you under undue stress, I urge you to take action—even if it's only to reduce some of the other coronary risk factors. After you think about it, however, you may be able to do more to change those external stress-inducing circumstances than you think. I frequently have my patients make a list of all the outside forces that are giving them difficulty, and together we go over the list for items that can be changed. Homes, cars, office routines, jobs—these can all be changed. Not all at once, of course, but gradually, item by item, the load of stress *can* be lightened.

3. *Inactivity*. There's so much evidence associating inactivity with heart disease that it's almost beyond question. Researchers have compared conductors on London's double-decker buses with the less-active drivers, farm workers with other occupational groups, active and sedentary members of Israeli *kibbutzim* (communes), active and sedentary longshoremen, and citizens in the Massachusetts town of Framingham. In these and in many other studies, the active had fewer heart problems than the sedentary.

If you find yourself getting up from the table after a heavy meal, sitting down in front of the TV, and dozing off until it's time to go to bed, consider the advice of Per-Orlaf Astrand, a noted Swedish physiologist. He says that anyone who intends to be sedentary should pass a careful medical examination "in order to establish whether one's state of health is good enough to stand the inactivity!"

4. *High Blood Pressure.* This has been generally recognized as one of the three major risk factors, along with cigarette smoking and cholesterol. Hypertension, or high blood pressure, stresses the circulatory system the way too much air stresses a balloon. Understandably, high blood pressure is the major cause of strokes, ruptured blood vessels in the brain. Most researchers feel that blood pressures under 140/90 are normal. They consider that anything above that is abnormal. Blood pressure above 160/95 is generally accepted as hypertension and should be treated. Part of the recent decline in strokes and heart fatalities has been attributed to the 100 percent rise in the number of people who now have their high blood pressure under control.

5. *Abnormal Resting ECG.* This is a valuable tool in detecting heart diseases such as heart attacks, blocks, and abnormal enlargements. It's a good warning against impending heart attack, but, as I've said before, a stress ECG has greater accuracy as a predictor because it views the heart in action.

6. *Obesity.* It's universally recognized that obesity puts a direct strain on the heart, along with the other systems of the body. Fat is relatively bloodless, as a look at the white fats in "marbled" beef will demonstrate. When the heart has to force blood through vessels that are squeezed by deposits of fat, there's a strain. When the body has to drag around extra pounds, that's more work—more weight for the muscles to lift and therefore more strain on the heart. If your percentage of body fat is over the median limits we list for your age and sex in our Coronary Risk Profile, you're doing your heart a disservice.

7. *Cigarette Smoking.* Before cigarette smoking was fashionable for women, sudden death from coronary heart

disease claimed only 1 woman for every 12 men. By the late sixties, when "baby" had "come a long way," the women's death ratio had tripled: to 3 women for every 12 men. New studies show that the average age for women dying from sudden heart attack are as follows:

nonsmokers: 67.9 years—light smokers: 55 years
—heavy smokers: 48 years.

Cigarette smoking is certainly a major cause of heart disease. A person who smokes over two packs of cigarettes a day has three times the likelihood of dying of heart attack as the nonsmoker, and a much greater risk that his heart attack will be fatal. If you survive the attack but continue to smoke, a recent study by Wilhelmsson on 564 postcardiac patients shows, your chance of another heart attack is twice as high as that of the cardiac patient who quits.

What do cigarettes do that produces such lethal results? A number of things. The carbon monoxide in the smoke, like that in your automobile exhaust, diminishes the red blood cells' capacity to carry oxygen. The result? The heart has to pump more blood to get the same amount of oxygen to your system. Cigarette-induced emphysema results in an increased workload for your heart: more blood has to be pumped through less resilient lungs to pick up the same amount of oxygen. And amyl hydrocarbons from the smoke may act as mutagens for arterial-wall cells, accelerating the process by which atherosclerotic plaques are formed.

The nicotine in cigarette smoke also affects the heart. It increases adrenalin flow—the body's response to the stress of an ingested poison. It speeds the heart rate by as much as 12 to 24 beats per minute, makes blood more likely to clot, and constricts the blood vessels, which may increase the systolic blood pressure by 8–10 mg/Hg. If you smoke, after a cigarette your hands may be colder because they're getting less blood—this can be demonstrated scientifically—whether the smoke is inhaled from your cigarette or from that of another smoker. As Aronow reported in the September 1974 issue of the *Journal of the American Medical Association,* it is important that "patients with coronary heart disease avoid the smoke from others. Inhaled smoke, even in a room where others are smoking, can be detrimental to a patient with heart disease." When someone asks, "Do you mind if I smoke?" more and more people are wisely answering, "Yes."

8. *Cholesterol.* For men, the risk of a first heart attack is more than doubled when cholesterol levels rise from between 225 and 250 up to 300 and over, according to National Heart and Lung Institute figures. And data from the Framingham study indicate that a man whose cholesterol changes from below 194 to over 250 will *triple* the risk of first attack.

Why should cholesterol be so dangerous? As most people know, high blood levels of cholesterol contribute to the formation of fatty plaques along the inside lining of the arteries. As these plaques slowly build up, layer upon layer, ultimately they choke off the flow of blood.

Looking at the risk factor odds makes it obviously prudent to lower the cholesterol to below 250, and preferably below 200. There are five known ways this can be done.

Nearly everyone knows the first way—lower the amount of cholesterol taken into the body. Cut down on egg yolks and animal fats, such as those found in meat, cheese, butter, cream, and whole milk. Also to be avoided are shellfish—shrimp, lobster, oysters, and crab meat. Lobster tails in drawn butter may be delicious, but also dangerous. Finally, saturated vegetable fats also raise cholesterol levels. Nondairy coffee creamers have these hardened or "hydrogenated" vegetable fats. So do solidified margarines, olive oil, some frozen desserts, and the fat in chocolate, cocoa butter.

As a general guideline, three cholesterol-rich meals per week should be your maximum, but if your cholesterol is above 250 you'll need to cut back even further. See Chapter 6, on diet, for more details and for menus.

The second way to lower cholesterol is to reduce the amount of cholesterol that your liver manufactures every day. It's a sad but proven fact that if there's no cholesterol in the diet, the liver may manufacture it. However, by a mechanism we don't yet fully understand, increased intake of polyunsaturated fats such as corn or safflower oil (two tablespoons/day) may slow down the liver's natural production of cholesterol, thereby lowering the level in the blood.

A third way to lower cholesterol is simply to lose weight, although this is not always effective. Nonetheless, since obesity is itself a risk factor, weight control is obviously a good step to take. Care in the *method* of weight loss must be taken, however, since some popular "quick weight loss" diets can send the cholesterol level up even higher than they were before the diet began. Again, check Chapter 6 for those to use and not to use.

A fourth way to lower cholesterol appears to be through exercise. I say "appears," because the extent to which exercise affects cholesterol has been debated. We do know, as I described in *Aerobics*, that after a cholesterol-rich meal an aerobically trained person gets rid of the cholesterol more rapidly than an untrained person does. We know that, after vigorous aerobic exercise, blood fat levels decrease for a twenty-four- to thirty-six-hour period. We also know, from studies at the Aerobics Center (which will be discussed later), that aerobic fitness correlated with lower levels of cholesterol in nearly 3,000 men. Further, a recent study by Lopez at Louisiana State University Medical School in New Orleans indicated marked reduction in serum cholesterol after a ten-week program of exercise.

Whether this lowered cholesterol level is sustained for a long period of time, and for how long, is still open to question. That's where the debate lies, and that's why I use the word "appears."

Aerobic exercise, however, can also lower cholesterol *risk*, even in cases where the cholesterol level stays the same. Though this may sound confusing at first, it's really quite simple: just another way of saying that cholesterol takes different forms in the blood and that some of the forms it takes are less dangerous than others. If we can change the cholesterol to a less dangerous form, one less often found in the blood of people who are suffering from heart disease, we can say that we've lowered the risk.

And we can change that form by changing the blood proteins that act as carriers for much of the cholesterol in the blood. These fat-carrying proteins, or lipoproteins as they're called, come in three sizes: small, or high-density (HDL); medium, or low-density (LDL); and large, or very-low-density (VLDL). The most dangerous appear to be the low-density lipoproteins—which are found in greater concentrations most often in men. The least dangerous appear to be the high-density lipoproteins— which are found in greater concentrations most often in women. (Even though the figures are changing, women continue to have heart attacks later in life than men.)

We also know that HDL and LDL proportions vary among women, depending on the amount of their aerobic exercise. As a recent study by Hames and Haskell at Stanford showed, a group of 43 female runners had less of the dangerous LDL and more of the protective HDL than did a control group of women who weren't exercising. Another Stanford study noted that the blood fat distribution of a group of male long-distance runners between the ages of 30 and 59 appeared to resemble the pattern for younger women more than that for middle-aged men.

Putting these results together, it makes sense to use aerobic exercise if your cholesterol is elevated. Regardless of whether or not we know the exact mechanism through which exercise works on cholesterol, as one of my patients likes to say, "I'm not young enough to sit around and wait until all the facts are in."

But if diet, weight control, and exercise don't lower cholesterol—and for some individuals they simply won't —cholesterol-reducing medication is indicated. At the Cooper Clinic we like to use the other methods first, but we don't hesitate to prescribe medication when it is indicated.

9. *Triglycerides*. These blood fats are more closely related to obesity and the intake of starches and carbohydrates than to the consumption of dairy products. They are another of the recognized coronary risk factors. A num-

ber of studies have linked high levels of triglycerides with increased heart attack risk. They appear particularly dangerous in women and in people who have elevated cholesterol along with VLDL, the extra-large lipoproteins. Perhaps one danger of this combination is as simple as a "sludging" effect—a thickening and slowing down of the blood by these fat globules, so that the cholesterol can adhere readily to the artery wall without being swept away. Another danger from triglycerides may be abnormal blood particles they form with VLDL, cholesterol, and cholesterol esters, though the exact mechanism here is not yet understood.

You can lower triglycerides in three ways. First, lose weight. In nearly all cases, weight loss is associated with a drop in triglycerides. Next, cut down on the saturated fats. Luncheon meats and poultry skin are particularly high in triglycerides. Trim off the fat from roasts and steaks, and cook them longer, to melt more of the fats away. Switch to skim milk and other low-fat dairy products. Use the leaner meats, such as fish, veal, and poultry (without the skin), as the main animal proteins in your diet.

Finally, lower triglycerides by cutting down on alcohol, starches, and refined sugars. When you eat these carbohydrates, your liver reacts by manufacturing triglycerides and sending them out into your bloodstream. Though the liver-synthesized fat particles aren't as large as the ones you get from a fried chicken dinner and a whipped-cream dessert, they're still triglycerides, and still a coronary risk.

When I explained to one of my patients how an increase in refined carbohydrates triggers an increase in triglycerides, she thought about it for a moment and then put it more simply. "Dr. Cooper," she said, "you mean that when I drink and eat sweets, my blood gets fat."

That about sums it up. And too many fats, either on your body or in your blood, are dangerous to your heart.

Exercise helps, too. Calorie-burning workouts help burn up both the fats in the blood and the fats that are stored in the body. As you'll see shortly, our studies at the Aerobics Center indicate a definite correlation between

aerobic fitness and a lowered blood triglyceride level.
10. *Fasting Blood Sugar.* Numerous studies have shown
how diabetes, the chronically raised level of sugar in the
blood, goes together with heart disease. High sugar levels
keep bad company and need to be brought down, with
medication, diet, weight control, and exercise. These last
three may eventually replace medication for many patients
after a regular program has been followed for several
months.

# The Secondary Risk Factors

In addition to the ten primary risk factors, the American
Heart Association lists three others as secondary. This
means that there's evidence against these three, but not
yet as overwhelming as the evidence against the first ten.
1. *Uric Acid.* Men and women with high levels of uric acid
in the blood suffer from gout. They also frequently have
heart disease. And they are also frequently overweight,
with high blood pressure. In Chapter 6, on diet, I've listed
the purine-rich foods such as legumes and the organ
meats that produce uric acid. I've also listed those that
may stimulate production of uric acid by the body, such
as alcohol and asparagus. Weight reduction and exercise
may also help lower uric acid level, though, in cases of
gout, medication is the accepted treatment.
2. *Vital Capacity.* The amount of air your lungs can hold
correlates with the incidence of heart disease. It appears
that the better the lungs can oxygenate the blood, the less
the demand will be on the heart.
3. *Body Build.* Endomorphic (fat) and mesomorphic
(muscular) people tend to have more frequent coronary
problems than ectomorphic (thin) people. Another case
where aerobic exercise and weight control are indicated
as safety factors.

This makes thirteen risk factors, but even the American
Heart Association would not claim this list as the last
word. There may very well be other factors that we do
not yet have enough data on to prove a correlation, and a

number of these factors are being studied right now.

For instance, a ten-year study of 1,329 men done by Jeremiah Stamler found that men with resting heart rates above 90 died from coronary disease at a rate 2½ times greater than those with resting heart rates under 70. At the Cooper Clinic we list the resting heart rate on our Coronary Risk Profile.

Other possibilities currently under investigation are blood type, with type O appearing the safest; an excess of zinc as compared with copper in the blood; drinking water, with soft and chlorinated water appearing as possible risk-inducers; and white flour, which a British study indicates may damage artery linings, making them more susceptible to the clogging effects of atherosclerosis.

So there are the risk factors, a deadly lot. We don't yet understand just exactly how they all link up with each other to cause heart disease: we don't even know precisely whether some are actually causes or only, shall we say, often-present bystanders. Family history, for instance, may indicate there is some genetic tendency toward heart disease passed along through generations, in the manner of colorblindness and hemophilia—perhaps the cellular mutation we've mentioned. Or it may just be more of a by-product, of sons and daughters eating, exercising, smoking, drinking, and living as stressfully as mothers and dads.

But, regardless of whether or not you look at these factors as causes, one message should come through loud and clear: *danger!* I wish I could tell you that you didn't have to worry about them, that you could, like many of the citizens of Framingham after their first few years of examinations, simply not bother to take the steps needed to make the danger signals go away.

The evidence, however, is before me: thousands of cases in documented scientific studies, all pointing the finger to these elements of risk, these threats to heart and life that kill millions every year. If you ignore the evidence, you do so only at your peril.

And, very likely, not for long.

## The Risk Profile Chart

Just knowing all the risk factors, of course, isn't enough. To answer the question "Is my heart in shape?" you need to see how the risks all add up in your particular case. At the Cooper Clinic we use a risk profile chart developed to do just that.

Since some of the risk factors seem to vary in danger according to age and sex, we have ten of these charts: five for men and five for women, adjusted according to norms for each decade from before age thirty on up to after age sixty. In addition, each of the sixteen variables is weighted from 0 to 8, based on the level and the importance of the risk factor. The sample we have here is for a man under thirty, but as you'll see when you turn to the appendix to find the chart that applies to your age and sex, the weighted values of a given coronary risk may vary from the example on the next page.

The chart for our young man has some good news and some bad news. From a standpoint of cholesterol, glucose, and blood pressure, he is doing well for a man under thirty. He has youth on his side, and his coronary blood vessels haven't yet stiffened up to a point where his heart shows any insufficiency or abnormality when put under a stress test.

Yet there's clear warning from this chart that this patient is headed in the wrong direction. His treadmill time is in the bottom ten percentile or in a word, terrible! He also has too much fat in his blood, and on his body. He's tense, and smoking nearly two packs a day, much of it out of nervousness. His cigarettes and his lack of exercise have his performing ability way down and his resting heart rate way up—to the point where he's wasting nearly thirty *thousand* heartbeats *every day*. And, of course, there's his family history.

So this young man, less than thirty, is potentially a candidate for heart disease. He is classified as a moderate risk, meaning there is a significant likelihood that he will develop some problem of a cardiac nature, in the not too distant future.

# COOPER CLINIC / Dallas, Texas

## Fitness Level and Coronary Risk Profile

Name: _____  MALES: *UNDER 30 YEARS OF AGE  2-22-77

| PERCENTILE RANKINGS / YOUR VALUES | BALKE TREADMILL TIME (min:sec) 12:48 | CHOLESTEROL (mg.%) 168 | TRIGLYCERIDE (mg.%) 172 | GLUCOSE (mg.%) 88 | URIC ACID (mg.%) 7.3 | % BODY FAT 21.8 | RESTING HEART RATE (bpm) 82 | SYSTOLIC (mm Hg) 116 | DIASTOLIC (mm Hg) 75 |
|---|---|---|---|---|---|---|---|---|---|
| 99 | 29:00 | 120.2 | 27.2 | 74.9 | 4.4 | 7.2 | 39.7 | 94.2 | 59.6 |
| 95 | 25:00 | 142.2 | 48.4 | 83.4 | 4.9 | 9.6 | 46.8 | 102.3 | 64.3 |
| 90 | 22:30 | 153.7 | 55.3 | 87.9 | 5.4 | 11.5 | 50.0 | 109.7 | 69.8 |
| 85 | 22:00 | 160.2 | 61.8 | 89.8 | 5.6 | 12.9 | 52.1 | 110.3 | 70.3 |
| 80 | 21:00 | 164.9 | 66.2 | 92.6 | 5.8 | 13.9 | 54.4 | 112.3 | 72.3 |
| 75 | 20:00 | 171.6 | 71.3 | 94.9 | 5.9 | 15.3 | 55.9 | 116.4 | 74.5 |
| 70 | 20:00 | 178.0 | 76.2 | 96.0 | 6.1 | 16.2 | 57.6 | 118.3 | 77.8 |
| 65 | 19:00 | 185.1 | 82.2 | 98.2 | 6.2 | 17.1 | 59.2 | 119.7 | 78.2 |
| 60 | 18:25 | 190.4 | 87.2 | 99.7 | 6.4 | 18.0 | 60.1 | 120.0 | 79.6 |
| 55 | 18:00 | 194.7 | 92.8 | 102.0 | 6.5 | 19.1 | 61.7 | 120.2 | 79.8 |
| 50 | 17:10 | 199.2 | 99.7 | 103.1 | 6.7 | 20.1 | 62.8 | 120.5 | 80.0 |
| 45 | 17:00 | 202.8 | 110.0 | 104.3 | 6.8 | 21.2 | 64.3 | 123.9 | 80.2 |
| 40 | 16:00 | 206.8 | 123.1 | 104.9 | 7.0 | 22.3 | 65.5 | 127.7 | 80.4 |
| 35 | 15:30 | 211.2 | 136.6 | 105.3 | 7.1 | 23.4 | 67.2 | 129.7 | 81.6 |
| 30 | 15:00 | 217.6 | 148.1 | 106.3 | 7.3 | 25.4 | 69.5 | 130.1 | 83.9 |
| 25 | 14:55 | 222.1 | 169.9 | 109.2 | 7.5 | 26.6 | 70.5 | 131.9 | 85.4 |
| 20 | 13:45 | 228.9 | 180.3 | 110.3 | 7.7 | 28.6 | 72.4 | 135.2 | 87.0 |
| 15 | 12:50 | 240.3 | 199.9 | 113.1 | 8.0 | 30.5 | 76.3 | 139.6 | 89.9 |
| 10 | 12:00 | 250.9 | 234.4 | 117.8 | 8.3 | 32.8 | 80.4 | 140.4 | 90.4 |
| 5 | 10:00 | 269.9 | 296.0 | 123.1 | 9.0 | 38.0 | 87.9 | 149.6 | 99.6 |
| 1 | 7:00 | 300.1 | 761.3 | | 10.1 | 49.0 | 99.7 | 158.3 | 109.7 |
| POP. SIZE | 371 | 273 | 271 | 271 | 271 | 248 | 358 | 367 | 367 |
| AVERAGE | 17:21 | 200.3 | 132.7 | 100.8 | 6.7 | 21.6 | 64.3 | 124.2 | 80.3 |
| STANDARD DEVIATION | 4:25 | 39.1 | 107.8 | 14.5 | 1.2 | 9.1 | 12.5 | 13.4 | 9.6 |
| NORMAL LIMITS** | 19:00* | (250.0) | (135.0) | (110.0) | (8.0) | (19.0) | (72.0) | (140.0) | (90.0) |

Percentile groupings (left margin): SUPERIOR (80–99), EXCELLENT (55–75), GOOD (35–50), FAIR (15–30), POOR (1–10). Coronary risk bands (V L / L / M / H / V H) are marked along the lower percentiles.

### Coronary Risk Factors

**PERSONAL HISTORY OF HEART ATTACK**
- 0 NONE
- 2 OVER 5 YEARS AGO
- 3 2 - 4 YEARS AGO
- 5 1 - 2 YEARS AGO
- 8 0 - 1 YEARS AGO

**FAMILY HISTORY OF HEART ATTACK**
- 0 NONE
- 2 YES, OVER 60 YEARS
- 4 YES, 50 YEARS OR UNDER

**SMOKING HABITS**
- 0 NONE
- 1 PIPE/CIGAR
- 1 PAST ONLY/QUIT
- 2 1 - 10 DAILY
- 3 11 - 30 DAILY
- 4 30+ DAILY

**TENSION — ANXIETY**
- 0 NO TENSION, VERY RELAXED
- 1 SLIGHT TENSION
- 1 MODERATE TENSION
- 2 HIGH TENSION
- 3 VERY TENSE, "HIGH STRUNG"

**RESTING ECG / EXERCISE ECG**
- 0 NORMAL / 0 NORMAL/NEGATIVE
- EQUIVOCAL (BORDERLINE) 8
- ABNORMAL (POSITIVE)

**AGE FACTOR**
- 0 UNDER 30 YEARS OF AGE
- 1 30-39 YEARS OF AGE
- 2 40-49 YEARS OF AGE
- 3 50-59 YEARS OF AGE
- 4 60+ YEARS OF AGE

**TOTAL CORONARY RISK**
- VERY LOW ( 0 - 4 )
- LOW ( 5 - 14 )
- MODERATE (15 - 24)
- HIGH (25 - 34)
- VERY HIGH (35+)

*Data based on first visit only
**Upper limits generally accepted by most physicians

© Institute for Aerobics Research — 1977

And as we told this patient, in comparison with other men in his age category, he did not compare favorably.

This is the purpose of the risk profile chart: to educate, to give you a clear picture of your present condition so that corrective action can be taken. Your chart, of course, will be filled out with the help of your physician after your next examination. In the event that he uses a treadmill stress test procedure other than the Balke, we have listed treadmill test conversion tables in the appendix of this book. Procedures for determining body fat percentages are also included.

Your total score indicates your present risk of developing a coronary problem within the next five years. As we accumulate more data at the Institute for Aerobics Research, these percentages probably will change, but at present, a score of 0–4 suggests less than a 2 percent chance of a major coronary problem (angina, fatal or nonfatal heart attack, or required coronary bypass procedure) within the next five years. Other suggested but not proven predictions are as follows:

Low (5–14) —less than 10 percent chance of a problem within the next five years.

Moderate (15–24) —up to 40 percent chance of a problem within the next five years.

High (25–34) —up to 70 percent chance of a problem within the next five years.

Very High (35 + ) —over 70 percent chance of a problem within the next five years.

We will continue to validate our weighting factors and predictability percentages, but right now it appears that this chart is more sensitive than any of the traditionally used risk factor tables as a predictor of impending heart problems. Why? The number of variables used is one reason, and the emphasis on treadmill stress testing is the other.

Checking the records of 48 men who came to the Cooper Clinic and subsequently had a major heart problem (15 died, 23 survived classic heart attacks, and 10 required coronary artery bypass surgery), we found that our most accurate predictor by far came from the results of the treadmill stress test. Of these 48 men, the number who had an abnormal exercise ECG or failed to walk more than 15 minutes on the Balke Test was 42—a predictor with 87.5 percent accuracy. No other risk factor came close. Of these men, 32 were overweight, 30 had a positive family history, 23 had cholesterol elevated over 250, and 21 were cigarette smokers. The other risk factors were found in even fewer numbers.

Perhaps the most significant item in this study, however, was that only 12 of the 48 men had an abnormal resting ECG pattern. In other words, 3 out of 4 of these men would have been told that their hearts were normal, only to have a major heart problem during the next five years.

We then made a larger study, looking at the examination records of nearly 3,000 men, average age 44.6, who had come to the Cooper Clinic between 1971 and 1974. With this large-scale study, we hoped to see if the time on the treadmill stress test correlated with any of the coronary risk factors. Men who were in very poor and poor condition showed uniformly poor results, across the board, in their risk factors of cholesterol, triglycerides, glucose, uric acid, blood pressure, and body fat. Men who were in fair condition appeared better than the poor or very poor in all these risk factors. And those in the good or excellent categories tested better still in every one of these risk factors. (See the table "Summary Data on Levels of Physical Fitness vs. Selected Risk Factors" on the following page.)

Let me also point out that these results have been statistically adjusted to factor out the influences of age, weight, and percentage of body fat. Older, heavier men who were in good or excellent condition *still* averaged better scores on these coronary risk factors than did the younger, slimmer men who were in fair, poor, or very poor physical condition.

These results offer welcome evidence that the time you spend getting your aerobic points is time well spent. As your aerobic fitness improves, so do your other coronary risk factors.

With this evidence, and with the Coronary Risk Profile chart, we find it much easier to motivate patients to better their condition without overwhelming them with a long

## SUMMARY DATA ON LEVELS OF PHYSICAL FITNESS VS. SELECTED RISK FACTORS: ADJUSTED MEAN SCORES [1]

### (2,998 MEN. AVERAGE AGE 44.6 YEARS)

|  | | | | CHD Risk Factors | | | |
|---|---|---|---|---|---|---|---|
| LEVELS OF PHYSICAL FITNESS (TREADMILL DETERMINED) | CHOLESTEROL (mg/100cc) | TRIGLYCERIDES (mg/100cc) | GLUCOSE (mg/100cc) | URIC ACID (mg/100cc) | SYSTOLIC B.P.[2] (mg/Hg) | DIASTOLIC B.P.[2] (mg/Hg) | BODY FAT (%) |
| Very poor | 229.9* | 176.8† | 111.0† | 6.7* | 127.6† | 83.4 | 26.1† |
| Poor | 232.9† | 163.8† | 107.3† | 6.8* | 124.9 | 82.4 | 25.3† |
| Fair | 226.9 | 138.7† | 105.6 | 6.7* | 124.4 | 83.2 | 24.0† |
| Good | 225.1 | 118.9† | 105.3 | 6.5 | 123.4 | 81.9 | 22.4† |
| Excellent | 221.1 | 98.3 | 103.4 | 6.4 | 122.9 | 81.4 | 20.8 |

[1] Scores are adjusted for age, body weight, and percent fat, since increasing age, weight and fat are all associated with increased CHD risk factors.

[2] Resting, sitting values.

* P 0.05 when compared to the excellent level of physical fitness.

† P 0.01 when compared to the excellent level of physical fitness.

(P values refer to the likelihood of this difference between values occurring strictly as a result of chance. For example P = 0.05 means only 5 times out of 100 or P = 0.01 means only 1 time out of 100 could this difference occur by chance. In statistical terms, both values are "significant" differences.)

42

list of "don'ts." Instead of saying, "Don't smoke, don't drink, don't eat what you've been eating, and don't get so emotionally stressed," we now can say something simple, and something positive.

This is a help because, in many cases, when a patient is overwhelmed with orders to stop practically everything he's been doing, he simply doesn't come back.

So we have one positive goal to give a patient, and you: improve your physical fitness category. Start one of the programs of aerobic exercise you'll find in our chart pack. As you get more fit, you'll gradually find your other risk factors are coming into line. Dieting will be easier and won't have to be so extreme. Your willpower, bolstered by regular exercise, will help you cope with urges for alcohol and tobacco. And the strength you feel, coupled with your decrease in adrenal hormone levels, will help you ride out stress situations with more calm and more confidence.

And once you've worked yourself into the "good" category of fitness as measured by your treadmill time, your prognosis for a future free from heart disease improves considerably.

How much? Well, we're going to have a definitive answer for this question before long, based on a ten-year longitudinal study we're conducting on 5,000 men. We should have some preliminary results in from this "Dallas study" at our Institute for Aerobics Research by 1980. In the meantime, however, a 1976 three-year study on 744 people, done by Margolis at Duke University Medical School, indicates that if a person has proven one-, two-, or three-vessel obstructive coronary artery disease (shown by coronary arteriography) but can walk the equivalent of 15:00 minutes or longer on the Balke treadmill test, he has a 98 percent chance of surviving the next three years.

The same study also shows that among these men who had comparable coronary artery disease but walked less than 10:00 on the Balke treadmill stress test (or its equivalent), 41 percent died within two years.

Not only is your level of fitness, according to this evidence, an independent coronary variable, it is probably the most important variable or predictor of impending disease!

Once you know the effects that aerobic exercise has on your cardiovascular system—those positive benefits we call the "training effect"—it becomes easier to understand why exercise is such a lifesaver. We've already spoken of the ways that aerobic exercise works to cut down the coronary risk factors, but there are four other effects, all well documented, that strengthen the heart and lighten its workload even further:

• Aerobic exercise increases the amount of blood in your system and increases the amount of oxygen-carrying hemoglobin in the blood. Your blood becomes, in a word, richer: it can bring in more oxygen to each cell and can take away more $CO_2$ and other wastes than it could before you started exercising. Your muscle cells, also, improve their ability to process the oxygen and eliminate wastes more efficiently. As a result, your heart doesn't have to pump as much blood to each cell as it did before.

• Aerobic exercise increases the working space and efficiency of your lungs and strengthens the muscles that make your lungs expand and contract. With each breath, you take in more air and get rid of more $CO_2$ than you did before. Your blood picks up more oxygen at your lungs than it did, and gets rid of more $CO_2$. The result, again, is richer, cleaner blood, and less work for your heart.

• Aerobic exercise makes your blood vessels more flexible, so that they don't tend to accumulate atherosclerotic deposits as readily. The result? Less resistance in the blood vessels, and again less work for your heart.

• Aerobic exercise increases the number of those tiny blood vessels that form a network throughout the cells of your body. New vessels may appear as if from nowhere —perhaps because of the physical stimulus of the vigorous circulation or perhaps by some chemical trigger: we don't know the cause. But the result is that when you get your heart rate up during an aerobic exercise workout, the cells throughout your body get a better cleansing and more life-sustaining oxygen than they did before.

There has been controversy in the medical profession over the phenomenon of coronary collateral circulation produced by exercise. Even though we can see the exercise-induced effects of the increased collateral such as a reduction in angina pain, and improved stress electrocardiograms, some physicians claim that the phenomenon is as yet unproven—that it has been shown only that exercise increases collateral circulation in animals, not in humans.

Why? Possibly because our techniques of determining the circulation in the living human heart are not sensitive enough to see these small vessels. They're too small to be visualized with our current angiographic techniques. And even when collateral vessels are visualized, some investigators question their value.

This prompted Maurice McGregor to publish in a 1975 editorial in the official *Journal of the American Heart Association:* "In view of the direct evidence that collateral vessels can at least partially compensate for the loss of normal coronary flow, it does not seem reasonable to infer that they may be functionless from the angiographic evidence supplied."

In lay terms, this means that collateral circulation in your heart may save your life.

## Rehabilitation

Because of the links of aerobic exercise with so many of the positive factors that work against heart disease, exercise is becoming more and more generally accepted as a primary part of a rehabilitation program for anyone who has had a heart problem. On my desk I have numerous studies from professional journals showing the results of such programs—studies from all over the world, and too numerous for all to be mentioned here.

It's a joy to see the beautiful results that the training effect produces in anyone, but it's especially gratifying to see the change in a person who's been through the ordeal of a heart attack. We have a number of men and women enrolled in our Aerobics Activity Center Controlled Exercise Class who have been through just such an ordeal. Along with others whose examinations have put them in the high-risk category, these people come to our gymnasium at 7 A.M. three to five mornings every week for stretching exercises, walking on our indoor track, and, as they progress, jogging, swimming, and competitive sports.

Some, of course, can't start the program until they've had surgery to bypass their occluded coronary arteries with other vessels. But that doesn't stop them once they've gotten back on their feet.

I think of Frank Salvato here at the Aerobics Center. In his early forties, Frank noted the onset of chest pain with exercise. He had not taken good care of himself; he was overweight and inactive, and he smoked heavily. He joined our rehabilitation program, but his disease was too extensive for him to progress well. Bypass surgery was recommended, and then days after a six-vessel bypass procedure he was able to rejoin our rehabilitation program. Since that time (January 1975), his progress has been amazing! Now he routinely runs 3–4 miles, five days a week and he is enjoying a robust, healthy, and symptom-free life. Twenty years ago, our medical practice would have put him to bed and made him an invalid. Yet, today he's stronger and healthier than he has ever been in his life!

Of course, the exercise treatment for coronary rehabilitation isn't anything new, really. As early as 1802 one of the great London physicians, William Heberdeen, recorded the history of one of his patients who had the painful insufficiency of blood to the heart we call angina. This man, wrote Heberdeen, set himself the task of sawing wood for a half an hour every day and "cured himself of the angina."

But the medical profession as a whole did not follow this lead. Even today, some doctors still treat their heart attack patients as invalids, which is now, in light of today's evidence, a questionable practice. To banish a person from life, and thereby shorten his life span rather than lengthen it, seems to me ill advised. Frequently after one of my lectures, a man or woman will walk slowly up to where

I'm standing with a group of people and ask, "Dr. Cooper, I've asked my doctor about an exercise program, but he's against it since I've had a heart attack. What should I do?"

I feel sympathy for these people. The best answer I can give them, and you if you're one of them, is this: Ask your doctor why your condition prohibits walking. If he has evidence that walking would indeed be dangerous for your heart, he should let you know what that evidence is. And he should also let you know whether or not the condition would be improved with bypass surgery. If he won't give you a clear and factual answer to these questions and back it up with the records of your clinical examination, then frankly I'd advise you to seek further consultation.

But I repeat, don't start exercise without a medical clearance.

Most cardiac patients these days, however, don't have this problem with their physicians. As my wife, Millie, likes to point out, practically every physician we meet (and we meet quite a number of them in our traveling) places his patients on a walking program after a heart attack. But why don't they put them on the walking program *before* they have the heart attack?

Why not, indeed?

We can't promise you absolute protection. We can only point to the odds, and to the risk factors, and say that your aerobics exercise program will greatly improve your chances of avoiding a heart attack.

We can also point to documented studies showing that exercise, even if it doesn't prevent the heart attack, will help you survive one if it does occur.

Dr. Charles W. Frank first documented this in 1966 by examining the exercise habits of 301 men who suffered heart attacks.

Of the men in Frank's "least active exercise" category, 47 percent died either on the day of the attack or within the first four weeks of hospitalization. But only 9 percent of the men in Frank's "most active" category did not survive the first four weeks after their attack. In other words, men who had been active were roughly five times more likely to survive their heart attacks than those who were totally inactive.

A beautiful illustration of this phenomenon is a fifty-eight-year-old patient of mine. He exercised regularly, jogging three to four times a week. I examined him early in 1974 and, while his stress test might be classified as borderline, he went over 18 minutes on the treadmill—a "good" category score, even for men under thirty years of age.

In the summer of 1974 he went on a safari in Africa. Just a day or so after arriving on site out on the African savannah he started feeling chest discomfort. Since the food was not too good, he attributed it to indigestion. He rested and took it easy for a day, and the symptoms subsided. He continued with the safari, walking great distances and chasing game for a month, out there in the wilds. After the hunt, he flew home, lugging his heavy duffel bags through customs, sweating profusely and not thinking anything about it, since his "indigestion" had disappeared.

But when he returned to Dallas, he mentioned the incident to his wife and she encouraged him to have a checkup. The resting ECG showed that he was recovering from a massive heart attack! It had laid him up one day—his coronary care unit was a tent in Africa. Obviously, his coronary heart disease had been developing slowly over the years, and most likely he had built up enough collateral circulation with his jogging that this "backup system" was able to hold the line when the obstruction finally occurred.

There are other comparable stories, and other cases where it seems that a preventive health program of diet and exercise is actually *reversing* the symptoms of coronary heart disease. At the Institute for Longevity Research in California, they're reporting results with a special diet (see the Pritikin Diet, in Chapter 6) combined with walking and jogging that have even me adopting a conservative "let's wait and see" attitude. As yet we don't have enough evidence, as I see it, to claim that diet and exercise can actually rebuild and open up clogged atherosclerotic arteries—only evidence that the process can be slowed down.

I hope we do get the evidence, some day, that the right diet and exercise can be a *cure* for heart disease. But right now I want to make it clear that there is evidence that preventive medicine will work, in the overwhelming majority of cases, to *prevent* or delay the onset of heart disease—to help you *survive* a heart attack—and to help immeasurably to *rehabilitate* you following a heart attack.

So, regardless of whether you're reading this before or after a problem, take action now. See your doctor. Check your Coronary Risk Profile. Get into your own exercise program.

And get your heart in shape.

# 4

# But Is It Safe
# to Exercise?

I am asked about safety at nearly all the lectures I give, by new patients at the Cooper Clinic, and by people I meet literally all over the world. Even after they understand the benefits of aerobic exercise, even after they see the fitness data and statistics, even after they hear how aerobics has changed the lives of so many people, they still have a lingering doubt.

It's almost as if they think that something so beneficial must have a hidden catch somewhere. "I'm really not in very good condition," they'll say. "I've never been athletic. Do you think aerobics would *really* be safe for me?"

Well, of course, I understand this feeling. I share the same concern for my wife, for my patients, and for the many, many friends I've made during the past years. They're all trying to exercise safely, within their tolerance, and I want them to keep exercising that way.

I want you to know how they do it. I also want you to know why, despite scattered claims and headlines about the dangers of jogging, the overwhelming evidence shows that you are safer with an aerobics program than you are without one.

So while I give you the safety guidelines we follow at the Aerobics Center, I'm going to discuss several of the claims made against exercise, giving the specific points they make and showing the abundance of specific data that disprove such claims.

Then you'll have a program that you can follow, and I think you'll also be able to answer the question of safety and exercise based on the evidence.

Our evidence from the Aerobics Center here in Dallas speaks for itself. At this writing, we have had more than 5,000 people exercising at the Aerobics Activity Center since 1971. We have recorded exercise data on these individuals, men and women of all ages, ranging in levels of fitness from superior down through very poor, and including patients in our cardiac rehabilitation and controlled-exercise programs.

We have recorded over 15,000 miles of cycling. We have recorded over 5,000 miles of swimming in our pool. We have logged over 15,000 hours of calisthenics in our gym, over 5,000 hours of handball and racquetball, and over 25,000 hours of tennis on our courts.

And on our tracks during the summer of 1976, we recorded the one millionth mile of running and jogging.

Yet we have not had a single fatality. And among those who followed our recommendations exactly, we have not had a single serious incident.

On the other hand, we have had two (nonfatal) instances, both cases where our guidelines had not been followed. These were men who tried to run hard after not exercising regularly in the four to six months preceding. Both men had cardiovascular complications, neither died, and both started back into a regular supervised program.

Needless to say, we're proud of this safety record. We feel we can assure you of the safest possible program—provided you follow the guidelines we use at the Aerobics Center. Here are the guidelines in six basic steps that I'm going to detail for you in this chapter:

1. Have a checkup by a physician.
2. Prepare with a proper diet, proper clothing and equipment, and proper workout conditions.
3. Warm up thoroughly, stretch adequately.
4. Choose your proper performance objective, and avoid overexertion.
5. Cool down thoroughly.
6. Monitor your exercise and recovery pulse regularly.

Following these six steps is the way our members have attained such an excellent safety record.

## The Physician's Checkup

All the six steps are essential, but the physician's checkup is probably the most important.

If you're under thirty, you should have a complete medical history and physical examination *within the preceding year* before you start exercising.

If you're between thirty and thirty-five, you should have the complete history and physical examination *within six months* before you start exercising, and the examination should include a resting electrocardiogram (ECG).

If you're over thirty-five, you should have the complete history, physical examination, and resting ECG *within three months* before you start. Additionally—and this is important—your physician should perform a *stress ECG*, as discussed in Chapter 2.

Based on the data he gets from your history, your examination, and your ECG, your doctor may give you the green light. He may say you can go ahead with an aerobics program that builds up to vigorous exercise in any form.

Or he may give you a yellow light: go ahead with caution. He may rule out vigorous competitive sports, such as handball, basketball, squash, paddleball, or racquetball. The intense competition of these sports, in a hot gym or closed court, may put too much strain on some hearts, and the quick movements required for competitive play may aggravate muscle or joint problems.

He may also recommend that you exercise only in a medically supervised program, if there's one in your community, until you've built up your body sufficiently with the training effect to earn your aerobic points on your own.

Or he may prohibit strenuous exercise altogether and recommend that you confine yourself to walking for your aerobic points. He will certainly make this recommendation if you have any of the following conditions:

a. Excessive obesity. If you are more than 50 pounds overweight according to standard charts, jogging and running are out. You must lose weight first on a walking program. (See the program for the excessively over-weight on page 124.)

b. Recent heart attack, or any irregularity of the heart, including disease of the valves, angina pectoris, enlarge-ment, or disorders of cardiac rhythm. In some cases even fast walking may be prohibited.

c. Uncontrolled sugar diabetes constantly fluctuating between too much and not enough blood sugar.

d. Blood pressure too high to control with medication.

e. Any recently active internal bleeding, or any infec-tious disease during its acute stage. For some of these patients, the rule is no exercise at all.

With other conditions, your doctor may limit your ex-ercise to a medically supervised program. If you have a chronic or convalescent-stage infection, kidney or lung disease, anemia, or insulin-controlled diabetes, you can count on getting some definite restrictions from your doc-tor. He or she will also give you strict boundaries for any workouts if you're on medication for high blood pressure, for convulsions, or arthritis (other than the hands), or if you get bad pain with walking caused by blood vessel disease of the legs.

Whatever your condition, once you get your doctor's approval—BEGIN. Even if he's limited you to walking (and walking can be recommended to almost anyone), you can still build up to full aerobic fitness. From the charts in Chapter 5, you'll see that walking can get you just as many points as any of the more strenuous exer-cises, and can give your body the same training effect benefits. It just takes longer.

Even Meyer Friedman, the opponent of vigorous ex-ercise whose *Type A Behavior and Your Heart* we dis-cussed in Chapter 3, has been quoted as saying that walking, cycling on level terrain, and easy swimming with rest breaks and inner tubes are okay, even for cardiac patients.

Yet since Dr. Friedman's objections to other forms of exercise have prompted hundreds of inquiries and requests for my comments, I would like to digress here briefly and consider his feelings toward jogging.

Dr. Friedman bases his objections to vigorous exercise primarily on a study of 64 patients who died instantaneously or suddenly of heart attacks, nearly all of whom had underlying severe heart disease. Of these 64 persons, 11 were engaged in or had just finished what Dr. Friedman classifies as "severe" exercise at the time of their heart attacks, and 6 after or during "moderate" exercise. The remaining 47 persons were stricken during sedentary activity such as standing, sitting, or sleeping. Out of the entire group of 64, only four deaths occurred that could be associated directly with jogging or running.

Following the publication of this article in the September 10, 1973, issue of the *Journal of the American Medical Association,* several rebuttals were published in subsequent journals. One letter to the editor was succinct and to the point:

After reading the article by Friedman, it seemed to me that they retrospectively saw a dangerous effect of uncontrolled exercise on subjects whom they later found to have severe coronary heart disease, and that they then vaulted to the astonishing conclusion that exercise is bad for everyone. This would be rather like finding that a given number of people die each year from the aspiration of food, and that, therefore, no one should eat.

R. Edward Dodge, Jr., M.D.

To generalize from this data that all jogging is dangerous seems unwarranted. But how dangerous is exercise for patients with diagnosed heart disease?

In the January 1976 issue of *Circulation,* an interesting article was published by Drs. Mead and Pyfer from the CAPRI program in Seattle, Washington. Since 1967 nearly 1,000 patients have participated in its medically supervised exercise programs, which meet for one hour three times per week. At least 85 percent of these patients have diagnosed heart disease, yet most are involved in fast walking or jogging. In the last nine years there have been 15 instances where a patient collapsed while exercising, but in all 15 cases the patients were successfully resuscitated. This makes exercise for heart patients sound dangerous until you realize that the patients have logged over 116,000 hours of supervised activity! This means that a problem requiring resuscitation occurred only once every 7,700 hours of exposure. Exercising one hour three times a week, it would take 50 years to accumulate this number of hours of exposure. But even those statistics may be high.

At the 1975 American Heart Association annual meeting, Haskell presented a paper documenting the frequency of problems in 25 cardiac rehabilitation programs involving 8,092 patients during the years 1960–1973. There were 949,568 hours of participation, and a problem requiring resuscitation occurred only once every 17,585 hours. A fatal problem occurred in a class once every 94,957 hours. He concluded that the risk of death for cardiac patients while exercising in medically supervised exercise programs is not much different from that reported for cardiac patients in general.

But what about the value of exercise in preventing or delaying the onset of heart disease in healthy people? Remember that inactivity is listed as a primary coronary risk factor and that both the Framingham study (5,127 men and women followed for 16 years) and the study of San Francisco longshoremen by Paffenberger (6,351 men followed for 22 years) found sedentary people have more than double the cardiac mortality rate of people in the active category. In reviewing the circumstances of sudden death in the Albany Study (a NIH study much like the one conducted in Framingham, Massachusetts), Dr. Joseph T. Doyle could recall no instance where physical activity could be implicated.

Against these studies of many thousands of people, Dr. Friedman's study of 64 individuals does not seem to justify claims that exercise is dangerous for everyone. I would say, however, that it should serve to underscore the caution we have given over the years to cardiac patients and primarily sedentary people: that unaccustomed, unsupervised, strenuous exercise may be dangerous.

Also, if your examination reveals a limiting condition,

keep in mind that in many cases an aerobic exercise program may help control the problem.

Maria Johnston's story is a good case in point. (Her husband, Bob, you remember, was the man who needed to go two more minutes on the treadmill just to fail!) After Bob ran his first 8-mile "Turkey Trot" on Thanksgiving Day, Maria knew she wanted to get involved in running. Bob said he could see it in her eyes when he finished the race.

But Maria had a bad back. She had injured it several years earlier, and at times the pain was almost unbearable. As she recalls it, when she tried running a year after the injury, "My back really hit me hard. My whole leg and foot would go numb."

But Maria was not a quitter. She waited for a month and then started playing tennis, even though her back and leg still bothered her. After a few months of tennis, the pain was gone, and she started running again. The pain didn't return, but her foot was still slightly numb. She decided she wasn't going to let that deter her. With a numb foot, she built up to running two miles a day.

Then she and Bob took up long-distance running. Slowly and agonizingly Maria built up to five miles a day, ultimately to marathon distances! And just about the time she reached the five-mile training level, the numbness in her foot began to disappear.

Over a two-year period, Maria was faithful and both her symptoms and her performance continued to improve. Her program climaxed recently when she was stress-tested and she established a new treadmill record for women tested at the Cooper Clinic! Twenty-seven minutes and thirty seconds!

We have performed over 5,000 tests on women, and the performance of this thirty-nine-year-old woman exceeds all! Certainly this should be a source of inspiration for other women, with or without back problems.

But, fortunately, most of us don't have to go through the pain of making a dramatic recovery, we just need to get started. Don't wait around. Make an appointment with your physician, get his approval, and get going!

## Preparation: Diet, Dress, Equipment, Workout Conditions

The type of *diet* to be consumed depends upon a variety of needs, such as weight loss, control of cholesterol, and blood sugar, which will be discussed in a later chapter. The important point to remember here is always wait at least *two hours* after a heavy meal before exercising vigorously. For at least 1½ hours following a meal, blood is diverted away from the brain (which makes you sleepy) and the heart. If you already have a problem with heart disease (either diagnosed or undiagnosed), exercise during this time may be more of a stress than the heart can stand. Frequently, patients with heart disease have the most angina or chest pain following a meal. Waiting two hours after a meal allows adequate time for the blood to resume its normal distribution and exercise is safe. Notice, I said a "heavy" meal. After a light meal, consisting primarily of fluids, exercise can be engaged in much sooner.

For early risers who get their points before breakfast, we find that there's no ill effect from working out on an empty stomach. Some of our people, though, like a glass of fruit juice ten or fifteen minutes before starting, and we find that's okay, too. It's a good way to get a little quick energy for waking up.

Also remember fluid intake. When you're working out regularly, you sweat and can lose copious amounts of fluid—sometimes up to 2 percent or more of your body weight. You need to replace this fluid, and sometimes your instinctive thirst, or your own habits, won't lead you to drink enough "replacement" fluids. Dehydration may occur, resulting in headaches, excess fatigue, and a general lack of energy. If this happens, concentrate on fluid replacement first, overcompensating for what you feel is adequate. A word of caution, though: avoid ice-cold drinks immediately after exercise. They may lead to some irritability or irregularity of the heart rhythm. Use cool or chilled fluids only.

Profuse sweating leads to excess loss of salt and other electrolytes. The simplest thing to do to compensate for this loss is to increase the amount of salt you use at mealtimes. There are also salt pills and liquid salt solutions, such as ERG and Gatorade, that will help your body to return its normal condition more rapidly. Avoid solutions with high sugar content if the sweat loss is excessive (with marathon running, for example) and utilize less concentrated solutions. ERG and Body Punch fit more in this category. Yet, again, the important thing is to replace the fluid first! Salt tablets without adequate fluid may aggravate or potentiate a heat stress condition.

At times, underlying medical problems may lead to unusual vulnerability to heat stress or fluid loss problems. While officiating at a marathon recently, I was summoned to the aid of a young runner who had collapsed. He was twenty-two years of age, highly conditioned, and the temperature was in the fifties. Yet he showed all the symptoms of severe heat stress and dehydration. Yes, he had consumed fluids at every aid station, but for two weeks preceding the race, he had suffered from a persistent diarrhea. Not realizing his dehydrated state, he entered the race and ran nearly twenty miles before the combined stress overtaxed his body. It was amazing to see how rapidly he responded to nothing more than intravenous fluids.

*Dress and Equipment.* Unless you're a swimmer, you are going to need a good pair of shoes particularly adapted to the exercise you select. The right footwear can make exercise more enjoyable, preventing problems with strains, blisters, sprains, and sore legs and ankles. If you're a jogger, consider several things in purchasing a pair of shoes. The sole must be adequately cushioned to absorb the impact of running on a hard surface. A shallow to deep ripple usually works best. I would suggest a slight elevation of the heel to take some of the strain off the Achilles tendons. In fact, a wide heel that tends to stabilize the foot works well for many people, and if the back of the shoe comes up high on the heel, this tends to distribute the pressure on the Achilles tendons more evenly. An adequate arch support is also necessary in a good jogging shoe. Finally, being able to buy a shoe for its width as well as length has merit.

The ripple-sole jogging shoes I use myself have a porous foam wedge built into the heel to reduce road impact further and cushion the run. These shoes soak up 40 percent of the force of my body's weight at every step, and when you consider that I take nearly 2,000 steps each mile, you can see the amount of "road shock" saved really adds up.

If you've ever had pain from shin splints, you may find that a pair of these cushion-sole shoes is the answer. Or you may need to switch from exercising on a hard surface, such as a gym floor or concrete, to softer turf.

If you have problems with the Achilles tendons, ankles, or arches, or difficulty with one specific area of your foot, one particular brand of shoe may be better for you than another. Consult the appendix for comparison ratings of the popular running shoes developed by the American Society of Podiatrists and *Runner's World* magazine.

Other tips on dress: two pairs of socks help avoid blisters, especially when you're just getting started. If your legs chafe around the thighs, cut down on the friction by rubbing them with vaseline prior to the workout. Wear loose clothing that doesn't restrict your movements. For men, jockey shorts give enough support and are recommended for long-distance running, but for short-distance running, handball, and other vigorous workout sports, you should use an athletic supporter. Cover the nipples with Band-Aids for long-distance runs; otherwise, friction from the shirt can cause irritation and bleeding.

Most women need a good supportive bra, not only for comfort but also to avoid strain on the ligaments supporting the breast.

Of course, you'll wash whatever clothing comes in contact with your body after each workout. That simple hygiene can save your skin from irritation and rashes later on.

If you're outdoors and it's cold, wear a hooded sweat shirt or a cap that comes over your ears. If it's really cold, down below zero, use a surgical or dental mask, a knitted ski mask, a loose muffler, or a terry-cloth "veil" over the mouth and nose to warm up the air a bit before it goes into your lungs. Loose-fitting mittens will keep your hands warmer than gloves, and a towel or scarf can keep the back of your neck feeling luxuriously good all during the workout time.

Two things to avoid, though, when it comes to dress: first, in cold weather, don't make the mistake of putting on too many clothes. They'll just hamper your movements and make you perspire excessively, making it hard to avoid chilling after exercise. And second, in hot weather stay away from those rubberized or impervious suits you see advertised so often. Their claim to give you weight loss is not only misleading, it's dangerous. It's misleading because the "pounds" you sweat off during a workout are pounds of water. This weight is regained as soon as you quench your thirst after the workout. And because these suits block the body's natural cooling mechanism by trapping perspiration, they're unsafe, especially on hot, humid days. Your body tries to cool off by perspiring, but the perspiration can't evaporate. Your temperature climbs and you may develop symptoms of heat exhaustion or sunstroke.

*Equipment* is really not necessary if you're exercising outdoors. And most of the fancy indoor equipment—"indoor gyms," pulleys, vibrators, springs, barbells—is worthless, aerobically speaking. I've seen too many people waste their money on something that works only on the muscle tone, and then after a few weeks, when they tire of it, just gathers dust. You're better off doing simple calisthenics and saving your money.

For indoor aerobic exercise, there are three items worth buying.

1. A cushioned floor mat, for indoor running in place or rope skipping. Remember still to wear a pair of the good running shoes to further absorb the impact.

2. A stationary bicycle. Avoid motorized bicycles; for aerobic exercise, you provide the horsepower. You can

get one that's adequate for between $60 and $130; more sophisticated models with calibrated resistance sell for $350 to $600. Make sure you can adjust the resistance, and that the bicycle has a speedometer with an odometer. Test out the seat and handlebar position for comfort before you buy, and look for a good chain guard so that your clothing won't get caught.

Adequate exercise on a stationary cycle is accomplished by considering the intensity and duration of the activity. The following combinations lead to an aerobic training effect if engaged in at least four times per week:

| HEART RATE | TIME (min: sec) |
|:---:|:---:|
| 150 | 10:00 |
| 140 | 15:00 |
| 130 | 30:00 |

Count the heart rate for 10 seconds immediately following exercise and multiply by 6. The heart rate should be at this level; if not, the next time adjust the resistance accordingly. Exercise comfortably, select a program that is within your capacity, not one leading to total exhaustion at the conclusion of the workout.

In Chapter 5 there are age-adjusted, progressive, stationary cycling exercise programs that can be used by both men and women of all ages. In the appendix, the aerobic point values are listed for this type of exercise, and also points have been determined, adjusted to weight and resistance, that can be used for the more expensive, calibrated-resistance bicycles (page 243).

3. A treadmill. With a motorized treadmill, you can come close to simulating regular running—indoors—and it is possible to obtain more aerobic benefit in a shorter period of time. How? By elevating the front of the treadmill. Holding the speed constant but elevating the treadmill may double or even triple the point value. Study the chart in the appendix (page 251) that awards points for treadmill walking and running based on the speed and incline.

Treadmills come in several varieties but are moderately expensive. They range from about $800 to several thousand dollars. Stability and durability are very important, so study the construction carefully before you buy. Some treadmills have adjustable inclines, either electrical or manual. Others have a standard built-in 5 percent incline. Since it is possible to increase the point value by elevating the front, an incline has an advantage. You can, however, elevate the front with blocks and get the same effect. Avoid treadmills with belts that run on rollers. Purchase one with a smooth surface if you wish to minimize foot problems.

*Workout conditions* affect your performance. Here are the guidelines that we recommend.

When it's more than 95 degrees out, or 90 degrees with over 60 percent humidity, don't exercise strenuously. Wait for your workout until the early morning or twilight, when it's cooler. Or swim for your points. Heat acclimatization (or the lack of it) also affects the temperature at which it is safe to exercise.

When it's below zero, use the mask, veil, or scarf we talked about to warm the air. Extra-cold air in your windpipe may cause coronary artery constriction in susceptible people, leading to chest pain. Also, airway obstruction or bronchoconstriction may occur with inhaled cool air. Yet if you're fit and observe some precautions, you can laugh at the cold as some of our Air Force men in Alaska do. They keep jogging right through the winter up there.

When it's smoggy out, if you live in the suburbs or the city, you don't have to stay in. Choose a place upwind or away from city traffic if you can, to help cut down on the irritation of air contaminants and fumes. Unless your doctor has examined you and advised differently, it's better to be exercising in the smog than sitting around letting your body deteriorate. If your city's "air quality" reading gets up to the "unsatisfactory" or "warning" level, though, I recommend in-place running or some other form of indoor workout until the atmosphere has cleared.

Altitude changes the oxygen-pressure in the air, and so changes your performance. See the tables in the appendix to adjust aerobic point requirements to your area.

If you're a jogger, choose a running surface that's as comfortable as you can find. Springy turf is best, followed by composition track, cinder track, dirt road, asphalt, and concrete, in just about that order. The sidewalk is a difficult place to exercise, with curbs, pedestrians, and other hazards to negotiate, but, from a safety standpoint, much better than a busy street.

And if you're going distances over a mile or two, avoid running on the slanted surface usually found at the side of the road. You'll avoid knee problems by running on the crown instead, but if this isn't possible, try alternating sides when it's safe and permissible.

If you're in a gym or an indoor handball or squash court, watch for inadequate ventilation and overheating, particularly in the summer. A few fast doubles matches in a closed racquetball or squash court can raise the heat, especially if the court's been busy all day. Running laps on a flat gym floor aggravates one side of the body unless you change directions on alternate days.

One further point about hot weather and difficult conditions: if they leave you fatigued, that's the time to cut down on speed and intensity and compensate with increased duration. Exercise at a lower rate, for a longer time. As you'll see from the chart packs, you'll still get the same number of points, but you'll get them more safely.

Depending on your exercise, too, you may get the same number of points with a little less speed, while you're going the *same amount* of distance. During the year here in Dallas, my afternoon run is generally 21 to 22 minutes for three miles. But on hot summer days I slow down to the upper range of the 17-point scale—closer to 24 minutes for the same three miles. I still get the same 17 points, but with much less strain and fatigue.

## The Warm-Up

At the Aerobics Center, nobody misses a warm-up before a workout. Even with the treadmill ECG test, we warm up at a slow speed and reduced incline. No matter who you are—even if you're a highly conditioned athlete—you need a good warm-up period before getting involved in any vigorous exercise. Warm-up helps guard against cramps, sprains, strains, and, especially important for people over thirty-five, heart irregularity.

Without a warm-up, any resting heart, if instantaneously stressed, may show signs of insufficient blood supply. This has been documented by ECG stress test on athletes in top condition. In one test, athletes went from a sitting position to all-out run at ten miles per hour on a 30 percent–inclined treadmill. Over 60 percent of these athletes showed cardiac abnormalities on their ECGs when their hearts were put to this sudden strain. Yet, when the *same test* was given to the same athletes after a two-minute warm-up, no such abnormalities occurred.

The warm-up routine we recommend for most people at the Aerobics Center focuses on *stretching* exercises rather than strengthening or conditioning exercises. We save the conditioning exercises until after the aerobic workout, so that you don't begin your aerobic exercise with an oxygen debt. We also find that the additional time spent in stretching helps to prevent cramps, shin splints, and other tendon and musculoskeletal problems.

Here is a 7- to 10-minute warm-up routine we recommend:

*Arm circles.* Arms extended straight out to the sides, rotate them counterclockwise 10 times, then clockwise 10 times. The circle described by your hands should have a diameter of at least 2 feet.

*Twisters.* Same position, arms extended, legs apart about 30 inches. Twist trunk all the way to the right, then all the way to the left, 10 times.

*Trunk circles.* Legs apart about 30 inches, hands together above head. With both hands together, touch the outside of your left foot, then the ground between the legs, then the outside of the right foot, then return to erect position, hands above your head. Repeat 10 times.

*Toe touches.* Sit with legs apart and flat on floor or ground. Reach for your toes with both hands, bringing your forehead as close to your knees as possible. Don't "bounce," even if you're not reaching your feet; just stretch, slowly, a total of 10 times.

An alternative to the sitting toe touches is the *standing leg stretcher*. Find a chair or table about 3 feet in height, and place one foot on the table so that the knee is straight and the leg is approximately parallel to the floor. Extend the fingertips toward the toe by stretching out slowly. After considerable training, placing the chin on the knee is not an unrealistic goal. This maneuver stretches the big muscles in the back of the upper part of the leg (hamstrings) and tends to protect them from injury. Stretching one leg for 15–30 seconds and then repeating with the other leg is all that is necessary.

*Knee-chest.* Lie flat on the floor on your back with the legs extended. First pull one knee up to the chest, hold for a count of 5, and then repeat with the other knee. Relax, then pull both knees together up to the chest. Hold for a count of 5. Repeat the cycle 5 times. This is not only a good stretching exercise, but also good for the back.

*Sprinter.* Assume a squatting position and then extend one leg straight back as far as possible, hands touching the floor. Hold momentarily and then repeat with the other leg. Repeat the cycle 5 times.

*Achilles tendon stretcher.* Lean forward, body straight, palms against a wall at about eye level. Step backwards, supporting your weight with your hands, staying flat-footed until you can feel your calf muscles stretching. Hold for 15 seconds. Repeat 5–10 times. Again, don't "bounce," just stretch out those calf and ankle tendons, *slowly*.

This is one of the best exercises for chronic Achilles tendon problems and should be done 2 to 3 times per day if a problem exists.

If time is at a premium, the two most important stretching exercises are the standing leg stretcher and the calf or Achilles tendon stretcher. Two to three minutes of these exercises before running will help immensely in avoiding the muscle and ligament injuries that incapacitate so many middle-aged runners.

After these warm-up stretching exercises, you are ready to begin the aerobic portion of your workout.

## Choose Your Proper Performance Objective

The cardinal rule of the aerobics point system is: *safely, slowly and progressively.* Follow the charts. Don't get ahead of them, and don't get ahead of yourself. More speed or intensity too soon is like taking a whole bottle of medicine instead of just the recommended dosage—an invitation to trouble, in this case from tendons, muscles, joints, and your heart. Classify yourself in consultation with your doctor, pick the Week 1 program that's right for your age and condition, and stick with it.

Several other things to remember: the goal for the week represents the objective you should aim for at the *end*, not the beginning, of the week. Work up gradually from where you were the week before. Remember also that there's no imperative that you reach that week's goal at that particular week: what counts is that you reach it eventually, and that you then move beyond it till you're getting 30 points. So if you find it too difficult to advance at some stage in your conditioning program, simply stay at the level you're in and work until you can *comfortably* move up to the next.

You may find that your performance, if we graphed it on a chart, would advance in a series of plateaus—like stair steps—rather than a straight upward line or curve. One day the training effect takes hold, and up you go.

Remember, too, that you can drop *down* in your ability to meet a week's objectives if illness or a trip or some other interruption keeps you away from your exercise routine. Don't try to pick up just where you left off. Backtrack on the charts. A general rule is to go back a week for every week you've been away from exercise, but since different people lose their aerobic capacities at different rates, you may have to adjust up or down. Gauge your performance objectives according to the way you feel when you're exercising, and don't push too hard to get back to where you were before. Your track or your gym or your pool will still be there next week.

Make sure you are there, too, and *without* muscle strains and sprains or fatigue from trying to catch up too quickly.

## Monitor Your Performance

"I'm pushing it pretty good out there, Doc," one of my runners said after a workout. "But how can I tell if I ought to slow down, or if I'm just being lazy and feeling sorry for myself?"

Good question. Here are the immediate signs of over-exertion to look for during exercise: tightness or pain in the chest, severe breathlessness, lightheadedness, dizziness, loss of muscle control, and nausea. When you experience any of these symptoms, stop exercising immediately. Your workouts are too vigorous. Try reducing the intensity or duration of the activity.

If chest pains occur, physician consultation is always advised before resuming your program.

Nausea or vomiting after exercise indicates that you've exceeded your capacity, or else you're exercising too soon after a meal.

Any time any symptom is persistent, medical consultation is advised.

Another result of exercising too hard is more of a chronic effect—overfatigue. This may be indicated by excessive drowsiness in the late afternoon or early evening, or by an inability to sleep restfully at night. Tossing and turning may result from an overfatigued state.

## Cooling Down

*A five-minute cool-down* period not only helps you avoid nausea and cramps, it's also an essential step in your exercise routine to avoid more serious problems.

When you're exercising, a lot of blood is being sent

to your legs to keep those big thigh and calf muscles adequately supplied with oxygen. While your legs are moving, so is the blood—helped on its way through the one-way valves of your veins and back to the heart by the squeezing action of the muscles.

If you stop suddenly, though, the squeezing action is gone. There's no movement in the muscles to help your heart circulate your blood. A "pooling" effect may keep the blood in your legs, depriving both your heart and your brain of much-needed oxygen.

When your heart isn't getting enough blood, consequences are more serious. The worst thing you can do right after a workout is to go into a steam room, a sauna, or a hot shower. Also, don't go sit down in your car, especially after a winter run, thinking you're going to drive away as soon as you get your breath. When you combine a sudden stop of activity with a sudden increase in warmth, the blood pools and the surface capillary vessels dilate, keeping an even greater percentage of blood away from the heart.

So taper off gradually. You should take at least as long to cool down as you did to warm up—as I've said, five minutes is the *minimum.*

If you've been jogging, walk at least a quarter of a mile.

If you've been playing basketball or tennis, resist the impulse to plunk down on the bench or flop under a tree. Walk around near the court.

If you've been swimming, walk back and forth across the shallow end of the pool.

If you've been cycling, finish up a mile or so from home, and pedal back slowly and easily. If you're using a stationary cycle, slow down and ease off the resistance.

Then you can enjoy your sauna or your shower, and feel good the rest of the day.

## Check Your Recovery Pulse and Breathing Rate

Five minutes after exercise, which includes the cool-down, check your pulse. If it's over 120, that's a sign that the exercise was too vigorous or extensive for a person in your condition. In that case, you should reduce either the intensity or the duration of the activity. Lower heart rates may be advisable in some people, especially the sick or aged, depending upon the results of the stress test.

The wrist is the best place to get a good pulse reading, but if you have trouble, feel the pulse in your throat, just below your ear or to one side of your larynx (voice box). Use your fingertips rather than your thumb and don't press too hard. With a watch that has a sweep second hand, count the pulse for 10 seconds, then multiply by 6, or count for 15 seconds and multiply by 4. This gives your pulse rate, accurate within 2 percent according to telemetry heart rate studies. Don't count for a whole minute; your pulse rate is dropping rapidly, particularly if you are highly conditioned.

In previous publications, we encouraged 10-minute monitoring and suggested a heart rate less than 100. There is so much variation among conditioned people that we no longer make that recommendation. All that is important is to be sure the 5-minute recovery rate is less than 120 beats per minute.

Your breathing or respiration rate is also an index to overexertion. Ten minutes after you stop exercising, you should be breathing at a fairly comfortable rate, somewhere around 12 to 16 breaths per minute. If you're still breathless, you've been pushing too hard in your workout or you may have some type of lung or respiratory problem.

## Conditioning Calisthenics

After you've cooled down, we recommend that you perform muscle-building or strengthening calisthenics. Start with 10 repetitions, and add 1 or 2 each week until a maximum of 25 can be performed. These exercises strengthen the muscles of the arms, the abdomen, and the back and may be of particular value in relieving pain in the lower back muscles.

*Sit-ups.* Lie supine, hands clasped behind the head, knees bent. Sit up, touching right elbow to left knee when sitting position is reached. Alternate from right to left knee. Push your toes under a bar or sofa if you need to anchor the feet.

*Arm lifts.* Sitting on the floor or ground, support your weight on your hands, positioned slightly behind you at either side. Keep your arms straight, elbows locked, and arch your head back, bringing your hips off the floor with your legs straight. All your weight should be on your hands and your heels. Then lower yourself back to the sitting position, and repeat.

*Pushups.* Men should do pushups from the toes, attempting to keep the body straight, touching only the nose. Older men and women should do the same, but from the knees rather than the toes. (An exercise mat is helpful here, if you're on a hard floor.)

A variety of other exercises can be used for muscle strengthening or conditioning either with or without equipment. These, however, are supplemental exercises and to be done only in addition to, not in place of, one of the primary aerobic exercises.

So there you have the guidelines we recommend for exercising safely. I can't promise you 100 percent freedom from problems, especially blisters and sore muscles, when you're starting out, but I can promise you'll encounter a lot *fewer* of these problems following our guidelines and our "starter" programs. Research you'll read about in subsequent chapters has demonstrated that.

Still, even if you're aerobically fit, you can have a fall, a sprain, or any other kind of accident. If you overdo exercise to the point of fatigue, you especially increase the odds of straining a muscle or twisting a knee.

In my years of working with runners, I've observed a variety of overuse ailments such as knee or ankle pain, hip soreness, and tendon problems. Most are self-limited and with rest disappear. I've noticed that the problems start developing when an attempt is being made to increase the weekly mileage. At a 10–15-mile/week schedule (moderate speed) very few problems occur. But when the threshold of 15–20 miles per week is exceeded, overuse problems begin to occur. It is the rare individual who can consistently run 75–100 miles per week or more without problems; those people usually become the top competitive distance runners. Mostly they are lean, asthenic individuals, and perhaps their genetic endowment has enabled them to accomplish such training goals without incapacitation. It was once said that "world-class distance runners are born, not made." From an anthropometric standpoint, perhaps that is true.

But remember, you don't have to exceed even 10 miles a week to get all the aerobic points you need—if your only goal is running to practice preventive medicine.

In a 1970 article published in the *Journal of the American Medical Association,* I asked physicians to send me documented cases of fatalities that occurred as a result of jogging. Although there were minimal responses, I found these common denominators: they were all men; nearly all over forty; in the first six weeks of their training program; jogging; and with no medical clearance.

Our guidelines have been designed as safeguards against this kind of incident, yet it's not possible to keep everyone within the safety of these boundaries. Accidents continue to happen, and when they do, they make the news. From time to time, I'm saddened to open my mail and find a local news clipping about a person (usually a middle-aged man) who died while exercising.

Exercise accidents will happen, just like automobile accident fatalities, or drownings, or fires.

But exercise accidents are no more a logical reason to stop exercise than other accidents are a reason to stop driving, or swimming, or heating our homes.

In fact, you've seen the overwhelming evidence that indicates that you're safer if you exercise than if you don't.

There are also some myths about exercise I would like to discuss—colorful theories, all entirely without evidence and in contradiction to the documentation in the medical literature. I've had hundreds of letters asking me to comment on three of these theories, so I'll take this opportunity to do so here.

The first is the myth of the "heartbeat bank," the idea

that your heart is programmed to beat only a certain number of times during your life. According to this theory, exercise is unsafe because it raises the heart rate and so uses up the beats in the "bank."

In the first place, of course, there's no evidence that the concept of the "bank" has any validity. But in the second place, and more importantly, aerobic exercise *saves* heartbeats in significantly large numbers. Your heart rate increases while you're exercising, but during the other twenty-three or more hours of the day and night, your heart rate will be lower than before. As the readers of *Aerobics for Women* will remember, after my wife, Millie, began her jogging program, her resting heart rate dropped from 82 to 57 beats per minute. Even when you allow for the 4,000 or so extra beats she sustains while she's warming up, exercising, and cooling down, Millie saves about *30,000* heartbeats every day.

If the "bank" theory were true, for every three years Millie kept exercising, she'd be adding an extra year's worth of heartbeats to her life.

Another of the "wear-out" theories is that, because the legs are in motion, jogging is unsafe for the hip joints. This theory also came without evidence, and when it was presented to Dr. Lowell Lutter, an active member of the American Medical Joggers Association, Dr. Lutter ordered a computer search done of the medical literature on hip osteoarthritis (deterioration). No reports were found in support of the theory, and one study, done on 74 world-class distance runners, showed the exact opposite effect.

According to X-ray examination, the hip joints of these distance runners, after an average of 20 years of distance running, showed only *half* as many instances of wear and tear (degenerative osteoarthritis) as the hips of a control group of non-runners.

The third of these "wear-out" theorists appeared in a national magazine with an article entitled "Jogging Can Kill You . . . and That's Not the Half of It." Again the material present was pure speculation, without a single reference to any reputable documented study. The claim was that jogging would jar the organs and the skeletal system, and so lead to a number of problems including varicose veins, "dropped" organs, and skeletal wear and tear.

There's no evidence to support this theory, either, and as with the other two, there's a large body of evidence to refute it. After one million miles of jogging here, we find that in most cases varicose veins tend to improve with jogging, as muscle tone improves—and recent Swedish studies have emphasized this. The "dropped" organs and skeletal deterioration described by this theory have yet to appear during my sixteen years' experience working with tens of thousands of people both in the Air Force and at the Aerobics Center. The longevity studies of endurance athletes mention none of these internal or skeletal problems. And a recent study of champion track athletes aged 40 to 75, performed at our Institute for Aerobics Research, showed Masters Track and Field athletes in general to have excellent cardiovascular function and body composition and function characteristics.

So if someone you know is staying away from exercise because of these "wear-out" theories, you can tell him or her that they simply don't hold up. The human body didn't evolve through millions of years to be fragile and sedentary. You'll wear out a lot faster from the stress of inactivity than you will from exercise.

## Competition

But, unfortunately, guidelines tend to be forgotten when a group has a competitive event. A race, a tournament, a big game can get the adrenalin flowing, leading some people to overdo. Or, worse, it can attract some players who really aren't in any shape to compete.

In order to avoid problems with competition, don't compete unless you are adequately prepared. If you are past thirty-five years of age, obtain physician's clearance, including a stress test, before entering. Remember to warm up and cool down properly *and run within your tolerance.* Pushing to the point of chest pain, excess fatigue, nausea, or light-headedness is not only foolish, but dangerous.

Compete for the enjoyment of it, not as if your life depended on it.

## The Real Competition

Remember that even though competition can give your incentive a boost, the real competition is with yourself. If you're exercising at least three times a week, exceeding 30 points, it is not necessary to compete, run a 12-minute test, or time yourself for a 1½-mile run. Accent the fact that you are in good shape, already a winner.

Remember, too, that when you're off your exercise routine because of illness or business trips, it is easy to quit. That is the time to use your competitive grit to get you out there exercising again slowly and progressively. There aren't any perfect humans. We all are creatures of inertia, and "a body at rest tends to remain at rest."

Also remember that at the beginning of any exercise program the first ten weeks are the hardest. That's when you'll get blisters, sore muscles, and *discouraged*. Other things in life will seem more important than your newly established workout routine.

But stick with it. If you have your doctor's approval, you *know* you can make it. Millions of others have, and so will you. They improved, as you will, in spurts, in plateaus. They sweated through those "stale" periods, when their performance didn't get better and their morale sagged. And they made it.

You can too. Even when you're wondering why you ever started an exercise program, you can get through those "stale" days. Just go through the motions. Soon your enthusiasm will return, your performance will go up, and you'll be over another hump.

But don't throw in the towel. As I've said often enough, the ugliest four-letter word in the language is "quit."

Don't quit.

Just take good care.

And stay safe.

# 5

# How to Get Started:
# The Theories, the Evidence,
# and the Chart Pack

Since the first publication of the *Aerobics* books, millions
of people throughout the world have started an aerobics
program, continued with it over the years, and achieved
most satisfying results. Let me give you an example of
what can happen, beautifully described in a letter I
received recently from Graham P. Stansbury of St.
Petersburg, Florida:

Dear Dr. Cooper:

Since you first published your book *Aerobics*, you must have
received many thousands of letters of praise. Nevertheless, I
feel that I must add to these because of what reading that book
has done for my well-being.

*Aerobics* was presented to me by my secretary on my 46th
birthday, June 10, 1969. After finishing only the third chapter,
your message came through so clearly I got up and jogged
around my office for 20 minutes. Thereafter, I jogged at home
every morning for 20 minutes, inside. After a month had
passed and leg pains had abated, I jogged on the street for
20 minutes every morning (2.2 miles) until June 10, 1971,
when I increased to 2.6 miles. I still jog this distance every
morning (22–24 minutes), allowing myself two misses a
month. When traveling, I jog 30–40 minutes in a motel or
hotel parking lot. I have jogged 6,087 miles and spent over
900 hours doing so in seven and one half (7½) years.

As I was overweight, overindulging and overanxious with a
history of arrhythmia at the start, similar to the coronary
candidates you so ably describe in your book, you can imagine
what all this aerobic exercise has done for me psychologically
and emotionally. Weight from 170 to 150; pulse from 80 to 55

(have clocked 48), blood pressure from 140 to 122 (forget the diastolic), vital capacity ? to 95 percent, plus all the other fringe benefits, including sleeping well, feeling and being fit, etc., that accompany regular aerobic conditioning.

I know this is an old story to you, Dr. Cooper, but please accept my sincere thanks for the aerobic message I received from your book. Without this book, I probably would never have gotten the message or out of my unconditional rut.

This is only one of thousands of such letters I have received during the past decade. The program does work, and these people are living testimonials as to its effectiveness.

But you may feel that your case is different—that you have an unusual problem or limitation. Let me respond first by saying that "where there is the will, there is a way."

If the will is there, these are the most commonly asked questions that I hope you will find answered in this chapter:

> What kind of exercise is most beneficial?
>
> How much exercise do I need?
>
> How often; how long; how strenuously?
>
> Where should I start if I am not in shape?
>
> Where should I level off?

These questions cannot be answered until we have asked and answered three more:

> How old am I?
>
> What shape am I in now?
>
> What are my goals?

Sorting out these questions and giving them hard, solid answers has been the key to the success of the aerobics program. For over fifteen years we have conducted studies involving large numbers of men and women, and have been able to establish quantified exercise requirements that apply, with a high degree of certainty, to large numbers of people.

This includes you.

Whatever your age or degree of fitness, it is likely that we have worked with hundreds, if not thousands, of people in your category. From analysis of these many responses, programs have been developed that will produce predictable levels of fitness (the training effect). The same data have made it possible to determine the amount of exercise you need to maintain adequate fitness.

But before we look at the details of the progressive programs, let's try to answer some of those basic questions about exercise mentioned earlier:

For example, what is the most beneficial kind of exercise?

To answer this question, you must understand that exercise can be used in three general ways:

1. *Rest and relaxation.* The weekend round of golf, the Wednesday night bowling, the after-dinner walk. You'll feel better after these, just as you will after a good night's sleep.

2. *Muscle-building or figure-contouring.* Isometrics, calisthenics, weight lifting, and other nonaerobic exercises are important here.

3. *Cardiovascular pulmonary conditioning.* These are the exercises that count. They condition the organs that you live with. Remember, you can get along without big muscles or a pretty figure, but you cannot get along without a good heart! All of these types of exercise have merit, but only one of them may prolong your life.

But if cardiovascular or aerobic conditioning is the most beneficial, how much do we need?

To answer this question, we must start at the fundamental level of the life process: the utilization of oxygen and the production of energy. "Aerobic" means "with air or with oxygen," and the objective of aerobics is to improve those organs and systems involved in the body's processing of oxygen: the heart, lungs, and blood vessels. Improved function means better utilization of oxygen and carries with it the benefits and protection we have already discussed in Chapter 3.

Through analysis of expired-air $CO_2$ and $O_2$ content, it is possible to measure numerically a subject's maximal oxygen utilization. In the early 1960s we established a satisfactory level of fitness of 42.0 ml/kg/min. (age- and sex-adjusted), based primarily on Scandinavian research data. Since then, that figure has not changed. All of our progressive programs are designed to train the subject to the extent that 85 percent of the participants will achieve at least the 42.0 ml/kg/min. level.

## The Point System

Having determined that aerobic exercise is the best for cardiovascular pulmonary conditioning and having established a goal for fitness based on oxygen utilization, it was then necessary to develop a system people could use to achieve these goals. From this research, the concept of points was established, based on the intensity and duration of physical activity.

For example, walking and running one mile at various speeds was evaluated by having subjects exercise on the treadmill, the energy cost being determined by collecting and analyzing all of the expired air. The following chart was developed from the results:

| TIME FOR ONE MILE (minutes) | OXYGEN CONSUMPTION (ml/kg/min.) | POINTS |
|---|---|---|
| 19:59–14:30 | 7 | 1 |
| 14:29–12:00 | 14 | 2 |
| 11:59–10:00 | 21 | 3 |
| 9:59– 8:00 | 28 | 4 |
| 7:59– 6:30 | 35 | 5 |
| under 6:30 | 42 | 6 |

As you can see, the faster the subjects ran the mile, the more oxygen their systems had to process.

You will probably also notice from the chart above that the increasing oxygen requirements * for these different speeds fall into multiples of 7. This made it easy to assign point values for walking and running 1 mile based on the multiple of 7.

For example, walking 1 mile between 19:59 and 14:30 minutes was awarded 1 point, since the energy cost for

---

* Some publications prefer to express the increase in energy requirements (oxygen consumption) in METs, which is an acronym for Multiples of the Resting Energy requirement, or metabolic rate. For a comparison between aerobic points and METs, refer to the discussion in the appendix of this book.

walking 1 mile in 19:59 minutes averages 7 ml/kg/min. The same is true for the other time intervals; that is, the expressed oxygen consumption is for the *slowest*, not the *fastest*, time in an interval.

In this way, you have to work harder to get the necessary points, assuring a better training response.

This same concept for awarding points was used with other exercises and types of physical activity, always using, as the foundation for 1 point, 7 ml/kg/min.

## Endurance Points

In the initial publication of the *Aerobics* books, running longer distances or exercising for greater periods resulted in only a simple multiple of the points. For example, running 1 mile in slightly less than 8:00 minutes was worth 5 points, whereas running 3 miles under 24:00 minutes was awarded 3 x 5, or 15 points. Many people questioned this relationship, since physiologically they felt greater stress running 3 continuous miles in less than 24:00 minutes than running three 8:00-minute miles with a brief rest in between. The question was certainly warranted and prompted additional research. Monitoring heart rate responses and oxygen costs for continuous versus interrupted activity showed an obvious difference and consequently endurance points were awarded. Now, as can be seen in the appendix of this book, running 1 mile slightly under 8:00 minutes is still worth 5 points, but running 3 miles in less than 24:00 minutes is worth 17, not 15, points. This concept of endurance points can be found in all of the point charts, again indicating that the longer the activity, the more aerobic benefit.

Having determined that aerobic exercise is the most beneficial from the standpoint of cardiovascular conditioning, and being able to show that aerobic exercises can be quantified by means of a point system, one additional question had to be answered. How many points are necessary, per day, per week, per month, and so on?

To answer that question, remember that our goal for aerobic conditioning is an oxygen consumption of 42.0

ml/kg/min., *age-* and *sex-*adjusted. For men under thirty years of age, the requirement is 42.0 ml/kg/min.; for older men, the requirement decreases each decade. A standard of 36.0 ml/kg/min. was established for women under thirty years. Again, the requirement decreases with age.

Many questions have arisen regarding the requirement for women, but that value was established because of smaller vital capacities, less muscle mass, and, in general, smaller frames.

Two approaches were used to determine how much exercise or how many points were necessary to achieve these fitness requirement goals. One group of people already conditioned were asked to list their daily and weekly physical activities. Another group went through a progressive training program. Using this approach, it was determined that with 30 points per week the majority of men would meet their goal, and with 24 points per week the women would reach theirs. It did not matter the type of aerobic exercise as long as the point goals were reached. This is the basis for the quantification of some twenty-eight different activities and the awarding of points, as seen in the appendix.

As you progress through one of the conditioning programs, remember that the important goal is to work up to 24 or 30 points per week. Don't worry about exercising at a certain speed or be concerned about what your performance might be on a 12-minute or 1½-mile test. Merely accept the fact that if you are getting the minimum points each week, your fitness is good.

Let me give you some examples:

George Mixon, Sr., is seventy-four years of age and exercises five times per week at the Aerobics Center. He walks five miles each time, averaging about 14 minutes per mile, and he made our 1000 Mile Club during the first year of his membership. He averages 70 points a week.

Jim Millerman, a thirty-seven-year-old insurance executive, regularly runs five miles—Tuesdays, Thursdays, and Saturdays. He runs at a 7-minute-per-mile pace and therefore averages 87 points per week.

Edna Fielding walks indoors at the Aerobics Center. It takes 24 laps to walk a mile, but she will average at least three miles per day 5 days a week. Her average speed is 14½ minutes per mile, and that is excellent for this woman, past sixty years of age. She accumulates at least 30 points per week and is also a member of our 1000 Mile Club.

Mary Scott plays singles tennis an average of seven hours a week, and she is earning 30 points that way.

All of these people are achieving 30 points per week or more. Is that desirable? What is the optimum number of points?

## The Evidence

In Chapter 3 I referred to an article that we published correlating levels of physical fitness determined by tread-mill stress testing with selected coronary risk factors. As you will recall, people in the good and excellent categories of fitness had consistently lower coronary risk factors than those in the poor and very poor categories. If you study the chart on page 42, you will notice that in most of the risks there is no significant difference between the good and excellent groups, whereas there is a highly significant difference between the excellent and the poor and very poor. In this group of nearly 3,000 men, tested for the first time at the Cooper Clinic, 574 had kept exercise records and we were able to compare their fitness level with the number of points they were averaging each week. The results were as follows:

### FITNESS AND AEROBIC POINTS/WEEK: 574 MALES, FIRST VISIT, AVERAGE AGE 44.5 YEARS
#### (INSTITUTE FOR AEROBICS RESEARCH)

| FITNESS CATEGORY | NUMBER | POINTS/WEEK |
|---|---|---|
| Very poor | 16 | 17.1 |
| Poor | 44 | 17.2 |
| Fair | 86 | 18.5 |
| Good | 226 | 34.6 |
| Excellent | 202 | 50.1 |

Studying the chart carefully, you will notice that the men in the three lowest categories were averaging fewer than 20 points per week. You would expect those in the very poor category to be the lowest, but the size of the group was too small to reach a valid conclusion. Yet it is obvious that a distinct difference exists at about 34 points per week. Remember, in the coronary risk chart no significant difference existed between the good and excellent categories, so the conclusion can be reached that, from a coronary risk standpoint, 50 points per week is no better than 34 points per week. If you average 34 points per week, the study shows that your coronary risks will be lower than those people averaging less.

But what about 75, 100, or more points per week? Do you get more protection the more points you get per week? We don't know the answer to that question yet, but we are conducting additional research that we hope will provide the answer.

## Some Theories: More or Less?

One prominent theory is that marathoners—that is, people actively participating in 26.2-mile road races—will never die of a heart attack. Complementing that theory is the requirement for running at least 6 miles six times a week to have any protection from coronary disease. I agree that long-endurance activities have a protective effect, although nothing currently known to mankind is *completely* protective. But in my years of doing human medical research, I have made one distinct observation: *never say "never" about anything!* For a marathoner, the chances of heart attack are remote, but there is always human variation. And since heart disease is a complex problem, exercise alone cannot be considered the panacea.

Recently it was brought to my attention that one of our forty-four-year-old patients was hospitalized after suffering a heart attack that occurred while he was relaxing at home. In reviewing his exercise records, we found that he had successfully completed several marathons, usually averaging faster than 7:30 minutes per mile. As I have said so many times, regular aerobic exercise is not an absolute guarantee against heart disease. However, it will very likely delay the onset, and we can document that a person who is exercising regularly has a better chance of surviving a heart attack, when and if it occurs.

Let me give you another interesting case history. Until age thirty-six, this physician was totally inactive, normal in weight, and smoking fewer than ten cigarettes per day. He had been a competitive swimmer in high school, but through college and during his medical training he had been totally inactive. At age thirty-six, he started in the aerobics program, progressed rapidly, and was quite faithful with his program over the next five years. In fact, he enjoyed running so much that he wanted to run a marathon. He was training hard and had reached a level of fitness enabling him to run 15 miles, averaging faster than 7:00 minutes per mile. Needless to say, this was superb conditioning for a forty-one-year-old man! Approximately three days after his best 15-mile run, he was running 1-mile wind sprints. After one, he was cooling down when he collapsed. A friend who was nearby attempted resuscitation unsuccessfully and then went for help. Meanwhile, the runner regained consciousness, confused but without other symptoms. Nonetheless, he was admitted to a coronary care unit in a local hospital and observed for three days. There were absolutely no signs of a heart attack and his heart rhythm was completely normal. At the end of the three-day observation, it was decided to stress-test him on the treadmill. He was, as expected, superbly conditioned. But after reaching a heart rate of 180, he was stopped abruptly. His heart rate immediately accelerated to above 400 as he went into a severe heart irregularity (ventricular flutter/fibrillation), and he collapsed. He responded well to emergency treatment and the episode lasted less than a minute. This prompted further diagnostic studies including a coronary arteriogram (X ray of the blood vessels of the heart). The examination revealed that one of the major arteries supplying blood to the heart was 95 percent obstructed. All of the other vessels were open and otherwise his heart function was normal. Following this study, a single vessel coronary bypass surgical procedure was performed and the man is now actively involved in a supervised rehabilitative program.

In reviewing his case history and coronary risk factors, we found he had almost no coronary risk, except that his father had died of a coronary at age forty-seven.

There are several important lessons to be learned from this case history.

1. People can perform remarkably well and without symptoms even in the presence of significant obstructive coronary disease.

2. Stress testing is desirable before entering a program and it should be repeated at yearly intervals for people past thirty-five years of age, even though they are highly conditioned. (This man had never been stress-tested before his problem—it was not felt that it was necessary in view of his outstanding physical condition.)

3. Familial history is probably a very important, if not the most important, coronary risk factor.

4. Obstructive coronary disease takes years to develop but only moments to cause symptoms. The obstruction in his coronary artery had probably been developing long before he started exercising, and perhaps his excellent conditioning program kept the attack from being fatal when it occurred.

This case exemplifies again the problem in accepting the theory that highly conditioned long-distance runners will have complete protection from heart disease. Even the advocates of the long-distance theory have nothing but presumptive data to document their claims. Perhaps in later years it will be shown that it takes long-distance marathon-type running to be protected from heart disease, but at this time the scientific data are not available to document this statement. To the contrary, we do have data to show that running 2 miles in less than 20:00 minutes, four times per week, gives you 36 points; and that people averaging 34 points per week or more have significantly lower coronary risks than the group averaging less. Are they protected from heart disease? Will they live longer? Only time will answer those questions.

I have talked about the *More* theory; now what about the *Less?*

It is human nature to dream of the instant, effortless, non-sweat-producing way to complete fitness. In fact, what most people want is a "pill," taken once a day, that will provide fitness with no effort. I sincerely hope that never occurs, since even if a pill could be used you would miss the great psychological benefit derived from regular exercise that is almost as beneficial as the physiological effects.

Yet the proponents of the effortless exercise were very happy to see *Total Fitness in 30 Minutes a Week*, published in 1975. In this book the author claims that with only 10 minutes of minimal activity, three times per week, you can reach a good level of fitness, and after 12 hours of this program be in excellent physical condition according to anyone's standards. The only question I would ask about this program is, where are the statistics to back up the statements? There are no references, and no statistics are published in the book. Until I can see documented evidence, I cannot accept this theory, particularly since its claims are directly contrary to the results of scientific investigations performed by many investigators over many years. Quoting Jack H. Wilmore, formerly of the National Health Institute, and R. James Barnard from the School of Medicine, University of California at Los Angeles: "It is difficult for those of us who must deal with the public on a daily basis to face the challenge of re-educating those who have read this book and want to believe that in physical fitness training, they should not even feel uncomfortable!"

To go directly against the proven results of years of research and to make dramatic claims without documentation is a disservice to the physical fitness movement in America, particularly for those individuals who want to use exercise in the practice of preventive medicine.

Too frequently, as in the case of *Total Fitness*, you will find no documentary data at all—no objective standards—no people tested—no measurements taken. That should make you suspicious in accepting any fitness claim unless it is backed up with documentary evidence. Be particularly suspicious of any program that "guarantees" results or "promises" *complete* protection from any type of medical problem. As I said before, there is too much variation among humans, and even though exercise has a beneficial effect in preventing or delaying the onset of heart disease, neither it nor anything else currently known to mankind will give you complete protection from heart disease.

## The Programs

With these words of preamble and caution, let's look at the programs. Nearly all progress up to 30 points per week, but *don't*, I repeat *don't*, attempt to get 30 points the first week unless you are already conditioned. Even though your heart could tolerate it, your legs and muscles would rebel. Work your way through the age-adjusted program you select, exactly as it is prescribed. Take more weeks if necessary, but do not try to accelerate the programs. They have built-in safety features.

If you read one of the previous *Aerobics* books, you will notice that the programs have been revised in four important ways:

1. The frequency per week of the initial workouts has been decreased in order to reduce those aches and musculoskeletal problems that tend to plague beginning exercisers.

2. More sports have been quantified, so that now there are over twenty-eight different activities that can be used in aerobic conditioning.

3. "Endurance points" are added to those sports and activities that qualify (first introduced in the later printings of *The New Aerobics*).

4. Better programs are provided for those with special problems, such as the excessively obese, the post–heart attack patients, or the patient who has undergone uncomplicated coronary artery bypass surgery.

As you will notice, we did not develop separate programs for women and men, since we have found that during the early weeks of conditioning women respond equally as well as men. During the later weeks of the program, some women may prefer to hold their workouts at 24 points a week, since that is their minimum level. Other women will want to progress on to the higher levels, and if those can be reached without strain, that also is permissible.

But do not get ahead of the charts. That's just asking for problems from fatigue and from overused muscles and joints. You want to get fit, not totally exhausted.

## The 12-Minute Test

Field testing of physical fitness is no longer a required part of the aerobics program and is in fact contraindicated initially in the deconditioned person over thirty-five years of age. Yet it is an easy way to measure the success of your program and continues to be a popular feature of the aerobics system. It gives you a reliable estimate of your aerobic capacity, or oxygen consumption, yet does not require expensive laboratory equipment. It can be used by people of all ages, and large groups can be tested at one time. It has also been used as a measuring tool to compare levels of fitness among people of different countries. Included here are 12-minute tests for running, walking, swimming, and cycling.

But do not go out and take any 12-minute test or other field test of fitness requiring maximal effort unless you are under thirty-five years of age, are already conditioned, or have progressed through at least the first six weeks of one of the programs.

If you qualify to take the test, you will find that it is quite simple. You cover the greatest distance that you can in 12:00 minutes, walking and running on a level surface, or just walking, or swimming, or cycling. Warm up before and cool down properly, as described in Chapter 4. If any unusual symptoms occur during the test, *do not continue*.

Based on the distance you cover in 12 minutes, you can measure your fitness level from the following tables.

# 12-MINUTE WALKING/RUNNING TEST
## Distance (Miles) Covered in 12 Minutes

| FITNESS CATEGORY | | 13–19 | 20–29 | 30–39 | 40–49 | 50–59 | 60+ |
|---|---|---|---|---|---|---|---|
| | | | | AGE (Years) | | | |
| I. Very poor | (men) | <1.30* | <1.22 | <1.18 | <1.14 | <1.03 | <.87 |
| | (women) | <1.0 | <.96 | <.94 | <.88 | <.84 | <.78 |
| II. Poor | (men) | 1.30–1.37 | 1.22–1.31 | 1.18–1.30 | 1.14–1.24 | 1.03–1.16 | .87–1.02 |
| | (women) | 1.00–1.18 | .96–1.11 | .95–1.05 | .88–.98 | .84–.93 | .78–.86 |
| III. Fair | (men) | 1.38–1.56 | 1.32–1.49 | 1.31–1.45 | 1.25–1.39 | 1.17–1.30 | 1.03–1.20 |
| | (women) | 1.19–1.29 | 1.12–1.22 | 1.06–1.18 | .99–1.11 | .94–1.05 | .87–.98 |
| IV. Good | (men) | 1.57–1.72 | 1.50–1.64 | 1.46–1.56 | 1.40–1.53 | 1.31–1.44 | 1.21–1.32 |
| | (women) | 1.30–1.43 | 1.23–1.34 | 1.19–1.29 | 1.12–1.24 | 1.06–1.18 | .99–1.09 |
| V. Excellent | (men) | 1.73–1.86 | 1.65–1.76 | 1.57–1.69 | 1.54–1.65 | 1.45–1.58 | 1.33–1.55 |
| | (women) | 1.44–1.51 | 1.35–1.45 | 1.30–1.39 | 1.25–1.34 | 1.19–1.30 | 1.10–1.18 |
| VI. Superior | (men) | >1.87 | >1.77 | >1.70 | >1.66 | >1.59 | >1.56 |
| | (women) | >1.52 | >1.46 | >1.40 | >1.35 | >1.31 | >1.19 |

* < Means "less than"; > means "more than."

Note: Other means of field testing, treadmill testing, and detailed instructions regarding the administration of the 12-minute running test can be found in the appendix (pages 277 and 280–283).

88

## 1.5-MILE RUN TEST
### Time (Minutes)

| FITNESS CATEGORY | | 13-19 | 20-29 | 30-39 | AGE (Years) 40-49 | 50-59 | 60+ |
|---|---|---|---|---|---|---|---|
| I. Very poor | (men) | >15:31* | >16:01 | >16:31 | >17:31 | >19:01 | >20:01 |
| | (women) | >18:31 | >19:01 | >19:31 | >20:01 | >20:31 | >21:01 |
| II. Poor | (men) | 12:11-15:30 | 14:01-16:00 | 14:44-16:30 | 15:36-17:30 | 17:01-19:00 | 19:01-20:00 |
| | (women) | 18:30-16:55 | 19:00-18:31 | 19:30-19:01 | 20:00-19:31 | 20:30-20:01 | 21:00-21:31 |
| III. Fair | (men) | 10:49-12:10 | 12:01-14:00 | 12:31-14:45 | 13:01-15:35 | 14:31-17:00 | 16:16-19:00 |
| | (women) | 16:54-14:31 | 18:30-15:55 | 19:00-16:31 | 19:30-17:31 | 20:00-19:01 | 20:30-19:31 |
| IV. Good | (men) | 9:41-10:48 | 10:46-12:00 | 11:01-12:30 | 11:31-13:00 | 12:31-14:30 | 14:00-16:15 |
| | (women) | 14:30-12:30 | 15:54-13:31 | 16:30-14:31 | 17:30-14:31 | 19:00-16:31 | 19:30-17:31 |
| V. Excellent | (men) | 8:37- 9:40 | 9:45-10:45 | 10:00-11:00 | 10:30-11:30 | 11:00-12:30 | 11:15-13:59 |
| | (women) | 12:29-11:50 | 13:30-12:30 | 14:30-13:00 | 15:55-13:45 | 16:30-14:30 | 17:30-16:30 |
| VI. Superior | (men) | < 8:37 | < 9:45 | <10:00 | <10:30 | <11:00 | <11:15 |
| | (women) | <11:50 | <12:30 | <13:00 | <13:45 | <14:30 | <16:30 |

*< Means "less than"; > means "more than."

Note: Detailed instructions regarding the administration of the 1.5-Mile Run Test can be found in the appendix (pages 282-283).

89

## 3-MILE WALKING TEST (NO RUNNING)
### Time (Minutes)

| FITNESS CATEGORY | | 13-19 | 20-29 | 30-39 | 40-49 | 50-59 | 60+ |
|---|---|---|---|---|---|---|---|
| | | | | AGE (Years) | | | |
| I. Very poor | (men) | >45:00* | >46:00 | >49:00 | >52:00 | >55:00 | >60:00 |
| | (women) | >47:00 | >48:00 | >51:00 | >54:00 | >57:00 | >63:00 |
| II. Poor | (men) | 41:01-45:00 | 42:01-46:00 | 44:31-49:00 | 47:01-52:00 | 50:01-55:00 | 54:01-60:00 |
| | (women) | 43:01-47:00 | 44:01-48:00 | 46:31-51:00 | 49:01-54:00 | 52:01-57:00 | 57:01-63:00 |
| III. Fair | (men) | 37:31-41:00 | 38:31-42:00 | 40:01-44:30 | 42:01-47:00 | 45:01-50:00 | 48:01-54:00 |
| | (women) | 39:31-43:00 | 40:31-44:00 | 42:01-46:30 | 44:01-49:00 | 47:01-52:00 | 51:01-57:00 |
| IV. Good | (men) | 33:00-37:30 | 34:00-38:30 | 35:00-40:00 | 36:30-42:00 | 39:00-45:00 | 41:00-48:00 |
| | (women) | 35:00-39:30 | 36:00-40:30 | 37:30-42:00 | 39:00-44:00 | 42:00-47:00 | 45:00-51:00 |
| V. Excellent | (men) | <33:00 | <34:00 | <35:00 | <36:30 | <39:00 | <41:00 |
| | (women) | <35:00 | <36:00 | <37:30 | <39:00 | <42:00 | <45:00 |

* < Means "less than"; > means "more than"

The *Walking test*, covering 3 miles in the fastest time possible *without running*, can be done on a track over any accurately measured distance. As with running, take the test after you have been training for at least six weeks, when you feel rested, and dress to be comfortable.

90

# 12-MINUTE SWIMMING TEST

### Distance (Yards) Swum in 12 Minutes

| FITNESS CATEGORY | | AGE (Years) | | | | | |
|---|---|---|---|---|---|---|---|
| | | 13–19 | 20–29 | 30–39 | 40–49 | 50–59 | 60+ |
| I. Very poor | (men) | <500* | <400 | <350 | <300 | <250 | <250 |
| | (women) | <400 | <300 | <250 | <200 | <150 | <150 |
| II. Poor | (men) | 500–599 | 400–499 | 350–449 | 300–399 | 250–349 | 250–299 |
| | (women) | 400–499 | 300–399 | 250–349 | 200–299 | 150–249 | 150–199 |
| III. Fair | (men) | 600–699 | 500–599 | 450–549 | 400–499 | 350–449 | 300–399 |
| | (women) | 500–599 | 400–499 | 350–449 | 300–399 | 250–349 | 200–299 |
| IV. Good | (men) | 700–799 | 600–699 | 550–649 | 500–599 | 450–549 | 400–499 |
| | (women) | 600–699 | 500–599 | 450–549 | 400–499 | 350–449 | 300–399 |
| V. Excellent | (men) | >800 | >700 | >650 | >600 | >550 | >500 |
| | (women) | >700 | >600 | >550 | >500 | >450 | >400 |

* < Means "less than"; > means "more than."

*The Swimming test* requires you to swim as far as you can in 12 minutes, using whatever stroke you prefer and resting as necessary, but trying for a maximum effort. The easiest way to take the test is in a pool with known dimensions, and it helps to have another person record the laps and time. Be sure to use a watch with a sweep second hand.

# 12-MINUTE CYCLING TEST

(3-Speed or less)

Distance (Miles) Cycled in 12 Minutes

| FITNESS CATEGORY | | 13-19 | 20-29 | 30-39 | 40-49 | 50-59 | 60+ |
|---|---|---|---|---|---|---|---|
| | | | | AGE (Years) | | | |
| I. Very poor | (men) | <2.75* | <2.5 | <2.25 | <2.0 | <1.75 | <1.75 |
| | (women) | <1.75 | <1.5 | <1.25 | <1.0 | <0.75 | <0.75 |
| II. Poor | (men) | 2.75-3.74 | 2.5-3.49 | 2.25-3.24 | 2.0-2.99 | 1.75-2.49 | 1.75-2.24 |
| | (women) | 1.75-2.74 | 1.5-2.49 | 1.25-2.24 | 1.0-1.99 | 0.75-1.49 | 0.75-1.24 |
| III. Fair | (men) | 3.75-4.74 | 3.5-4.49 | 3.25-4.24 | 3.0-3.99 | 2.50-3.49 | 2.25-2.99 |
| | (women) | 2.75-3.74 | 2.5-3.49 | 2.25-3.24 | 2.0-2.99 | 1.50-2.49 | 1.25-1.99 |
| IV. Good | (men) | 4.75-5.74 | 4.5-5.49 | 4.25-5.24 | 4.0-4.99 | 3.50-4.49 | 3.0-3.99 |
| | (women) | 3.75-4.74 | 3.5-4.49 | 3.25-4.24 | 3.0-3.99 | 2.50-3.49 | 2.0-2.99 |
| V. Excellent | (men) | >5.75 | >5.5 | >5.25 | >5.0 | >4.5 | >4.0 |
| | (women) | >4.75 | >4.5 | >4.25 | >4.0 | >3.5 | >3.0 |

* < Means "less than"; > means "more than."

*The Cycling test* can be used as a test of fitness if you are utilizing the cycling program. Cycle as far as you can in 12 minutes in an area where traffic is not a problem. Try to cycle on a hard, flat surface, with the wind (less than 10 mph), and use a bike with no more than 3 gears. If the wind is blowing harder than 10 mph take the test another day. Measure the distance you cycle in 12 minutes by either the speedometer/odometer on the bike (which may not be too accurate) or by another means, such as a car odometer or an engineering wheel.

92

## The Personal Progress Charts

Record keeping is a great motivational tool, and at the end of the chart pack you will find several charts. Keep your records, monitor your daily progress, and determine your points. If you want a more sophisticated way to keep your records, fill out progress cards like those we use at the Aerobics Center (appendix, page 291) or consider becoming an active member of the Aerobics International Research Society (AIRS). Information on how to join AIRS also is in the appendix (page 290). In addition to the motivation record keeping provides, you will become a part of our longitudinal study in which we are trying to document the role that exercise plays in the maintenance of good health and the prevention of disease.

So now, the rest is up to you. Select the program that fits your age and condition. And get started!

# The Aerobics Chart Pack

1. Read all the chapters preceding this chart pack before starting into one of the following progressive exercise programs.
2. Then select one of the nine programs compatible with your age, health and personal desires.

| If you are: | Your programs are found on pages: |
|---|---|
| Under 30 years of age | 95– 99 |
| 30–39 years of age | 99–104 |
| 40–49 years of age | 104–111 |
| 50–59 years of age | 112–119 |
| Age 60 and older | 120–123 |

3. Remember, the time goals are to be reached at the end, not at the beginning, of the week. And if you have a problem with the requirements of the week, repeat it until that week's goals can be met.
4. When you have completed one of the age-adjusted programs, continue averaging a minimum of 24 to 30 points a week, utilizing one or a variety of different exercises. Either continue with the final program in a chosen exercise, or select one of the 30-point-per-week maintenance programs listed on pages 129–131, or develop a program of your own from the point value charts beginning on page 228.
5. Remember the objective of aerobics is to get the required number of points per week, not to exercise in any particular way or at any particular speed or intensity. Accept the fact that your condition is good even without testing if you are averaging 24 points per week (women) or 30 points per week (men). The number of weekly points you earn correlates well with your level of physical fitness.

## FITNESS CATEGORIES AND WEEKLY POINTS

| | WOMEN | MEN |
|---|---|---|
| Very poor | $< 1$ | $< 1$ |
| Poor | 1–9 | 1–14 |
| Fair | 10–23 | 15–29 |
| Good | 24–40 | 30–50 |
| Excellent | $> 40$ | $> 50$ |

$<$ Means "less than"; $>$ means "more than."

## WALKING EXERCISE PROGRAM
### (under 30 years of age)

| WEEK | DISTANCE (miles) | TIME GOAL (min) | FREQ/WK | POINTS/WK |
|---|---|---|---|---|
| 1 | 2.0 | 35:00 | 3 | 9 |
| 2 | 2.0 | 34:00 | 3 | 9 |
| 3 | 2.0 | 33:00 | 3 | 9 |
| 4 | 2.0 | 32:00 | 4 | 12 |
| 5 | 2.0 | 31:00 | 4 | 12 |
| 6 | 2.0 | 30:00 | 4 | 20 |
| 7 | 2.0 | 29:00 | 4 | 20 |
| 8 | 2.0 | 28:00 | 4 | 20 |
| 9 | 2.5 | 34:00 | 4 | 26 |
| 10 | 2.5 | 33:00 | 4 | 26 |
| 11 | 3.0 | 42:00 | 4 | 32 |
| | 3.0 | 41:00 | 4 | 32 |
| 12 | or | | | |
| | 2.5 | 33:00 | 5 | 32.5 |

## RUNNING EXERCISE PROGRAM *
### (under 30 years of age)

| WEEK | DISTANCE (miles) | TIME GOAL (min) | FREQ/WK | POINTS/WK |
|---|---|---|---|---|
| 1 | 2.0 | 32:00 | 3 | 9 |
| 2 | 2.0 | 30:30 | 3 | 9 |
| 3 | 2.0 | 27:00 | 3 | 15 |
| 4 | 2.0 | 26:00 | 3 | 15 |
| 5 | 2.0 | 25:00 | 3 | 15 |
| 6 | 2.0 | 24:30 | 3 | 15 |
| 7 | 2.0 | 24:00 | 3 | 21 |
| 8 | 2.0 | 22:00 | 3 | 21 |
| 9 | 2.0 | 21:00 | 3 | 21 |
| 10 | 2.0 | 19:00 | 3 | 27 |
| 11 | 2.0 | 18:00 | 4 | 36 |
| | 2.0 | <17:00 | 4 | 36 |
| 12 | or | | | |
| | 2.5 | <22:00 | 3 | 34.5 |

* Start the program by walking, then walk and run, or run, as necessary to meet the changing time goals.

## CYCLING EXERCISE PROGRAM
### (under 30 years of age)

| WEEK | DISTANCE (miles) | TIME GOAL (min) | FREQ/WK | POINTS/WK |
|---|---|---|---|---|
| 1 | 2 | 9:00 | 3 | 1.5 |
| 2 | 2 | 8:00 | 3 | 4.5 |
| 3 | 3 | 10:45 | 3 | 9 |
| 4 | 3 | 10:00 | 4 | 12 |
| 5 | 4 | 15:00 | 4 | 18 |
| 6 | 4 | 14:30 | 4 | 18 |
| 7 | 5 | 18:30 | 4 | 24 |
| 8 | 5 | 18:00 | 4 | 24 |
| 9 | 5 | 17:30 | 5 | 30 |
| 10 | 6 | 22:30 | 4 | 30 |
| 11 | 6 | 22:00 | 4 | 30 |
| 12 | 6 | 21:30 | 4 | 30 |

During the first six weeks, warm up by cycling slowly for 3:00 minutes before attempting the specified distance and time. Cool down by cycling slowly for 3:00 minutes at the conclusion of exercise.

## SWIMMING EXERCISE PROGRAM
### (under 30 years of age)

#### Overhand Crawl *

| WEEK | DISTANCE (yards) | TIME GOAL (min) | FREQ/WK | POINTS/WK |
|---|---|---|---|---|
| 1 | 300 | 12:00 | 4 | 0 |
| 2 | 300 | 10:30 | 4 | 0 |
| 3 | 300 | 10:15 | 4 | 0 |
| 4 | 500 | 20:00 | 5 | 0 |
| 5 | 500 | 18:00 | 5 | 0 |
| 6 | 500 | 17:00 | 5 | 0 |
| 7 | 200 | 4:00 | 5 | 8.35 |
| 8 | 300 | 6:00 | 5 | 12.5 |
| 9 | 400 | 8:00 | 5 | 16.65 |
| 10 | 500 | 10:30 | 5 | 20.85 |
| 11 | 600 | 12:30 | 5 | 25 |
| 12 | 800 | 15:30 | 4 | 30.68 |

Before each workout, warm up by walking back and forth across the shallow end of the pool for a minimum of 5:00 minutes. Cool down by walking slowly for 3:00 minutes at the end of the exercise.

During the first six weeks, the objective is to swim the distance, *but not continuously*. Swim a distance that is comfortable, rest, then continue the swimming-resting cycle until the required distance is covered. Beginning with the seventh week, attempt to cover the distance without stopping.

* Breaststroke is less demanding, as is the backstroke. The butterfly is considerably more demanding.

## HANDBALL/RACQUETBALL/SQUASH/
## BASKETBALL/SOCCER/HOCKEY/LACROSSE EXERCISE PROGRAM
### (under 30 years of age)

| WEEK | TIME GOAL (min) | FREQ/WK | POINTS/WK |
|------|------|------|------|
| 1 | 30:00 | 3 | 0 |
| 2 | 30:00 | 3 | 0 |
| 3 | 30:00 | 3 | 0 |
| 4 | 45:00 | 3 | 0 |
| 5 | 45:00 | 3 | 0 |
| 6 | 45:00 | 3 | 0 |
| 7 | 20:00 | 4 | 12 |
| 8 | 25:00 | 4 | 16 |
| 9 | 30:00 | 4 | 20 |
| 10 | 40:00 | 4 | 28 |
| 11 | 45:00 | 4 | 32 |
| 12 | 60:00 | 3 | 33 |

During the first six weeks, the objective is to exercise the required time, *but not continuously*. Rest frequently. The time goals represent the combined exercise and rest periods. Beginning with the seventh week, the time goals represent continuous exercise. Do not count breaks, time-outs, etc.

## STATIONARY RUNNING EXERCISE PROGRAM
### (under 30 years of age)

| WEEK | TIME GOAL (min) | STEPS/MIN * | FREQ/WK | POINTS/WK |
|------|------|------|------|------|
| 1 | 10:00 | 70–80 | 3 | 0 |
| 2 | 10:00 | 70–80 | 3 | 0 |
| 3 | 10:00 | 70–80 | 3 | 0 |
| 4 | 15:00 | 70–80 | 3 | 0 |
| 5 | 15:00 | 70–80 | 3 | 0 |
| 6 | 15:00 | 70–80 | 3 | 0 |
| 7 | 10:00 | 70–80 | 4 | 12 |
| 8 | 10:00 | 70–80 | 5 | 15 |
| 9 | 12:30 | 80–90 | 4 | 20 |
| 10 | 12:30 | 80–90 | 5 | 25 |
| 11 | 15:00 | 80–90 | 4 | 28 |
| 12 | 15:00 | 90–100 | 4 | 34 |

During the first six weeks, the requirement is to exercise the required number of minutes, *but not continuously*. Rest frequently and as long as necessary, *but continue to walk slowly while resting*. The time goals represent the combined stationary running and rest periods. Beginning with the seventh week, the time goals represent continuous exercise. Warm up for 3:00 minutes by walking briskly. Cool down for 3:00 minutes after exercise by walking slowly. Exercise on a cushioned surface (e.g., a thick carpet) in athletic shoes that have either a ripple or deep-cushioned sole.

* Count only when left foot hits the floor. Feet must be lifted at least eight inches off the floor.

## STATIONARY CYCLING EXERCISE PROGRAM
### (under 30 years of age)

| WEEK | SPEED (mph/rpm) | TIME GOAL (min) | PR AFTER EXERCISE * | FREQ/WK | POINTS/WK |
|------|------|------|------|------|------|
| 1 | 15/55 | 8:00 | <140 | 3 | 3 |
| 2 | 15/55 | 10:00 | <140 | 3 | 3¾ |
| 3 | 15/55 | 12:00 | <140 | 3 | 4⅛ |
| 4 | 17½/65 | 12:00 | <150 | 4 | 6½ |
| 5 | 17½/65 | 14:00 | <150 | 4 | 8 |
| 6 | 17½/65 | 16:00 | <150 | 4 | 9 |
| 7 | 17½/65 | 16:00 | >150 | 5 | 11¼ |
| 8 | 17½/65 | 16:00 | >150 | 5 | 11¼ |
| 9 | 20/75 | 18:00 | >160 | 5 | 18⅛ |
| 10 | 20/75 | 18:00 | >160 | 5 | 18⅛ |
| 11 | 25/90 | 20:00 | >160 | 5 | 28⅓ |
| 12 | 25/90 | 25:00 | >160 | 4 | 30 |

During the first six weeks, warm up by cycling for 3:00 minutes, 17½ to 20 mph, with no resistance, before beginning the actual workout. At the conclusion of the exercise, cool down by cycling for 3:00 minutes with no resistance.

* Add enough resistance so that the pulse rate (PR) counted for 10 seconds immediately after exercise and multiplied by 6 equals the rate specified. If it is higher, lower the resistance before cycling again; if it is lower, increase the resistance.

## STAIR-CLIMBING EXERCISE PROGRAM
### (under 30 years of age)

| WEEK | ROUND TRIPS (average number per min) | TIME GOAL (min) | FREQ/WK | POINTS/WK |
|------|------|------|------|------|
| 1 | 5 | 10:00 | 3 | 0 |
| 2 | 5 | 10:00 | 3 | 0 |
| 3 | 5 | 10:00 | 3 | 0 |
| 4 | 5 | 12:00 | 3 | 0 |
| 5 | 5 | 12:00 | 3 | 0 |
| 6 | 5 | 12:00 | 3 | 0 |
| 7 | 6 | 8:30 | 4 | 8 |
| 8 | 6 | 9:30 | 4 | 9 |
| 9 | 7 | 10:00 | 5 | 16¼ |
| 10 | 7 | 10:30 | 5 | 17½ |
| 11 | 8 | 11:30 | 5 | 26¼ |
| 12 | 8 | 13:00 | 5 | 30 |

During the first six weeks, the requirement is to exercise the required number of minutes, *but not continuously*. Rest frequently, and as long as necessary, but walk slowly while resting. The time goal is the combined time for both stair climbing and resting. Beginning with the seventh week, the time goals refer to continuous exercise. Warm up for 3:00 minutes by walking briskly. Cool down for 3:00 minutes after exercise by walking slowly.

This program applies to 10 steps, 6″ to 7″ in height, 25° to 30° incline. Use of banister is encouraged.

## ROPE-SKIPPING EXERCISE PROGRAM
### (under 30 years of age)

| WEEK | TIME GOAL (min) | STEPS/MIN | FREQ/WK | POINTS/WK |
|------|------|------|------|------|
| 1 | 10:00 | 70–90 | 3 | 0 |
| 2 | 10:00 | 70–90 | 3 | 0 |
| 3 | 10:00 | 70–90 | 3 | 0 |
| 4 | 15:00 | 70–90 | 3 | 0 |
| 5 | 15:00 | 70–90 | 3 | 0 |
| 6 | 15:00 | 70–90 | 3 | 0 |
| 7 | 7:30 | 90–110 | 4 | 12 |
| 8 | 7:30 | 90–110 | 5 | 15 |
| 9 | 10:00 | 90–110 | 4 | 16 |
| 10 | 10:00 | 90–110 | 5 | 20 |
| 11 | 12:30 | 90–110 | 5 | 25 |
| 12 | 15:00 | 90–110 | 5 | 30 |

During the first six weeks, the requirement is to exercise the required number of minutes, *but not continuously*. Rest frequently, and as long as necessary, but continue either to skip very slowly or to walk while resting; the time goals represent the combined time for rope skipping and resting. Beginning with the seventh week, the time goals refer to continuous exercise. Warm up for 3:00 minutes by slow skipping or walking briskly. Cool down for 3:00 minutes after exercise by slow walking.

Exercise on a cushioned surface (e.g., a thick carpet) in athletic shoes. Skip with both feet together, or step over the rope, alternating feet.

## WALKING EXERCISE PROGRAM
### (30–39 years of age)

| WEEK | DISTANCE (miles) | TIME GOAL (min) | FREQ/WK | POINTS/WK |
|------|------|------|------|------|
| 1 | 2.0 | 36:00 | 3 | 9 |
| 2 | 2.0 | 35:00 | 3 | 9 |
| 3 | 2.0 | 34:00 | 3 | 9 |
| 4 | 2.0 | 32:30 | 4 | 12 |
| 5 | 2.0 | 31:00 | 4 | 12 |
| 6 | 2.0 | 30:00 | 4 | 20 |
| 7 | 2.0 | 29:00 | 4 | 20 |
| 8 | 2.0 | 28:30 | 4 | 20 |
| 9 | 2.5 | 35:30 | 4 | 26 |
| 10 | 2.5 | 34:30 | 4 | 26 |
| 11 | 3.0 | 43:15 | 4 | 32 |
| | 3.0 | 42:30 | 4 | 32 |
| 12 | or | | | |
| | 2.5 | 34:00 | 5 | 32.5 |

## RUNNING EXERCISE PROGRAM *
### (30–39 years of age)

| WEEK | DISTANCE (miles) | TIME GOAL (min) | FREQ/WK | POINTS/WK |
|------|------------------|-----------------|---------|-----------|
| 1 | 2.0 | 32:00 | 3 | 9 |
| 2 | 2.0 | 31:00 | 3 | 9 |
| 3 | 2.0 | 28:00 | 3 | 15 |
| 4 | 2.0 | 27:00 | 3 | 15 |
| 5 | 2.0 | 26:00 | 3 | 15 |
| 6 | 2.0 | 25:00 | 3 | 15 |
| 7 | 2.0 | 24:00 | 3 | 21 |
| 8 | 2.0 | 23:00 | 3 | 21 |
| 9 | 2.0 | 22:00 | 3 | 21 |
| 10 | 2.0 | 21:00 | 4 | 28 |
| 11 | 2.0 | 20:00 | 4 | 36 |
| | 2.0 | <18:00 | 4 | 36 |
| 12 | or | | | |
| | 2.5 | <23:00 | 3 | 34.5 |

* Start the program by walking, then walk and run, or run, as necessary to meet the changing time goals.

## CYCLING EXERCISE PROGRAM
### (30–39 years of age)

| WEEK | DISTANCE (miles) | TIME GOAL (min) | FREQ/WK | POINTS/WK |
|------|------------------|-----------------|---------|-----------|
| 1 | 2.0 | 10:30 | 3 | 1.5 |
| 2 | 2.0 | 9:30 | 3 | 1.5 |
| 3 | 2.0 | 9:00 | 4 | 2 |
| 4 | 3.0 | 12:15 | 3 | 4.5 |
| 5 | 3.0 | 10:30 | 3 | 9 |
| 6 | 3.0 | 10:15 | 4 | 12 |
| 7 | 4.0 | 15:15 | 4 | 18 |
| 8 | 4.0 | 14:45 | 5 | 22.5 |
| 9 | 5.0 | 19:00 | 4 | 24 |
| 10 | 6.0 | 23:00 | 4 | 30 |
| 11 | 6.0 | 22:30 | 4 | 30 |
| 12 | 6.0 | 22:00 | 4 | 30 |

During the first six weeks, warm up by cycling slowly for 3:00 minutes before attempting the specified distance and time. Cool down by cycling slowly for 3:00 minutes at the conclusion of exercise.

## SWIMMING EXERCISE PROGRAM
### (30–39 years of age)

#### Overhand Crawl *

| WEEK | DISTANCE (yards) | TIME GOAL (min) | FREQ/WK | POINTS/WK |
|------|------------------|-----------------|---------|-----------|
| 1 | 200 | 8:00 | 4 | 0 |
| 2 | 300 | 12:00 | 4 | 0 |
| 3 | 300 | 10:30 | 4 | 0 |
| 4 | 500 | 20:00 | 5 | 0 |
| 5 | 500 | 18:00 | 5 | 0 |
| 6 | 500 | 17:00 | 5 | 0 |
| 7 | 200 | 4:00 | 5 | 8.35 |
| 8 | 300 | 6:00 | 5 | 12.5 |
| 9 | 400 | 8:30 | 5 | 16.65 |
| 10 | 500 | 10:30 | 5 | 20.85 |
| 11 | 600 | 12:30 | 5 | 25 |
| 12 | 800 | 16:00 | 4 | 30.68 |

Before each workout, warm up by walking back and forth across the shallow end of the pool for a minimum of 5:00 minutes. Cool down by walking slowly for 3:00 minutes at the end of the exercise.

During the first six weeks, the objective is to swim the distance, *but not continuously*. Swim a distance that is comfortable, rest, then continue the swimming-resting cycle until the required distance is covered. Beginning with the seventh week, attempt to cover the distance without stopping.

* Breaststroke is less demanding, as is the backstroke. The butterfly is considerably more demanding.

## HANDBALL/RACQUETBALL/SQUASH/
## BASKETBALL/SOCCER/HOCKEY/LACROSSE EXERCISE PROGRAM
### (30–39 years of age)

| WEEK | TIME GOAL (min) | FREQ/WK | POINTS/WK |
|------|-----------------|---------|-----------|
| 1 | 25:00 | 3 | 0 |
| 2 | 30:00 | 3 | 0 |
| 3 | 30:00 | 3 | 0 |
| 4 | 35:00 | 3 | 0 |
| 5 | 40:00 | 3 | 0 |
| 6 | 40:00 | 3 | 0 |
| 7 | 20:00 | 4 | 12 |
| 8 | 25:00 | 4 | 16 |
| 9 | 30:00 | 4 | 20 |
| 10 | 35:00 | 4 | 24 |
| 11 | 40:00 | 4 | 28 |
| 12 | 60:00 | 4 | 33 |

During the first six weeks, the objective is to exercise the required time, *but not continuously*. Rest frequently. The time goals represent the combined exercise and rest periods. Beginning with the seventh week, the time goals represent continuous exercise. Do not count breaks, time-outs, etc.

# STATIONARY RUNNING EXERCISE PROGRAM
## (30–39 years of age)

| WEEK | TIME GOAL (min) | STEPS/MIN * | FREQ/WK | POINTS/WK |
|------|------|------|------|------|
| 1 | 10:00 | 70–80 | 3 | 0 |
| 2 | 10:00 | 70–80 | 3 | 0 |
| 3 | 12:30 | 70–80 | 3 | 0 |
| 4 | 12:30 | 70–80 | 3 | 0 |
| 5 | 15:00 | 70–80 | 3 | 0 |
| 6 | 15:00 | 70–80 | 3 | 0 |
| 7 | 10:00 | 70–80 | 4 | 12 |
| 8 | 10:00 | 70–80 | 4 | 12 |
| 9 | 12:30 | 70–80 | 4 | 15 |
| 10 | 12:30 | 80–90 | 4 | 20 |
| 11 | 15:00 | 80–90 | 4 | 28 |
| 12 | 15:00 | 90–100 | 4 | 34 |

During the first six weeks, the requirement is to exercise the required number of minutes, *but not continuously*. Rest frequently and as long as necessary, *but continue to walk slowly while resting*. The time goals represent the combined stationary running and rest periods. Beginning with the seventh week, the time goals represent continuous exercise. Warm up for 3:00 minutes by walking briskly. Cool down for 3:00 minutes after exercise by walking slowly. Exercise on a cushioned surface (e.g., a thick carpet) in athletic shoes that have either a ripple or deep-cushioned sole.

* Count only when left foot hits the floor. Feet must be lifted at least eight inches off the floor.

## STATIONARY CYCLING EXERCISE PROGRAM
### (30–39 years of age)

| WEEK | SPEED (mph/rpm) | TIME GOAL (min) | PR AFTER EXERCISE * | FREQ/WK | POINTS/WK |
|------|------|------|------|------|------|
| 1 | 15/55 | 8:00 | <140 | 3 | 3 |
| 2 | 15/55 | 10:00 | <140 | 3 | 3¾ |
| 3 | 15/55 | 12:00 | <140 | 3 | 4⅛ |
| 4 | 15/55 | 14:00 | <150 | 4 | 7 |
| 5 | 15/55 | 16:00 | <150 | 4 | 8 |
| 6 | 15/55 | 18:00 | <150 | 4 | 9 |
| 7 | 15/55 | 20:00 | >150 | 5 | 12½ |
| 8 | 17½/65 | 18:00 | >150 | 5 | 13⅛ |
| 9 | 17½/65 | 20:00 | >150 | 5 | 14½ |
| 10 | 20/75 | 18:00 | >150 | 5 | 18⅛ |
| 11 | 20/75 | 22:30 | >160 | 5 | 22½ |
| 12 | 25/90 | 25:00 | >160 | 4 | 30 |

During the first six weeks, warm up by cycling for 3:00 minutes, 17½ to 20 mph, with no resistance, before beginning the actual workout. At the conclusion of the exercise, cool down by cycling for 3:00 minutes with no resistance.

* Add enough resistance so that the pulse rate (PR) counted for 10 seconds immediately after exercise and multiplied by 6 equals the rate specified. If it is higher, lower the resistance before cycling again; if it is lower, increase the resistance.

## STAIR-CLIMBING EXERCISE PROGRAM
### (30–39 years of age)

| WEEK | ROUND TRIPS (average number per min) | TIME GOAL (min) | FREQ/WK | POINTS/WK |
|------|------|------|------|------|
| 1 | 5 | 10:00 | 3 | 0 |
| 2 | 5 | 10:00 | 3 | 0 |
| 3 | 5 | 10:00 | 3 | 0 |
| 4 | 5 | 12:00 | 3 | 0 |
| 5 | 5 | 12:00 | 3 | 0 |
| 6 | 5 | 12:00 | 3 | 0 |
| 7 | 6 | 7:30 | 4 | 7 |
| 8 | 6 | 8:30 | 4 | 8 |
| 9 | 7 | 9:00 | 4 | 12 |
| 10 | 7 | 10:30 | 5 | 17½ |
| 11 | 8 | 11:00 | 5 | 25 |
| 12 | 8 | 13:00 | 5 | 30 |

During the first six weeks, the requirement is to exercise the required number of minutes, *but not continuously.* Rest frequently, and as long as necessary, but walk slowly while resting. The time goal is the combined time for both stair climbing and resting. Beginning with the seventh week, the time goals refer to continuous exercise. Warm up for 3:00 minutes by walking briskly. Cool down for 3:00 minutes after exercise by walking slowly.

This program applies to 10 steps, 6" to 7" in height, 25° to 30° incline. Use of banister is encouraged.

# ROPE-SKIPPING EXERCISE PROGRAM
## (30–39 years of age)

| WEEK | TIME GOAL (min) | STEPS/MIN | FREQ/WK | POINTS/WK |
|------|------|------|------|------|
| 1 | 10:00 | 70–90 | 3 | 0 |
| 2 | 10:00 | 70–90 | 3 | 0 |
| 3 | 12:30 | 70–90 | 3 | 0 |
| 4 | 12:30 | 70–90 | 3 | 0 |
| 5 | 15:00 | 70–90 | 3 | 0 |
| 6 | 15:00 | 70–90 | 3 | 0 |
| 7 | 7:30 | 90–110 | 4 | 12 |
| 8 | 7:30 | 90–110 | 4 | 12 |
| 9 | 10:00 | 90–110 | 4 | 16 |
| 10 | 10:00 | 90–110 | 5 | 20 |
| 11 | 12:30 | 90–110 | 5 | 25 |
| 12 | 15:00 | 90–110 | 5 | 30 |

During the first six weeks, the requirement is to exercise the required number of minutes, *but not continuously*. Rest frequently, and as long as necessary, but continue either to skip very slowly or walk while resting; the time goals represent the combined time for rope skipping and resting. Beginning with the seventh week, the time goals refer to continuous exercise. Warm up for 3:00 minutes by slow skipping or walking briskly. Cool down for 3:00 minutes after exercise by slow walking.

Exercise on a cushioned surface (e.g., a thick carpet) in athletic shoes. Skip with both feet together, or step over the rope, alternating feet.

# WALKING EXERCISE PROGRAM
## (40–49 years of age)

| WEEK | DISTANCE (miles) | TIME GOAL (min) | FREQ/WK | POINTS/WK |
|------|------|------|------|------|
| 1 | 2.0 | 38:00 | 3 | 9 |
| 2 | 2.0 | 36:00 | 3 | 9 |
| 3 | 2.0 | 35:00 | 3 | 9 |
| 4 | 2.0 | 34:00 | 3 | 9 |
| 5 | 2.0 | 32:00 | 4 | 12 |
| 6 | 2.0 | 30:30 | 4 | 12 |
| 7 | 2.0 | 29:30 | 4 | 20 |
| 8 | 2.0 | 28:45 | 4 | 20 |
| 9 | 2.5 | 36:00 | 4 | 26 |
| 10 | 2.5 | 35:45 | 4 | 26 |
| 11 | 2.5 | 35:30 | 4 | 26 |
| 12 | 3.0 | 43:15 | 4 | 32 |
| 13 | 3.0 | 43:00 | 4 | 32 |
| | 3.0 | 42:45 | 4 | 32 |
| 14 | or | | | |
| | 2.5 | 35:30 | 5 | 32.5 |

## RUNNING EXERCISE PROGRAM *
### (40–49 years of age)

| WEEK | DISTANCE (miles) | TIME GOAL (min) | FREQ/WK | POINTS/WK |
|------|------------------|-----------------|---------|-----------|
| 1 | 2.0 | 34:00 | 3 | 9 |
| 2 | 2.0 | 32:00 | 3 | 9 |
| 3 | 2.0 | 30:00 | 3 | 15 |
| 4 | 2.0 | 28:00 | 3 | 15 |
| 5 | 2.0 | 27:00 | 3 | 15 |
| 6 | 2.0 | 26:00 | 3 | 15 |
| 7 | 2.0 | 25:00 | 4 | 20 |
| 8 | 2.0 | 24:30 | 4 | 20 |
| 9 | 2.0 | 24:00 | 4 | 28 |
| 10 | 2.0 | 23:00 | 4 | 28 |
| 11 | 2.0 | 22:00 | 4 | 28 |
| 12 | 2.0 | 21:00 | 4 | 28 |
| 13 | 2.0 | 20:00 | 4 | 36 |
|  | 2.0 | <19:00 | 4 | 36 |
| 14 | or |  |  |  |
|  | 2.5 | <24:00 | 3 | 34.5 |

* Start the program by walking, then walk and run, or run, as necessary to meet the changing time goals.

## CYCLING EXERCISE PROGRAM
### (40–49 years of age)

| WEEK | DISTANCE (miles) | TIME GOAL (min) | FREQ/WK | POINTS/WK |
|------|------------------|-----------------|---------|-----------|
| 1 | 2 | 11:00 | 3 | 1.5 |
| 2 | 2 | 10:00 | 3 | 1.5 |
| 3 | 2 | 9:30 | 4 | 2 |
| 4 | 3 | 11:15 | 3 | 9 |
| 5 | 3 | 10:45 | 4 | 12 |
| 6 | 3 | 10:30 | 4 | 12 |
| 7 | 4 | 15:30 | 4 | 18 |
| 8 | 4 | 15:00 | 4 | 18 |
| 9 | 5 | 19:30 | 4 | 24 |
| 10 | 5 | 19:00 | 4 | 24 |
| 11 | 5 | 18:30 | 5 | 30 |
| 12 | 6 | 23:30 | 4 | 30 |
| 13 | 6 | 23:00 | 4 | 30 |
| 14 | 6 | 22:30 | 4 | 30 |

During the first six weeks, warm up by cycling slowly for 3:00 minutes before attempting the specified distance and time. Cool down by cycling slowly for 3:00 minutes at the conclusion of exercise.

# SWIMMING EXERCISE PROGRAM
## (40–49 years of age)

### Overhand Crawl *

| WEEK | DISTANCE (yards) | TIME GOAL (min) | FREQ/WK | POINTS/WK |
|------|------------------|-----------------|---------|-----------|
| 1 | 200 | 8:00 | 4 | 0 |
| 2 | 200 | 7:00 | 4 | 0 |
| 3 | 300 | 12:00 | 4 | 0 |
| 4 | 300 | 10:30 | 5 | 0 |
| 5 | 400 | 16:00 | 5 | 0 |
| 6 | 400 | 14:00 | 5 | 0 |
| 7 | 200 | 6:30 | 5 | 6.25 |
| 8 | 200 | 5:30 | 5 | 6.25 |
| 9 | 300 | 6:15 | 5 | 12.5 |
| 10 | 400 | 9:00 | 5 | 16.65 |
| 11 | 500 | 11:00 | 5 | 20.85 |
| 12 | 600 | 13:00 | 5 | 25 |
| 13 | 700 | 15:00 | 4 | 25.32 |
| 14 | 800 | 16:30 | 4 | 30.68 |

Before each workout, warm up by walking back and forth across the shallow end of the pool for a minimum of 5:00 minutes. Cool down by walking slowly for 3:00 minutes at the end of the exercise.

During the first six weeks, the objective is to swim the distance, *but not continuously.* Swim a distance that is comfortable, rest, then continue the swimming-resting cycle until the required distance is covered. Beginning with the seventh week, attempt to cover the distance without stopping.

* Breaststroke is less demanding, as is the backstroke. The butterfly is considerably more demanding.

# HANDBALL/RACQUETBALL/SQUASH/
# BASKETBALL/SOCCER/HOCKEY/LACROSSE EXERCISE PROGRAM
## (40–49 years of age)

| WEEK | TIME GOAL (min) | FREQ/WK | POINTS/WK |
|------|------|------|------|
| 1 | 20:00 | 3 | 0 |
| 2 | 25:00 | 3 | 0 |
| 3 | 30:00 | 3 | 0 |
| 4 | 30:00 | 3 | 0 |
| 5 | 40:00 | 3 | 0 |
| 6 | 40:00 | 3 | 0 |
| 7 | 20:00 | 4 | 12 |
| 8 | 25:00 | 4 | 16 |
| 9 | 25:00 | 4 | 16 |
| 10 | 30:00 | 4 | 20 |
| 11 | 35:00 | 4 | 24 |
| 12 | 40:00 | 4 | 28 |
| 13 | 45:00 | 4 | 32 |
| 14 | 60:00 | 3 | 33 |

During the first six weeks, the objective is to exercise the required time, *but not continuously*. Rest frequently. The time goal represents the combined exercise and rest periods. Beginning with the seventh week, the time goal represents continuous exercise. Do not count breaks, time-outs, etc.

# STATIONARY RUNNING EXERCISE PROGRAM
## (40–49 years of age)

| WEEK | TIME GOAL (min) | STEPS/MIN * | FREQ/WK | POINTS/WK |
|------|-----------------|-------------|---------|-----------|
| 1 | 7:30 | 70–80 | 3 | 0 |
| 2 | 10:00 | 70–80 | 3 | 0 |
| 3 | 10:00 | 70–80 | 3 | 0 |
| 4 | 12:30 | 70–80 | 3 | 0 |
| 5 | 12:30 | 70–80 | 3 | 0 |
| 6 | 15:00 | 70–80 | 3 | 0 |
| 7 | 7:30 | 70–80 | 4 | 9 |
| 8 | 7:30 | 70–80 | 5 | 11.25 |
| 9 | 10:00 | 70–80 | 4 | 12 |
| 10 | 10:00 | 80–90 | 4 | 16 |
| 11 | 12:30 | 70–80 | 5 | 18.75 |
| 12 | 12:30 | 80–90 | 4 | 20 |
| 13 | 15:00 | 80–90 | 4 | 28 |
| 14 | 15:00 | 90–100 | 4 | 34 |

During the first six weeks, the requirement is to exercise the required number of minutes, *but not continuously*. Rest frequently and as long as necessary, *but continue to walk slowly while resting*. The time goals represent the combined stationary running and rest periods. Beginning with the seventh week, the time goals represent continuous exercise. Warm up for 3:00 minutes by walking briskly. Cool down for 3:00 minutes after exercise by walking slowly. Exercise on a cushioned surface (e.g., a thick carpet) in athletic shoes that have either a ripple or deep-cushioned sole.

* Count only when left foot hits the floor. Feet must be raised at least eight inches off the floor.

## STATIONARY CYCLING PROGRAM
### (40–49 years of age)

| WEEK | SPEED (mph/rpm) | TIME GOAL (min) | PR AFTER EXERCISE * | FREQ/WK | POINTS/WK |
|------|-----------------|-----------------|---------------------|---------|-----------|
| 1 | 15/55 | 6:00 | <140 | 3 | 2¼ |
| 2 | 15/55 | 8:00 | <140 | 3 | 3 |
| 3 | 15/55 | 10:00 | <140 | 3 | 3¾ |
| 4 | 15/55 | 12:00 | <150 | 4 | 5½ |
| 5 | 15/55 | 14:00 | <150 | 4 | 7 |
| 6 | 15/55 | 16:00 | <150 | 4 | 8 |
| 7 | 15/55 | 18:00 | <150 | 5 | 11¼ |
| 8 | 15/55 | 20:00 | <150 | 5 | 12½ |
| 9 | 17½/65 | 18:00 | >150 | 5 | 13 |
| 10 | 17½/65 | 20:00 | >150 | 5 | 14½ |
| 11 | 20/75 | 18:00 | >150 | 5 | 18⅛ |
| 12 | 20/75 | 20:00 | >150 | 5 | 19⅜ |
| 13 | 20/75 | 22:30 | >150 | 5 | 22½ |
| 14 | 25/90 | 25:00 | >150 | 5 | 30 |

During the first six weeks, warm up by cycling for 3:00 minutes, 17½ to 20 mph, with no resistance, before beginning the actual workout. At the conclusion of the exercise, cool down by cycling for 3:00 minutes with no resistance.

* Add enough resistance so that the pulse rate (PR) counted for 10 seconds immediately after exercise and multiplied by 6 equals the rate specified. If it is higher, lower the resistance before cycling again; if it is lower, increase the resistance.

## STAIR-CLIMBING EXERCISE PROGRAM
### (40–49 years of age)

| WEEK | ROUND TRIPS (average number per min) | TIME GOAL (min) | FREQ/WK | POINTS/WK |
|------|------|------|------|------|
| 1 | 5 | 7:30 | 3 | 0 |
| 2 | 5 | 7:30 | 3 | 0 |
| 3 | 5 | 10:00 | 3 | 0 |
| 4 | 5 | 10:00 | 3 | 0 |
| 5 | 5 | 12:00 | 3 | 0 |
| 6 | 5 | 12:00 | 3 | 0 |
| 7 | 6 | 6:30 | 4 | 6 |
| 8 | 6 | 7:30 | 4 | 7 |
| 9 | 6 | 8:30 | 5 | 10 |
| 10 | 7 | 9:00 | 4 | 12 |
| 11 | 7 | 10:30 | 4 | 14 |
| 12 | 7 | 10:30 | 5 | 17½ |
| 13 | 8 | 11:00 | 5 | 25 |
| 14 | 8 | 13:00 | 5 | 30 |

During the first six weeks, the requirement is to exercise the required number of minutes, *but not continuously*. Rest frequently, and as long as necessary, but walk slowly while resting. The time goal is the combined time for both stair climbing and resting. Beginning with the seventh week, the time goals refer to continuous exercise. Warm up for 3:00 minutes by walking briskly. Cool down for 3:00 minutes after exercise by walking slowly.

This program applies to 10 steps, 6″ to 7″ in height, 25° to 30° incline. Use of banister is encouraged.

## ROPE-SKIPPING EXERCISE PROGRAM
### (40–49 years of age)

| WEEK | TIME GOAL (min) | STEPS/MIN | FREQ/WK | POINTS/WK |
|------|-----------------|-----------|---------|-----------|
| 1 | 7:30 | 70–90 | 3 | 0 |
| 2 | 10:00 | 70–90 | 3 | 0 |
| 3 | 10:00 | 70–90 | 3 | 0 |
| 4 | 12:30 | 70–90 | 3 | 0 |
| 5 | 12:30 | 70–90 | 3 | 0 |
| 6 | 15:00 | 70–90 | 3 | 0 |
| 7 | 5:00 | 90–110 | 4 | 8 |
| 8 | 7:30 | 90–110 | 4 | 12 |
| 9 | 7:30 | 90–110 | 4 | 12 |
| 10 | 10:00 | 90–110 | 4 | 16 |
| 11 | 10:00 | 90–110 | 5 | 20 |
| 12 | 12:30 | 90–110 | 5 | 25 |
| 13 | 12:30 | 90–110 | 5 | 25 |
| 14 | 15:00 | 90–110 | 5 | 30 |

During the first six weeks, the requirement is to exercise the required number of minutes, *but not continuously*. Rest frequently, and as long as necessary, but continue either to skip very slowly or to walk while resting; the time goals represent the combined time for rope skipping and resting. Beginning with the seventh week, the time goals refer to continuous exercise. Warm up for 3:00 minutes by slow skipping or walking briskly. Cool down for 3:00 minutes after exercise by slow walking.

Exercise on a cushioned surface (e.g., a thick carpet) in athletic shoes. Skip with both feet together, or step over the rope, alternating feet.

## WALKING EXERCISE PROGRAM
### (50–59 years of age)

| WEEK | DISTANCE (miles) | TIME GOAL (min) | FREQ/WK | POINTS/WK |
|---|---|---|---|---|
| 1 | 1.5 | 29:30 | 4 | 8 |
| 2 | 1.5 | 28:00 | 4 | 8 |
| 3 | 1.5 | 26:00 | 4 | 8 |
| 4 | 2.0 | 36:00 | 4 | 12 |
| 5 | 2.0 | 35:00 | 4 | 12 |
| 6 | 2.0 | 34:00 | 4 | 12 |
| 7 | 2.0 | 32:00 | 4 | 12 |
| 8 | 2.0 | 31:00 | 4 | 12 |
| 9 | 2.5 | 38:30 | 4 | 16 |
| 10 | 2.5 | 37:45 | 4 | 16 |
| 11 | 2.5 | 37:00 | 3 | 19.5 |
| 12 | 2.5 | 37:00 | 4 | 26 |
| 13 | 3.0 | 44:00 | 4 | 32 |
| 14 | 3.0 | 43:00 | 4 | 32 |
| 15 | 3.0 | 43:00 | 4 | 32 |
| | 3.0 | 42:30 | 4 | 32 |
| 16 | or | | | |
| | 2.5 | 36:00 | 5 | 32.5 |

## RUNNING EXERCISE PROGRAM *
### (50–59 years of age)

| WEEK | DISTANCE (miles) | TIME GOAL (min) | FREQ/WK | POINTS/WK |
|---|---|---|---|---|
| 1 | 2.0 | 36:00 | 3 | 9 |
| 2 | 2.0 | 34:00 | 3 | 9 |
| 3 | 2.0 | 32:00 | 3 | 9 |
| 4 | 2.0 | 30:00 | 3 | 15 |
| 5 | 2.0 | 29:00 | 3 | 15 |
| 6 | 2.0 | 28:00 | 3 | 15 |
| 7 | 2.0 | 27:00 | 4 | 20 |
| 8 | 2.0 | 26:00 | 4 | 20 |
| 9 | 2.0 | 25:00 | 4 | 20 |
| 10 | 2.0 | 24:00 | 4 | 28 |
| 11 | 2.0 | 23:00 | 4 | 28 |
| 12 | 2.0 | 22:00 | 4 | 28 |
| 13 | 2.0 | 21:30 | 4 | 28 |
| 14 | 2.0 | 21:00 | 4 | 28 |
| 15 | 2.0 | 20:30 | 4 | 28 |
| | 2.0 | <20:00 | 4 | 36 |
| 16 | or | | | |
| | 2.5 | <25:00 | 3 | 34.5 |

* Start the program by walking, then walk and run, or run, as necessary to meet the changing time goals.

# CYCLING EXERCISE PROGRAM
## (50–59 years of age)

| WEEK | DISTANCE (miles) | TIME GOAL (min) | FREQ/WK | POINTS/WK |
|------|------------------|-----------------|---------|-----------|
| 1 | 2 | 12:00 | 3 | 0 |
| 2 | 2 | 11:00 | 3 | 1.5 |
| 3 | 2 | 10:00 | 4 | 2 |
| 4 | 3 | 12:30 | 4 | 6 |
| 5 | 3 | 11:15 | 4 | 12 |
| 6 | 3 | 11:00 | 4 | 12 |
| 7 | 4 | 15:45 | 4 | 18 |
| 8 | 4 | 15:30 | 4 | 18 |
| 9 | 4 | 15:15 | 5 | 22.5 |
| 10 | 4 | 15:00 | 5 | 22.5 |
| 11 | 5 | 19:45 | 4 | 24 |
| 12 | 5 | 19:30 | 4 | 24 |
| 13 | 5 | 19:00 | 4 | 24 |
| 14 | 6 | 23:45 | 4 | 30 |
| 15 | 6 | 23:30 | 4 | 30 |
| 16 | 6 | 23:00 | 4 | 30 |

During the first six weeks, warm up by cycling slowly for 3:00 minutes before attempting the specified distance and time. Cool down by cycling slowly for 3:00 minutes at the conclusion of exercise.

# SWIMMING EXERCISE PROGRAM
(50–59 years of age)

### Overhand Crawl *

| WEEK | DISTANCE (yards) | TIME GOAL (min) | FREQ/WK | POINTS/WK |
|------|------------------|-----------------|---------|-----------|
| 1 | 150 | 6:00 | 4 | 0 |
| 2 | 200 | 8:00 | 4 | 0 |
| 3 | 200 | 7:00 | 4 | 0 |
| 4 | 300 | 12:00 | 5 | 0 |
| 5 | 300 | 10:30 | 5 | 0 |
| 6 | 400 | 16:00 | 5 | 0 |
| 7 | 100 | 2:30 | 5 | 0 |
| 8 | 150 | 3:45 | 5 | 0 |
| 9 | 200 | 4:45 | 5 | 8.35 |
| 10 | 250 | 5:30 | 5 | 10.4 |
| 11 | 300 | 6:45 | 5 | 12.5 |
| 12 | 400 | 9:15 | 5 | 16.65 |
| 13 | 500 | 11:30 | 5 | 20.85 |
| 14 | 600 | 13:45 | 5 | 25 |
| 15 | 700 | 16:00 | 4 | 25.32 |
| 16 | 800 | 18:00 | 4 | 30.68 |

Before each workout, warm up by walking back and forth across the shallow end of the pool for a minimum of 5:00 minutes. Cool down by walking slowly for 3:00 minutes at the end of the exercise.

During the first six weeks, the objective is to swim the distance, *but not continuously*. Swim a distance that is comfortable, rest, then continue the swimming-resting cycle until the required distance is covered. Beginning with the seventh week, attempt to cover the distance without stopping.

* Breaststroke is less demanding, as is the backstroke. The butterfly is considerably more demanding.

# HANDBALL/RACQUETBALL/SQUASH/ BASKETBALL/SOCCER/HOCKEY/LACROSSE EXERCISE PROGRAM
## (50–59 years of age)

| WEEK | TIME GOAL (min) | FREQ/WK | POINTS/WK |
|------|-----------------|---------|-----------|
| 1 | 10:00 | 3 | 0 |
| 2 | 15:00 | 3 | 0 |
| 3 | 20:00 | 3 | 0 |
| 4 | 25:00 | 3 | 0 |
| 5 | 30:00 | 3 | 0 |
| 6 | 30:00 | 3 | 0 |
| 7 | 15:00 | 4 | 9 |
| 8 | 20:00 | 4 | 12 |
| 9 | 25:00 | 4 | 16 |
| 10 | 30:00 | 4 | 20 |
| 11 | 35:00 | 4 | 24 |
| 12 | 40:00 | 4 | 28 |
| 13 | 45:00 | 4 | 32 |
| 14 | 45:00 | 4 | 32 |
| 15 | 45:00 | 4 | 32 |
| 16 | 60:00 | 3 | 33 |

During the first six weeks, the objective is to exercise the required time, *but not continuously.* Rest frequently. The time goal represents the combined exercise and rest periods. Beginning with the seventh week, the time goal represents continuous exercise. Do not count breaks, time-outs, etc.

# STATIONARY RUNNING EXERCISE PROGRAM
### (50–59 years of age)

| WEEK | TIME GOAL (min) | STEPS/MIN * | FREQ/WK | POINTS/WK |
|------|------|------|------|------|
| 1 | 5:00 | 70–80 | 3 | 0 |
| 2 | 7:30 | 70–80 | 3 | 0 |
| 3 | 10:00 | 70–80 | 3 | 0 |
| 4 | 10:00 | 70–80 | 3 | 0 |
| 5 | 12:30 | 70–80 | 3 | 0 |
| 6 | 12:30 | 70–80 | 3 | 0 |
| 7 | 5:00 | 70–80 | 4 | 6 |
| 8 | 7:30 | 70–80 | 4 | 9 |
| 9 | 10:00 | 70–80 | 4 | 12 |
| 10 | 10:00 | 70–80 | 5 | 15 |
| 11 | 10:00 | 70–80 | 5 | 15 |
| 12 | 12:30 | 70–80 | 5 | 18.75 |
| 13 | 12:30 | 70–80 | 5 | 18.75 |
| 14 | 15:00 | 70–80 | 5 | 27.5 |
| 15 | 15:00 | 70–80 | 5 | 27.5 |
| 16 | 17:30 | 80–90 | 4 | 34 |

During the first six weeks, the requirement is to exercise the required number of minutes, *but not continuously*. Rest frequently and as long as necessary, *but continue to walk slowly while resting*. The time goals represent the combined stationary running and rest periods. Beginning with the seventh week, the time goals represent continuous exercise. Warm up for 3:00 minutes by walking briskly. Cool down for 3:00 minutes after exercise by walking slowly. Exercise on a cushioned surface (e.g., a thick carpet) in athletic shoes that have either a ripple or deep-cushioned sole.

* Count only when left foot hits the floor. Feet must be raised at least eight inches off the floor.

## STATIONARY CYCLING EXERCISE PROGRAM
### (50–59 years of age)

| WEEK | SPEED (mph/rpm) | TIME GOAL (min) | PR AFTER EXERCISE * | FREQ/WK | POINTS/WK |
|------|-----------------|-----------------|---------------------|---------|-----------|
| 1 | 15/55 | 4:00 | <135 | 3 | 1½ |
| 2 | 15/55 | 6:00 | <135 | 3 | 2¼ |
| 3 | 15/55 | 8:00 | <135 | 3 | 3 |
| 4 | 15/55 | 10:00 | <140 | 4 | 5 |
| 5 | 15/55 | 10:00 | <140 | 4 | 5 |
| 6 | 15/55 | 12:00 | <140 | 4 | 5½ |
| 7 | 15/55 | 14:00 | <140 | 5 | 8¾ |
| 8 | 15/55 | 16:00 | <140 | 5 | 10 |
| 9 | 15/55 | 18:00 | <140 | 5 | 11¼ |
| 10 | 15/55 | 20:00 | <140 | 5 | 12½ |
| 11 | 17½/65 | 18:00 | <150 | 5 | 13⅛ |
| 12 | 17½/65 | 20:00 | <150 | 5 | 14⅜ |
| 13 | 20/75 | 20:00 | <150 | 5 | 19⅜ |
| 14 | 20/75 | 20:00 | >150 | 5 | 19⅜ |
| 15 | 20/75 | 25:00 | >150 | 5 | 25 |
| 16 | 20/75 | 30:00 | >150 | 4 | 26 |

During the first six weeks, warm up by cycling for 3:00 minutes, 17½ to 20 mph, with no resistance, before beginning the actual workout. At the conclusion of the exercise, cool down by cycling for 3:00 minutes with no resistance.

From the tenth week on, the exercise periods can be divided into two equal periods, performed twice daily.

* Add enough resistance so that the pulse rate (PR) counted for 10 seconds immediately after exercise and multiplied by 6 equals the rate specified. If it is higher, lower the resistance before cycling again; if it is lower, increase the resistance.

# STAIR-CLIMBING EXERCISE PROGRAM
## (50–59 years of age)

| WEEK | ROUND TRIPS (average number per min) | TIME GOAL (min) | FREQ/WK | POINTS/WK |
|---|---|---|---|---|
| 1 | 4 | 5:00 | 3 | 0 |
| 2 | 4 | 5:00 | 3 | 0 |
| 3 | 4 | 7:30 | 3 | 0 |
| 4 | 4 | 7:30 | 3 | 0 |
| 5 | 4 | 10:00 | 3 | 0 |
| 6 | 4 | 10:00 | 3 | 0 |
| 7 | 5 | 5:00 | 4 | 2 |
| 8 | 5 | 7:00 | 5 | 5 |
| 9 | 5 | 9:00 | 5 | 7½ |
| 10 | 5 | 11:00 | 5 | 10 |
| 11 | 6 | 9:30 | 5 | 11¼ |
| 12 | 6 | 11:00 | 5 | 12½ |
| 13 | 7 | 10:30 | 5 | 17½ |
| 14 | 7 | 12:00 | 5 | 20 |
| 15 | 8 | 11:00 | 5 | 25 |
| 16 | 8 | 13:00 | 5 | 30 |

During the first six weeks, the requirement is to exercise the required number of minutes, *but not continuously*. Rest frequently, and as long as necessary, but walk slowly while resting. The time goal is the combined time for both stair climbing and resting. Beginning with the seventh week, the time goals refer to continuous exercise. Warm up for 3:00 minutes by walking briskly. Cool down for 3:00 minutes after exercise by walking slowly.

This program applies to 10 steps, 6″ to 7″ in height, 25° to 30° incline. Use of banister is encouraged.

## ROPE-SKIPPING EXERCISE PROGRAM
### (50–59 years of age)

| WEEK | TIME GOAL (min) | STEPS/MIN | FREQ/WK | POINTS/WK |
|------|-----------------|-----------|---------|-----------|
| 1 | 5:00 | 70–90 | 3 | 0 |
| 2 | 7:30 | 70–90 | 3 | 0 |
| 3 | 10:00 | 70–90 | 3 | 0 |
| 4 | 10:00 | 70–90 | 3 | 0 |
| 5 | 12:30 | 70–90 | 3 | 0 |
| 6 | 12:30 | 70–90 | 3 | 0 |
| 7 | 5:00 | 70–90 | 4 | 6 |
| 8 | 5:00 | 70–90 | 5 | 7½ |
| 9 | 7:30 | 70–90 | 4 | 9 |
| 10 | 7:30 | 70–90 | 5 | 11¼ |
| 11 | 10:00 | 70–90 | 4 | 12 |
| 12 | 10:00 | 70–90 | 5 | 15 |
| 13 | 12:30 | 70–90 | 5 | 18¾ |
| 14 | 12:30 | 70–90 | 5 | 18¾ |
| 15 | 15:00 | 70–90 | 5 | 22½ |
| 16 | 15:00 | 90–110 | 5 | 30 |

During the first six weeks, the requirement is to exercise the required number of minutes, *but not continuously*. Rest frequently, and as long as necessary, but continue either to skip very slowly or to walk while resting; the time goals represent the combined time for rope skipping and resting. Beginning with the seventh week, the time goals refer to continuous exercise. Warm up for 3:00 minutes by slow skipping or walking briskly. Cool down for 3:00 minutes after exercise by slow walking.

Exercise on a cushioned surface (e.g., a thick carpet) in athletic shoes. Skip with both feet together, or step over the rope, alternating feet.

## WALKING EXERCISE PROGRAM
### (age 60 and over)

| WEEK | DISTANCE (miles) | TIME GOAL (min) | FREQ/WK | POINTS/WK |
|------|------------------|-----------------|---------|-----------|
| 1 | 1.0 | 20:00 | 4 | 4 |
| 2 | 1.0 | 19:00 | 4 | 4 |
| 3 | 1.0 | 18:00 | 4 | 4 |
| 4 | 1.5 | 29:00 | 4 | 8 |
| 5 | 1.5 | 28:00 | 4 | 8 |
| 6 | 1.5 | 27:00 | 4 | 8 |
| 7 | 2.0 | 38:00 | 4 | 12 |
| 8 | 2.0 | 36:00 | 4 | 12 |
| 9 | 2.0 | 34:00 | 4 | 12 |
| 10 | 2.5 | 42:30 | 4 | 16 |
| 11 | 2.5 | 41:30 | 4 | 16 |
| 12 | 2.5 | 40:00 | 4 | 16 |
| 13 | 3.0 | 55:00 | 4 | 20 |
| 14 | 3.0 | 52:30 | 4 | 20 |
| 15 | 3.0 | 50:00 | 4 | 20 |
| 16 | 3.0 | 48:00 | 5 | 25 |
| 17 | 3.5 | 56:00 | 4 | 24 |
| 18 | 3.5 | 55:00 | 5 | 30 |

## RUNNING EXERCISE PROGRAM
### (age 60 and over)

NOT RECOMMENDED

## CYCLING EXERCISE PROGRAM
### (age 60 and over)

| WEEK | DISTANCE (miles) | TIME GOAL (min) | FREQ/WK | POINTS/WK |
|------|--------|--------|---------|-----------|
| 1 | 1 | 8:00 | 3 | 0 |
| 2 | 1 | 6:00 | 3 | 0 |
| 3 | 2 | 14:00 | 4 | 0 |
| 4 | 2 | 12:00 | 4 | 2 |
| 5 | 2 | 11:30 | 4 | 2 |
| 6 | 3 | 17:45 | 4 | 6 |
| 7 | 3 | 16:45 | 5 | 7.5 |
| 8 | 3 | 15:00 | 5 | 7.5 |
| 9 | 4 | 23:00 | 4 | 10 |
| 10 | 4 | 21:30 | 5 | 12.5 |
| 11 | 4 | 20:00 | 5 | 12.5 |
| 12 | 5 | 28:00 | 4 | 14 |
| 13 | 5 | 27:00 | 5 | 17.5 |
| 14 | 5 | 26:00 | 5 | 17.5 |
| 15 | 5 | 25:00 | 5 | 17.5 |
| 16 | 6 | 35:00 | 5 | 22.5 |
| 17 | 6 | 33:00 | 5 | 22.5 |
| 18 | 7 | 40:00 | 5 | 27.5 |

*Note:* Three-wheeled cycling is encouraged.

During the first six weeks, warm up by cycling slowly for 3:00 minutes before attempting the specified distance and time. Cool down by cycling slowly for 3:00 minutes at the conclusion of exercise.

# SWIMMING EXERCISE PROGRAM
(age 60 and over)

### Overhand Crawl *

| WEEK | DISTANCE (yards) | TIME GOAL (min) | FREQ/WK | POINTS/WK |
|------|------------------|-----------------|---------|-----------|
| 1 | 100 | 5:00 | 4 | 0 |
| 2 | 150 | 7:30 | 4 | 0 |
| 3 | 200 | 10:00 | 4 | 0 |
| 4 | 200 | 9:00 | 5 | 0 |
| 5 | 300 | 15:00 | 5 | 0 |
| 6 | 300 | 12:00 | 5 | 0 |
| 7 | 100 | 4:00 | 5 | 0 |
| 8 | 100 | 3:30 | 5 | 0 |
| 9 | 150 | 5:30 | 5 | 0 |
| 10 | 200 | 6:30 | 5 | 6.25 |
| 11 | 250 | 7:00 | 5 | 7.8 |
| 12 | 300 | 8:30 | 5 | 9.4 |
| 13 | 350 | 9:00 | 5 | 10.95 |
| 14 | 400 | 10:30 | 5 | 12.5 |
| 15 | 450 | 11:10 | 5 | 18.75 |
| 16 | 500 | 12:25 | 5 | 20.85 |
| 17 | 550 | 13:30 | 5 | 22.9 |
| 18 | 600 | <15:00 | 5 | 25 |

Before each workout, warm up by walking back and forth across the shallow end of the pool for a minimum of 5:00 minutes. Cool down by walking slowly for 3:00 minutes at the end of the exercise.

During the first six weeks, the objective is to swim the distance, *but not continuously.* Swim a distance that is comfortable, rest, then continue the swimming-resting cycle until the required distance is covered. Beginning with the seventh week, attempt to cover the distance without stopping.

* Breaststroke is less demanding, as is the backstroke. The butterfly is considerably more demanding.


# HANDBALL/RACQUETBALL/SQUASH/ BASKETBALL/SOCCER/HOCKEY/LACROSSE EXERCISE PROGRAM
(age 60 and over)

### NOT RECOMMENDED


# STATIONARY RUNNING EXERCISE PROGRAM
(age 60 and over)

### NOT RECOMMENDED

## STATIONARY CYCLING EXERCISE PROGRAM
### (age 60 and over)

| WEEK | SPEED (mph/rpm) | TIME GOAL (min) | PR AFTER EXERCISE * | FREQ/WK | POINTS/WK |
|------|-----------------|-----------------|---------------------|---------|-----------|
| 1 | 15/55 | 4:00 | <100 | 3 | 1½ |
| 2 | 15/55 | 4:00 | <100 | 3 | 1½ |
| 3 | 15/55 | 6:00 | <100 | 3 | 2¼ |
| 4 | 15/55 | 6:00 | <110 | 4 | 3 |
| 5 | 15/55 | 8:00 | <110 | 4 | 4 |
| 6 | 15/55 | 10:00 | <110 | 4 | 5 |
| 7 | 15/55 | 12:00 | <110 | 4 | 5½ |
| 8 | 15/55 | 14:00 | <110 | 4 | 7 |
| 9 | 15/55 | 16:00 | <110 | 4 | 8 |
| 10 | 15/55 | 16:00 | <120 | 5 | 10 |
| 11 | 15/55 | 18:00 | <120 | 5 | 11¼ |
| 12 | 15/55 | 20:00 | <120 | 5 | 12½ |
| 13 | 17½/65 | 18:00 | <120 | 5 | 13⅛ |
| 14 | 17½/65 | 20:00 | <120 | 5 | 14⅜ |
| 15 | 20/75 | 20:00 | <130 | 5 | 19⅜ |
| 16 | 20/75 | 22:30 | <130 | 5 | 22½ |
| 17 | 20/75 | 25:00 | <130 | 5 | 25 |
| 18 | 20/75 | 30:00 | <130 | 4 | 26 |

During the first six weeks, warm up by cycling for 3:00 minutes, 17½ to 20 mph, with no resistance, before beginning the actual workout. At the conclusion of the exercise, cool down by cycling for 3:00 minutes with no resistance.

From the tenth week on, the exercise periods can be divided into two equal periods, performed twice daily.

* Add enough resistance so that the pulse rate (PR) counted for 10 seconds immediately after exercise and multiplied by 6 equals the rate specified. If it is higher, lower the resistance before cycling again; if it is lower, increase the resistance.

## STAIR-CLIMBING EXERCISE PROGRAM
### (age 60 and over)

#### NOT RECOMMENDED

## ROPE-SKIPPING EXERCISE PROGRAM
### (age 60 and over)

#### NOT RECOMMENDED

## PROGRESSIVE WALKING PROGRAM FOR THE
## EXCESSIVELY OVERWEIGHT INDIVIDUAL *
(to be used in conjunction with dieting)

| WEEK | DISTANCE (miles) | TIME GOAL (min) | FREQ/WK | POINTS/WK |
|------|------------------|-----------------|---------|-----------|
| 1 | 2.0 | 40:30 | 3 | 3 |
| 2 | 2.0 | 39:00 | 3 | 9 |
| 3 | 2.0 | 38:00 | 4 | 12 |
| 4 | 2.0 | 37:00 | 4 | 12 |
| 5 | 2.0 | 36:00 | 5 | 15 |
| 6 | 2.0 | 35:00 | 5 | 15 |
| 7 | 2.5 | 45:00 | 5 | 20 |
| 8 | 2.5 | 43:00 | 5 | 20 |
| 9 | 3.0 | 52:00 | 5 | 25 |
| 10 | 3.0 | 51:00 | 5 | 25 |
| 11 | 3.0 | 50:00 | 5 | 25 |
| 12 | 3.0 | 49:00 | 5 | 25 |
| 13 | 3.0 | 48:00 | 5 | 25 |
| 14 | 3.0 | 47:00 | 5 | 25 |
| 15 | 3.0 | 46:00 | 5 | 25 |
| 16 | 3.0 | <45:00 | 4 | 32 |

After completing the progressive program, either continue with the final program listed above, or select one of the 30-point-per-week maintenance programs listed on pages 129–131; or develop a program of your own from the point value charts beginning on page 228.

* At least 50 pounds above the maximum weights listed according to sex and height in the Metropolitan Life Insurance tables on page 141.

# PROGRESSIVE WALKING PROGRAM FOLLOWING UNCOMPLICATED CORONARY ARTERY BYPASS SURGERY *

| WEEK | DISTANCE (miles) | TIME GOAL (min) | FREQ/WK | POINTS/WK |
|------|------------------|-----------------|---------|-----------|
| 1 | 0.5 | 12:00 | 3 | 0 |
| 2 | 0.5 | 10:00 | 3 | 0 |
| 3 | 1.0 | 22:00 | 3 | 0 |
| 4 | 1.0 | 20:00 | 3 | 3 |
| 5 | 1.0 | 19:00 | 4 | 4 |
| 6 | 1.0 | 18:00 | 4 | 4 |
| 7 | 1.5 | 29:30 | 4 | 8 |
| 8 | 1.5 | 28:00 | 4 | 8 |
| 9 | 1.5 | 26:00 | 5 | 10 |
| 10 | 1.5 | 24:00 | 5 | 10 |
| 11 | 2.0 | 32:00 | 5 | 15 |
| 12 | 2.0 | 31:00 | 5 | 15 |
| 13 | 2.5 | 38:00 | 5 | 20 |
| 14 | 2.5 | 37:00 | 5 | 20 |
| 15 | 3.0 | 48:00 | 5 | 25 |
| 16 | 3.0 | 47:00 | 5 | 25 |
| 17 | 3.0 | 46:00 | 5 | 25 |
| | 3.0 | <45:00 | 4 | 32 |
| 18 | or | | | |
| | 4.0 | <60:00 | 3 | 33 |

*This program should not be started until at least three weeks following surgery. After this 18-week program, some patients can progress to a standard running program, *but only with their physician's approval!* If approval is given, start the progressive running program at the 2.0-miles-in-30:00-minute level in your age-adjusted category (e.g., week 3 of the 40–49 age group).

# PROGRESSIVE WALKING PROGRAM FOLLOWING AN UNCOMPLICATED HEART ATTACK AND FOR CARDIAC PATIENTS WITH MINIMAL DISEASE *

| WEEK | DISTANCE (miles) | TIME GOAL (min) | FREQ/WK | POINTS/WK |
|------|------------------|------------------|---------|-----------|
| 1 | 1.0 | 22:00 | 3 | 0 |
| 2 | 1.0 | 21:00 | 3 | 0 |
| 3 | 1.0 | 20:00 | 3 | 3 |
| 4 | 1.0 | 18:00 | 4 | 4 |
| 5 | 1.0 | 17:00 | 4 | 4 |
| 6 | 1.0 | 16:00 | 4 | 4 |
| 7 | 1.5 | 24:00 | 4 | 8 |
| 8 | 1.5 | 23:00 | 4 | 8 |
| 9 | 2.0 | 32:00 | 4 | 12 |
| 10 | 2.0 | 31:30 | 5 | 15 |
| 11 | 2.0 | 31:00 | 5 | 15 |
| 12 | 2.5 | 39:00 | 5 | 20 |
| 13 | 2.5 | 38:00 | 5 | 20 |
| 14 | 2.5 | 37:45 | 5 | 20 |
| 15 | 3.0 | 48:00 | 5 | 25 |
| 16 | 3.0 | 47:00 | 5 | 25 |
| 17 | 3.0 | 46:00 | 5 | 25 |
| 18 | 3.0 | <45:00 | 4 | 32 |
|  | or |  |  |  |
|  | 4.0 | <60:00 | 3 | 33 |

* This program is to be started two months following the heart attack, *only with physician's approval,* and only if the patient is asymptomatic and not requiring medication for relief of pain or prevention of heart irregularities. If these prerequisites cannot be met, the program for patients with moderate to severe heart disease should be used. After this 18-week program, some patients can progress to a standard running program, *but only with their physician's approval!* If approval is given, start the progressive running program at the 2.0-miles-in-30:00-minute level in your age-adjusted category (e.g., week 3 of the 40–49 age group).

## PROGRESSIVE EXERCISE PROGRAM FOR CARDIAC PATIENTS, MODERATE TO SEVERE DISEASE (SYMPTOMATIC) *

| WEEK | DISTANCE (miles) | MAX HR † | FREQ/WK |
|---|---|---|---|
| 1 | 1/8 | 100 | |
| | rest 1:00 | | |
| | 1/8 | 100 | |
| | rest 1:00 | | 3 |
| | 1/8 | 100 | |
| | rest 1:00 | | |
| | 1/8 | 100 | |
| 2 | 1/8 | 105 | |
| | rest 1:00 | | |
| | 2/8 | 105 | |
| | rest 1:00 | | 3 |
| | 2/8 | 105 | |
| | rest 1:00 | | |
| | 1/8 | 105 | |
| 3 | 1/8 | 110 | |
| | rest 1:00 | | |
| | 2/8 | 110 | |
| | rest 1:00 | | 3 |
| | 2/8 | 110 | |
| | rest 1:00 | | |
| | 1/8 | 110 | |
| 4 | 1/8 | 110 | |
| | rest 1:00 | | |
| | 3/8 | 115 | |
| | rest 1:00 | | 3 |
| | 3/8 | 115 | |
| | rest 1:00 | | |
| | 1/8 | 110 | |
| 5 | 1/8 | 110 | |
| | rest 1:00 | | |
| | 4/8 | 120 | |
| | rest 1:00 | | 3–4 |
| | 4/8 | 120 | |
| | rest 1:00 | | |
| | 1/8 | 100 | |

* This program is designed for those patients with symptoms requiring medication for relief, and should be used only in a medically supervised class.

† Maximum heart rate is determined during the rest periods by counting the pulse for 10 seconds and multiplying by 6.

## Moderate to Severe Disease Program (continued)

| WEEK | DISTANCE (miles) | MAX HR | FREQ/WK |
|---|---|---|---|
| 6 | 1/8 | 110 | |
| | rest 1:00 | | |
| | 5/8 | 120 | |
| | rest 1:00 | | 3–4 |
| | 5/8 | 120 | |
| | rest 1:00 | | |
| | 1/8 | 100 | |
| 7 | 1/8 | 110 | |
| | rest 1:00 | | |
| | 6/8 | 125 | |
| | rest 1:00 | | 3–4 |
| | 6/8 | 125 | |
| | rest 1:00 | | |
| | 1/8 | 100 | |
| 8 | 1/8 | 110 | |
| | rest 1:00 | | |
| | 7/8 | 125 | 3–4 |
| | rest 0:30 | | |
| | 1/8 | 100 | |
| 9 | 1/8 | 110 | |
| | rest 1:00 | | |
| | 7/8 | 130 | 3–5 |
| | rest 0:30 | | |
| | 1/8 | 100 | |
| 10 | 1/8 | 110 | |
| | rest 1:00 | | |
| | 1 | 130 | 3–5 |
| | rest 0:30 | | |
| | 1/8 | 110 | |
| 11 | 2/8 | 110 | |
| | rest 1:00 | | |
| | 1 | 130 | 3–5 |
| | rest 0:30 | | |
| | 1/8 | 120 | |
| 12 | 2/8 | 110 | |
| | rest 1:00 | | |
| | 1 | 135 | 3–5 |
| | rest 0:30 | | |
| | 1/8 | 120 | |

At the conclusion of this program, progress to the program of cardiac patients with minimal disease (if no problems or complications have occurred).

# MAINTENANCE PROGRAMS FOR THE PERSON ALREADY CONDITIONED
(all ages)

## WALKING

| DISTANCE (miles) | TIME REQUIREMENT (min) | FREQ/WK | POINTS/WK |
|---|---|---|---|
| 2.0 | 24:01–30:00 | 6 | 30 |
| or | | | |
| 3.0 | 36:01–45:00 | 4 | 32 |
| or | | | |
| 4.0 | 48:01–60:00 | 3 | 33 |
| or | | | |
| 4.0 | 60:01–80:00 | 5 | 30 |

## RUNNING

| DISTANCE (miles) | TIME REQUIREMENT (min) | FREQ/WK | POINTS/WK |
|---|---|---|---|
| 1.0 | 6:41–8:00 | 6 | 30 |
| or | | | |
| 1.5 | 10:01–12:00 | 4 | 32 |
| or | | | |
| 1.5 | 12:01–15:00 | 5 | 32.5 |
| or | | | |
| 2.0 | 16:01–20:00 | 4 | 36 |
| or | | | |
| 2.0 | 13:21–16:00 | 3 | 33 |

## CYCLING

| DISTANCE (miles) | TIME REQUIREMENT (min) | FREQ/WK | POINTS/WK |
|---|---|---|---|
| 5.0 | 15:01–20:00 | 5 | 30 |
| or | | | |
| 6.0 | 18:01–24:00 | 4 | 30 |
| or | | | |
| 7.0 | 21:01–28:00 | 4 | 36 |
| or | | | |
| 8.0 | 24:01–32:00 | 3 | 31.5 |

## SWIMMING

| DISTANCE (yards) | TIME REQUIREMENT (min) | FREQ/WK | POINTS/WK |
|---|---|---|---|
| 600 | 10:01–15:00 | 6 | 30 |
| or | | | |
| 800 | 13:21–20:00 | 4 | 30.5 |
| or | | | |
| 900 | 15:01–22:30 | 4 | 36 |
| or | | | |
| 1000 | 16:41–25:00 | 3 | 31 |

## HANDBALL/RACQUETBALL/SQUASH/ BASKETBALL/SOCCER/HOCKEY/LACROSSE

| TIME REQUIREMENT (min) | FREQ/WK | POINTS/WK |
|---|---|---|
| 30:00 | 6 | 30 |
| 35:00 | 5 | 30 |
| 45:00 | 4 | 32 |
| 60:00 | 3 | 33 |

## STATIONARY RUNNING

| TIME REQUIREMENT (min) | STEPS/MIN * | FREQ/WK | POINTS/WK |
|---|---|---|---|
| 12:30 | 80–90 | 6 | 30 |
| or | | | |
| 15:00 | 80–90 | 5 | 35 |
| or | | | |
| 15:00 | 90–100 | 4 | 34 |
| or | | | |
| 20:00 | 70–80 | 4 | 32 |
| or | | | |
| 20:00 | 80–90 | 3 | 30 |

* Count only when left foot hits the floor. Feet must be lifted at least eight inches off the floor.

### STATIONARY CYCLING *

| SPEED (mph/rpm) | TIME REQUIREMENT (min) | FREQ/WK | POINTS/WK |
|---|---|---|---|
| 17½/65 | 30:00 | 6 | 30 |
| or | | | |
| 17½/65 | 35:00 | 5 | 30 |
| or | | | |
| 20/75 | 30:00 | 5 | 32½ |
| or | | | |
| 25/90 | 20:00 | 5 | 28½ |
| or | | | |
| 25/90 | 25:00 | 4 | 30 |
| or | | | |
| 30/105 | 25:00 | 3 | 30 |

* Add enough resistance so that the pulse rate counted for 10 seconds immediately after exercise and multiplied by 6 equals or exceeds 140 beats per minute.

### STAIR CLIMBING

| ROUND TRIPS (min) * | TIME REQUIREMENT (min) | FREQ/WK | POINTS/WK |
|---|---|---|---|
| 7 | 12:00 | 8 | 32 |
| or | | | |
| 7 | 15:00 | 6 | 28½ |
| or | | | |
| 8 | 11:00 | 6 | 30 |
| or | | | |
| 8 | 13:00 | 5 | 30 |
| or | | | |
| 9 | 14:30 | 4 | 35 |

* Count round trips on 10 steps, 6″ to 7″ in height, 25° to 30° incline.

### ROPE SKIPPING

| TIME REQUIREMENT (min) | STEPS/MIN | FREQ/WK | POINTS/WK |
|---|---|---|---|
| 12:30 | 90–110 | 6 | 30 |
| or | | | |
| 15:00 | 90–110 | 5 | 30 |
| or | | | |
| 17:30 | 70–90 | 5 | 33¾ |
| or | | | |
| 17:30 | 90–110 | 4 | 34 |
| or | | | |
| 20:00 | 90–110 | 3 | 30 |

## PERSONAL PROGRESS CHART

| DATE | EXERCISE | DISTANCE | DURATION | POINTS | CUMULAT. POINTS |
|------|----------|----------|----------|--------|-----------------|
|      |          |          |          |        |                 |
|      |          |          |          |        |                 |
|      |          |          |          |        |                 |
|      |          |          |          |        |                 |
|      |          |          |          |        |                 |
|      |          |          |          |        |                 |
|      |          |          |          |        |                 |
|      |          |          |          |        |                 |
|      |          |          |          |        |                 |
|      |          |          |          |        |                 |
|      |          |          |          |        |                 |
|      |          |          |          |        |                 |
|      |          |          |          |        |                 |
|      |          |          |          |        |                 |
|      |          |          |          |        |                 |
|      |          |          |          |        |                 |
|      |          |          |          |        |                 |
|      |          |          |          |        |                 |
|      |          |          |          |        |                 |
|      |          |          |          |        |                 |
|      |          |          |          |        |                 |
|      |          |          |          |        |                 |
|      |          |          |          |        |                 |
|      |          |          |          |        |                 |
|      |          |          |          |        |                 |
|      |          |          |          |        |                 |
|      |          |          |          |        |                 |
|      |          |          |          |        |                 |

## PERSONAL PROGRESS CHART

| DATE | EXERCISE | DISTANCE | DURATION | POINTS | CUMULAT. POINTS |
|------|----------|----------|----------|--------|-----------------|
|      |          |          |          |        |                 |
|      |          |          |          |        |                 |
|      |          |          |          |        |                 |
|      |          |          |          |        |                 |
|      |          |          |          |        |                 |
|      |          |          |          |        |                 |
|      |          |          |          |        |                 |
|      |          |          |          |        |                 |
|      |          |          |          |        |                 |
|      |          |          |          |        |                 |
|      |          |          |          |        |                 |
|      |          |          |          |        |                 |
|      |          |          |          |        |                 |
|      |          |          |          |        |                 |
|      |          |          |          |        |                 |
|      |          |          |          |        |                 |
|      |          |          |          |        |                 |
|      |          |          |          |        |                 |
|      |          |          |          |        |                 |
|      |          |          |          |        |                 |
|      |          |          |          |        |                 |
|      |          |          |          |        |                 |
|      |          |          |          |        |                 |
|      |          |          |          |        |                 |
|      |          |          |          |        |                 |
|      |          |          |          |        |                 |
|      |          |          |          |        |                 |
|      |          |          |          |        |                 |
|      |          |          |          |        |                 |
|      |          |          |          |        |                 |
|      |          |          |          |        |                 |
|      |          |          |          |        |                 |
|      |          |          |          |        |                 |
|      |          |          |          |        |                 |

## PERSONAL PROGRESS CHART

| DATE | EXERCISE | DISTANCE | DURATION | POINTS | CUMULAT. POINTS |
|------|----------|----------|----------|--------|-----------------|
|      |          |          |          |        |                 |
|      |          |          |          |        |                 |
|      |          |          |          |        |                 |
|      |          |          |          |        |                 |
|      |          |          |          |        |                 |
|      |          |          |          |        |                 |
|      |          |          |          |        |                 |
|      |          |          |          |        |                 |
|      |          |          |          |        |                 |
|      |          |          |          |        |                 |
|      |          |          |          |        |                 |
|      |          |          |          |        |                 |
|      |          |          |          |        |                 |
|      |          |          |          |        |                 |
|      |          |          |          |        |                 |
|      |          |          |          |        |                 |
|      |          |          |          |        |                 |
|      |          |          |          |        |                 |
|      |          |          |          |        |                 |
|      |          |          |          |        |                 |
|      |          |          |          |        |                 |
|      |          |          |          |        |                 |
|      |          |          |          |        |                 |
|      |          |          |          |        |                 |
|      |          |          |          |        |                 |
|      |          |          |          |        |                 |
|      |          |          |          |        |                 |
|      |          |          |          |        |                 |
|      |          |          |          |        |                 |
|      |          |          |          |        |                 |
|      |          |          |          |        |                 |
|      |          |          |          |        |                 |
|      |          |          |          |        |                 |

## PERSONAL PROGRESS CHART

| DATE | EXERCISE | DISTANCE | DURATION | POINTS | CUMULAT. POINTS |
|------|----------|----------|----------|--------|-----------------|
|      |          |          |          |        |                 |
|      |          |          |          |        |                 |
|      |          |          |          |        |                 |
|      |          |          |          |        |                 |
|      |          |          |          |        |                 |
|      |          |          |          |        |                 |
|      |          |          |          |        |                 |
|      |          |          |          |        |                 |
|      |          |          |          |        |                 |
|      |          |          |          |        |                 |
|      |          |          |          |        |                 |
|      |          |          |          |        |                 |
|      |          |          |          |        |                 |
|      |          |          |          |        |                 |
|      |          |          |          |        |                 |
|      |          |          |          |        |                 |
|      |          |          |          |        |                 |
|      |          |          |          |        |                 |
|      |          |          |          |        |                 |
|      |          |          |          |        |                 |
|      |          |          |          |        |                 |
|      |          |          |          |        |                 |
|      |          |          |          |        |                 |
|      |          |          |          |        |                 |
|      |          |          |          |        |                 |
|      |          |          |          |        |                 |
|      |          |          |          |        |                 |
|      |          |          |          |        |                 |
|      |          |          |          |        |                 |
|      |          |          |          |        |                 |
|      |          |          |          |        |                 |
|      |          |          |          |        |                 |
|      |          |          |          |        |                 |

## PERSONAL PROGRESS CHART

| DATE | EXERCISE | DISTANCE | DURATION | POINTS | CUMULAT. POINTS |
|------|----------|----------|----------|--------|-----------------|
|      |          |          |          |        |                 |
|      |          |          |          |        |                 |
|      |          |          |          |        |                 |
|      |          |          |          |        |                 |
|      |          |          |          |        |                 |
|      |          |          |          |        |                 |
|      |          |          |          |        |                 |
|      |          |          |          |        |                 |
|      |          |          |          |        |                 |
|      |          |          |          |        |                 |
|      |          |          |          |        |                 |
|      |          |          |          |        |                 |
|      |          |          |          |        |                 |
|      |          |          |          |        |                 |
|      |          |          |          |        |                 |
|      |          |          |          |        |                 |
|      |          |          |          |        |                 |
|      |          |          |          |        |                 |
|      |          |          |          |        |                 |
|      |          |          |          |        |                 |
|      |          |          |          |        |                 |
|      |          |          |          |        |                 |
|      |          |          |          |        |                 |
|      |          |          |          |        |                 |
|      |          |          |          |        |                 |
|      |          |          |          |        |                 |
|      |          |          |          |        |                 |
|      |          |          |          |        |                 |

## PERSONAL PROGRESS CHART

| DATE | EXERCISE | DISTANCE | DURATION | POINTS | CUMULAT. POINTS |
|------|----------|----------|----------|--------|-----------------|
|      |          |          |          |        |                 |
|      |          |          |          |        |                 |
|      |          |          |          |        |                 |
|      |          |          |          |        |                 |
|      |          |          |          |        |                 |
|      |          |          |          |        |                 |
|      |          |          |          |        |                 |
|      |          |          |          |        |                 |
|      |          |          |          |        |                 |
|      |          |          |          |        |                 |
|      |          |          |          |        |                 |
|      |          |          |          |        |                 |
|      |          |          |          |        |                 |
|      |          |          |          |        |                 |
|      |          |          |          |        |                 |
|      |          |          |          |        |                 |
|      |          |          |          |        |                 |
|      |          |          |          |        |                 |
|      |          |          |          |        |                 |
|      |          |          |          |        |                 |
|      |          |          |          |        |                 |
|      |          |          |          |        |                 |
|      |          |          |          |        |                 |
|      |          |          |          |        |                 |
|      |          |          |          |        |                 |
|      |          |          |          |        |                 |
|      |          |          |          |        |                 |
|      |          |          |          |        |                 |
|      |          |          |          |        |                 |
|      |          |          |          |        |                 |
|      |          |          |          |        |                 |

## PERSONAL PROGRESS CHART

| DATE | EXERCISE | DISTANCE | DURATION | POINTS | CUMULAT. POINTS |
|------|----------|----------|----------|--------|-----------------|
|      |          |          |          |        |                 |
|      |          |          |          |        |                 |
|      |          |          |          |        |                 |
|      |          |          |          |        |                 |
|      |          |          |          |        |                 |
|      |          |          |          |        |                 |
|      |          |          |          |        |                 |
|      |          |          |          |        |                 |
|      |          |          |          |        |                 |
|      |          |          |          |        |                 |
|      |          |          |          |        |                 |
|      |          |          |          |        |                 |
|      |          |          |          |        |                 |
|      |          |          |          |        |                 |
|      |          |          |          |        |                 |
|      |          |          |          |        |                 |
|      |          |          |          |        |                 |
|      |          |          |          |        |                 |
|      |          |          |          |        |                 |
|      |          |          |          |        |                 |
|      |          |          |          |        |                 |
|      |          |          |          |        |                 |
|      |          |          |          |        |                 |
|      |          |          |          |        |                 |
|      |          |          |          |        |                 |
|      |          |          |          |        |                 |
|      |          |          |          |        |                 |
|      |          |          |          |        |                 |
|      |          |          |          |        |                 |
|      |          |          |          |        |                 |
|      |          |          |          |        |                 |
|      |          |          |          |        |                 |

# 6

# How Important Is Diet?
# Mathematics, Miracles,
# Safety, and Supplements

If you turned to this chapter first, that probably means you're concerned about your weight.

Well, you should be. Obesity is dangerous for your heart. On our Coronary Risk Profiles, a high percentage of body fat carries with it as many as 4 coronary risk points, or 8.5 percent of the total risk points allocated. Other diet-related factors—glucose, uric acid, cholesterol, and triglycerides—carry with them an additional 13 points. Seventeen out of forty-seven points, then, or 36 percent of your coronary risk as measured by our risk profile chart, will be directly affected by your diet and/or your weight.

In this chapter I'm going to give you several medically safe programs for weight loss, taking into account that you will be supplementing your program with regular aerobic exercise. I'm going to evaluate several of the popular diets and also list some principles to follow when preparing meals that will make your daily diet safer for your heart. Then I'll discuss specific foods that can create problems for your heart, such as refined sugars, coffee, and alcohol, and finally give you some "straight talk" about vitamin supplements.

So let's discuss what is most likely your first concern: are you overweight? The best way to tell is by measuring your percent body fat, either by specific gravity determination or by measuring skinfold thickness. Underwater weighing and total body volumetric techniques are used in research centers to measure specific gravity, whereas calipers are more commonly used to measure skinfold thickness.* Yet a good indicator of your percent body fat is whether your tendency while swimming is to sink or float. Remember, *fat floats* and *muscle sinks!*

If your body fat can be measured, acceptable levels are: for men, less than 19 percent; for women, less than 22 percent. Athletes should be under 15 percent, and outstanding distance runners under 5 percent. I can recall one world-class marathoner who was 1.1 percent fat! A walking skeleton? Not at all—he was just amazingly lean. An idea of the average percent body fat for men and women, according to age, can be determined from the median level in the Coronary Risk Profile charts.

If it is not possible to have your body fat measured, then look at one of the standard height-weight charts such as the one from the Metropolitan Life Insurance Company: "Desirable Weights."

If using one of these techniques, or merely looking in a mirror (sideways if necessary), convinces you that your body weight is excessive, let's look at your problem and see what can be done about it.

Basically, there are two types of obesity.

The first is obesity of early onset—obesity that begins in childhood and results in a marked increase in the *total number* of fat cells. For example, between 25 and 30 billion fat cells are normal, but a fat child may end up as an adult with *100* billion fat cells. That person is going to have a problem with weight all of his or her life.

Early-onset obesity accounts for only a small percentage of all obesity, but it is extremely difficult to treat, especially in later life. Yet *prevention*, with exercise, can be helpful. Animal experiments have shown that, if physical activity is increased in early life, the final number of fat cells is less. It seems clear that fat children need exercise even more than other children.

* The technique for measuring skinfold thickness is described in the appendix, page 278.

## DESIRABLE WEIGHTS
(Weight in Pounds According to Frame, in Indoor Clothing)

MEN OF AGES 25 AND OVER

| HEIGHT Feet | Inches | SMALL FRAME | MEDIUM FRAME | LARGE FRAME |
|---|---|---|---|---|
| 5 | 1 | 112–120 | 118–129 | 126–141 |
| 5 | 2 | 115–123 | 121–133 | 129–144 |
| 5 | 3 | 118–126 | 124–136 | 132–148 |
| 5 | 4 | 121–129 | 127–139 | 135–152 |
| 5 | 5 | 124–133 | 130–143 | 138–156 |
| 5 | 6 | 128–137 | 134–147 | 142–161 |
| 5 | 7 | 132–141 | 138–152 | 147–166 |
| 5 | 8 | 136–145 | 142–156 | 151–170 |
| 5 | 9 | 140–150 | 146–160 | 155–174 |
| 5 | 10 | 144–154 | 150–165 | 159–179 |
| 5 | 11 | 148–158 | 154–170 | 164–184 |
| 6 | 0 | 152–162 | 158–175 | 168–189 |
| 6 | 1 | 156–167 | 162–180 | 173–194 |
| 6 | 2 | 160–171 | 167–185 | 178–199 |
| 6 | 3 | 164–175 | 172–190 | 182–204 |

WOMEN OF AGES 25 AND OVER

| HEIGHT Feet | Inches | SMALL FRAME | MEDIUM FRAME | LARGE FRAME |
|---|---|---|---|---|
| 4 | 8 | 92– 98 | 96–107 | 104–119 |
| 4 | 9 | 94–101 | 98–110 | 106–122 |
| 4 | 10 | 96–104 | 101–113 | 109–125 |
| 4 | 11 | 99–107 | 104–116 | 112–128 |
| 5 | 0 | 102–110 | 107–119 | 115–131 |
| 5 | 1 | 105–113 | 110–122 | 118–134 |
| 5 | 2 | 108–116 | 113–126 | 121–138 |
| 5 | 3 | 111–119 | 116–130 | 125–142 |
| 5 | 4 | 114–123 | 120–135 | 129–146 |
| 5 | 5 | 118–127 | 124–139 | 133–150 |
| 5 | 6 | 122–131 | 128–143 | 137–154 |
| 5 | 7 | 126–135 | 132–147 | 141–158 |
| 5 | 8 | 130–140 | 136–151 | 145–163 |
| 5 | 9 | 134–144 | 140–155 | 149–168 |
| 5 | 10 | 138–148 | 144–159 | 153–173 |

*Note:* For girls between 18 and 25, subtract 1 pound for each year under 25.

Copyright 1968, Metropolitan Life Insurance Company.
Courtesy of Metropolitan Life Insurance Company.

The second and most common type of obesity is adult-onset obesity, which is marked, not by an increased number of fat cells, but by an increase in the size of existing fat cells.

People with adult-onset obesity gain weight simply because the caloric intake of the food they eat exceeds the calories used in their routine daily activity.

People lose weight because they reverse that process—taking in fewer calories than they need and/or burning more calories than they did before.

That sounds easy enough, but how does the average person know where the cutoff point is? How does he measure his intake and then determine his needs?

Go to one of the standard calorie charts (or the abbreviated one in the appendix) and estimate your daily intake. Be as accurate as possible in determining portion sizes and weights. A common error is *underestimating the actual food intake.*

Then, if you are a normally active person, the basic number of calories it takes just to maintain your present weight (neither gaining nor losing) can be determined by multiplying your weight in pounds times 15. (If you are quite sedentary, multiply your weight times 12, since you are burning fewer calories during the course of the day. If you are pregnant or are a lactating mother, multiply your weight times 18. If you are doing manual labor, multiply your weight times 20.)

Take, for example, a normally active man who weighs 170 pounds. His weight multiplied by 15 comes to 2,550. That's how many calories he needs a day just to maintain his weight. If his caloric intake goes much above that, he's going to start gaining weight. If it is much below that, he'll start losing weight.

Yet a loss of 3,500 calories is necessary to shed a pound of fat. So if his goal is a loss of two pounds a week—as I recommended—he'll need a net loss of 7,000 calories a week, or 1,000 calories a day.

With an aerobic exercise program, you are burning up calories in addition to those consumed as a part of your daily activities. How many calories? Well that depends on how many aerobic points are earned, the type of physical activity, and the initial weight of the person. There are simply too many variables involved to establish an exact calories-per-aerobic-point figure, as is clear from looking at the table below:

## CALORIES USED PER MILE OF RUNNING

| WEIGHT (lbs.) | PACE PER MILE | | |
|---|---|---|---|
| | 6:00 min. | 8:00 min. | 10:00 min. |
| 120 | 83 | 79 | 76 |
| 130 | 89 | 85 | 82 |
| 140 | 95 | 92 | 88 |
| 150 | 102 | 98 | 94 |
| 160 | 109 | 104 | 100 |
| 170 | 115 | 111 | 106 |
| 180 | 121 | 117 | 112 |
| 190 | 128 | 123 | 118 |
| 200 | 135 | 129 | 124 |
| 210 | 141 | 136 | 130 |
| 220 | 148 | 142 | 136 |

As you can see, our 170-pound man would burn 9 more calories with a 6-minute mile than with a 10-minute mile. If he were getting his 30 weekly aerobic points with 6-minute miles, he'd run five of them, for a total caloric output of 575. If he were getting his points from running a mile in slightly less than 10 minutes, he'd need to run over seven of them to reach 30 points, for a total caloric output of close to 750.

On the average, though, you won't be too far wrong estimating a caloric expenditure of 20 calories per aerobic point (600 calories for a 30-point week) and that, coupled with a 1,000- to 1,500-calorie diet, enables most people to lose two pounds per week.

As you can see, the calories you're allowed on a weight-loss diet will vary according to your size and daily activity. The smaller the person, the fewer calories will be allowed. A normally active 125-pound woman, for example, is going to have to go on a 1,000-calorie diet to lose her two pounds a week. A 220-pound person should be able to lose two pounds a week with a 1,500-calorie diet.

You obviously can't lose very much weight through exercise alone, unless you're a lumberjack, a longshoreman, or a marathon runner. It is clear that the more rapid and sensible way to lose weight is by decreasing food intake while simultaneously increasing physical activity.

Harvard's Dr. Jean Mayer points out the critical relationship between exercise and weight loss with the fact that U.S. men today weigh an average of seven pounds more than they did fifty years ago, even though they consume fewer calories. The reason? They have cut down on exercise even more than on food. This phenomenon has long been exploited by farmers who keep animals cooped up to fatten them, according to Dr. Mayer. In fact, Dr. Mayer did a study of Boston schoolgirls and found that obese girls ate less than normal-weight girls of the same age and height. But the obese girls expended only one third as much energy!

Another important phenomenon of exercise is the seemingly contradictory fact that vigorous exercise actually depresses the appetite, thus making dieting easier.

Some people find this hard to believe. They'll cite the example of going out for a long walk and coming back ravenous. Well, there's no contradiction. Low-energy exercise does stimulate the appetite. But vigorous, sweat-producing exercise—aerobics exercise—reduces the appetite. Studies on men performing vigorous exercise—say, forty-five minutes to an hour—tend to show that food intake and appetite are not increased. In another study, very little exercise was associated with high appetite, and moderate forms of exercise with low appetite. That's why I recommend that dieters do their aerobics shortly before their big meal of the day.

But why do I recommend only a two-pound weight loss a week? Because I think it is a realistic approach—one that anyone can follow—and a safe approach. I've had patients say to me, "Well, Dr. Cooper, if I can lose two pounds a week by cutting my caloric intake in half and exercising 30 points' worth a week, why can't I fast, earn 60 points a week, and lose a lot more than two pounds a week?"

The answer is, you can. But I don't recommend it for two reasons. First, slow weight loss allows time for learning and adapting to a new eating pattern. Then, when ideal weight is reached, you will be more comfortable eating a more controlled diet and find the weight loss easier to maintain. Second, fasting (and by fasting, I mean abstaining from anything but water and vitamin tablets for days at a time) tends to confuse the body and it starts burning up the wrong tissues.

A group of physicians from Georgetown University reported a study in which four obese subjects voluntarily went on an intermittent starvation and caloric restricted diet for 96 days. At the end of that time, the patients had lost an average of seventy pounds. But careful measurements established that only one third of the weight loss was fatty tissue, *while two thirds was lean body mass or muscle.*

This phenomenon has been demonstrated in numerous other studies. A Cornell University experiment showed that in a total starvation study about half the weight loss was attributable to a loss of lean body mass.

On the other hand, a study by Zuti and Golding showed that where people combined caloric restriction and exercise, they gained muscle and lost only fat.

But loss of lean body mass is not the only problem with fasting. People who go on a strict fast show changes at times in their ECGs. And those who combine fasting with vigorous exercise sometimes do so with undesirable results. Many of the World War II POWs who were starved for prolonged periods died on forced marches, probably from cardiac arrhythmia (severe heart irregularities).

So I do not recommend fasting—nor do I recommend having your mouth wired shut by an orthodontist so you *can't* eat.

Another extreme that some people go to is having bypass surgery performed to short-circuit the bowel and reduce food absorption. This is an extreme procedure used at times in people who are excessively overweight and can't control their weight any other way. Except in those rare cases, however, this method should be approached with extreme caution. Severe, postoperative complications occasionally occur that at times are fatal.

Millions of people have tried to lose weight by the use of dietary pills. I cannot recommend any type of appetite suppressants, especially amphetamines. In the first place, they do not get to the heart of weight problems—eating habits. A person can lose weight using appetite suppressants, and gain it all back (and frequently more) when he or she stops using them. In addition, if the suppressants are used over an extended period of time, they can be addictive. Some even contain digitalis, a heart medicine that should be used only under strict medical supervision.

That's why the Food and Drug Administration issued a warning on these "anorectic" drugs in 1972 and noted that such drugs "have a limited usefulness in the treatment of obesity, and because of their significant potential for dependence and abuse should be used with extreme care."

Still another questionable weight loss method—to my mind—is the Simeons Technique, which combines a diet with daily injections of the hormone human chorionic gonadotrophin (HCG). The theory is that HCG has the peculiar effect of transferring, or "mobilizing," the abnormal fat previously locked away in fixed deposits into the bloodstream, making it available for energy. The fact is, however, that there are no scientific data to indicate that you can "mobilize" fat with HCG or with any other medication. In addition, several recent studies have shown absolutely no effect where HCG injections were compared with a placebo. It is the diet alone that causes the weight loss seen in these experiments.

Fads will come and go, and there will always be plenty of people to try them: people lured by the promise of "easy" weight loss or "eat-what-you-want" weight loss. But for good health, dieters must go back to the sensible —and safe—diets.

I'd like to discuss some of the more popular diets, and their good and bad points.

A popular *high-fat diet* is the Atkins diet, from Dr. Robert C. Atkins' *Diet Revolution*. It is also a low-carbohydrate diet. Atkins contends—quite rightly—that some of our most severe dietary problems are the result of an excess of carbohydrates in our daily diets. He calls it "carbohydrate poisoning" and points out that we consume more sugar now in two weeks than we did in a year two centuries ago. Carbohydrates—not fat—he says, are the principle elements in food that fatten people. So he eliminates carbohydrates *entirely* from the diet (at least in the early stage of the diet), forcing the body to convert from being a carbohydrate-burning engine to a fat-burning engine. Along with this conversion, Atkins says, comes another change: the pituitary gland starts putting out a substance known as the "fat mobilizing hormone" (FMH).

In place of carbohydrates, Atkins substitutes foods that are high in animal fat—foods such as cream, bacon, cheese, and butter. "As long as you don't take in carbohydrates," Atkins says, "you can eat any amount of this 'fattening' food and it won't put a single ounce of fat on you."

Frankly, this diet can be dangerous. At a time when heart disease has reached epidemic proportions and the vast majority of medical experts are warning us to get off high-cholesterol diets, Atkins suggests that we go on the highest cholesterol diet of them all. He claims that, on his diet, cholesterol levels and triglyceride levels almost always go down. That may or may not be true. I have seen no scientific data to back this claim up, and it is certainly not based on any known scientific principle. But under any circumstance, for persons who have a history of high cholesterol and triglyceride this diet could cause problems. For example, one of my patients lost twenty-six pounds on the Atkins diet. But his cholesterol level went from 164 to 252 mg%! Other patients have lost weight and their cholesterol did not increase. Yet it is impossible to predict a patient's cholesterol response.

So I cannot recommend a high-fat diet. Nor can I recommend a diet that eliminates carbohydrates entirely. The human body requires a balanced diet, and carbohydrates—in moderation—maintain that balance. When daily intakes of carbohydrates fall below 30 grams, fatigue often results.

Dr. John Yudkin's low-carbohydrate diet is a more sensible way to approach the problem. He limits carbohydrates to 50 grams a day (reduced from an average of 350 grams) and eliminates the intake of refined sugar, which he considers harmful and totally unnecessary.

Still, there are several disadvantages even to this approach. First, it pays too little attention to caloric intake (and in the long run, calories *do* count). And second, it does not restrict the kinds of fat that should be eaten. It is *not* a high-fat diet, but it doesn't limit fat, either. Again, I feel that a *balance* is important in any diet.

Dr. Irwin Stillman's *The Doctor's Quick Weight Loss Diet* is another very popular diet. This is essentially a high-protein, high-water-intake diet.

The Stillman diet is based on the theory that the body deals differently with proteins than with fats and carbohydrates. In effect, the body uses up extra energy to burn up protein—and that extra effort ("the fires of metabolism") burns up stored fat. Stillman calls this phenomenon "specific dynamic action," or "SDA," and he estimates that this action causes the body to burn up 275 extra calories per day. Thus Stillman lets you eat all you want of foods that are high in protein: lean meats and fish; poultry; low-fat cheeses; eggs. High-fat and high-carbohydrate foods are prohibited.

The Stillman diet also requires you to drink at least eight glasses of water a day—in addition to the coffee or tea you ordinarily drink—to wash away the ketones (or "ashes") left after the fat in your body is burned.

There is plenty of evidence to show that the Stillman diet *is* effective in weight reduction and is probably safe for most dieters. However, it should be used only under a doctor's supervision and it is ill-advised for people with kidney problems, pregnant women, and people who suffer from gout. There is also a pronounced sense of fatigue usually associated with it.

But again, my main objection is that it is not a balanced diet.

What do I mean by a "balanced diet"? I mean a diet:

1. That provides other needed nutrients as well as carbohydrates, protein, and fat while restricting calories to promote slow but steady weight loss.

2. That is low in carbohydrates, but not carbohydrate-restricted, allowing at least 50 to 60 grams per day.

3. That is high in protein to take advantage of the SDA effect that Stillman speaks of (even though it probably plays an insignificant role in weight reduction).

4. That allows some fats, but because their main function is providing a source for energy, they should be restricted to no more than 1 to 3 teaspoons per day—polyunsaturated only.

5. That calls for plenty of liquids (a good idea whether you're losing weight or not).

6. That calls for a good, one-a-day multiple vitamin and mineral supplement (mandatory when consuming fewer than 1,000 calories per day).

7. That eliminates concentrated sweets and sugars, which are not essential to a nutritious diet because they usually provide calories only and no other nutrients and are "empty calorie"–type foods such as candy, regular soft drinks, and alcohol.

8. That includes fresh fruits, vegetables, and whole grain breads to provide adequate roughage in the diet.

Yet, with all these recommendations, it is amazing how easily most people can lose weight by merely eliminating desserts, bread, and potatoes!

## A Safe Maintenance Diet for Your Heart

Once you've lowered your weight to the point where both you and your physician are happy about it, you'll still be concerned with keeping the blood-serum risk factors (cholesterol, triglycerides, glucose, uric acid) at acceptable levels. The dietary patterns you follow for this purpose will vary according to what the test results indicate, of course, but there are some general principles that do apply here.

The best all-around maintenance diet that I know of is called *The Prudent Diet,* developed by the late Dr. Norman Jolliffe and carried on in book form by Iva Bennett and Martha Simon. This diet suggests limiting the consumption of red meat to four portions per week, eating no more than two eggs a week, limiting the intake of organ foods, and avoiding fat-rich dairy products and saturated fats, in order to reduce cholesterol and triglycerides. These dietary limitations are, in a word, prudent, considering what we know about heart disease, but they may be a bit on the restrictive side for persons who are getting 30 or more aerobic points each week. If you're exercising regularly, you may find you can still maintain a satisfactory risk factor profile without adhering so strictly to these guidelines, especially those concerning meat and eggs.

For example, I consume at least one glass of homogenized milk daily, and four to six eggs and up to four servings of meat other than fish or fowl each week. Occasionally, I will consume some butter. Yet my weight has not fluctuated more than five pounds up or down in the past fifteen years, and recently my cholesterol was 187 mg%, and my triglycerides were 41 mg%. With blood lipids at that level, there is no data to indicate that dietary restriction is necessary. Nonetheless, I cannot maintain my weight or keep such low cholesterol and triglyceride levels unless I run a minimum of 12 to 15 miles each week.

The same principles that apply to your choice of menu carry over into the preparation of your food. You can go a long way toward making your everyday meals safe for your heart by making changes in the way you prepare them. Here are some recommendations from the Cooper Clinic dietician that you should study carefully:

1. Read labels on packaged foods, since many foods are vague as to their content. For example, nondairy cream substitutes sound good, but they usually contain coconut oil, which is a *saturated* vegetable fat.

2. Foods can be prepared using certain amounts and types of fat. For example, a cream soup prepared with

skim milk, vegetable, and corn oil margarine is acceptable, as is fish broiled with a teaspoon of corn oil margarine and other seasonings.

3. Meat should be prepared by first *trimming off all visible fat before cooking.* Then place the meat on a rack and bake, broil, or roast. The remaining fat will drain from the cooking meat. Using fat-free broth or tomato juice instead of meat drippings for basting will not put fat back into the meat. If stewing or boiling meat for soup stock or other dishes, cook it a day ahead. After refrigeration, the fat that has hardened at the top can easily be removed.

4. Use a non-stick coated pan for pan-frying.

5. Vegetables may be baked, boiled, broiled, or steamed. To retain maximum vitamin and mineral content, do not overcook. Fat-free broth, seasonings, lemon juice, vinegar, and even allowed fat may be added. Keep raw vegetables on hand for low-calorie snacks.

6. Dairy products should be made from skim or non-fat milk. Use whipped evaporated skim milk or non-fat dry milk instead of whipping cream. To whip evaporated skim milk, chill in freezer until icy and beat until stiff.

7. Use fresh, frozen, or canned fruits and juices without sugar added.

8. Sugar-free products such as gelatin, pudding mix (prepared with skim milk), soft drinks, jams, and jellies may be used.

Following the principles and cooking tips we've outlined above, and by counting calories and earning 30 aerobic points a week, the goal of a two-pound-per-week weight reduction can be achieved without either damaging the system or taking all the pleasure out of mealtimes. A 170-pound man, for example, is allowed 1,650 calories a day for his weight reduction program (if he exercises at a 30 point/week level). On the following page is a menu for one of those days, recommended by the American Heart Association. As you can see, it's far from a gloom-ridden starvation diet, yet it adds up to 1,650 calories:

### BREAKFAST

Chilled half grapefruit
¾ cup dry cereal
1 cup skim milk
1 soft-cooked egg
1 slice toast
1 teaspoon diet margarine
1 teaspoon marmalade
2 teaspoons sugar for cereal,
  fruit, or beverage
Coffee or tea

### LUNCH

Tomato stuffed with chicken
  salad (use 1 tomato; ½ cup
  diced chicken, 2 tablespoons
  mayonnaise; capers; parsley;
  celery; lettuce)
1 large or 2 small hard rolls
1 teaspoon diet margarine
1 cup skim milk
1 small banana, sliced
Coffee or tea

### DINNER

Baked fish fillet (4 ounces—
  use 1 teaspoon oil and ¼
  cup bread crumbs)
Broccoli with 1½ teaspoons
  Hollandaise sauce
Scalloped tomatoes (use ½
  cup canned tomatoes; 1
  slice diced bread; 1 teaspoon oil; salt; pepper;
  basil)
1 slice Boston brown bread
1 teaspoon diet margarine
1 canned pear, unsweetened
Coffee or tea

### SNACKS

Raw vegetables, such as
  carrot and celery sticks,
  as desired

# The Cooper Clinic Low-Cal Diet

If you are starting a long-term program, you may want to begin by using a diet of 600–900 calories that will result initially in an 8–10-pound weight loss during the first two weeks. Since it borders on fasting, I would suggest that it be used only with the approval of your physician, for a maximum of two weeks. And that a multivitamin tablet be used daily. A maximum of six weeks and preferably longer should elapse before it is begun again.

Persons with cholesterol levels of above 250 should not use this diet since it is relatively high in cholesterol-containing foods and saturated fats.

Some people cannot tolerate diets of this type and chronic nausea occurs. If so, stop the diet and use a more balanced approach.

Finally, there is a great tendency to lose successfully with this diet and then to rapidly regain the weight once the diet is over. You must follow this diet with a balanced 1,000–1,500-calorie diet for 4–6 weeks before you resume normal eating habits.

Keeping these points in mind, here is the diet:

## COOPER CLINIC LOW-CAL DIET

### MONDAY

| BREAKFAST | LUNCH | DINNER |
|---|---|---|
| ½ small grape-fruit | ½ cup water-packed tuna | ¼ small broiled chicken |
| 1 soft-cooked egg | on lettuce with | Tossed salad with |
| 1 slice dry toast | tomato wedges | lemon wedge |
| (water, black tea | (1 small) | Steamed green |
| or coffee is en- | 4 long melba | beans with |
| couraged at every | toast | mushrooms |
| meal) | Water/beverage | 1 small apple |
| | | Water/beverage |

| BREAKFAST | LUNCH | DINNER |
|---|---|---|

## TUESDAY

| BREAKFAST | LUNCH | DINNER |
|---|---|---|
| ½ small grapefruit<br>1 soft-cooked egg<br>1 slice dry toast<br>(water, black tea or coffee is encouraged at every meal) | ¾ cup cottage cheese<br>Tossed salad with lemon wedge<br>1 small dinner roll<br>Water/beverage | 5 oz. broiled steak<br>Steamed broccoli<br>Tossed salad with lemon wedge<br>Water/beverage |

## WEDNESDAY

| BREAKFAST | LUNCH | DINNER |
|---|---|---|
| ½ small grapefruit<br>1 soft-cooked egg<br>1 slice dry toast<br>(water, black tea or coffee is encouraged at every meal) | 2 oz. sliced cheese<br>Tossed salad with lemon wedge<br>4 long melba toast<br>Water/beverage | 6 oz. baked fish with 1 teaspoon butter or margarine<br>Stewed zucchini squash with tomatoes<br>Lettuce wedge with lemon wedge<br>1 small pear<br>Water/beverage |

## THURSDAY

| BREAKFAST | LUNCH | DINNER |
|---|---|---|
| ½ small grapefruit<br>1 soft-cooked egg<br>1 slice dry toast<br>(water, black tea or coffee is encouraged at every meal) | 3 oz. broiled beef patty<br>Lettuce & tomato salad with lemon wedge<br>1 small dinner roll<br>Water/beverage | 3 small broiled lamb chops<br>Steamed asparagus<br>Tossed salad with lemon wedge<br>Water/beverage |

| BREAKFAST | LUNCH | DINNER |
|---|---|---|

## FRIDAY

| | | |
|---|---|---|
| ½ small grape-fruit<br>1 soft-cooked egg<br>1 slice dry toast<br>(water, black tea or coffee is encouraged at every meal) | Small baked chicken leg & thigh<br>Tossed salad with lemon wedge<br>1 small dinner roll<br>Water/beverage | 5 oz. broiled steak<br>Steamed brussels sprouts<br>Tossed salad with lemon wedge<br>1 small apple<br>Water/beverage |

## SATURDAY

| | | |
|---|---|---|
| ½ small grape-fruit<br>1 soft-cooked egg<br>1 slice dry toast<br>(water, black tea or coffee is encouraged at every meal) | 2 oz. sliced cheese<br>Tossed salad with lemon wedge<br>1 slice bread (toasted if desired)<br>Water/beverage | 6 oz. baked fish with 1 teaspoon of butter or margarine<br>Steamed broccoli<br>Tossed salad with lemon wedge<br>1 small pear<br>Water/beverage |

## SUNDAY

| | | |
|---|---|---|
| ½ small grape-fruit<br>1 soft-cooked egg<br>1 slice dry toast<br>(water, black tea or coffee is encouraged at every meal) | ½ cup cottage cheese<br>Tossed salad with lemon wedge<br>1 teaspoon margarine or butter<br>1 small dinner roll<br>Water/beverage | 5 oz. steak<br>Spinach<br>Tossed salad with lemon wedge<br>1 small apple<br>Water/beverage |

*Repeat the menu exactly the second week.*

With your doctor's approval, this is a safe way to lose up to ten pounds rapidly (real weight loss, not just fluid loss). But remember, two weeks *only!*

Many patients particularly like this diet at the beginning of a weight-loss program. It gives them visible results early, which helps in motivation for the long weeks of calorie-counting that lie ahead. Many have told me it was easier to adhere to the long-term balanced diet knowing they'd already dropped a size or two in their dresses or slacks!

## The Pritikin Diet

The food ratio recommended by the American Heart Association is 14 percent protein, 35 percent fat, and 51 percent carbohydrates. At the Longevity Research Institute in Santa Barbara, California, however, Nathan Pritikin and other researchers have been claiming dramatic results with heart disease patients using (along with exercise) a diet that is 80 percent complex carbohydrates, excluding refined or simple carbohydrates such as sugar and alcohol. The remaining calories in this diet are 10 percent protein and 10 percent fat, with a cholesterol intake kept below 100 mg per day.

The theory behind this diet is that an increase in blood flow can come about more readily when the fat content in the blood is dramatically reduced. As we have already discussed, high cholesterol, lipoproteins, and triglycerides can induce a sludging effect that inhibits circulation. Adding to this impediment could also be clusters of red blood cells which, like a traffic jam, can block off an artery. This erythrocyte aggregation, to use the medical terminology, can be induced by fats in the blood that are absorbed from the diet. In addition, according to the Pritikin theory, if the cholesterol level in the blood drops low enough, some of the cholesterol plaques or obstructions in the arteries will dissolve, opening up previously blocked or partially blocked vessels.

The Longevity Research Institute uses this low-fat diet for long-term angina patients whose conditions have deteriorated to the point where coronary bypass surgery is indicated. The patient eats mainly whole grain bread and other natural complex carbohydrates, getting his protein from grains, nuts, and minimal portions of meat. Green salads and other fresh vegetables are of course used abundantly. According to the institute's findings, the lipid content of the blood drops rapidly with this diet, which helps increase blood flow and the oxygen-carrying capacity of the blood. After a few days of this diet and aerobics exercise (generally walking or stationary cycling) some patients find that the angina has decreased, and that they can exercise a bit more. Soon the training effect begins to take hold, and within thirty days, in the cases the institute reports, medication is no longer required.

Published scientific data are still lacking to document the claimed results of the combined diet and exercise program and, at this time, I am not too optimistic about its "reversing arteriosclerosis." We know that low-fat diets combined with exercise are beneficial to most coronary patients, but certainly not "100 percent successful," as some of the press releases from the Longevity Research Institute have claimed.

## The Problem Foods

*Refined Sugars.* As we've just noted, many of the diets avoid refined sugars. They do so for the reasons we have already discussed: primarily, the elevation of blood sugar and secondarily the elevation of blood triglycerides. There is also the possibility that dietary sugar may stimulate the liver to produce more cholesterol.

But refined sugar carries with it another problem for the average person. And since the "average American" now ingests between 99 and 170 pounds of sugar every year, this is a fairly widespread problem. I'm not talking about the enormous number of calories that so much sugar represents, either, even though an estimated 50 million

Americans are currently overweight to the point of obesity.

I am referring to the "yo-yo" mechanism, which can produce problems in addition to obesity.

The "yo-yo" mechanism is activated because sucrose (table sugar) is quickly converted into glucose and quickly gets into your bloodstream. For a short period this may produce a feeling of "quick energy," but as this is happening your pancreas is turning out a rush of insulin to metabolize the elevated sugar—so that the level that was up comes rapidly down. In some cases, there are symptoms of dizziness, light-headedness, and near fainting noted with this rebound phenomenon which usually are transient.

If low-glucose level becomes chronic, the result is hypoglycemia, and a whole range of symptoms both physical and mental. However, let me add that even though the diagnosis of true hypoglycemia is frequently made, clinical, symptomatic hypoglycemia is quite rare.

It is wiser, therefore, to avoid excess quantities of refined sugar and so reduce the "peaks and valleys" of blood glucose level that they produce. Aerobics exercise is of value here, too, in controlling to some extent the extreme highs or lows in blood sugar. In other words, both adult onset diabetes and true hypoglycemia may improve.

## Coffee

Unfortunately, there is much that we don't know yet about the effects of stimulants, such as coffee and tea and colas, on the body. One study showed no link between coffee and heart disease. But two Boston studies suggest a strong correlation between the two.

In one of those studies, involving 716 patients with heart attacks, those who drank one to five cups of coffee a day ran a 50 percent greater risk of developing heart problems than those who drank no coffee. Those who drank six or more cups of coffee a day ran a 110 percent greater risk.

But those studies found no greater risk from tea consumption. This was surprising, since tea contains 12 milligrams of caffeine per ounce. This suggests that there may be something else in coffee besides caffeine that is harmful to the heart.

Colas also contain caffeine, but again we don't know enough about their side effects.

However, we do know that caffeine does stimulate the heart—and that's cause enough for caution. We learned several years ago to restrict coffee intake before resting or stress ECGs because of the increased frequency of premature or "skipped" heartbeats.

So while I can't pass hard and fast judgment on colas and tea, I recommend no more than two or three cups of coffee a day and an absolute maximum of five cups per day.

## High-Purine Foods

As we mentioned earlier, foods high in the purines can elevate blood levels of uric acid—a coronary risk factor. Other foods, such as alcohol, stimulate the body to produce higher levels of uric acid, which creates the same problem.

Here is a list of foods that must be taken only infrequently by patients with high uric acid levels:

| | |
|---|---|
| Alcohol | Kidney |
| Asparagus | Liver |
| Mushrooms | Sweetbreads |
| Peas | Lentils |
| Anchovies, sardines | Meat extracts |
| Heart | |

Weight reduction, as we said earlier, does help lower uric acid, as does aerobic exercise. Care must be taken, though, to avoid a crash diet, since destruction of body cells involved in abrupt weight loss will release cellular purine and increase the uric acid level, aggravating the condition rather than helping.

## Alcohol

Of all the problem foods, alcohol is the only one that's regularly discussed on a moral as well as a medical level. And in fact the radical behavior changes produced by excessive alcohol intake can damage far more a man or woman and his or her family than can a whole host of diseases.

But let's look at the medical side. Alcohol, like carbon monoxide, interferes with the body's ability to utilize oxygen. Oxygen can get to the tissues, but it can't move effectively from the blood to the cells where it is to be used if there is a significant blood alcohol level.

Also, alcohol is a depressant. It anesthetizes the nerves so that a person feels relaxed, but alcohol *does not really relax the muscles* when taken at the levels we associate with social drinking. Electromyography tests done at the University of Maryland showed no change in muscle activity even though blood alcohol levels were elevated, after intake of from one to five cocktails, depending on the subject's weight. People who participated in the study had the feeling of relaxation after drinking, but they weren't really relaxed—the physiological tension that could keep them on edge and induce stress symptoms, in other words, was still around to cause problems.

Another problem is cirrhosis, the liver disease that ranks in the top five causes of adult death in the United States.

And a third, of course, is obesity. An ounce and one half of 100-proof alcohol has 75 calories, and a 12-ounce can of beer, 150 (light beer, 96).

Moreover, a person who is a chronic alcoholic will nearly always have some serious nutritional deficiency, since alcohol destroys many essential nutrients, especially the B vitamins.

Finally, regular intake of large amounts of alcohol has a cumulative effect on the tissues and organs of the body. It disrupts the mechanism of glucose metabolism, so that the brain tissue may become glucose-deprived and become dependent on alcohol as a substitute.

According to recent studies at the University of Texas Clayton Foundation done by Dr. Roger J. Williams, this impairment of glucose metabolism in the brain is a primary factor in the dependency state we know as alcoholism.

And it is here that alcohol becomes a moral problem as well as a medical one. We're familiar with the personality changes we associate with alcoholism: the insults, the outbursts of temper, the defensiveness, the psychological debilitation, the increased dependence on drink, and the inability to get along with people.

One aid for problem drinking, as you might suspect, is aerobic exercise. The discipline of an exercise routine, the improvement in circulation to the brain and other organs, the increased oxygen available—all produce a positive effect. One San Diego psychiatrist, Dr. Thaddeus K. Kostrubala, has been recommending jogging for his alcoholic patients, especially over three miles and more than a half hour daily. He reports, "I have never had such a breakthrough in medical knowledge in my whole life. I am intrigued beyond belief by what I am seeing." People have also sent me numerous letters and case histories indicating that exercise made the critical difference in curing a drinking problem.

But I still recommend Alcoholics Anonymous for problem drinkers, because if they don't stop drinking first, they're not going to stay on either a diet or an exercise program. A.A. provides the direct intervention that is so often necessary, and it also helps cure by example.

I also recommend that anyone who drinks has blood studies done annually, including glucose level and enzyme screening for early detection of liver disease. It's important to remember that you don't have to be an alcoholic to develop liver trouble. Heavy drinkers are all susceptible.

Finally, for someone who wants *really* to relax after a hard day, I recommend an aerobic exercise workout. Not only is this more effective than alcohol, it's also been shown by controlled experimental studies to be more effective than a tranquilizer. And it's less expensive. So, as

*The Physician and Sports Medicine* recently advised, "Make the next round around the block."

## Vitamin and Mineral Supplements

Megavitamin therapy, especially with vitamin C and vitamin E, has been widely publicized during recent years as a cure for illnesses ranging from heart disease to the common cold. While I share the hope of many that cures will soon be found for these problems, it must be said that vitamin therapy is presently in the stage where more promises than scientific proofs are available.

From a preventive medicine standpoint, however, I recommend a vitamin-mineral supplement taken daily. This may sound odd, when one considers that the diet recommendations you have read would *already* give a person 100 percent of the daily allowances for vitamins and minerals recommended by the National Research Council of the National Academy of Sciences in 1974. In fact, the following simple menu, hardly elaborate, will give 100 percent of the recommended requirements of all vitamins, minerals, protein, fat, and carbohydrate:

Orange juice, 8 ounces
Fortified skim milk, 1 quart
Meat, fish, or poultry, 7 ounces
Wheat flakes, 1 cup
Whole wheat bread, 4 slices
Cooked green peas, 1 cup
Cooked spinach, 1 cup

If this is all you need, why take a vitamin supplement? Basically, for two reasons. First, depending on the stresses and physical activities of the day, your body's demand for vitamins may increase. Even though all vitamins but C are stored in the liver and available to meet an increase in requirements, it makes sense to keep these reserves well stocked. Second, your intake of natural vitamins from your diet may vary, particularly when you're eating away from home, or because of consuming alcoholic beverages. A stressful business trip could deplete the liver's vitamin

stores while it keeps you from replenishing them naturally
—and for this reason a supplement makes sense.

*Vitamin C* supplements in addition to a multivitamin-
mineral may also be advisable, particularly since vitamin
C is not stored in the body.

Yet, don't overdo the vitamin C intake. Massive doses
of several grams have been associated with bowel irritation, diarrhea, and attacks of gout. It may also irritate
the bladder and cause kidney stones. Persons with diabetes
should remember, too, that a large vitamin C intake may
invalidate their tests for sugar in the urine. Another study
indicates that the large amounts of vitamin C are simply
excreted, so that the amount in the bloodstream cannot
be increased any more by taking 1,000 milligrams a day
than it can by taking 100 milligrams a day.

To get to the most widely publicized point about
vitamin C, though, what about its use as a cold preventive?
Does it work, or doesn't it?

Well, there is some evidence that it does work—at least
as well as, and in one instance better than, a placebo
(inert pill). That latter instance was a study of 818
subjects at the University of Toronto, where 1 gram of
vitamin C or a placebo was given daily, with neither the
subjects nor the persons dispensing the pills knowing who
was getting what. Both groups had the same number
of colds, but the vitamin C group needed to stay home
with their colds only 70 percent of the number of days
that the placebo group required.

Of course, the placebo effect is not to be discounted
either. Many people in the placebo group undoubtedly felt
they were getting protection from colds and so may have
protected themselves—actually getting fewer colds that
winter than they were accustomed to. Back in 1949, when
a similar study was done at the University of Minnesota,
one of the subjects who had unknowingly been taking a
placebo came back the following winter asking for more
of the wonder drug that had kept him from getting a
cold! So just the act of taking something may help, even
if the chemical action of the vitamin C against the cold
turns out to be negligible.

How much, then? For adults, I recommend 500 mg–1,000 mg daily, decreasing to 250 mg–500 mg during the summer months. Taken apart from your other vitamins, it won't hurt and it may help.

*Vitamin E* has been highly publicized as a means of improving physical performance as well as a miracle cure for heart disease, impotence, blood clots, and aging. The placebo effect may be operating in a great many cases where such responses and cures have been reported, since subsequent double-blind studies by many serious investigators have failed to repeat the results. One laboratory study that may be significant, however, was done on human tissue culture at the University of California at Berkeley in 1974. There investigators were able to double the life of cells placed under light and high-oxygen conditions, thought to stimulate environmental stress. This appears to support the idea that vitamin E has an anti-oxidative role, the basis of claims that it "smooths out" the oxidation process of fatty acids and so provides a steadier flow of energy during the day.

Do you need supplements of vitamin E? Since it's abundant in cereals and in soybean, cottonseed, and corn oils, if you're getting these you're getting vitamin E. I doubt that supplemental vitamin E is necessary with a prudent diet, and I don't recommend it. I especially caution patients with heart disease not to rely on treatment with vitamin E. This could waste valuable time and may be dangerous!

Vitamin E may be of value in reducing night leg cramps if taken in large doses (up to 1,000 I.U. daily). At least one study documents a significant difference, and I have had several patients respond favorably. They start with 200 I.U. daily and, at two-week intervals, increase the dosage 200 I.U. until either the leg cramps disappear or 1,000 I.U. daily dosage is reached. If at 1,000 I.U. there is no improvement, discontinue taking the vitamin.

Finally, *lecithin* has also been publicized as a cure-all for heart disease. The theory is that, since lecithin acts as an emulsifier for cholesterol, it will dissolve cholesterol particles in the bloodstream and prevent them from contributing to the atherosclerotic process of clogging your arteries. Unfortunately, this theory has yet to be proven with controlled, double-blind experiments. Meanwhile, however, there are two other facts to remember about lecithin. First, lecithin is manufactured by your liver. Unless you have liver damage, if you're eating a prudent, balanced diet you're manufacturing your own lecithin for your bloodstream. Second, remember that the lecithin in the pills you might take as supplements does not go directly into your bloodstream to work any miracles dissolving serum cholesterol. It goes into your stomach, where it is chemically altered by the digestive process, and then into the intestine, where it undergoes further chemical breakdown.

So there you have the dietary suggestions we make to patients at the Cooper Clinic. We don't claim they're miraculous; all we claim is that we get results.

Not that you won't feel better after you've been on this balanced, prudent, weight-reduction or maintenance program for a few months. You will. After three months, you may have lost twenty pounds or more, and you'll have gained in circulatory health and lean muscle mass by continuing your aerobic exercise. But you won't have done it by any instant miracle or fad. You'll have worked at it steadily, without strain on your system, without elevating your coronary risk, and without taking any exotic dietary supplements. The biggest aggravation you'll have faced is the necessity to count calories, and to see that your aerobic exercise and your caloric intake match up to the right weight loss or maintenance formula for you.

After a long period, of course, you may find the results miraculous. Many have, and that's as it should be.

But as I hope I indicated with the title to this chapter, a lot of mathematics comes before that particular miracle.

# 7

# Preventive Medicine and You

In 1772, Benjamin Franklin began a letter to his son, William Franklin, this way:

Dear Son,

In yours of May 14th, you acquaint me with your indisposition which gave me great concern. The resolution you have taken to use more exercise is extremely proper. It is of the greatest importance to prevent disease, since the cure of them by physic is so very precarious. . . .

Benjamin Franklin had a great insight into both preventive medicine and the important role of regular exercise. But it has taken us over 200 years to grasp the full meaning of his words.

In December 1975, Dr. Irving Tabershaw, president of the American College of Preventive Medicine, said:

There is evidence that we are in a state of social transition from overwhelming public interest in the care of the sick and disabled to recognition and support for preventive medicine. Perhaps the single most important development which favors an upsurge in interest in preventive medicine is the increasing disillusionment of the American people with health care.

As the American Health Foundation has said so clearly: "Ours is a legacy of a medical system which provides too much care, too late!"

In 1974 the five leading causes of death in Americans 35 to 54 years of age were as follows:

| MEN | WOMEN |
|---|---|
| 1. Heart disease | 1. Breast cancer |
| 2. Lung cancer | 2. Heart disease |
| 3. Accidents | 3. Strokes |
| 4. Cirrhosis of the liver | 4. Accidents |
| 5. Strokes | 5. Cirrhosis of the liver |

How many of those deaths resulted from an act of God and how many from an act of man?

Strokes are primarily the end result of high blood pressure, and at least 15 million Americans have this problem. An estimated 50 percent of the women are under adequate control, but only 25 percent of the men. Also, it is well known that hypertension (high blood pressure) and obesity go hand in hand. With 50 million Americans overweight, obviously there is a great potential for hypertensive problems as well as a great opportunity for prevention.

Cirrhosis of the liver, in the vast majority of cases, is secondary to excess alcohol consumption, and obviously this is a condition that is self-inflicted. In nearly half of the fatal automobile accidents, alcohol is a predisposing factor.

If we were to use our seat belts and shoulder harnesses, deaths from auto accidents could be cut in half. Yet in 1975 only 25 percent of Americans used their seat belts and 4 percent used their shoulder harnesses. In countries like Canada and Switzerland, there are laws regarding the use of seat belts and shoulder harnesses and stiff penalties if you are caught not wearing them, particularly if an injury-producing accident occurs.

If 60 million Americans were to quit smoking cigarettes, deaths from lung cancer could be reduced. Yet, since 95 percent of smokers start before age 21, the greatest potential is in educating and motivating young people not to start. In 1975 the U.S. Public Health Service estimated that 360,000 deaths were directly related to the use of tobacco. And from 1949 to 1975 the U.S. government subsidized the tobacco industry with $275 million! Preventive medicine has to be realistic, and the source must be attacked before results can be expected.

Not only is the use of tobacco related to lung cancer, but it is a major factor in heart disease. With proper weight, diet, exercise, and avoidance of tobacco, heart disease can be controlled, and those four factors are the foundation for any good preventive medicine program. A fifth is also important: the regular physical examination. Past thirty-five years of age and particularly past forty, the annual, comprehensive, preventive health exam is one of the most important parts of a good preventive program.

At the Aerobics Center we hope to provide data that will lead to a "boom" in preventive medicine in America. By gathering more data and formulating more specific programs, we hope to help people guard against disease not only in the heart, but in other areas of the body. Of course, we don't have the space here to go into a detailed program for all the problems that today's studies now suggest are preventable. However, I would like to share with you some of the more recent findings in one important area: cancer prevention.

Since it is first on the list of causes of death for women thirty-five to fifty-four years of age, let's discuss cancer of the breast. As I noted earlier, monthly self-examination is highly recommended. The majority of breast cancers diagnosed at a time when surgical correction is effective are found by the women themselves. More sophisticated techniques are now available to X-ray the breast, such as mammography or xeroradiography. A tumor in the breast grows slowly, and it has been estimated that up to eight years is required before the mass can be palpated. With good radiographic techniques, the tumor can at times be picked up two years before it can be palpated. In those cases, the results are usually quite good and a complete cure more likely.

Recently there has been considerable discussion about X rays of the breast being a cause of cancer. There are good arguments on both sides, but if a woman past thirty-five years of age has a suspicious mass, an X ray is indicated. I do not feel that routine mammography, performed annually as a part of a preventive care examination, is yet justified. There has even been some question about frequent fluoroscopic examinations of the chest as being a cause of breast cancer. At one time (1930–1954) air collapse therapy of the lung was used to treat tuberculosis. In conjunction with the treatment, the 1,047 women in one study were fluoroscoped an average of 102 times over a period of several years. In this group an excess of breast cancer developed.

Our diagnostic techniques in this area may be questioned but, intriguingly enough, there may be preventive practices that will help decrease the incidence of breast cancer.

The length of time spent in nursing children may have some effects: cancer of the breast is more frequent in unmarried than in married women, and in Japan, where women spend more time in lactation, they have only one seventh the incidence of breast cancer that we have here in the United States. Early menstruation, brought on, some researchers suspect, by an increase in the average weight of girls approaching puberty, may also be linked to malignancy in the breast. Epidemiologists have shown that in Western populations during the last one hundred years menstrual flow has begun in girls at increasingly younger ages—and correlated with an increasing rate of breast cancer.

Recent studies from the Harvard School of Public Health have shown a relationship between the use of female hormones after the menopause and a significant increase in breast cancer. For several years we have known of a relationship between postmenopausal estrogens (hormones) and an increased incidence of uterine cancer, but only recently has the relationship to breast cancer been shown. When we try to change the body's normal physiology, we can expect some problems. Another example is the use of birth control pills. There is a causal relationship between use of the pill and blood clots, high blood pressure, strokes, and heart disease, as well as the possibility that a relationship exists between the pill and liver tumors (hepatomas) and gall bladder disease. It has not been shown that the pill causes breast cancer; only postmenopausal estrogens have been related to that problem.

The American Cancer Society states that, each year, over 47,000 American men and women die of cancer of the bowel. Yet it is estimated that if every person, asymptomatic, over forty years of age, had a proctosigmoidoscopy done annually, 27,000 lives could be saved. With proctoscopy (direct visualization of the lower twelve inches of the colon and rectum) up to 75 percent of the cancers of the bowel can be picked up, and usually at a stage where they can be removed in a physician's office. Bowel cancers are usually slow-growing, and it takes up to 600 days before they start spreading. During the past six years at the Cooper Clinic, over fifty cases of early potentially malignant lesions have been discovered and successfully removed in a physician's office, and not one of those patients has had any further problems related to the malignancy.

Does that sound like the annual examination is worthless as has been suggested in recent periodicals?

Here is more documentary evidence: as a part of a twenty-five-year study at the University of Minnesota Cancer Detection Center, 18,158 patients were examined annually, and when a polyp or early lesion was seen, it was removed, whether it appeared to be benign or not.

The results showed that 85 percent of the malignancies one would statistically anticipate to develop in a population of this size did *not* develop, and that those few malignancies which did develop were all removed successfully.

But while examinations are important, there are studies that suggest the importance also of diet and exercise in this area. First is the well-publicized need for dietary fiber and roughage, which speeds up the movement of intestinal waste through the system. Two recent studies, one in England and one in America, show that patients with colon cancer have more anaerobic bacteria in their fecal matter than does the general population. And epidemiological studies consistently show that populations with high-fiber diets have a lower incidence of intestinal malignancy than Americans. One of these studies, done on Japanese immigrants, shows that when a Japanese moves to Hawaii or California and adopts an Americanized diet, his or her risk of developing cancer of the colon increases —from 4 in 100,000 in Japan to 30.9 in 100,000 in America.

Other studies demonstrate that smokers who are heavy consumers of alcohol develop cancer of the upper alimentary tract at a rate higher than that of the general population, and that patients with colon cancer have an above-average amount of bile acid and cholesterol metabolites in their fecal matter. Bile acid and cholesterol metabolites are known to be increased by diets high in fat and cholesterol.

What about exercise? Does that play a role in reducing intestinal cancers? Well, we don't have any firm evidence in this area—though from a theoretical standpoint, this does appear to be a potential area for investigation. Regular exercise is associated with lowered cholesterol, as we saw in Chapter 3. It lowers gastric hyperacidity, as we saw when we discussed stress. And by its massaging action on the intestines, aerobic exercise speeds up transit time, reducing the problems of constipation, which may be a factor in bowel cancer and other intestinal disorders.

With some cancers of the reproductive system, there is further evidence that screening and preventive techniques can greatly reduce the present risk. Fatalities from cervical cancers have already decreased by 50 percent after the introduction of the Papanicolaou test (Pap smear). These cancers are also known to be related to early intercourse, promiscuity, and poor genital hygiene—all indisputably preventable. Vitamin A deficiency, also preventable, may be another factor influencing this disease, some researchers feel, since vitamin A helps preserve the integrity of the epithelial covering of the cervix. For males in the United States, penile cancer has been tallied at between 1 and 3 percent of all cancer—yet it is demonstrably avoidable. Circumcision before puberty, done as part of a religious rite by Moslems and Jews, reduces the incidence of this malignancy almost entirely among these two religious groups. In countries where circumcision is not regularly performed, incidence of this cancer is higher —up to 10 percent of all male cancers in India and up to 20 percent in China. Here in the United States, according to one study done on 120 penile cancer patients, *not one* had been circumcised in infancy.

No preventable-cancer discussion, of course, would be complete without mention of tobacco. We have noted the correlation earlier between cigarette smoking and lung cancer in seven out of eight cases. We have noted the correlation between tobacco and cancer of the upper digestive tract, and should add that cigarette smoking *doubles* the risk of bladder malignancy. But we should also note another tobacco hazard that is unfortunately receiving more and more television advertising publicity these days: chewing tobacco and snuff. Persons who habitually use tobacco in this form expose their mouths to prolonged contact with tobacco—and to prolonged contact with whatever carcinogen is present in the tobacco. The figures indicate a definite correlation between snuff usage and mouth cancer. One study on 394 cases found that 3 out of 4 women with these cancers were snuff users and held the "pinch" of snuff in the same place inside the mouth where the malignancy began. Another study found that among the women in 525 oral cancer cases, 9 out of 10 had the snuff-dipping habit. These cancers are just as needless as those oral cancers common in India, the Philippines, Sri Lanka, Burma, Pakistan, and Guam, where the tobacco to be chewed is mixed with slaked lime and betel nut. The habit is just as preventable.

Overall, it has been estimated that three out of every four instances of cancer of all types are connected with an extrinsic, environmental factor. This means that 75 percent of cancer cases have the *potential* for being prevented—and if not prevented before they begin, then screened by examination, and caught in time for excision or other medical treatment.

I have had two patients die of lung cancer, and both of them skipped their annual physical (and chest X rays) two years in a row. In each case, their last examination showed no trace of cancer on the X ray. If they had come the following year, perhaps the cancer would have been picked up at a stage where their lives could have been saved. We have several patients who are still alive after having their cancer of the lung diagnosed early and successfully removed surgically.

Glaucoma is the second most important cause of blindness in the United States, and glaucoma screening is recommended for all persons older than forty years. And yet glaucoma screening is rarely performed as a part of most routine physical examinations.

With all of this information about the importance of preventive medicine and the value of annual examinations, why is there such poor acceptance? According to Ashley Montagu's article in *The New York Times*, December 1, 1975: "Too many of us will not see a doctor when we are well for fear that something may be discovered that is wrong with us. Most people come to regard health as something one goes to the doctor to be restored to when one is sick. Hence health becomes a function of disease and one sees a doctor only when one is sick."

Even if there were a great increase in interest among patients, there are too few people qualified to practice good preventive medicine—or even to think in terms of preventive medicine. And, in general, medical schools aren't doing much to correct the situation. They just aren't teaching courses in comprehensive preventive medicine. One school of public health is taking up the slack and training medical health specialists to work alongside physicians. These students are taught the same courses that medical students take, but they are taught from a different point of view. They study pharmacy, but concentrate on toxicology and the harmful effects of medications. They study obstetrics, not to deliver babies, but to work in the important prenatal care. Anatomy is studied, not to operate, but to be able to give better advice regarding musculoskeletal problems that occur with exercise. Nutrition is a big area, primarily in the control of obesity, and quit-smoking clinics and alcohol-control programs are all a part of their training.

Yes, there has been progress made in recent years. But we still have a long way to go. Despite the obvious logic of keeping people well rather than getting sick people healthy, preventive medicine is still in its infancy and is the Cinderella of the medical specialities.

And remember, in the words of Péguy, "When a man dies, he does not just die of the disease he has, he dies of his entire life!"

# 8

# I Know It's Good for My Body, But Will It Help Me?

A patient asked me this question not long ago, and followed it up with, "Will *I* feel better?"

For a moment I was going to say, "What do you mean? Of *course* you'll feel better!" But then I saw his point.

He wasn't talking about feelings in his body.

It's common to separate the mind, or the spirit, from the body. Perhaps that's one reason why some of us neglect our bodies, even when they hurt, and still feel as if we were doing something virtuous: "carrying on," without "giving in."

Yet I can assure you that there is an interrelation between the body and the mind.

To begin with, as we saw in the chapter on diet, chemical substances taken into the body have a measurable effect on the mind. Alcohol, glucose imbalance, and vitamin deficiency all change one's mental outlook and performance, just as do the prescription chemical stimulants and depressants, the "mood elevators" and "tranquilizers."

Likewise, positive or negative thoughts from the mind affect the body, as countless studies of psychosomatic illness have shown—not to mention the many instances in our histories and legends where people have grown ill and died from the emotional wounds we call a "broken heart."

Yet what about the reverse? Supposing we strengthen the heart, improve cardiovascular fitness: will that affect the mind just as surely as a chemical stimulant or depressant?

Both our theory and our research evidence indicate "yes."

In the first place, improved cardiovascular fitness—through diet, exercise, weight control, and proper rest—has a direct chemical effect on the brain. The increased circulatory flow to the brain makes available more oxygen and more glucose, both of which are necessary for the mind to function. A man whose oxygen supply is cut off will "black out" quickly, just as will a man whose glucose supply is lowered during insulin shock.

Conversely, someone whose circulation has improved, giving his brain more oxygen and more glucose, will feel more wide awake and alert, more ready to handle whatever stresses or challenges the day has in store. Many times I have noted, after hours of writing or working on a difficult problem, mental fatigue and dullness. If I take an exercise break, it is amazing how quickly the alertness and mental productivity improves. Hours of dullness can be replaced by moments of effective creativity.

I've often asked people at the Aerobics Center why they started their exercise programs, and the answers usually have to do with something connected with physical health: a bad physical examination, a friend or relative who had a heart attack, and so on.

But when I ask, "All right, *now* what makes you *keep* running or swimming or cycling?" I nearly always hear the same answer: "It makes me feel so much better." In fact, if there's one benefit of aerobic exercise I hear about more than any other, it's this improvement in a person's own capability and capacity, this feeling that the "fuzziness" has cleared and that he's ready for anything.

So strong is this positive feeling that, I suspect, for many people the improvement in coronary risk factors and the weight reduction and all the other physical benefits are almost secondary. Many of them have told me, "Dr. Cooper, even if you came out here and said that aerobics was doing my body no good at all, I'd *still* work out tomorrow because I know how bad I feel when I stop exercising."

A study by the California Human Performance Laboratory confirmed this connection between physical health and psychological well-being. From data taken by survey from 6,298 adults, there was a direct correlation between physical health and mental well-being. In the same study, social health was also directly related to physical health in the responses of these 6,298 persons.

A 1976 report from the Mayo Clinic makes the same connection between physical improvement and emotional well-being. Reporting on the results of a one-year graduated exercise program for men with angina pectoris, the investigators conclude: "All had a decrease in angina, an increase in self-esteem, and a more positive attitude toward their work and their disability." We have seen comparable results in the members of our controlled exercise class.

Now, of course, the question: was the improvement in their attitude due to the decrease in angina, or did the exercise really have an effect beyond the body?

A study on sixty middle-aged men done at Purdue University indicates that exercise does operate to change the mind toward a more positive direction, independent of any curative effect on bodily disease. The men studied were free from clinical conditions that would prevent them from obtaining medical clearance for a vigorous exercise program, but most of them were definitely not in good shape according to tests of oxygen intake capability, lean body mass, heart rate, and blood pressure.

The Purdue researchers put them through a strenuous program: 1½ hours of exercise three times a week. These men would jog for 10 minutes, take a half hour of calisthenics, then run (working up to 2-5 miles) and then play basketball, squash, or volleyball, or swim, for the final half hour.

While I don't recommend a program of this intensity, especially for beginning exercisers, it's clear from the results of the personality tests administered before and after the program that the regimen was helpful. More significantly, the personality scores of the men who were in the worst condition to begin with showed the greatest level of improvement. Their scores went up on personality tests that measured emotional stability, imagination, self-assurance, and self-sufficiency. The scores of those who were in the "high-fitness" category at the beginning of the program showed little change.

For the men who went from least-fit to a higher level of fitness, there was, in other words, a personality change documented through psychological testing—even though there has long been a belief among psychologists that the personality shaped during youth is nearly impervious to change by the time of middle age.

Did the benefits all come from more oxygen and glucose to the brain?

Looking at classical psychology theory, it's a fairly safe bet that there's more connected with the process than that. Whichever of the classic "theories" of human psychology we examine, we can see that an aerobic exercise program would strengthen the human psyche in ways apart from the physiological. According to theories of several psychologists, we all have a built-in urge for physical pleasure, for power and achievement, for helping others, and for meaningful goals to make life worthwhile.

Just looking at a few of the letters that come in every day, I find testimonials that fit into these categories. On physical pleasure, they speak of the aerobic "glow" that comes after exercise—that period of time when "my circulation's humming and I feel so awake and alive!" On achievement, they speak of the personal records they've broken—the things they can do now that they could never do before—not only in exercise, but in their social and business lives as well. They talk of increased ability to think clearly in conferences, to show stamina during late-afternoon and evening negotiations. And an Indiana man writes an indirect testimonial I'm particularly fond of:

> Our minister runs up to twelve miles a day several days a week as he can find the time. He used to be a THREE pack a day, gasping, coughing wreck—what a change in a human, unreal. He is now drawing the largest crowds in the history of our church.

On the concern for others, there are numerous testimonials that this quality relates to aerobic fitness. Perhaps the ones I am most proud of are the comments we receive about the "atmosphere" of the Aerobics Center here in Dallas. As one man puts it: "It's not like a health club or a country club. It's different here—everybody tries to help the other guy succeed, to help him get the job done, to reach his goal. The way I feel is, they helped me get started; now I'm helping others get to the same point. And there's always someone here to look up to—some way to strive for more. Some people see jogging as a loner's activity, but I don't. We're in this together."

Today's psychologists, influenced by behaviorism and ideas such as "altered states of consciousness" and "self-image," also offer views to explain why exercise has such merit.

Take self-image. Of course, it's easy to understand how that would improve in a person who changed a lot of flab to muscle through aerobic exercise, whose skin began to glow and whose eyes began to sparkle. That person could see his or her own *actual* image change to one more attractive. But another benefit of a regular exercise program in this area may have nothing to do with these visible results.

Rather it's the discipline itself, the fact that one's set a challenge and has overcome it by sticking regularly to the exercise program, that seems also to affect the self-image in a positive way. People get a sense that they *can* do what they set out to do, according to the Purdue psychologists, and this gives a sense of accomplishment and independence many haven't felt so strongly in a long time.

As another benefit, the use of an exercise "break" in the routine level of consciousness (as I mentioned earlier) in order to increase creativity and mental strength has been advocated this year by a number of psychologists. William Glasser, in his book *Positive Addiction,* cites the benefits of "losing oneself in a positive activity on a regular basis." He calls running "the hardest but surest way" to achieve what he calls "the PA state" of consciousness, described by one of his research subjects as follows: "I feel good, I don't think at all. My awareness is only of the present, but even that cannot be called awareness. Brain chatter is gone."

University of Chicago psychologist Dr. Csikszentmihalyi, after studying forms of "flow-inducting" activity, gives a similar description. He reports a loss of self-consciousness, an increase in concentration, and, as one person told him, a state of mind where "I become one with the atmosphere." Physical activity is a good way to induce this state, according to this theory, because we can control the difficulty and adjust the challenge to fit our skills, avoiding the distractions of frustration or boredom.

Along the same line, I find it's good to vary the *real* terrain when you can, and to run in the most attractive surroundings available. Especially after a long day's work, to take the pressure off with a good long run up in the hills or out in a park can be richly enjoyable, whether or not you slip into a different state of consciousness. After you've built up your cardiovascular reserves to the point where you can do this kind of running for a half hour or more, you may find that the rhythm of your pace carries you off to where you're feeling both peaceful and intense at the same time—a sort of euphoria—and if that happens, fine. I wouldn't work at making it happen, though. Just do the running and let the mind take care of itself. You're going to feel better from your workout, anyway, no matter whether or not your mind "shifts gears."

I was getting this kind of mental enjoyment from the sheer act of running years ago, during my marathoning days, yet I must admit I was thinking more of physiological matters than psychological when I wrote *Aerobics*. And as a scientist, I wish there were more data on this kind of experience, so that we wouldn't have to rely so heavily on subjective reports.

Yet regardless of the theory you ascribe to, it makes sense to get aerobic exercise on a regular basis. As my wife, Millie, has long told her audiences: "How many positive things do you do for yourself—things that no one can take away from you?" The only risk you run is that you'll feel too good to be able to tolerate quitting. As running authority Dr. George Sheehan put it: "The jogger's main concern is the 'dark night of the soul' he experiences on those days when he is unable to run."

And when you do start an exercise program, you soon will find that some of the symptoms you may have associated with tensions of psychological difficulty are gone—headaches, for example. Working with a group of men over fifty years of age who had a history of migraine headaches, researchers at the University of Southern California, quoted in the *Executive Fitness Newsletter*, found that the headaches improved without medication after a few weeks of physical exercise. They also found that, for tension headaches, a fifteen-minute walk brought more relief than a mild tranquilizer.

Exercise has also been shown effective in reducing allergy and asthma, long associated with emotional stress. Though the mechanism isn't clear, speculation is that the improved circulation helps relieve the congestion that "stuffs up" the respiratory tract.

Also, as we discussed when talking about stress and the heart, exercise has a direct chemical effect on the adrenal hormones in the system, keeping them in balance. When you get out for your workout, you literally burn up the tensions of the day and so get better rest at night. Moreover, you have a greater ability to resist all types of stress. Take, for example, this amazing story that came from Lt. Cdr. Everett Alvarez, Jr., one of the prisoners of war in Vietnam:

The physical fitness training we received in high school and college athletic programs proved beyond a doubt to be extremely valuable in our ability to cope with our situation and the conditions which we, as prisoners, were forced to live with.

The maintenance of top physical fitness was a key to survival and certainly very necessary for our continuing mental stability as well.

Because of our knowledge and training, we were able to institute rigorous daily exercise programs and adapt these same programs to the varying situations we found ourselves in, no matter how severe they might have been. You would have been extremely moved to see a man, with legs in stocks, unable to move the lower portion of his body, daily doing hundreds of situps and isometric exercises. Though our captors felt that he should be "punished" because of his unwillingness to "cooperate," this gave him the physical and mental balance to continue the resistance.

To the athletic coaches of our early days, my fellow POWs and myself say a special "thank you" for instilling in us the spirit and determination that the game isn't over until the final whistle blows.

Also in the realm of human survival, we've seen the longevity studies that indicate men who are more fit live longer—as in the case of the 6,351 San Francisco longshoremen. And from hundreds of my patients, especially during these last few years of fluctuation in the economy, I learn that they're coping with more stress than ever before—and handling it better because of their exercise programs. A new business full of risk, a divorce, death of a spouse, or some other major crisis in adult life takes real strength to face up to, and as one of my patients who had come through two of these crises in one year said recently, "What pulls you through is the fitness and discipline you get from exercise."

I've heard the story so many times, told in different words by different patients. "The discipline of exercise." "A routine to hang on to." "A way to cut fatigue," "to build strength," "to rejuvenate the spirit."

However they tell it, it's a story I'm always glad to hear.

Still, it's one thing to talk about fitness giving longevity, relief from tension-induced pain, and improved emotional well-being, but it's another to say that fitness will improve your performance and ability *while* you're feeling good. Do we have evidence for that?

Of course, we have testimonials. We know that businesses that have begun preventive health and fitness programs report increased productivity, as well as a rise in the morale of their employees and a drop in absences. I saw that happen myself, when I was working with groups of men in the Air Force.

In departments where men were running in our aerobics conditioning program, supervisors claimed that production improved—even though the men were losing a half hour of work time every day. The difference was a change

in attitude, a team spirit and enthusiasm that developed
out of their daily exercise program.

We saw the same correlation between fitness and
achievement at the high school level, during an aerobics
training program we conducted for five Fort Worth
schools. Among 475 boys who participated in the study,
we found that those who did better on the 12-minute test
had higher average grades, as shown below:

| DISTANCE RUN (12 minutes) | AVERAGE GRADES (4.0 = A) |
|---|---|
| 1.75 miles or above | 2.72 |
| 1.5 –1.74 | 2.68 |
| 1.25–1.49 | 2.44 |
| 1.00–1.24 | 2.30 |
| Less than 1.00 | 1.91 |

A study done in Iowa indicates a similar correlation.
There, as reported by the President's Council on Physical
Fitness and Sports in the *Physical Fitness Research Digest*,
boys on the basketball teams had a grade point average of
2.57 compared to a 2.19 average for a similar group of
nonathletic boys. Girls playing basketball had averages
of 2.89, compared with 2.29 for nonathletic girls.

It stands to reason. Cardiovascular fitness would make
these students more alert in class and more receptive to
ideas, as well as giving them more mental stamina to
study more effectively in the evenings. Of course, we can't
overlook another point: the students who were more fit
would miss class less often, because they'd be sick less
often. In the Fort Worth study, we have the correlations
to prove it:

| DISTANCE RUN (12 minutes) | AVERAGE DAYS ABSENT FOR SEMESTER |
|---|---|
| 1.75 miles or above | 4.0 |
| 1.5 –1.74 | 4.6 |
| 1.25–1.49 | 5.2 |
| 1.00–1.24 | 5.8 |
| Under 1.00 | 5.9 |

What about sheer ability, though, ruling out factors
such as motivation and stamina? Does fitness make a
difference here? In my judgment, we don't have enough
data to really say one way or the other, but there are

some interesting indications. One study done by clinical psychologists at the Veterans Administration Hospital in New York, found that breathing 100 percent oxygen under pressure had a positive effect on a group of elderly patients. Two weeks of exposure for brief periods twice a day produced an improvement in standard memory test scores of up to 25 percent. Unfortunately, these changes did not persist. Theoretically, we should get the same improvement from aerobics conditioning in these same patients, since it has been demonstrated that the training effect improves oxygen supply and that such improvement can be gained regardless of age. In practice, however, we don't have the data—yet. That's one of the areas our Institute for Aerobic Research hopes to investigate.

In Florida, though, psychiatrist Ray Killinger has done work in this area. He reports that aerobic fitness results in improvement in the following seven categories of the thinking process: originality of thought; duration of concentration; mental response time; ability to change topics and subjects quickly; depth of thinking; duality of thought —the ability to entertain a number of ideas at once; and finally, mental tenacity.

Think harder, think longer. As Senator Proxmire said back in 1968, "There's little question that your mind works more swiftly, and your stamina at work at a desk, in a conference, anywhere is improved by following the Cooper prescription."

Or as novelist Joseph Heller put it in a 1976 interview, his lunchtime run at the YMCA "clears my mind, flushes out the pressures and starts a free flow of ideas. There is no time in a week when I feel so good. . . . It's a pure, clean, tired feeling."

Or as Mary Redding of Oral Roberts University said in a letter I received just recently, "*Aerobics for Women* is standard equipment around our office. We go to the aerobics building at lunchtime and work out, and come back with clear minds (and no drowsiness) to tackle the afternoon's work."

Why take a tranquilizer or a stimulant when you can get the benefits of both with no destructive side effects

—and help your body in the bargain?

Two other benefits of fitness might also be mentioned here when we're talking of the psychological bonuses: first, it will likely improve your self-image if your career is important to you, because it not only will help you work better but also, if a survey of 15,000 executive salaries is any indication, will net you more money. The Robert Half Personnel Agencies of New York, which did the survey, found a correlation between amount of salary earned and number of pounds overweight. According to Robert Half, "Some fat people pay a penalty of $1,000 a pound," with less than 10 percent of those in the upper-income brackets more than ten pounds overweight. In the lower incomes, nearly 40 percent of those surveyed were more than ten pounds too heavy.

Even if all this doesn't move someone you're trying to convince, though—even if he's not interested in longer life, better health, better work performance, improved emotional harmony, clearer thinking, and more money—you might have him consider one last point: fitness is becoming more and more fashionable. According to *Harper's Bazaar,* "Now everyone is in the act. Jackie does it, Senator Proxmire does it, actress Sylvia Miles does it. Every day another prominent name is added to the list of devotees." If the trend continues, instead of chasing celebrities into restaurants, fans may begin chasing them around the local tracks—which, considering the problem that we have in this country with obesity, might be quite a healthy trend.

Seriously, though, no matter what the next person is doing, no matter how much more money you may make or what grades you may earn, you owe it to yourself to get the benefits of fitness. Why? Because there's more to life than just going disease-free. As my wife, Millie, is fond of saying, "Your doctor can tell you that you're in great shape, but if you don't feel good, what difference does it make?"

Both on a chemical level and on a psychological-emotional level, fitness will put more energy into you. More years in your life, as we say, and more life in your years.

# 9

# You Still Have a Question?

I have received at least 10,000 letters since the publication of *Aerobics,* and many have asked the same questions. In this chapter I want to answer some of the most commonly asked questions, emphasize answers already given, and discuss some of the questions dealing with special problems and situations. These are typical questions frequently asked.

## The Point Charts

*Q.* Why are the points awarded in *Aerobics for Women* different from those awarded in *The New Aerobics?* Do women receive fewer points than men?

*A.* Women and men receive the same number of points for aerobic exercise. Points awarded in *The New Aerobics* contain endurance points, whereas the old point charts were mistakenly printed in *Aerobics for Women.* To clarify the matter, study the points in this book, which are the latest and most accurate.

*Q.* My buddy runs on the school track, but I like to do my running on the beach, when the weather is good. I maintain I get more exercise for the same distance, but he says it doesn't make any difference. Who's right?

*A.* You are. Running in the sand (if it is soft) is certainly more difficult than running on a solid surface. We have not worked out a point adjustment, but I would expect there to be about a 20 percent difference. For example, a sand mile in 9:30 would be equivalent to a hard-surface mile in 8:30.

*Q.* Why don't I get the same number of points for running three separate miles as running three continuous miles?

*A.* Our lab studies show that the energy cost is much

greater for running continuously than for running the same distance with rests in between. This is the reason we award endurance points after the second mile (or its equivalent in other sports).

*Q.* I am a fourth-year medical student and I have recently begun jogging and am earning between 40 and 50 points per week. I do have a question for you. I sometimes wear 2½-pound weights around each ankle and am wondering if this entitles me to extra points.

*A.* Since you add 2½-pound weights to each leg while running, you are utilizing the "overload principle" and can add about a third more points for the extra energy cost. I would give you 7 points for an eight-minute mile, as compared with 5 points without weights.

Please understand that this is strictly an estimate, since we have not done any studies to determine the oxygen consumption with the overload principle. However, it does appear to be realistic.

On this same basis, I would award 25 percent more points for running in combat boots and 50 percent more points for running while carrying a 35-pound pack.

*Q.* One thing about your point system still puzzles me. I know it's harder to run 8:00-minute miles than it is to run 10:00-minute miles, yet you give me the same 4 points whether I do the mile in 10:00 minutes or 8:01 minutes. And then you say that if I can go just one second faster, and run the mile in 8:00 minutes, you'll give me a whole additional point. That extra second can't be worth all *that* much, can it?

*A.* You're right; it can't be worth that much. As you'll see in our chapter explaining the chart pack, our point values are geared to the *slowest*, not the fastest time in any given interval, to make you work harder and assure a better training response. Each single, whole-number aerobic point represents an oxygen consumption of 7 milliliters per kilogram of body weight, per minute. That is, when you're running the mile at a 10:00-minute pace, you're utilizing oxygen at a rate of 28 ml/kg/min., the energy cost for which we award 4 points. To go faster, you must increase your energy cost, but you won't see this reflected in the chart pack until you get down to 8:00 minutes. At that speed, your oxygen consumption rate is 35 ml/kg/min., and we award 5 points.

If we had unlimited space in this book, we could give you a fractional point value for the speeds in between 10:00 minutes and 8:01 minutes and for all the other chart-pack time intervals. Since we don't, however, the best we can offer those of you interested in getting fractional point values is a printout of your monthly exercise performance from our AIRS (Aerobics International Research Society) computer. The AIRS computer has been programmed to take fractional point values into account. For more information on AIRS, see page 290.

## Heat

*Q.* Why shouldn't I exercise when it's really hot? Working in the heat doesn't seem to bother me.

*A.* If you're acclimatized to the heat, you have some protection from the dangers of hyperthermia (rectal temperature above 104 degrees). Yet hyperthermia may lead to loss of consciousness and ultimately death. When you exercise, only one fourth of the energy you produce is converted into movement; the other 75 percent is converted into heat. If your body can't get rid of this heat, you'll overheat just like a car with a broken radiator. If you feel a throbbing in your temples and a cold sensation around your chest, sides, and back, your temperature is rapidly approaching the harmful level. Cool off *immediately* with a tepid shower, cool (not cold) fluids, or a swimming pool if one is available.

Dehydration that occurs in a hot, humid environment can lead to circulatory collapse, hyperthemia, and death —as happens almost every year in high school football training camps. We recommend forcing fluids when exercising or running in a heat stress situation, even though the exerciser may not feel really thirsty. The type of fluid is also important, since it must replace the electrolytes lost during exercise. These include sodium chloride, magnesium, and potassium, the loss of which can interfere with muscle contraction and other body functions. Salting your food and taking a multivitamin with minerals and a glass of orange juice daily help keep these electrolytes normal.

When you're acclimatized to heat, your body conserves electrolytes and the main thing you need to think about is consuming adequate amounts of fluids. To get acclimatized, simply exercise in the heat at approximately *half* your maximum output, about an hour each workout for eight to ten days.

*Q.* What do you think of salt tablets and the commercial electrolyte-replacement drinks?

*A.* Nearly all the bottled electrolyte drinks should be diluted about half strength, because they contain a high concentration of sugar. Sugar has been shown to interfere with the absorption of fluid from the stomach if the concentration is too high.

Salt tablets, unless they're taken with large amounts of fluids, will also slow down the absorption process and may aggravate a heat stress problem.

## Cold

*Q.* I live in a northern climate but enjoy running outdoors in winter. Is that dangerous? Is there a chance my lungs can become frostbitten?

*A.* I have never heard of a frostbitten lung, although some people suffer from spasms in their windpipe when exposed to very cold air. Their most common symptom is wheezing, and this disappears when rewarming occurs. Heart patients may notice chest pain or angina, particularly when walking into a cold wind. Such exposures must be avoided as much as possible. Yet, for the healthy jogger, running or exercising in cold or even subzero weather is possible, provided clothing is adequate. Avoid either over- or underdressing and getting chilled. You can use a dental or surgical mask over the mouth and nose, but this may cause too much resistance to breathing. If so, a terrycloth "veil" over the mouth and nose

may work well. Even though it may be difficult to frostbite the lungs, it is easy to frostbite the nose, fingers,
or male genitals, so dress warmly.

*Q.* Is there any harm in swimming in cold water?

*A.* If the water is too cold, it could be fatal—particularly
for someone with a heart problem. The shock of entering
cold water could bring on a severe cardiac arrhythmia,
which can, of course, be fatal if not treated immediately.
Also, just the sensation of cold on the face, whether from
air or water, can produce a suppression of the heart rate
and thereby increase the load on the heart. Finally, body
heat is lost much more rapidly in water than in air. On
land, you can exercise and keep warm, but in cold water
you can't.

To sum it up, I would not recommend that anyone
with a known heart condition swim in water colder than
75 degrees.

# Altitude

*Q.* I know the air's thinner at high altitudes, but what
effect does this have on my exercise?

*A.* For anaerobic exercise where you're basically going
on stored oxygen you won't notice much. But for aerobic
exercise where your body must utilize the oxygen in the
air continuously, you will see detrimental effect. For example, the 1968 Olympics in Mexico City showed near-
world-record performances for events that took up to 3½
minutes, but showed performances significantly below this
level for events that took longer.

As the altitude goes up, your body works to compensate for the reduced pressure of oxygen. There is an
increase in red blood cell production of hemoglobin and
blood volume in response to altitude acclimatization,
compensating for the decreased amount of available oxygen. Rapid breathing is also characteristic of altitude exposure, again as your body tries to compensate for the
lack of oxygen. The air is usually quite dry and dehydration can become a problem. Heart patients especially

should avoid vigorous exercise at high altitudes. Yet, if you consider these potential problems and adequately compensate for them, exercise at high altitudes can be safe, particularly following acclimatization. Ideally, you should take two days to acclimatize for every 3,000 feet of ascent.

*Q.* I live at an altitude of 6,200 feet. Shouldn't I be earning more points than a person performing the same amount of exercise at sea level?

*A.* Yes, you should. Although we have not measured it, we do know that you get more benefit from exercising at higher altitudes. As a rule of thumb, I'd add one fourth more points for exercising at 5,000 to 7,000 feet, one third more points for 7,000 to 10,000 feet, and one half more points above 10,000 feet.

So, if you're earning 30 points a week at 6,200 feet, you can add an extra 7 or 8 points.

*Q.* Having had a single heart attack in October 1974, and having made an excellent recovery, is it safe for me to make a trip to La Paz, Bolivia (altitude 12,000 feet)?

*A.* If you have no postcoronary symptoms and require no medication, I see no reason why such altitudes would be a problem to you, provided you take it easy for the first twenty-four hours. But if you experience any pain or discomfort after minimal activity, or require medication for your heart, I would advise against such exposure and in fact discourage any prolonged exposure to an altitude above 5,000 feet unless adequately acclimatized.

*Q.* I was an avid skier before my heart attack three years ago. I'd like to take it up again, but I'm concerned about all the stories I read about people having heart attacks at high altitudes. My wife says, "Forget it," and my doctor says, "Okay, but take it easy." What do you say?

*A.* I have many postcoronary patients who are skiing without any problems. If you are asymptomatic—if you have no chest pains and do not experience any shortness of breath—if you are not taking any pain-relieving medication for your heart, and if you are involved at least in a regular walking program, then I think you can safely engage in downhill skiing. To be on the safe side, though,

I'd recommend a treadmill stress test first, if you haven't already had one.

But I'm much more hesitant to recommend cross-country skiing for postcoronary patients, since it requires considerably more energy than downhill skiing.

I'd apply the same rules to postcoronary patients who want to scuba-dive or backpack in the mountains.

The thing to remember is this: use caution in everything you do. It's not wise to force yourself to the extent that you're chronically fatigued or your heart rate is still high five minutes after you finish exercising (above 120).

## The Exercise Program

*Q.* I'm forty-one years old, in good condition, healthy (I've even been stress-tested), and have been on an aerobics program for three years. But I just can't meet the time and distance goals that I've set for myself. Any suggestions?

*A.* Don't worry about it. I'm not concerned about speed. I'm concerned about duration and intensity. The more research I conduct, the more convinced I become that the "long, slow distance" is the way to go. Our most popular jogging program here at the Aerobics Center is two miles in less than twenty minutes—and there are very few people who can't work up to that level. It is much more important to total 25–35 points per week than it is to perform at a particular speed.

*Q.* I'm forty-five years old and would like to begin an aerobics program. But my doctor won't give me a treadmill stress test. Should I insist on one?

*A.* No. I never try to second-guess another person's physician. There's always the possibility that you might have a medical condition that would make a stress test dangerous.

Under any circumstance, while I believe that a stress test is *important* for persons over thirty-five who want to exercise, I do not insist on it unless there is a known heart problem. As an alternative, however, I do insist on people over thirty-five using a slowly progressive starter program, which can be found in the chart packs, and working up to 30 points a week gradually. If you develop any problems along the way, STOP. Then go see your doctor again.

*Q.* I distribute a copy of *The New Aerobics* to every patient who passes the treadmill stress test and encourage them to begin a regular walking program. But I have a problem. Unless the patient is on a measured course, how do I tell him to measure the increase in his rate of speed?

*A.* The rough rule of thumb that we use to determine the speed of walking is by steps per minute. If the patient is walking at 90 steps per minute, he should cover the mile in approximately 20 minutes. A 15-minute mile is 120 steps per minute. A 14-minute mile is 130 steps per minute. These are standard military paces and can be used in prescribing walking problems. (For people under five feet in height, this rule will not be valid).

*Q.* When I run a mile, I find it much easier to run a little faster for two minutes, then walk briskly for thirty seconds, and keep doing this until I have completed the mile —which I do in around seven minutes. Doesn't this give me the same results as if I ran the whole seven minutes at a slower pace?

*A.* It is better to reduce the speed and jog continuously for a certain distance. Even though you can run fast for two minutes, walk briskly for thirty seconds, and cover a mile in seven minutes, I would suggest that you run continuously and cover the mile nonstop in about eight minutes. Both are worth the same number of points, but there will be less strain on the heart at the slower speed.

*Q.* I've read that while running you should breathe in through the nose and out through the mouth. Is that right?

*A.* No, but it is a common misconception. We find that it restricts athletic performance, as does pursed-lip breathing, gasping, and trying to run at a pace where you take a certain number of steps for each breath.

Accordingly, we encourage people to breathe in and out through both the mouth and nose, at a rate that feels comfortable.

*Q.* From reading your books on aerobics, I have concluded that one of the following is true:

1. Exercising seven days a week is harmful.
2. Exercising seven days a week is no more beneficial than six.
3. Exercising seven days is better than six, but it's nice psychologically to reward yourself with a day off.

Which is correct?

*A.* As you surmise, I do consider exercising seven days a week undesirable. You need one day of rest in order to replace your glycogen stores. The psychological benefits of a day off are important, but there is also some physiological gain.

In a recent study conducted by our Institute for Aerobics Research, we were able to show, during the initial weeks of a program, that the best improvement, the least number of injuries, and the most faithful participation occurred in the group working thirty minutes a day, three days per week.

Most of us who have been exercising for many years have settled on four to five times per week.

*Q.* I believe in the aerobics concept, but I hate to exercise. I just can't stay with it. Any suggestions?

*A.* Try to find someone to exercise with, or join a group. I have found over the years that those are the two best substitutes for self-discipline.

*Q.* In your book *The New Aerobics* you say that when you run you should "let the arms swing comfortably at your side, parallel to your body movement." I am having a difficult time letting my arms relax in the above manner. Any suggestions?

*A.* The swing of an arm is important during running and should assume a different position according to speed. For long-distance running—that is, two miles or longer— the arm should be held at roughly a right angle and should swing slightly across the chest. For shorter distances and faster speeds, the arms should be parallel to the body, although still in a right-angle position.

*Q.* At what speed does jogging become running?

*A.* Anything faster than a nine-minute mile I call running. Anything slower I call jogging.

*Q.* I read someplace recently that the heart can be damaged by forcing it to beat too fast. Doesn't this apply to aerobics exercise as well?

*A.* The heart has a natural, built-in governing system, and the normal heart can't be "forced" to beat too fast, or damaged by vigorous erercise. In fact, some world-class distance runners have maximal heart rates about 200 beats per minute!

*Q.* Dr. Cooper, you say that the rapidity with which your heart rate returns to normal after exercise is an indicator of your fitness. Yet my heart rate an hour and a half after exercising is still not back to the 50–55 at which I started. So what's the problem? Am I out of shape?

*A.* Not necessarily. You build up an oxygen debt during strenuous exercise and it usually takes a while to repay that debt.

As a general rule, we feel that your heart rate should be below 120 beats per minute within five minutes after exercising. But it may take an hour or two to return completely to normal, depending on the intensity and duration of the exercise, the heat stress you've undergone, and your general state of health.

*Q.* How do you account for the fact that some people will score in the excellent category in one fitness test, but only in the good or fair category in another?

*A.* In most cases, there really won't be that much difference. A person who has been regularly earning 30 points a week by swimming, cycling, playing basketball, tennis, or racquetball, ought to score in the good category on the treadmill. If he's been earning 50 points, he ought to score in the excellent category. This is what we call the "crossover effect."

Now, it is true that a 50-point-a-week swimmer or tennis player will usually place behind the jogger on a two-mile run. But that doesn't have anything to do with his fitness or his oxygen consumption; his legs just aren't conditioned to run that far. It should be noted, in fact, that our treadmill record for men over sixty years of age —twenty-eight minutes—is held by a cyclist.

*Q.* What is the swimming equivalent for the twelve-minute running test?

*A.* For the twelve-minute swimming test, we consider 600 yards in twelve minutes as the excellent category of fitness, and 500 yards as the good category.

*Q.* Frankly, I consider exercise one great big pain. But I know it's important, so I've taken up cycling. My problem is that I live in a cold climate and there just aren't many days during the winter when I can ride. So I'm thinking of getting an indoor, stationary cycle. Do I get the same benefit on a stationary cycle?

*A.* In my experience, stationary cycling has just not been very effective in helping people to develop a good aerobics program. There's too much temptation to exercise minimally—without resistance—on a stationary cycle, so that the heart rate may never get above 100 beats per minute.

To determine if stationary cycling is effective, you have to measure the intensity and the duration of the exercise. This is the basic rule of thumb we use:

If you're going to cycle ten minutes a day, the exercise should be strenuous enough to get your heart rate up to 150 beats per minute (counted for ten seconds immediately after exercise, and multiplied by 6).

If you cycle fifteen minutes a day, your heart rate should get up to 140.

If you cycle thirty minutes a day, your heart rate should get up to 130. If you meet these standards, and exercise at least four times per week, indoor cycling can be just as effective as regular cycling or jogging. But you really have to work at it!

*Q.* In your opinion, what's the value of yoga exercises?

*A.* As I have said before, exercise can be used in three different ways: (1) for rest and relaxation; (2) for muscle building and figure contouring; and (3) for cardiovascular and pulmonary conditioning. Yoga fits in the "rest and relaxation" category, since deep-breathing and stretching exercises don't increase the demand for oxygen at the cellular level. I know of no data to show that yoga has any cardiovascular effect or that it produces any training effect benefits.

*Q.* I am fifty-six years old and do my running in the evening. Sometimes our family doesn't eat dinner until eight or nine o'clock. How long should I wait after dinner before exercising? I don't like to run too late.

*A.* I would strongly discourage vigorous physical activity within ninety minutes after a heavy meal. If you desire to run closer to meals, you must consume a light meal consisting mostly of liquids.

Men of fifty-six years of age very commonly have undiagnosed heart disease. Aggravating this condition by running too soon after eating can be dangerous. Why not try running before dinner? This is safer, and it will help you keep your weight down by cutting your appetite.

*Q.* At what point does pollution of the air become harmful to you when you're running?

*A.* We can't give a precise answer to that question at the present time. That's why we've established an environmental protection branch at our Institute for Aerobics Research. In our special chamber, people will exercise at various levels of controlled air pollution. We do know that the older person is more susceptible to chest and lung problems from exercising in smog—and that the person who is deconditioned is more likely to have problems than the person who is conditioned. As a rule of thumb, I'd advise you not to exercise in a smoggy environment if you have any form of lung disease, if you have not been exercising regularly, or if you are past sixty years of age. Also, I would advise *anyone* against exercise outdoors in the case of a smog alert. Exercise indoors instead.

## Clothing

*Q.* What's the proper shoe to wear for jogging?

*A.* In selecting a shoe, there are several things you have to consider.

First, the sole. If you're running on a hard surface, it should be a cushioned sole, and preferably one that is rippled.

Second, the size. The shoe should be wide enough, as well as long enough. If it's too narrow, it will squeeze your foot together and you'll end up with foot problems.

Third, it's of utmost importance to have a good arch support, particularly for those who have flat feet. Many runners develop painful knees and never realize that it is the result of poor arch supports in their shoes.

Fourth, you should have adequate support in the heel—a good, firm fit around the heel, and a little elevation of the heel.

For specific strong points of various shoe brands, check the charts included in the appendix.

*Q*. What kind of footwear do you recommend for jogging in the snow? This is important to me, since we have snow for four or five months out of the year where I live.

*A*. First of all, you should always try to jog on a smooth place, such as a sidewalk or a road. But if you *have* to run in deep snow, you need to protect your legs. I'd advise wearing sweat pants and tucking the legs into the socks. You should wear the same kind of shoe you ordinarily jog in.

## Medical Problems

*Q*. What can I do to get rid of a heel spur?

*A*. First of all, have an X ray made to make sure it *is* a heel spur. A true heel spur is calcification, caused by the tendon pulling away from the bone.

It could be just a jogger's heel, caused by the impact of coming down hard on the heel. A change in running style will cure this.

Or it could be a stone bruise, caused by striking the heel on a hard object. Time will cure this.

But even if you're certain it is a heel spur, I would advise surgery only as a last resort. Some doctors have had success with cortisone injections, but I am a little leery of this treatment, particularly multiple injections.

The most successful treatment that I have found is to keep the patient off the heel until the acute pain disappears, and then place an insert (doughnut or sports orthotics) in the heel of the shoe to keep the pressure off the spur. Any podiatrist can fit such an insert in your shoe.

*Q.* I've been jogging for about four months now and suddenly I've developed soreness and leg pains. Is this normal?

*A.* It's certainly not uncommon. Even today, after all the years I've been running, I'm sometimes sore and stiff when I get up in the morning after a vigorous run the preceding day.

I strongly urge everyone to do stretching exercises before running. The basic exercises that we use can be found in Chapter 4 under "warm-up."

*Q.* My problem is that my legs and shins hurt two or three inches above the ankle every time I run. Is that natural?

*A.* No, it's not. When you have leg problems in general —but particularly shin splints and ankle problems— there are three things that you have to consider.

1. Wearing the correct shoe. We have already discussed that.

2. The running surface. If you're having leg pains, try to get onto a softer surface—off concrete and onto a spongy track or grass.

3. Your running style. If you're coming down too hard on the heel of the foot, chances are that's your problem. Try to run as if you're running on fresh eggs. Run softly and smoothly and hit with the heel only slightly ahead of the rest of the foot.

*Q.* My wife is a registered nurse and is on her feet all day. She has varicose veins. Because of her veins she will not jog with me. She feels it would only make them worse. What do you think?

*A.* It may make them worse. But in the majority of cases it can improve both the symptoms and the appearance of the veins. All I can suggest is that she give it a try.

*Q.* I recently read a magazine article by a doctor who claims that jogging can cause damage to the sacroiliac joint, can bring on varicose veins, can cause the breasts to collapse and sag, and can result in a herniated disc, a displaced uterus, and a hernia. How do you answer that?

*A.* I think I know the magazine article you refer to. As I pointed out in Chapter 4, the author of that article conducted no tests and has no data to back up any of his statements. He merely says those things *could* happen.

But my data, based on fifteen years of intensive study, indicate that they *don't* happen—at least, not as a result of jogging.

Unfortunately, people still use sensationalism and scare tactics to sell magazines.

*Q.* When I get a cold, it sometimes hangs on for weeks and weeks. Is it okay to exercise with a cold? I hate to lose all that good training effect.

*A.* You can exercise as long as you don't have a fever. After a fever, your temperature must be down to normal and remain normal for twenty-four hours before you exercise again. Otherwise, it may cause problems.

*Q.* Four weeks ago, I underwent surgery to repair a hernia. I had been running two miles daily before my operation. Your direction as to when to start exercising again would be greatly appreciated.

*A.* Most patients who have surgery must avoid vigorous activity, including jogging, for some time afterward. I discourage any type of vigorous activity for six weeks, then a progressive walking program, working up to two miles for the next four weeks. Generally by the tenth or twelfth week following surgery the jogging program can be reinitiated with ease. By the sixth month following surgery you should be running the same speeds and the same distances achieved prior to surgery.

*Q.* Are there any good aerobic exercises for paraplegics?

*A.* In 1975 a paraplegic finished the Boston Marathon in less than three hours, *pushing himself in a wheelchair.* I can assure you that that man's cardiovascular fitness is fantastic, even though I've never examined him. There are all sorts of wheelchair athletic events for paraplegics— including basketball games—that I would recommend. It's more difficult to get the training effect by exercising with your arms, but it can be done.

# Men

*Q.* I'm forty-five, don't smoke, and have a heart rate of 63. Do you think my heart's in shape?

*A.* As you'll read in Chapter 3, there's more to your question than that. To answer it, take the Coronary Risk Profile that applies to your age group in to your physician, and fill it out after your examination. You'll find the charts in the appendix. As you can see, a resting heart rate of 63 for your age group is close to the median.

*Q.* I'm not even thirty yet. Why should I have to worry about coronary disease?

*A.* You may not show any symptoms until years later, but the odds are high that you're building coronary disease right now. Autopsies done on U.S. soldiers killed in Korea and Vietnam showed that an average of 77 percent (Korea) and 55 percent (Vietnam) had evidence of atherosclerosis. These were healthy young men, average age 22.1 years.

*Q.* Is there anything I can do about baldness?

*A.* If you're talking about some hair loss due to a scalp infection, your doctor can help. But if you're talking about hereditary baldness, the answer is still no. There's no documented evidence that any of the vitamin supplements and hair oils now marketed will have any effect, and neither will exercise, for that matter. About the only consolation I can offer is that there *is* a positive correlation between baldness and virility.

# Women

*Q.* What's your advice to women who develop unwanted calf and thigh muscles from jogging?

*A.* Most women who jog regularly actually *lose* unwanted inches from the thighs and hips.

As far as calf muscles are concerned, women just don't tend to develop the same kind of muscles as men. And you should see the legs on some of the women marathoners! Occasionally a very athletic-type woman will develop masculine muscle traits, but it is definitely the exception to the rule.

*Q.* You've said before that aerobic exercise may increase fertility. Have you any new evidence on this?

*A.* No, and I still don't want to imply that aerobics will have an assured positive effect. But the letters do continue to come in. One I received just the other day from Tulsa, Oklahoma, has this to say:

I had been married several years, and we decided we wanted a baby. This was just a few months after I'd begun running. But I couldn't get pregnant. Then last spring, when I'd been running for about a year, we achieved pregnancy. My obstetrician was very supportive, even encouraging me to stick with the running right up to the end. And I did. The day before Elizabeth was born I ran two miles. I felt absolutely great throughout the pregnancy and the delivery was a snap. In fact, I came to work the day she was born, and delivered before quitting time that afternoon. I ran again when she was twelve days old. (She's now five months old.)

Then about four weeks ago I began feeling ill. At first I thought it was a virus, but when it didn't go away I began to fear that it might be something more. I went in for a pregnancy test, and sure enough it was something more—the something is due in January. The doctor told me that I have the dubious honor of being the very first patient they've had to become pregnant while having this new type of IUD (the "copper 7"). When I went in for my first examination, his first words were, "Well, this is what aerobics will do for you."

*Q.* Have you changed your recommendations about jogging or exercising during and after pregnancy?

*A.* I still feel it's up to your doctor. As a general rule, I recommend switching to a milder form of aerobic exercise, such as walking or swimming, after the sixth month. After delivery, again it's up to your doctor. Six weeks is a generally acceptable waiting time.

As I've said before, though, and as you've read, we have many exceptions to these recommendations in our files. Another that comes to mind is a twenty-nine-year-old woman from California who stated that she regularly ran two miles in sixteen minutes or less up through the ninth month of her pregnancy. She said it was fun to go up to the high school track where men were already running, run her two miles in sixteen minutes, and notice the amazed expressions on the faces of the men when they were passed by this nine-months-pregnant woman!

*Q.* I've just started getting my aerobic points each week. Do I need to do any other exercises for figure toning? If so, which ones and how often?

*A.* We recommend the exercises listed in Chapter 4 for strengthening and conditioning, particularly if you have a tendency to back trouble, as most people do. Keep in mind that your aerobic exercises also work to tone the muscles; the more points you earn, the more of these benefits you'll experience.

*Q.* I know it's old-fashioned, but I still feel "unladylike" when I go out to run. Any suggestions?

*A.* You may be experiencing a natural feeling of awkwardness, if you're just starting an exercise program. That will disappear as you become more conditioned. You'll also notice that you become more attractive as you begin feeling more alive. As a lady of forty-seven writes from Shaker Heights, Ohio: "The greatest result is the muscle tone and tighter skin I have noticed. That loose area under the chin that I used to play with while reading a book suddenly disappeared!" You might also think of women such as Dinah Shore and Jacqueline Onassis—they're hardly unladylike, and they exercise regularly.

Aside from these matters of attitude, though, there are other things you can do if you want to "feminize" your exercise program. An attractive warm-up suit costs no more than a good blouse or handbag, yet it may make a significant difference in your appearance and the way you feel. You might think of simplifying your hairstyle to one that doesn't require elaborate setting or come "unglued" during exercise—a first-rate stylist can give you a "wash-and-wear" cut no matter what your type of hair. Or you might pin up your hair under a cap, or use an attractive scarf to tie it up, as Millie does. It also helps to find other women you can exercise with, for friendship and group support.

If you're still feeling painfully self conscious (and not

just using this as an excuse to avoid the effort of exercise) you might consider some other form of aerobic workout. Walking, swimming, and cycling are possibilities, as are the indoor exercises of stationary cycling, rope skipping, and so on. With these, no one will see you, so there's no cause for embarrassment.

I still feel, however, that a woman with the glow of health is naturally more beautiful and gracious than a woman who's not fit.

*Q.* My doctor says now that I'm fifty-three I need exercise more than ever. Why is this?

*A.* Two problems, bone weakening and heart disease, tend to increase after the menopause. Exercise will help counteract the tendency to brittle bones. Regarding heart disease, women over fifty have an increase in coronary risk factors (as we have seen from our examinations at the Cooper Clinic), which makes the protection of an exercise program all the more desirable.

Here are the specific comparisons between women and men that we have measured. The first chart compares the varying median levels of cholesterol:

### CHOLESTEROL

|  | AGE | | | |
|---|---|---|---|---|
|  | Under 30 | 30–39 | 40–49 | 50–59 |
| Women | 190 | 205 | 215 | 233 |
| Men | 200 | 219 | 233 | 238 |

In both men and women the cholesterol levels rise with age. The women start out at a lower level and stay at a much lower level through the forties. But then the female level jumps dramatically and almost reaches the male level.

This same correlation appears in the other tests.

### TRIGLYCERIDES

|  | AGE | | | |
|---|---|---|---|---|
|  | Under 30 | 30–39 | 40–49 | 50–59 |
| Women | 70 | 70 | 85 | 109 |
| Men | 90 | 106 | 119 | 119 |

## PERCENT BODY FAT *

|        | Under 30 | 30–39 | 40–49 | 50–59 |
|--------|----------|-------|-------|-------|
|        | AGE      |       |       |       |
| Women  | 31.9     | 30.4  | 33.7  | 35.1  |
| Men    | 20.6     | 22.4  | 24.4  | 25.1  |

* Women naturally have a higher percent of body fat than men. What is important here is the rate of increase over the years.

## BLOOD PRESSURE

|        | Under 30 | 30–39 | 40–49 | 50–59 |
|--------|----------|-------|-------|-------|
|        | AGE      |       |       |       |
| Women  | 113/75   | 113/78 | 114/79 | 125/80 |
| Men    | 124/80   | 120/80 | 120/80 | 120/80 |

As you can see, the natural protection that women enjoy against heart disease decreases after menopause.

To find your overall coronary risk, take the Coronary Risk Profile chart that applies to your age group to your physician during your next examination. You will find the charts in the appendix.

Q. I find it hard to quit smoking, but I've been told to quit by my doctor now that I'm expecting a baby. Is smoking really that much worse for me during pregnancy? A. It's bad for you, but it's worse for your child. A study in Britain showed that pregnant women who smoke have, on the average, smaller babies, lighter babies, and babies with lower IQs. They also show a higher incidence of stillbirths, and there is a significant increase in infant deaths among their babies.

Let me take a moment and elaborate on some ideas that may help you break the habit. People start smoking because of one or more smoking parents, or because of peer pressure. There is no inherited tendency or desire for tobacco. People continue smoking because of its stimulation effect (10 percent), the enjoyment of handling a cigarette (10 percent), or because it is a pleasurable relaxation (15 percent). If you fit into this category, it is not hard to quit. However, if your smoking is a crutch or reliever of tension (30 percent), a craving or psychological addiction (25 percent), or merely a habit (10 percent), it will be much harder to quit.

Even if you can't quit, then smoke fewer cigarettes each day; take fewer puffs on each cigarette; reduce the depth of inhalation; choose a brand low in tar and nicotine; and smoke less of each cigarette. But without question, quitting is best! If you stop "cold turkey," you can expect symptoms of a physiological withdrawal for about seven days. These include headaches, irritability, muscle aches and cramps, anxiety, visual and sleep disturbances, and an intense craving for tobacco.

Yet these symptoms are transient. The psychological withdrawal is the big problem. It is critical for the first two to three months and may last weeks to years. Obstacles in overcoming the psychological withdrawal are social pressures (you may have to change friends); lack of a plan to help you stop; the use of alcohol; the expectation of failure (61 percent of smokers have tried to quit); and the fear of weight gain. Yet you would have to gain about one hundred pounds to have the same harmful effects of smoking over one pack of cigarettes per day.

Finally, if you do some "bridge burning," this may be of considerable help. For example, actively encourage and help others to quit smoking; associate with former smokers; dispose of ashtrays and the other paraphernalia of smoking; make a cash bet or a social pact with a friend; make a public commitment, put your ego on the line; put a bumper sticker on your car: "Cancer Cures Smoking"; and if you work in an office, put up a sign: "Thank you for not smoking."

But the most important and helpful things to do are: (1) attend a five-day quit-smoking course, or a quit-smoking class sponsored by the American Cancer Society or other organizations, and (2) *substitute* exercise for your smoking. Freud once said, "Whoever understands the human mind knows that hardly anything is harder for a man to give up than a pleasure he has once experienced. Actually, we can never give anything up; we only exchange one thing for another. What appears to be a renunciation is really the formation of a substitute or surrogate." Many people have written stating they could never break the cigarette smoking habit until they started exercising. If you haven't started exercising, give it a try!

*Q*. Exercise seems like such a bother to go through for a good figure. Can't I just be sensible about my diet?

*A*. You should be sensible about your diet. But if you're on a weight-loss diet and don't exercise, you will lose approximately 50 percent fat and 50 percent muscle, and the figure you end up with will be weak and flabby. With exercise, you'll lose only fat, or almost entirely fat. Additionally, you'll help avoid the fatigue and the tension-frustration cycle that often accompany diets, by burning up the day's tensions with your workouts.

*Q*. I have a baby-sitting problem during the day, and when my husband comes home there's too much to do with dinner and getting the kids to bed. What to do?

*A*. You could exercise indoors, with stair climbing, rope skipping, or running in place. Or you could do as my wife, Millie, and her friends have done the past six years. They get together early in the morning (five-thirty) before their husbands leave for work, and run four miles at about a nine- to ten-minute-mile pace. Millie says they talk nearly all the way because "that's what makes it interesting." When a woman new in the neighborhood joined their group recently, she ran an extra half mile she hadn't planned to run one morning because she "wanted to hear the end of the story"!

*Q*. My husband's been dabbling with an exercise program, but he finds it's often inconvenient and I know he skips too many times. My question is should I say anything about this, or just leave him alone? I don't want to turn him off exercise by nagging.

*A*. You're right not to nag, but you should definitely be encouraging. A study of 188 faculty members followed for two years at three universities showed that the men whose wives had a positive attitude toward their exercise program continued exercising at *double* the rate of those whose wives were negative or neutral.

## Children

### AGE UNDER TEN YEARS

*Q.* I read somewhere that kids really don't need exercise until they're almost grown. Is that really true? My nine-year-old spends a lot more time just sitting in front of the TV than I think would be healthy.

*A.* What you probably read was that kids don't need *competitive* or *highly structured* exercise until they're ten or eleven years old. They do need exercise, though, and most of them get it just from their usual state of perpetual motion around the house and the yard. Oxygen consumption tests of young children indicate that most are in superb condition from their daily activities up to ten years of age.

The child who's deprived of exercise may suffer for it in later years. For instance, a child without exercise may have a greater tendency toward obesity in later life because his (or her) body has literally developed more and larger fat cells. The number and size of fat cells, these researchers have found, multiply rapidly at certain stages. If the child's exercising during these high-growth phases, he will have fewer and smaller fat cells, and much less difficulty with his diet when he grows up. But 80 percent of obese children, according to one study, will be obese adults.

The thing to remember is to make certain your child gets enough *enjoyable* activity. Instill in him or her a love of sports by teaching techniques and skills, and by giving space and time for free play. Regular trips to the park, hikes, walks, picnics, and so on are also good, as would be the example of fitness you would present from your own exercise program.

*Q.* How do you feel about organized sports for kids, such as Little League baseball and Pop Warner League football?

*A.* Children under ten are pretty young for any hard body contact, and every year doctors are seeing more joint injuries in young children from contact sports, particularly football. However, if a child really *wants* to participate—for the enjoyment of it—then it can certainly be beneficial. You should discourage the competitive pressures, however. When he comes home, instead of asking, "Did you win?" or "How did *you* do?" ask, "How was it?" or "Did you have a good time?" If your children don't want to participate in organized sports, don't push the issue. Tell them that all you care about is that they're getting enough exercise. Above all, don't let your children's performance become a manifestation of your hidden desires. I have seen parents reduce their children to tears for not doing as well as the parents *thought* they should do.

*Q.* I heard that kids have to watch cholesterol and fats just as adults do. Aren't they too young for any of that to be dangerous?

*A.* Heart disease has its origins in infancy and children, said an article in the *American Journal of Pathology.* Autopsy studies on children killed accidentally have shown fatty or cholesterol streaks in their aortas even at less than ten years of age!

You'll remember that, in the chapter on the heart, I said that the blood lipoproteins combine with cholesterol and triglycerides to form dangerous patterns, with some being more dangerous than others. These dangerous patterns, or phenotypes as they're called, are often passed on from generation to generation.

I urge parents to ask their pediatrician to obtain a blood-lipid profile on their children. This is particularly important for parents who have abnormal blood lipids themselves, or who have a history of heart disease. Learn at an early age if your child has a potential problem and take corrective action.

One study done at the University of Miami School of Medicine showed that children whose fathers have had heart attacks before age fifty are likely to have high cholesterol levels.

So ask for the blood screening, if your pediatrician isn't doing it as a routine part of the examination. One note of caution, however. For some reason, among children with elevated cholesterol on one test, 80 percent will revert to normal in a subsequent test. So children with a high cholesterol need at least two determinations before any sort of a decision is reached.

But when lipid abnormalties have definitely been diagnosed, there is no age that is too young for sensible weight control and dietary programs. For some children with dangerous phenotypes, a dietary program from infancy could well prevent a premature death some thirty to forty years later.

*Q.* My child has asthma. Should I keep him out of gym class?

*A.* No. Just make sure the instructor knows that your child should rest frequently until he builds up his fitness. Brief periods of activity will help the condition, and being left out of sports because of asthma can make a child feel isolated and inferior. Asthmatic children can respond well to exercise programs provided that they are slowly progressive and do not lead to excess fatigue. If such children are not encouraged to develop some degree of fitness, more serious pulmonary problems may develop as an adult.

*Q.* How can I tell if my ten-year-old is in shape? Should I give him the 12-minute test?

*A.* I don't recommend it. It's hard to get a true maximum effort from children before the age of thirteen, and the competitive overtones of a fitness test administered by a parent can take the fun out of running. I'd rather see you let your boy run for fun; you might buy him a watch if he wants to keep track of the time. (We are evaluating a 9-minute test of fitness for younger children but I am not ready to recommend it yet.)

## AGES TEN THROUGH TWELVE

*Q.* My daughter is twelve and doesn't seem to like exercise. What do you suggest?

*A.* Girls at this age are usually more physically mature than boys and could probably do better in some sports, such as tennis, volleyball, and swimming, than their male classmates. Your daughter may be reacting to our cultural conditioning of these "young ladies" to avoid vigorous exercise. You can help her break the unhealthy cycle by setting an example, and by encouraging regular running, tennis, swimming, or any of the other aerobic activities. If she has a good physical education class at school, that will be of considerable merit. Look into it and see if the weekly activity there totals at least 24 points/week. If not, see if it can't be improved.

*Q.* How do you recommend I talk about the dangers of smoking with my son?

*A.* Before you talk, set the example by not smoking. Then just be as factual as possible; don't make it a moral issue and turn tobacco into a "forbidden fruit." Many pertinent facts you'll find in the chapter on the heart, although these mortality statistics may seem a bit far away to a young boy. Your son might be more interested in a study we conducted in Forth Worth on 771 senior high school boys in which we had them run the 12-minute test and then compared their results with their habits and life-style. There was a direct relationship between their level of fitness and their cigarette smoking habits:

| CIGARETTES SMOKED | AVERAGE DISTANCE RUN (12 MINUTES) |
| --- | --- |
| None | 1.51 miles |
| Fewer than 10 per day | 1.42 miles |
| 10–20 per day | 1.38 miles |
| More than 20 per day | 1.16 miles |

A comparable study was published in 1968 showing this relationship in young Air Force recruits, and another in 1971 in Austrian military men. Even with intensive training, smokers simply cannot reach the performance level of nonsmokers.

Young girls, in particular, need a good educational program with regard to smoking, since the greatest increase in cigarette smoking since 1969 has been in young girls twelve to seventeen years of age.

# Teenagers

*Q.* I know my sixteen-year-old isn't getting enough exercise in school. And she says she hates gym class. What should I do?

*A.* I want to elaborate at some length in answering this question because it's an important subject for our daughters and sons alike.

To begin with, what does she do during gym class? One of the earliest memories I have of my gym class is playing basketball, without supervision, while an overweight phys. ed. instructor sat up in the bleachers smoking a cigarette and reading a newspaper. But even if the supervision is good, the quality may be lacking. When we conducted our study in Fort Worth, we gave one group an aerobics program, and another had the school's standard gym class. When we tested at the end of the semester, the aerobics group showed a marked improvement in cardiovascular fitness, but those in the standard gym class showed no cardiovascular improvement whatsoever.

So if your daughter says that gym classes are a waste of time, you should check into it.

Also, does she really hate to exercise, or is this an indication of peer pressure? This was brought home to me quite dramatically in 1970 when I was invited to deliver a lecture at an eastern girls' school. At the afternoon reception before the lecture, I was surprised to have the head of the physical education department warn me to expect a very resistant audience. "These girls," she said, "don't want to have anything to do with physical education." It seems that the college required only one semester of physical education during the entire four years, but the girls were circulating petitions to eliminate even *that* requirement.

That evening my wife and I walked into the auditorium, expecting to find an empty house. Imagine our surprise when we walked in and found that we had to weave our way down to the stage; every seat was taken and girls were sitting in the aisles. There wasn't even standing room left!

The girls were quiet, receptive, and attentive. I spoke for an hour and fifteen minutes and Millie spoke for another fifteen minutes. Then they bombarded us with questions—good questions, questions that showed that they were really thinking about the facts we had given them.

Afterward, I turned to the head of the physical education department and said, "I just don't understand. You told us to expect a completely different type of audience."

She said she was just as surprised as we were and had no ready explanation.

It wasn't until about two weeks later that she wrote to explain. She said that they had discovered since our visit that there were only two or three girls who were leading the fight to phase out physical education. The rest of the girls had become the "silent majority." But she said our appearance on the campus turned the entire situation around. We gave the majority of girls a will and a reason to resist the vocal minority, and that ended, at that time, the effort to do away with physical education on the campus.

So I don't believe that the majority of young men and women are against physical education as such. And in an age when students are demanding a lot more relevance in their *academic* courses, they're not going to accept anything less in their physical education courses.

Not only must a physical education program be sufficiently demanding to produce a training effect, it must generate a degree of enthusiasm on the part of the students. This is too often neglected. We accept without question the necessity for enthusiasm on a football team or a basketball team. But we tend to forget that enthusiasm is just as important for individuals as it is for teams.

A few years ago, Brigham Young University developed a new wrinkle to this idea of distance running. It organized teams of young men and women to compete against each other in running "around the world in eighty days." When I was there to speak in the field house during this contest, they had to stop the runners so I could be heard. That's how hard they were trying to get their miles in.

Recently I received a letter from a physical education instructor at a Boulder, Colorado, high school. Several years ago she organized a voluntary cross-country class in which the students run from three to five miles during the forty-minute class, four days a week. The fact that she runs with them, I am sure, is a great motivating factor.

During the semester, half of their grade is determined by the number of miles they have run, the other half on their 12-minute test scores. For example:

$$A = 70\text{--}84 \text{ miles}$$
$$B = 60\text{--}69 \text{ miles}$$
$$C = 50\text{--}59 \text{ miles}$$
$$D = 40\text{--}49 \text{ miles}$$

"I have never had one student make an F on either the tests or the daily work," she wrote me recently.

Finally, a good physical fitness program must be enjoyable—and must be something the students will continue for the rest of their lives.

Not everybody is a jogger—or wants to be.

Not everybody is a swimmer—or wants to be.

That's why I think the cycling craze is so encouraging. People all over the country are cycling their way to cardiovascular fitness—but, just as important, they are having a good time doing it.

The tennis craze is accomplishing the same result. People have found it to be an enjoyable way to keep fit. Now racquetball is becoming quite popular, and it is an excellent aerobic activity.

Fitness is the reason the "aerobic dance" is so popular these days, especially with young women and girls. This consists of sustained and strenuous dance movements for fifteen to twenty to thirty minutes at a time, without stopping. It's too strenuous for most older women but is gaining very wide acceptance with younger ones. We don't have any good data as yet to determine how much cardiovascular benefit is derived from "aerobic dancing," but it is an interesting concept.

As you can see from the list below, there are many other ways to earn 30 points a week beside the "traditional" aerobics programs of jogging, swimming, walking, and cycling:

Football is worth 6 points per hour.
Badminton is worth 4½ points per hour.
Tennis (singles) is worth 4½ points per hour.
Fencing is worth 6 points per hour.
Golf is worth 1½ points for nine holes (walking only).
Hockey is worth 3 points for 20 minutes.
Soccer is worth 6 points for 40 minutes.
Rope skipping is worth 3 points for 10 minutes.
Volleyball is worth 2 points for 30 minutes.
Basketball and racquetball are worth 4½ points for 30 minutes.
Rowing is worth 4 points for 18 minutes.

Exercise doesn't have to be a drudgery. It isn't *supposed* to be! Fitness isn't just for highly skilled athletes. It's for all of us. It's our natural state of being, particularly when we're young. Being out of shape is really being out of sorts with ourselves.

I mentioned in another chapter the compulsory aerobics program at Oral Roberts University in Oklahoma. I like President Roberts' motto for that program: "Get fit; keep fit, and develop the whole man." I'd add to that, "Develop the whole woman, too."

Getting back to what you as a parent should do, though.

Of course you should support and encourage your daughter to exercise outside school, and to participate in any extracurricular activities that will give her the aerobic points she needs.

But, more important, I suggest you bring the information in this chapter and throughout this book to the attention of other parents, and then make an organized effort to get this evidence before your school board. The data from Chapter 8 in which we showed how fitness level correlates with higher grades and better attendance should be particularly helpful here.

*Q.* How many points a week should my fourteen-year-old boy be getting?

*A.* Ages thirteen through nineteen are critical years for the health of most children. This is the time when exercise should be systematic and vigorous, for these are the years when natural fitness levels begin to fall off for both boys and girls. From age thirteen on, for boys, 30 aerobic points a week *should be the minimum,* for girls, 24. And I hasten to add that this is just a base: weight lifting, gymnastics, and organized sports can and should be done *in addition to* the regular aerobic exercise program.

The early teens is the time when boys and girls should be developing the exercise habits that will remain with them throughout their lives. They should concentrate on developing proficiency in the "lifetime sports."

## Senior Citizens

*Q.* At seventy-three, I don't get around much these days, and I've been thinking that a program of exercise might help limber me up. But isn't it really too late for me to get any of those training effect benefits that you talk about?

*A.* It will take you longer to get the training effect, but you can still show a response. We recommend that you choose one of the starter programs in consultation with your doctor, and progress as slowly or as rapidly from week to week as feels comfortable.

Many of the symptoms that keep you from "getting around" are the results of deconditioning as much as of true aging. Young, healthy adults detrained by prolonged bed rest exhibit the same functional losses that many older people take as a matter of course.

When 112 men aged fifty-two to eighty-seven (mean age 69.5) were trained with an hour of stretching, calisthenics, and jogging three times each week, however, substantial training effect benefits were recorded after forty-two weeks. Oxygen utilization improved by approximately 30 percent, and vital capacity by about 20 percent. Significant improvement was also found in percent body fat, physical work capacity, and blood pressure. A three-month program for women in the same age range also showed significant improvement, though the time interval was not what I would call sufficient to give optimum results.

Studies conducted by Dr. Pollock of our Institute for Aerobics Research while at Wake Forest University showed an 18 percent improvement in oxygen utilization in men between forty-nine and sixty-five years of age after twenty weeks of an exercise program.

As you grow older, then, it takes longer to get fit, but you can do it. I like the statement I heard from one senior citizen. He said, "I can still run—things just go by slower."

*Q.* I wish I could start exercising, but it seems as if my arthritis bothers me whenever I do anything. What do you suggest?

*A.* If you're like most people with this complaint, you'll have good days and bad days. Start on one of the good days and keep at it, walking, swimming, or one of the other exercises where movements are smooth and continuous.

The odds are that your arthritis will improve. One example that comes to mind is retired TV producer Tony D'Aleo, who at sixty had to quit shuffleboard because his hands shook so badly he couldn't play. Tony was diabetic, arthritic, fifty pounds overweight, and unable to walk without the aid of a cane when he began his aerobics program. Now he jogs ten miles in the morning, leads an exercise class at the Beverly Hills YMCA, and in 1975 was earning between 300 and 500 points *a week!*

*Q.* I've heard that there's organized track competition for senior citizens on a national level. Is this true?

*A.* Regional and national Masters Track and Field meets are getting more and more popular. To obtain a schedule of events near you, write David Pain, 1160 Via Espana, La Jolla, California 92037.

A gold-medal winner at the 1975 Senior Olympics at Irvine, California, was Mrs. Eula Weaver, age eighty-six. At age eighty-one, after a fourteen-year history of cardio-

vascular problems, she was treated for congestive heart
failure. Her circulation was so impaired she wore gloves
in the summertime to keep her hands warm. Sometimes
walking only fifty feet gave her such severe leg cramps
she had to be carried home. Yet after a four-year program of diet and exercise, Mrs. Weaver jogs over a mile
most days and goes fifteen miles on her stationary bicycle daily. She has been off medication since the end of
her first year on the program.

## Athletes

*Q.* I am a distance runner, training for a spot on the 1980
U.S. Olympic team. I have been told by several sports
physicians that in order to sufficiently condition my heart
I should, in the off season, run all my workouts at a much
slower pace (say, at eight minutes per mile) for months on
end until by this method I have built up enough reserves
to withstand the intensive interval training I would subject
myself to in the spring. What's your opinion?
*A.* A comment once made by a world-class distance runner was that "If you train at a slow pace, you will run
at a slow pace." I tend to agree—and feel that you should
be running quality miles (5:45–6:30 pace) and a lot of
them.
*Q.* As a distance runner, do I need sprinting in my training program? Or should I just concentrate on distance?
*A.* Competitive athletes, distance runners included, need
weight training for strengthening, intervals for speed, and
aerobics for the endurance base. The 1970 Brazilian World
Cup soccer team (mentioned in Chapter 1) earned 80–100
aerobic points per week for one year before the competition in Mexico City. This helped them outscore every
team they played in the second half of their games and
ultimately win the championship. Yet those 80–100 aerobic
points were over and above the points they earned playing
soccer, and of course that didn't include their interval
work. Points are not awarded for interval work, but this
is an important part of competitive training.

In your area of distance running, Olympic medalist

Frank Shorter trains at 120–140 miles per week for distance. But in preparation for the 1976 Olympics he was also running intervals once or twice a week: specifically, 16 consecutive quarter miles at 62 seconds each, with a 35-second rest in between.

*Q.* Do the pro teams in the United States use aerobics?

*A.* I know of several AFL–NFL football teams who use the 12-minute test as part of the summer conditioning or testing program. The Dallas Cowboys, for example, encouraged aerobic training during the off-season last year and required all of their players to run 1.50–1.75 miles in 12:00 minutes, according to the requirements of their position. The cardiovascular endurance base aerobics builds up helps players outlast the opposition and also reduces the injuries that come from playing while fatigued.

Another sports pro, Kyle Rote, Jr., of the Dallas Tornado soccer team, trains regularly at the Aerobics Center. In 1974, 1976 and 1977, he won the TV "Superstar" competition.

*Q.* I know I shouldn't eat heavily just before my high school football game. But what about the traditional steak and potatoes breakfast?

*A.* No good. Your digestive system before a game falls behind schedule, due to pregame tensions. Add the normal four hours to digest that steak to the four-hour delay from tension, and you may get pregame nausea and cramps, even though you had breakfast at eight. Then when you're out on the field at three o'clock, the steak is *still* digesting, so that your muscles have to compete with your stomach for their blood supply.

Researcher Dr. Kenneth Rose of the University of Nebraska recommends a basically liquid pregame meal to avoid this problem.

*Q.* Is there a pregame diet that can improve an athlete's performance?

*A.* Yes, if you're an athlete who needs sustaining power over a long period of time. But the diet must be started a week before the game or athletic event.

The process is known as carbohydrate loading, and it

works on the principle discovered in the 1960s that glycogen in the muscles, the "fuel" for endurance, can be built up with a high-carbohydrate diet.

There are three points to remember. First, stay away from sweets—the refined sugars are not the carbohydrates that work here. Second, don't gain weight! Finally, before the muscles can be loaded with glycogen, they must be exhausted of glycogen first. The entire "loading" process takes a full week.

For the first three days, the carbohydrate intake should be *low,* and the diet, aside from that, should be a normal one. This lowers the supply of glycogen in the muscles.

On the fourth day, you should exercise to exhaustion the muscles you will use in your event. This is what exhausts the already low supply of glycogen.

During the last three days, your workouts should be reduced and your carbohydrate intake should be high. You should eat large amounts of cereals, bread, fruit, vegetables, honey, and potatoes, but not the refined sugars. These natural carbohydrates will cause a superconcentration of glycogen stores and should enable you to improve your endurance capacity.

*Q.* Do women athletes have an advantage over men in any Olympic event?

*A.* No, but distance running is gaining in popularity with women, because it's here that their disadvantage of less muscle (for speed) is compensated for. Women, well trained, have 5–10 percent more body fat than trained men, and there are theories that they are able to burn this fat during a distance run. This theory, if proven, would mean that a woman would be carrying more "fuel" than a man and would thus have an advantage for long endurance events. At marathon and longer distances, women's records are continuing to drop, consistently reducing the gap with men.

# Summary

I have answered and elaborated on a variety of questions in this chapter about the application of and, at times, problems associated with aerobics. I hope that you have found answers to your questions but, if not, don't use that as an excuse not to exercise. Concentrate on the reasons why you should, don't try to find excuses why you shouldn't. As I said before, "Where there is the will, there is a way," and millions of Americans are now enjoying "their way."

# 10

# A Look to the Future

First, let's talk about *your* future.

How much of it will there be?

According to today's insurance actuarial standards, if you exercise regularly, you'll gain four years of future. If you don't smoke, you'll gain from three to eight years. If you're moderate in your drinking, you'll gain one year. If you practice weight control, you'll add between two and eight years, depending on how many pounds you aren't overweight. And if you'll simply take time every year for a preventive medical checkup, you'll add two more years to your future.

That's a minimum of twelve years and a possible twenty-three years added to your life, based on the inexorable tallies compiled from life insurance company records. Just from preventive medicine.

The question is, what *kind* of years are you going to have in your future?

By this time I hope you're just as much concerned with the *quality* of the years you have ahead of you as you are about their number. You don't want to spend your future evenings asleep in front of the TV set, or your future days afraid to climb the stairs.

You also don't want to spend your life savings paying for hospital care, or for an extended stay in a nursing home.

What you more likely have in mind is the kind of future John McQuaid—an Indiana man who began aerobics after heart surgery—is looking forward to. He writes: "I mowed the grass right through the summer heat, and also was able to once again go fishing and tramping along Eel River—things I had begun to believe I would never do again."

221

Frederic Berg, in Huntington, New York, sees the same kind of future, after he began an aerobics swimming program at age forty-two: "Without exaggeration, it is fair to say that I am probably more physically fit today than I was at age twenty. In addition to the cardiovascular benefits, I lost nineteen pounds with the help of a moderate diet, trimmed my waistline from 37 to 33, and the overall muscle tone of my body has improved beyond belief. But equally as important is the new vitality and general feeling of well-being that I enjoy each day. Aerobics has become a way of life for me."

And a letter from Mrs. Anne Knight of Shaker Heights, Ohio, makes the point exactly: "It's really terrific! I have no intention of falling away from my running routine. My only nephew says I'll probably live to be ninety, but I don't care how long I live (forty-seven now) just so I 'live.'"

These are people who got the same message that John H. Knowles, president of the research-oriented Rockefeller Foundation, had to give about the quality of American life in the year 2000: "The next major advance in the health of the American people will result only from what the individual is willing to do for himself."

And what the individual will do for himself, of course, is what I hope you're going to do for yourself: practice preventive care, according to the principles that we've discussed. Don't wait until you're disease-ridden to begin.

As Dr. Knowles also said, "A perpetuation of the present system of high-cost, after-the-fact medicine will only result in higher costs and more frustration."

And American medicine has made some good progress in moving toward a preventive, rather than a "treatment-only," frame of mind. As I said earlier, the preventive medicine boom has begun, aided especially by American business.

When it really gets moving, just think for a moment about what that's going to mean for America.

Think of the time we're now spending in recovery from diseases that could have been prevented. Think of what we could be doing constructively with that time.

Think of the $114.9 *billion* we spent in 1975, not on preventive care, but on treatment for existing ailments. Imagine what could be done with the large proportion of those billions of dollars that might have been saved through prevention.

Think too, of the time lost, the energy lost every day in everyday foul-ups, brought on because someone was "too tired" to do something right the first time, or "just not feeling well enough" to make the effort to cooperate. We could be accomplishing so much more as a nation where fitness was the rule rather than the exception.

Imagine where we'd be today if we felt as strongly about fitness as do the people in East Germany. There fitness training is required for all, to the point where children only in the second grade have already become proficient in at least two swimming strokes. It's not by accident that the East Germans, with a country the size of Ohio, currently hold seven out of the fifteen world records in women's track, and an astonishing thirteen out of fourteen world records in women's swimming. They *plan* for fitness.

And when I think of the way the Germans require fitness. I can't help thinking also about what is being done in Communist China. Over there, people are out in the streets every morning for regular supervised exercise. And why? This is what the late Chairman Mao had to say on that subject: "The youth of China are encouraged to get fit, keep fit, and spur on the revolution."

Sometimes I wonder what would have happened here during the late sixties if so many of the student radicals hadn't been heavy smokers and basically sedentary, and many of them aggravating their poor condition with drugs.

"Well, all right, Dr. Cooper," people ask me sometimes, "do you think we ought to *require* fitness here in America?"

As I hope I made clear when I was talking about children, my answer is still a firm no. I feel that the young especially should get into the habit of fitness naturally, and not be turned away from exercise by coercion. For adults, again I feel that the best way to motivate is through example and incentive. Also, as an American, I cherish my freedom of choice far too highly to advocate giving it up, even for a cause as worthy and as beneficial as fitness.

Yet I can understand it when a business requires fitness of its management personnel. With the amount of money it invests in an executive's training, I think it's justified in protecting that investment with preventive medicine.

Or, as one corporation president put it when interviewed by *The Wall Street Journal:* "If you can't take thirty minutes or an hour out of your day to work out in our health club, you're not very well organized and shouldn't be working for this company."

That may sound stiff, but I know it's true. I frequently need to put in a seventy-hour week, and sometimes more. But I can assure you I can always find time for the workout. In fact, if I didn't find time for it, it wouldn't be long before I wouldn't be able to handle the workload I do now. Without exercise, my body would deteriorate; that's simply a basic law of physiology.

So I can understand it when a company lays down the law. But I also know, as I wrote in 1968, that Americans hate to be told what to do. It's better to move them by example, the way I'm pleased to see a number of my colleagues in the medical profession are doing, including the one hundred plus who run in the Boston Marathon.

It's more effective, though, to move people by incentive. And now we may have a way to do that which adds to the rewards of better health and more achievement.

## Superselect Life Insurance

For several years I have been working on the development of a superselect life insurance policy. If a person can qualify, he or she would be the recipient of a sizable reduction in the annual life insurance premium. The principle behind it is the same as that behind the "safe driver" concept. If the initial examination reveals a low or very low coronary risk (from the Coronary Risk Profile), the patient would qualify for lowered rates. The exact amount of the reduction has not yet been determined, nor has the way the program would be implemented. Yet the concept has already been approved by the Texas State Insurance Commission and, I hope, will be available in the near future. Such a policy "could encourage the boom" in preventive medicine.

## Other Incentives

There is more that we could be doing in this area, and I hope to see it accomplished within the next five years.

I would like to see the availability of superselect health insurance as well as life insurance. If a person works hard practicing preventive medicine, his or her sickness and absenteeism from work should drop considerably, and if illness is less, shouldn't health insurance premiums be less?

Another possibility is having the health insurance cover the cost of the annual health examination. Some insurance companies presently do this, but not many. Our health insurance premiums are in reality not covering health, they are limited to disease! Likewise, life insurance is really death insurance. I would like to see those concepts changed.

There is the story of the enterprising young man who many years ago moved to a foreign country and started selling life insurance. His business was booming until someone died . . . and then they ran him out of the country.

With the cost of bypass surgery between $10,000 and $15,000 and the cost of treadmill stress testing being about $100, the figures plainly add up on the side of early detection, risk intervention, and, in general, prevention. As I said earlier, the West Germans have already made preventive medical centers available at *no cost whatever*.

For another thing, with the help of the media, preventive medical criteria, methods, and goals can be brought to millions of people who are now unaware of the things they can accomplish for themselves. The anti-smoking commercials, while they lasted, showed how great a positive effect can be gained when prevention is brought before the public at a professional level.

And third, with the government's share in the $114.9 billion worth of disease treatment up 22 percent in the last year and to go up even further, it seems, with national health insurance, doesn't it make sense that there should be a tax incentive for fitness? We currently allow income-tax deductions for a number of things that have far less potential for saving the government's revenues. And the administration of such a program could be expense-free: a taxpayer who had passed the superselect life insurance annual examination could simply claim a deduction every April.

It's only common sense, and I think we're going to be practicing more of that in the next few years, as the preventive medicine boom grows larger and larger.

I hope you're part of the millions who will lead yet more and more Americans to fitness.

I hope you'll be able to say—to paraphrase the words of one of our Bicentennial speakers—that "the great days of our republic have only just begun."

And I hope that, by taking better care of yourself, you will find that the great days of your own life have just begun. Once again, good luck, and God bless you both physically and spiritually.

# Appendix

# The Point System

## WALKING/RUNNING

| TIME (min:sec) | POINT VALUE | TIME (min:sec) | POINT VALUE |
|---|---|---|---|
| **1.0 Mile** | | **1.4 Miles** | |
| over 20:01 | 0 | over 42:01 | 0 |
| 20:00–15:01 | 1.0 | 42:00–28:01 | 0.4 |
| 15:00–12:01 | 2.0 | 28:00–21:01 | 1.8 |
| 12:00–10:01 | 3.0 | 21:00–16:49 | 3.2 |
| 10:00– 8:01 | 4.0 | 16:48–14:01 | 4.6 |
| 8:00– 6:41 | 5.0 | 14:00–11:13 | 6.0 |
| 6:40– 5:44 | 6.0 | 11:12– 9:21 | 7.4 |
| under 5:43 | 7.0 | 9:20– 8:01 | 8.8 |
| | | under 8:00 | 10.2 |
| **1.1 Miles** | | **1.5 Miles** | |
| over 33:01 | 0 | over 45:01 | 0 |
| 33:00–22:01 | 0.1 | 45:00–30:01 | 0.5 |
| 22:00–16:31 | 1.2 | 30:00–22:31 | 2.0 |
| 16:30–13:13 | 2.3 | 22:30–18:01 | 3.5 |
| 13:12–11:01 | 3.4 | 18:00–15:01 | 5.0 |
| 11:00– 8:49 | 4.5 | 15:00–12:01 | 6.5 |
| 8:48– 7:21 | 5.6 | 12:00–10:01 | 8.0 |
| 7:20– 6:19 | 6.7 | 10:00– 8:35 | 9.5 |
| under 6:17 | 7.8 | under 8:34 | 11.0 |
| **1.2 Miles** | | **1.6 Miles** | |
| over 36:01 | 0 | over 48:01 | 0 |
| 36:00–24:01 | 0.2 | 48:00–32:01 | 0.6 |
| 24:00–18:01 | 1.4 | 32:00–24:01 | 2.2 |
| 18:00–14:25 | 2.6 | 24:00–19:13 | 3.8 |
| 14:24–12:01 | 3.8 | 19:12–16:01 | 5.4 |
| 12:00– 9:37 | 5.0 | 16:00–12:49 | 7.0 |
| 9:36– 8:01 | 6.2 | 12:48–10:41 | 8.6 |
| 8:00– 6:53 | 7.4 | 10:40– 9:10 | 10.2 |
| under 6:52 | 8.6 | under 9:08 | 11.8 |
| **1.3 Miles** | | **1.7 Miles** | |
| over 39:01 | 0 | over 51:01 | 0 |
| 39:00–26:01 | 0.3 | 51:00–34:01 | 0.7 |
| 26:00–19:31 | 1.6 | 34:00–25:31 | 2.4 |
| 19:30–15:37 | 2.9 | 25:30–20:25 | 4.1 |
| 15:36–13:01 | 4.2 | 20:24–17:01 | 5.8 |
| 13:00–10:25 | 5.5 | 17:00–13:37 | 7.5 |
| 10:24– 8:41 | 6.8 | 13:36–11:21 | 9.2 |
| 8:40– 7:27 | 8.1 | 11:20– 9:44 | 10.9 |
| under 7:26 | 9.4 | under 9:43 | 12.6 |

| TIME (min:sec) | POINT VALUE |
|---|---|
| **1.8 Miles** | |
| over 54:01 | 0 |
| 54:00–36:01 | 0.8 |
| 36:00–27:01 | 2.6 |
| 27:00–21:37 | 4.4 |
| 21:36–18:01 | 6.2 |
| 18:00–14:25 | 8.0 |
| 14:24–12:01 | 9.8 |
| 12:00–10:19 | 11.6 |
| under 10:17 | 13.4 |
| **1.9 Miles** | |
| over 57:01 | 0 |
| 57:00–38:01 | 0.9 |
| 38:00–28:31 | 2.8 |
| 28:30–22:49 | 4.7 |
| 22:48–19:01 | 6.6 |
| 19:00–15:13 | 8.5 |
| 15:12–12:41 | 10.4 |
| 12:40–10:53 | 12.3 |
| under 10:52 | 14.2 |
| **2.0 Miles** | |
| over 40:01 | 1.0 |
| 40:00–30:01 | 3.0 |
| 30:00–24:01 | 5.0 |
| 24:00–20:01 | 7.0 |
| 20:00–16:01 | 9.0 |
| 16:00–13:21 | 11.0 |
| 13:20–11:27 | 13.0 |
| under 11:26 | 15.0 |
| **2.1 Miles** | |
| over 42:01 | 1.1 |
| 42:00–31:31 | 3.2 |
| 31:30–25:13 | 5.3 |
| 25:12–21:01 | 7.4 |
| 21:00–16:49 | 9.5 |
| 16:48–14:01 | 11.6 |
| 14:00–12:01 | 13.7 |
| under 12:00 | 15.8 |
| **2.2 Miles** | |
| over 44:01 | 1.2 |
| 44:00–33:01 | 3.4 |
| 33:00–26:25 | 5.6 |

| TIME (min:sec) | POINT VALUE |
|---|---|
| **2.2 Miles (Cont.)** | |
| 26:24–22:01 | 7.8 |
| 22:00–17:37 | 10.0 |
| 17:36–14:41 | 12.2 |
| 14:40–12:35 | 14.4 |
| under 12:34 | 16.6 |
| **2.3 Miles** | |
| over 46:01 | 1.3 |
| 46:00–34:31 | 3.6 |
| 34:30–27:37 | 5.9 |
| 27:36–23:01 | 8.2 |
| 23:00–18:25 | 10.5 |
| 18:24–15:21 | 12.8 |
| 15:20–13:10 | 15.1 |
| under 13:08 | 17.4 |
| **2.4 Miles** | |
| over 48:01 | 1.4 |
| 48:00–36:01 | 3.8 |
| 36:00–28:49 | 6.2 |
| 28:48–24:01 | 8.6 |
| 24:00–19:13 | 11.0 |
| 19:12–16:01 | 13.4 |
| 16:00–13:44 | 15.8 |
| under 13:43 | 18.2 |
| **2.5 Miles** | |
| over 50:01 | 1.5 |
| 50:00–37:31 | 4.0 |
| 37:30–30:01 | 6.5 |
| 30:00–25:01 | 9.0 |
| 25:00–20:01 | 11.5 |
| 20:00–16:41 | 14.0 |
| 16:40–14:19 | 16.5 |
| under 14:17 | 19.0 |
| **2.6 Miles** | |
| over 52:01 | 1.6 |
| 52:00–39:01 | 4.2 |
| 39:00–31:13 | 6.8 |
| 31:12–26:01 | 9.4 |
| 26:00–20:49 | 12.0 |
| 20:48–17:21 | 14.6 |
| 17:20–14:53 | 17.2 |
| under 14:52 | 19.8 |

# WALKING/RUNNING (CONTINUED)

| TIME (hr:min:sec) | POINT VALUE | TIME (hr:min:sec) | POINT VALUE |
|---|---|---|---|
| **2.7 Miles** | | **3.2 Miles** | |
| over 54:01 | 1.7 | over 1:04:01 | 2.2 |
| 54:00–40:31 | 4.4 | 1:04:00– 48:01 | 5.4 |
| 40:30–32:25 | 7.1 | 48:00– 38:25 | 8.6 |
| 32:24–27:01 | 9.8 | 38:24– 32:01 | 11.8 |
| 27:00–21:37 | 12.5 | 32:00– 25:37 | 15.0 |
| 21:36–18:01 | 15.2 | 25:36– 21:21 | 18.2 |
| 18:00–15:27 | 17.9 | 21:20– 18:19 | 21.4 |
| under 15:26 | 20.6 | under 18:17 | 24.6 |
| **2.8 Miles** | | **3.3 Miles** | |
| over 56:01 | 1.8 | over 1:06:01 | 2.3 |
| 56:00–42:01 | 4.6 | 1:06:00– 49:31 | 5.6 |
| 42:00–33:37 | 7.4 | 49:30– 39:37 | 8.9 |
| 33:36–28:01 | 10.2 | 39:36– 33:01 | 12.2 |
| 28:00–22:25 | 13.0 | 33:00– 26:25 | 15.5 |
| 22:24–18:41 | 15.8 | 26:24– 22:01 | 18.8 |
| 18:40–16:01 | 18.6 | 22:00– 18:53 | 22.1 |
| under 16:00 | 21.4 | under 18:52 | 25.4 |
| **2.9 Miles** | | **3.4 Miles** | |
| over 58:01 | 1.9 | over 1:08:01 | 2.4 |
| 58:00–43:31 | 4.8 | 1:08:00– 51:01 | 5.8 |
| 43:30–34:49 | 7:7 | 51:00– 40:49 | 9.2 |
| 34:48–29:01 | 10.6 | 40:48– 34:01 | 12.6 |
| 29:00–23:13 | 13.5 | 34:00– 27:13 | 16.0 |
| 23:12–19:21 | 16.4 | 27:12– 22:41 | 19.4 |
| 19:20–16:35 | 19.3 | 22:40– 19:27 | 22.8 |
| under 16:34 | 22.2 | under 19:26 | 26.2 |
| **3.0 Miles** | | **3.5 Miles** | |
| over 1:00:01 | 2.0 | over 1:10:01 | 2.5 |
| 1:00:00– 45:01 | 5.0 | 1:10:00– 52:31 | 6.0 |
| 45:00– 36:01 | 8.0 | 52:30– 42:01 | 9.5 |
| 36:00– 30:01 | 11.0 | 42:00– 35:01 | 13.0 |
| 30:00– 24:01 | 14.0 | 35:00– 28:01 | 16.5 |
| 24:00– 20:01 | 17.0 | 28:00– 23:21 | 20.0 |
| 20:00– 17:10 | 20.0 | 23:20– 20:01 | 23.5 |
| under 17:08 | 23.0 | under 20:00 | 27.0 |
| **3.1 Miles** | | **3.6 Miles** | |
| over 1:02:01 | 2.1 | over 1:12:01 | 2.6 |
| 1:02:00– 46:31 | 5.2 | 1:12:00– 54:01 | 6.2 |
| 46:30– 37:13 | 8.3 | 54:00– 43:13 | 9:8 |
| 37:12– 31:01 | 11.4 | 43:12– 36:01 | 13.4 |
| 31:00– 24:49 | 14.5 | 36:00– 28:49 | 17.0 |
| 24:48– 20:41 | 17.6 | 28:48– 24:01 | 20.6 |
| 20:40– 17:44 | 20.7 | 24:00– 20:35 | 24.2 |
| under 17:43 | 23.8 | under 20:34 | 27.8 |

| TIME (hr:min:sec) | POINT VALUE | TIME (hr:min:sec) | POINT VALUE |
|---|---|---|---|
| **3.7 Miles** | | **4.2 Miles** | |
| over 1:14:01 | 2.7 | over 1:24:01 | 3.2 |
| 1:14:00– 55:31 | 6.4 | 1:24:00–1:03:01 | 7.4 |
| 55:30– 44:25 | 10.1 | 1:03:00– 50:25 | 11.6 |
| 44:24– 37:01 | 13.8 | 50:24– 42:01 | 15.8 |
| 37:00– 29:37 | 17.5 | 42:00– 33:37 | 20.0 |
| 29:36– 24:41 | 21.2 | 33:36– 28:01 | 24.2 |
| 24:40– 21:10 | 24.9 | 28:00– 24:01 | 28.4 |
| under 21:08 | 28.6 | under 24:00 | 32.6 |
| **3.8 Miles** | | **4.3 Miles** | |
| over 1:16:01 | 2.8 | over 1:26:01 | 3.3 |
| 1:16:00– 57:01 | 6.6 | 1:26:00–1:04:31 | 7.6 |
| 57:00– 45:37 | 10.4 | 1:04:30– 51:37 | 11.9 |
| 45:36– 38:01 | 14.2 | 51:36– 43:01 | 16.2 |
| 38:00– 30:25 | 18.0 | 43:00– 34:25 | 20.5 |
| 30:24– 25:21 | 21.8 | 34:24– 28:41 | 24.8 |
| 25:20– 21:44 | 25.6 | 28:40– 24:35 | 29.1 |
| under 21:43 | 29.4 | under 24:34 | 33.4 |
| **3.9 Miles** | | **4.4 Miles** | |
| over 1:18:01 | 2.9 | over 1:28:01 | 3.4 |
| 1:18:00– 58:31 | 6.8 | 1:28:00–1:06:01 | 7.8 |
| 58:30– 46:49 | 10.7 | 1:06:00– 52:49 | 12.2 |
| 46:48– 39:01 | 14.6 | 52:48– 44:01 | 16.6 |
| 39:00– 31:13 | 18.5 | 44:00– 35:13 | 21.0 |
| 31:12– 26:01 | 22.4 | 35:12– 29:21 | 25.4 |
| 26:00– 22:19 | 26.3 | 29:20– 25:10 | 29.8 |
| under 22:17 | 30.2 | under 25:08 | 34.2 |
| **4.0 Miles** | | **4.5 Miles** | |
| over 1:20:01 | 3.0 | over 1:30:01 | 3.5 |
| 1:20:00–1:00:01 | 7.0 | 1:30:00–1:07:31 | 8.0 |
| 1:00:00– 48:01 | 11.0 | 1:07:30– 54:01 | 12.5 |
| 48:00– 40:01 | 15.0 | 54:00– 45:01 | 17.0 |
| 40:00– 32:01 | 19.0 | 45:00– 36:01 | 21.5 |
| 32:00– 26:41 | 23.0 | 36:00– 30:01 | 26.0 |
| 26:40– 22:53 | 27.0 | 30:00– 25:44 | 30.5 |
| under 22:52 | 31.0 | under 25:43 | 35.0 |
| **4.1 Miles** | | **4.6 Miles** | |
| over 1:22:01 | 3.1 | over 1:32:01 | 3.6 |
| 1:22:00–1:01:31 | 7.2 | 1:32:00–1:09:01 | 8.2 |
| 1:01:30– 49:13 | 11.3 | 1:09:00– 55:13 | 12.8 |
| 49:12– 41:01 | 15.4 | 55:12– 46:01 | 17.4 |
| 41:00– 32:49 | 19.5 | 46:00– 36:49 | 22.0 |
| 32:48– 27:21 | 23.6 | 36:48– 30:41 | 26.6 |
| 27:20– 23:27 | 27.7 | 30:40– 26:19 | 31.2 |
| under 23:26 | 31.8 | under 26:17 | 35.8 |

| TIME (hr:min:sec) | POINT VALUE | TIME (hr:min:sec) | POINT VALUE |
|---|---|---|---|
| **4.7 Miles** | | **6.0 Miles** | |
| over 1:34:01 | 3.7 | over 2:00:01 | 5.0 |
| 1:34:00–1:10:31 | 8.4 | 2:00:00–1:30:01 | 11.0 |
| 1:10:30– 56:25 | 13.1 | 1:30:00–1:12:01 | 17.0 |
| 56:24– 47:01 | 17.8 | 1:12:00–1:00:01 | 23.0 |
| 47:00– 37:37 | 22.5 | 1:00:00– 48:01 | 29.0 |
| 37:36– 31:21 | 27.2 | 48:00– 40:01 | 35.0 |
| 31:20– 26:53 | 31.9 | 40:00– 34:19 | 41.0 |
| under 26:52 | 36.6 | under 34:17 | 47.0 |
| **4.8 Miles** | | **6.5 Miles** | |
| over 1:36:01 | 3.8 | over 2:10:01 | 5.5 |
| 1:36:00–1:12:01 | 8.6 | 2:10:00–1:37:31 | 12.0 |
| 1:12:00– 57:37 | 13.4 | 1:37:30–1:18:01 | 18.5 |
| 57:36– 48:01 | 18.2 | 1:18:00–1:05:01 | 25.0 |
| 48:00– 38:25 | 23.0 | 1:05:00– 52:01 | 31.5 |
| 38:24– 32:01 | 27.8 | 52:00– 43:21 | 38.0 |
| 32:00– 27:27 | 32.6 | 43:20– 37:10 | 44.5 |
| under 27:26 | 37.4 | under 37:08 | 51.0 |
| **4.9 Miles** | | **7.0 Miles** | |
| over 1:38:01 | 3.9 | over 2:20:01 | 6.0 |
| 1:38:00–1:13:31 | 8.8 | 2:20:00–1:45:01 | 13.0 |
| 1:13:30– 58:49 | 13.7 | 1:45:00–1:24:01 | 20.0 |
| 58:48– 49:01 | 18.6 | 1:24:00–1:10:01 | 27.0 |
| 49:00– 39:13 | 23.5 | 1:10:00– 56:01 | 34.0 |
| 39:12– 32:41 | 28.4 | 56:00– 46:41 | 41.0 |
| 32:40– 28:01 | 33.3 | 46:40– 40:01 | 48.0 |
| under 28:00 | 38.2 | under 40:00 | 55.0 |
| **5.0 Miles** | | **7.5 Miles** | |
| over 1:40:01 | 4.0 | over 2:30:01 | 6.5 |
| 1:40:00–1:15:01 | 9.0 | 2:30:00–1:52:31 | 14.0 |
| 1:15:00–1:00:01 | 14.0 | 1:52:30–1:30:01 | 21.5 |
| 1:00:00– 50:01 | 19.0 | 1:30:00–1:15:01 | 29.0 |
| 50:00– 40:01 | 24.0 | 1:15:00–1:00:01 | 36.5 |
| 40:00– 33:21 | 29.0 | 1:00:00– 50:01 | 44.0 |
| 33:20– 28:35 | 34.0 | 50:00– 42:53 | 51.5 |
| under 28:34 | 39.0 | under 42:25 | 59.0 |
| **5.5 Miles** | | **8.0 Miles** | |
| over 1:50:01 | 4.5 | over 2:40:01 | 7.0 |
| 1:50:00–1:22:31 | 10.0 | 2:40:00–2:00:01 | 15.0 |
| 1:22:30–1:06:01 | 15.5 | 2:00:00–1:36:01 | 23.0 |
| 1:06:00– 55:01 | 21.0 | 1:36:00–1:20:01 | 31.0 |
| 55:00– 44:01 | 26.5 | 1:20:00–1:04:01 | 39.0 |
| 44:00– 36:41 | 32.0 | 1:04:00– 53:21 | 47.0 |
| 36:40– 31:27 | 37.5 | 53:20– 45:44 | 55.0 |
| under 31:26 | 43.0 | under 45:43 | 63.0 |

# WALKING/RUNNING (CONTINUED)

| TIME (hr:min:sec) | POINT VALUE | TIME (hr:min:sec) | POINT VALUE |
|---|---|---|---|
| **8.5 Miles** | | **12.0 Miles** | |
| over 2:50:01 | 7.5 | over 4:00:01 | 11.0 |
| 2:50:00–2:07:31 | 16.0 | 4:00:00–3:00:01 | 23.0 |
| 2:07:30–1:42:01 | 24.5 | 3:00:00–2:24:01 | 35.0 |
| 1:42:00–1:25:01 | 33.0 | 2:24:00–2:00:01 | 47.0 |
| 1:25:00–1:08:01 | 41.5 | 2:00:00–1:36:01 | 59.0 |
| 1:08:00– 56:41 | 50.0 | 1:36:00–1:20:01 | 71.0 |
| 56:40– 48:35 | 58.5 | 1:20:00–1:08:35 | 83.0 |
| under 48:34 | 67.0 | under 1:08:34 | 95.0 |
| **9.0 Miles** | | **13.0 Miles** | |
| over 3:00:01 | 8.0 | over 4:20:01 | 12.0 |
| 3:00:00–2:15:01 | 17.0 | 4:20:00–3:15:01 | 25.0 |
| 2:15:00–1:48:01 | 26.0 | 3:15:00–2:36:01 | 38.0 |
| 1:48:00–1:30:01 | 35.0 | 2:36:00–2:10:01 | 51.0 |
| 1:30:00–1:12:01 | 44.0 | 2:10:00–1:44:01 | 64.0 |
| 1:12:00–1:00:01 | 53.0 | 1:44:00–1:26:41 | 77.0 |
| 1:00:00– 51:27 | 62.0 | 1:26:40–1:14:19 | 90.0 |
| under 51:26 | 71.0 | under 1:14:17 | 103.0 |
| **9.5 Miles** | | **14.0 Miles** | |
| over 3:10:01 | 8.5 | over 4:40:01 | 13.0 |
| 3:10:00–2:22:31 | 18.0 | 4:40:00–3:30:01 | 27.0 |
| 2:22:30–1:54:01 | 27.5 | 3:30:00–2:48:01 | 41.0 |
| 1:54:00–1:35:01 | 37.0 | 2:48:00–2:20:01 | 55.0 |
| 1:35:00–1:16:01 | 46.5 | 2:20:00–1:52:01 | 69.0 |
| 1:16:00–1:03:21 | 56.0 | 1:52:00–1:33:21 | 83.0 |
| 1:03:20– 54:19 | 65.5 | 1:33:20–1:20:01 | 97.0 |
| under 54:17 | 75.0 | under 1:20:00 | 111.0 |
| **10.0 Miles** | | **15.0 Miles** | |
| over 3:20:01 | 9.0 | over 5:00:01 | 14.0 |
| 3:20:00–2:30:01 | 19.0 | 5:00:00–3:45:01 | 29.0 |
| 2:30:00–2:00:01 | 29.0 | 3:45:00–3:00:01 | 44.0 |
| 2:00:00–1:40:01 | 39.0 | 3:00:00–2:30:01 | 59.0 |
| 1:40:00–1:20:01 | 49.0 | 2:30:00–2:00:01 | 74.0 |
| 1:20:00–1:06:41 | 59.0 | 2:00:00–1:40:01 | 89.0 |
| 1:06:40– 57:10 | 69.0 | 1:40:00–1:25:44 | 104.0 |
| under 57:08 | 79.0 | under 1:25:43 | 119.0 |
| **11.0 Miles** | | **16.0 Miles** | |
| over 3:40:01 | 10.0 | over 5:20:01 | 15.0 |
| 3:40:00–2:45:01 | 21.0 | 5:20:00–4:00:01 | 31.0 |
| 2:45:00–2:12:01 | 32.0 | 4:00:00–3:12:01 | 47.0 |
| 2:12:00–1:50:01 | 43.0 | 3:12:00–2:40:01 | 63.0 |
| 1:50:00–1:28:01 | 54.0 | 2:40:00–2:08:01 | 79.0 |
| 1:28:00–1:13:21 | 65.0 | 2:08:00–1:46:41 | 95.0 |
| 1:13:20–1:02:53 | 76.0 | 1:46:40–1:31:27 | 111.0 |
| under 1:02:52 | 87.0 | under 1:31:26 | 127.0 |

| TIME (hr:min:sec) | POINT VALUE | TIME (hr:min:sec) | POINT VALUE |
|---|---|---|---|
| **17.0 Miles** | | **22.0 Miles** | |
| over 5:40:01 | 16.0 | over 7:20:01 | 21.0 |
| 5:40:00–4:15:01 | 33.0 | 7:20:00–5:30:01 | 43.0 |
| 4:15:00–3:24:01 | 50.0 | 5:30:00–4:24:01 | 65.0 |
| 3:24:00–2:50:01 | 67.0 | 4:24:00–3:40:01 | 87.0 |
| 2:50:00–2:16:01 | 84.0 | 3:40:00–2:56:01 | 109.0 |
| 2:16:00–1:53:21 | 101.0 | 2:56:00–2:26:41 | 131.0 |
| 1:53:20–1:37:10 | 118.0 | 2:26:40–2:05:44 | 153.0 |
| under 1:37:08 | 135.0 | under 2:05:43 | 175.0 |
| **18.0 Miles** | | **23.0 Miles** | |
| over 6:00:01 | 17.0 | over 7:40:01 | 22.0 |
| 6:00:00–4:30:01 | 35.0 | 7:40:00–5:45:01 | 45.0 |
| 4:30:00–3:36:01 | 53.0 | 5:45:00–4:36:01 | 68.0 |
| 3:36:00–3:00:01 | 71.0 | 4:36:00–3:50:01 | 91.0 |
| 3:00:00–2:24:01 | 89.0 | 3:50:00–3:04:01 | 114.0 |
| 2:24:00–2:00:01 | 107.0 | 3:04:00–2:33:21 | 137.0 |
| 2:00:00–1:42:53 | 125.0 | 2:33:20–2:11:27 | 160.0 |
| under 1:42:52 | 143.0 | under 2:11:26 | 183.0 |
| **19.0 Miles** | | **24.0 Miles** | |
| over 6:20:01 | 18.0 | over 8:00:01 | 23.0 |
| 6:20:00–4:45:01 | 37.0 | 8:00:00–6:00:01 | 47.0 |
| 4:45:00–3:48:01 | 56.0 | 6:00:00–4:48:01 | 71.0 |
| 3:48:00–3:10:01 | 75.0 | 4:48:00–4:00:01 | 95.0 |
| 3:10:00–2:32:01 | 94.0 | 4:00:00–3:12:01 | 119.0 |
| 2:32:00–2:06:41 | 113.0 | 3:12:00–2:40:01 | 143.0 |
| 2:06:40–1:48:35 | 132.0 | 2:40:00–2:17:10 | 167.0 |
| under 1:48:34 | 151.0 | under 2:17:08 | 191.0 |
| **20.0 Miles** | | **25.0 Miles** | |
| over 6:40:01 | 19.0 | over 8:20:01 | 24.0 |
| 6:40:00–5:00:01 | 39.0 | 8:20:00–6:15:01 | 49.0 |
| 5:00:00–4:00:01 | 59.0 | 6:15:00–5:00:01 | 74.0 |
| 4:00:00–3:20:01 | 79.0 | 5:00:00–4:10:01 | 99.0 |
| 3:20:00–2:40:01 | 99.0 | 4:10:00–3:20:01 | 124.0 |
| 2:40:00–2:13:21 | 119.0 | 3:20:00–2:46:41 | 149.0 |
| 2:13:20–1:54:19 | 139.0 | 2:46:40–2:22:53 | 174.0 |
| under 1:54:17 | 159.0 | under 2:22:52 | 199.0 |
| **21.0 Miles** | | **26.22 Miles** | |
| over 7:00:01 | 20.0 | over 8:44:25 | 25.22 |
| 7:00:00–5:15:01 | 41.0 | 8:44:24–6:33:19 | 51.44 |
| 5:15:00–4:12:01 | 62.0 | 6:33:18–5:14:40 | 77.66 |
| 4:12:00–3:30:01 | 83.0 | 5:14:38–4:22:13 | 103.88 |
| 3:30:00–2:48:01 | 104.0 | 4:22:12–3:29:47 | 130.10 |
| 2:48:00–2:20:01 | 125.0 | 3:29:46–2:54:49 | 156.32 |
| 2:20:00–2:00:01 | 146.0 | 2:54:48–2:29:51 | 182.54 |
| under 2:00:00 | 167.0 | under 2:29:50 | 208.76 |

# CYCLING

| TIME (min:sec) | POINT VALUE | TIME (hr:min:sec) | POINT VALUE |
|---|---|---|---|
| **2.0 Miles** | | **9.0 Miles** | |
| over 12:01 | 0 | over 54:01 | 4.8 |
| 12:00– 8:01 | 0.5 | 54:00–36:01 | 7.5 |
| 8:00– 6:01 | 1.5 | 36:00–27:01 | 12.0 |
| under 6:00 | 2.5 | under 27:00 | 16.5 |
| **3.0 Miles** | | **10.0 Miles** | |
| over 18:01 | 0 | over 1:00:01 | 5.5 |
| 18:00–12:01 | 1.5 | 1:00:00– 40:01 | 8.5 |
| 12:00– 9:01 | 3.0 | 40:00– 30:01 | 13.5 |
| under 9:00 | 4.5 | under 30:00 | 18.5 |
| **4.0 Miles** | | **11.0 Miles** | |
| over 25:01 | 0 | over 1:06:01 | 6.2 |
| 24:00–16:01 | 2.5 | 1:06:00– 44:01 | 9.5 |
| 16:00–12:01 | 4.5 | 44:00– 33:01 | 15.0 |
| under 12:00 | 6.5 | under 33:00 | 20.5 |
| **5.0 Miles** | | **12.0 Miles** | |
| over 30:01 | 2.0 | over 1:12:01 | 6.9 |
| 30:00–20:01 | 3.5 | 1:12:00– 48:01 | 10.5 |
| 20:00–15:01 | 6.0 | 48:00– 36:01 | 16.5 |
| under 15:00 | 8.5 | under 36:00 | 22.5 |
| **6.0 Miles** | | **13.0 Miles** | |
| over 36:01 | 2.7 | over 1:18:01 | 7.6 |
| 36:00–24:01 | 4.5 | 1:18:00– 52:01 | 11.5 |
| 24:00–18:01 | 7.5 | 52:00– 39:01 | 18.0 |
| under 18:00 | 10.5 | under 39:00 | 24.5 |
| **7.0 Miles** | | **14.0 Miles** | |
| over 42:01 | 3.4 | over 1:24:01 | 8.3 |
| 42:00–28:01 | 5.5 | 1:24:00– 56:01 | 12.5 |
| 28:00–21:01 | 9.0 | 56:00– 42:01 | 19.5 |
| under 21:00 | 12.5 | under 42:00 | 26.5 |
| **8.0 Miles** | | **15.0 Miles** | |
| over 48:01 | 4.1 | over 1:30:01 | 9.0 |
| 48:00–32:01 | 6.5 | 1:30:00–1:00:01 | 13.5 |
| 32:00–24:01 | 10.5 | 1:00:00– 45:01 | 21.0 |
| under 24:00 | 14.5 | under 45:00 | 28.5 |

*Note:* Points are determined considering an equal uphill and downhill course, and considering an equal time with and against the wind. For cycling a one-way course against a wind exceeding 5 mph, add ½ point per mile to the total point value.

| TIME (hr:min:sec) | POINT VALUE | TIME (hr:min:sec) | POINT VALUE |
|---|---|---|---|
| **16.0 Miles** | | **24.0 Miles** | |
| over 1:36:01 | 9.7 | over 2:24:01 | 15.3 |
| 1:36:00–1:04:01 | 14.5 | 2:24:00–1:36:01 | 22.5 |
| 1:04:00– 48:01 | 22.5 | 1:36:00–1:12:01 | 34.5 |
| under 48:00 | 30.5 | under 1:12:00 | 46.5 |
| **17.0 Miles** | | **25.0 Miles** | |
| over 1:42:01 | 10.4 | over 2:30:01 | 16.0 |
| 1:42:00–1:08:01 | 15.5 | 2:30:00–1:40:01 | 23.5 |
| 1:08:00– 51:01 | 24.0 | 1:40:00–1:15:01 | 36.0 |
| under 51:00 | 32.5 | under 1:15:00 | 48.5 |
| **18.0 Miles** | | **26.0 Miles** | |
| over 1:48:01 | 11.1 | over 2:36:01 | 16.7 |
| 1:48:00–1:12:01 | 16.5 | 2:36:00–1:44:01 | 24.5 |
| 1:12:00– 54:01 | 25.5 | 1:44:00–1:18:01 | 37.5 |
| under 54:00 | 34.5 | under 1:18:00 | 50.5 |
| **19.0 Miles** | | **27.0 Miles** | |
| over 1:54:01 | 11.8 | over 2:42:01 | 17.4 |
| 1:54:00–1:16:01 | 17.5 | 2:42:00–1:48:01 | 25.5 |
| 1:16:00– 57:01 | 27.0 | 1:48:00–1:21:01 | 39.0 |
| under 57:00 | 36.5 | under 1:21:00 | 52.5 |
| **20.0 Miles** | | **28.0 Miles** | |
| over 2:00:01 | 12.5 | over 2:48:01 | 18.1 |
| 2:00:00–1:20:01 | 18.5 | 2:48:00–1:52:01 | 26.5 |
| 1:20:00–1:00:01 | 28.5 | 1:52:00–1:24:01 | 40.5 |
| under 1:00:00 | 38.5 | under 1:24:00 | 54.5 |
| **21.0 Miles** | | **29.0 Miles** | |
| over 2:06:01 | 13.2 | over 2:54:01 | 18.8 |
| 2:06:00–1:24:01 | 19.5 | 2:54:00–1:56:01 | 27.5 |
| 1:24:00–1:03:01 | 30.0 | 1:56:00–1:27:01 | 42.0 |
| under 1:03:00 | 40.5 | under 1:27:00 | 56.5 |
| **22.0 Miles** | | **30.0 Miles** | |
| over 2:12:01 | 13.9 | over 3:00:01 | 19.5 |
| 2:12:00–1:28:01 | 20.5 | 3:00:00–2:00:01 | 28.5 |
| 1:28:00–1:06:01 | 31.5 | 2:00:00–1:30:01 | 43.5 |
| under 1:06:00 | 42.5 | under 1:30:00 | 58.5 |
| **23.0 Miles** | | **35.0 Miles** | |
| over 2:18:01 | 14.6 | over 3:30:01 | 23.0 |
| 2:18:00–1:32:01 | 21.5 | 3:30:00–2:20:01 | 33.5 |
| 1:32:00–1:09:01 | 33.0 | 2:20:00–1:45:01 | 51.0 |
| under 1:09:00 | 44.5 | under 1:45:00 | 68.5 |

# CYCLING (CONTINUED)

| TIME (hr:min:sec) | POINT VALUE | TIME (hr:min:sec) | POINT VALUE |
|---|---|---|---|
| **40.0 Miles** | | **75.0 Miles** | |
| over 4:00:01 | 26.5 | over 7:30:01 | 51.0 |
| 4:00:00–2:40:01 | 38.5 | 7:30:00–5:00:01 | 73.5 |
| 2:40:00–2:00:01 | 58.5 | 5:00:00–3:45:01 | 111.0 |
| under 2:00:00 | 78.5 | under 3:45:00 | 148.5 |
| **45.0 Miles** | | **80.0 Miles** | |
| over 4:30:01 | 30.0 | over 8:00:01 | 54.5 |
| 4:30:00–3:00:01 | 43.5 | 8:00:00–5:20:01 | 78.5 |
| 3:00:00–2:15:01 | 66.0 | 5:20:00–4:00:01 | 118.5 |
| under 2:15:00 | 88.5 | under 4:00:00 | 158.5 |
| **50.0 Miles** | | **85.0 Miles** | |
| over 5:00:01 | 33.5 | over 8:30:01 | 58.0 |
| 5:00:00–3:20:01 | 48.5 | 8:30:00–5:40:01 | 83.5 |
| 3:20:00–2:30:01 | 73.5 | 5:40:00–4:15:01 | 126.0 |
| under 2:30:00 | 98.5 | under 4:15:00 | 168.5 |
| **55.0 Miles** | | **90.0 Miles** | |
| over 5:30:01 | 37.0 | over 9:00:01 | 61.5 |
| 5:30:00–3:40:01 | 53.5 | 9:00:00–6:00:01 | 88.5 |
| 3:40:00–2:45:01 | 81.0 | 6:00:00–4:30:01 | 133.5 |
| under 2:45:00 | 108.5 | under 4:30:00 | 178.5 |
| **60.0 Miles** | | **95.0 Miles** | |
| over 6:00:01 | 40.5 | over 9:30:01 | 65.0 |
| 6:00:00–4:00:01 | 58.5 | 9:30:00–6:20:01 | 93.5 |
| 4:00:00–3:00:01 | 88.5 | 6:20:00–4:45:01 | 141.0 |
| under 3:00:00 | 118.5 | under 4:45:00 | 188.5 |
| **65.0 Miles** | | **100.0 Miles** | |
| over 6:30:01 | 44.0 | over 10:00:01 | 68.5 |
| 6:30:00–4:20:01 | 63.5 | 10:00:00– 6:40:01 | 98.5 |
| 4:20:00–3:15:01 | 96.0 | 6:40:00– 5:00:01 | 148.5 |
| under 3:15:00 | 128.5 | under 5:00:00 | 198.5 |
| **70.0 Miles** | | | |
| over 7:00:01 | 47.5 | | |
| 7:00:00–4:40:01 | 68.5 | | |
| 4:40:00–3:30:01 | 103.5 | | |
| under 3:30:00 | 138.5 | | |

# SWIMMING

| TIME (min:sec) | POINT VALUE | TIME (min:sec) | POINT VALUE |
|---|---|---|---|
| **200 Yards** | | **550 Yards** | |
| over 6:41 | 0 | over 18:21 | 0 |
| 6:40–5:01 | 1.25 | 18:20–13:46 | 3.44 |
| 5:00–3:21 | 1.67 | 13:45– 9:11 | 4.58 |
| under 3:20 | 2.50 | under 9:10 | 6.87 |
| **250 Yards** | | **600 Yards** | |
| over 8:21 | 0 | over 20:01 | 0 |
| 8:20–6:16 | 1.56 | 20:00–15:01 | 3.75 |
| 6:15–4:11 | 2.08 | 15:00–10:01 | 5.00 |
| under 4:10 | 3.12 | under 10:00 | 7.50 |
| **300 Yards** | | **650 Yards** | |
| over 10:01 | 0 | over 21:41 | 0 |
| 10:00– 7:31 | 1.88 | 21:40–16:16 | 4.31 |
| 7:30– 5:01 | 2.50 | 16:15–10:51 | 5.67 |
| under 5:00 | 3.75 | under 10:50 | 8.38 |
| **350 Yards** | | **700 Yards** | |
| over 11:41 | 0 | over 23:21 | 0 |
| 11:40– 8:46 | 2.19 | 23:20–17:31 | 4.88 |
| 8:45– 5:51 | 2.92 | 17:30–11:41 | 6.33 |
| under 5:50 | 4.38 | under 11:40 | 9.25 |
| **400 Yards** | | **750 Yards** | |
| over 13:21 | 0 | over 25:01 | 0 |
| 13:20–10:01 | 2.50 | 25:00–18:46 | 5.44 |
| 10:00– 6:41 | 3.33 | 18:45–12:31 | 7.00 |
| under 6:40 | 5.00 | under 12:30 | 10.13 |
| **450 Yards** | | **800 Yards** | |
| over 15:01 | 0 | over 26:41 | 0 |
| 15:00–11:16 | 2.81 | 26:40–20:01 | 6.00 |
| 11:15– 7:31 | 3.75 | 20:00–13:21 | 7.67 |
| under 7:30 | 5.63 | under 13:20 | 11.00 |
| **500 Yards** | | **850 Yards** | |
| over 16:41 | 0 | over 28:21 | 0 |
| 16:40–12:31 | 3.12 | 28:20–21:16 | 6.56 |
| 12:30– 8:21 | 4.17 | 21:15–14:11 | 8.33 |
| under 8:20 | 6.25 | under 14:10 | 11.87 |

*Note:* Points are calculated on overhand crawl, considering average skill in swimming, i.e., 9.0 kcal (kilo calories) per minute. Breaststroke is less demanding: 7.0 kcal per minute. Backstroke, a little more than breaststroke: 8.0 kcal per minute. Butterfly is the most demanding, i.e., 12.0 kcal per minute.

## SWIMMING (CONTINUED)

| TIME (min:sec) | POINT VALUE | TIME (min:sec) | POINT VALUE |
|---|---|---|---|
| **900 Yards** | | **1300 Yards** | |
| over 30:01 | 0 | over 43:21 | 0 |
| 30:00–22:31 | 7.13 | 43:20–32:31 | 11.63 |
| 22:30–15:01 | 9.00 | 32:30–21:41 | 14.33 |
| under 15:00 | 12.75 | under 21:40 | 19.75 |
| **950 Yards** | | **1350 Yards** | |
| over 31:41 | 0 | over 45:01 | 0 |
| 31:40–23:46 | 7.69 | 45:00–33:46 | 12.19 |
| 23:45–15:51 | 9.67 | 33:45–22:31 | 15.00 |
| under 15:50 | 13.63 | under 22:30 | 20.63 |
| **1000 Yards** | | **1400 Yards** | |
| over 33:21 | 0 | over 46:41 | 0 |
| 33:20–25:01 | 8.25 | 46:40–35:01 | 12.75 |
| 25:00–16:41 | 10.33 | 35:00–23:21 | 15.67 |
| under 16:40 | 14.50 | under 23:20 | 21.50 |
| **1050 Yards** | | **1450 Yards** | |
| over 35:01 | 0 | over 48:21 | 0 |
| 35:00–26:16 | 8.81 | 48:20–36:16 | 13.31 |
| 26:15–17:31 | 11.00 | 36:15–24:11 | 16.33 |
| under 17:30 | 15.38 | under 24:10 | 22.37 |
| **1100 Yards** | | **1500 Yards** | |
| over 36:41 | 0 | over 50:01 | 0 |
| 36:40–27:31 | 9.37 | 50:00–37:31 | 13.88 |
| 27:30–18:21 | 11.67 | 37:30–25:01 | 17.00 |
| under 18:20 | 16.25 | under 25:00 | 23.25 |
| **1150 Yards** | | **1550 Yards** | |
| over 38:21 | 0 | over 51:41 | 0 |
| 38:20–28:46 | 9.94 | 51:40–38:46 | 14.44 |
| 28:45–19:11 | 12.33 | 38:45–25:51 | 17.67 |
| under 19:10 | 17.12 | under 25:50 | 24.13 |
| **1200 Yards** | | **1600 Yards** | |
| over 40:01 | 0 | over 53:21 | 0 |
| 40:00–30:01 | 10.50 | 53:20–40:01 | 15.00 |
| 30:00–20:01 | 13.00 | 40:00–26:41 | 18.33 |
| under 20:00 | 18.00 | under 26:40 | 25.00 |
| **1250 Yards** | | **1650 Yards** | |
| over 41:41 | 0 | over 55:01 | 0 |
| 41:40–31:16 | 11.06 | 55:00–41:16 | 15.56 |
| 31:15–20:51 | 13.67 | 41:15–27:31 | 19.00 |
| under 20:50 | 18.88 | under 27:30 | 25.88 |

| TIME (hr:min:sec) | POINT VALUE | TIME (hr:min:sec) | POINT VALUE |
|---|---|---|---|

### 1700 Yards

| over 56:41 | 0 |
|---|---|
| 56:40–42:31 | 16.12 |
| 42:30–28:21 | 19.67 |
| under 28:20 | 26.75 |

### 2300 Yards

| over 1:16:41 | 0 |
|---|---|
| 1:16:40– 57:31 | 22.87 |
| 57:30– 38:21 | 27.67 |
| under 38:20 | 37.25 |

### 1750 Yards

| over 58:21 | 0 |
|---|---|
| 58:20–43:46 | 16.69 |
| 43:45–29:11 | 20.33 |
| under 29:10 | 27.62 |

### 2400 Yards

| over 1:20:01 | 0 |
|---|---|
| 1:20:00–1:00:01 | 24.00 |
| 1:00:00– 40:01 | 29.00 |
| under 40:00 | 39.00 |

### 1800 Yards

| over 1:00:01 | 0 |
|---|---|
| 1:00:00– 45:01 | 17.25 |
| 45:00– 30:01 | 21.00 |
| under 30:00 | 28.50 |

### 2500 Yards

| over 1:23:21 | 0 |
|---|---|
| 1:23:20–1:02:31 | 25.13 |
| 1:02:30– 41:41 | 30.33 |
| under 41:40 | 40.75 |

### 1850 Yards

| over 1:01:41 | 0 |
|---|---|
| 1:01:40– 46:16 | 17.81 |
| 46:15– 30:51 | 21.67 |
| under 30:50 | 29.38 |

### 2600 Yards

| over 1:26:41 | 0 |
|---|---|
| 1:26:40–1:05:01 | 26.25 |
| 1:05:00– 43:21 | 31.67 |
| under 43:20 | 42.50 |

### 1900 Yards

| over 1:03:21 | 0 |
|---|---|
| 1:03:20– 47:31 | 18.38 |
| 47:30– 31:41 | 22.33 |
| under 31:40 | 30.25 |

### 2700 Yards

| over 1:30:01 | 0 |
|---|---|
| 1:30:00–1:07:31 | 27.38 |
| 1:07:30– 45:01 | 33.00 |
| under 45:00 | 44.25 |

### 2000 Yards

| over 1:06:41 | 0 |
|---|---|
| 1:06:40– 50:01 | 19.50 |
| 50:00– 33:21 | 23.67 |
| under 33:20 | 32.00 |

### 2800 Yards

| over 1:33:21 | 0 |
|---|---|
| 1:33:20–1:10:01 | 28.50 |
| 1:10:00– 46:41 | 34.33 |
| under 46:40 | 46.00 |

### 2100 Yards

| over 1:10:01 | 0 |
|---|---|
| 1:10:00– 52:31 | 20.63 |
| 53:30– 35:01 | 25.00 |
| under 35:00 | 33.75 |

### 2900 Yards

| over 1:36:41 | 0 |
|---|---|
| 1:36:40–1:12:31 | 29.62 |
| 1:12:30– 48:21 | 35.67 |
| under 48:20 | 47.75 |

### 2200 Yards

| over 1:13:21 | 0 |
|---|---|
| 1:13:20– 55:01 | 21.75 |
| 55:00– 36:41 | 26.33 |
| under 36:40 | 35.50 |

### 3000 Yards

| over 1:40:01 | 0 |
|---|---|
| 1:40:00–1:15:01 | 30.75 |
| 1:15:00– 50:01 | 37.00 |
| under 50:00 | 49.50 |

## HANDBALL/RACQUETBALL/SQUASH/
## BASKETBALL/SOCCER/HOCKEY/LACROSSE *

| TIME (hr:min:sec) | POINT VALUE |
|---|---|
| under 4:59 | 0 |
| 5:00– 9:59 | 0.75 |
| 10:00– 14:59 | 1.50 |
| 15:00– 19:59 | 2.25 |
| 20:00– 24:59 | 3.00 |
| 25:00– 29:59 | 4.00 |
| 30:00– 34:59 | 5.00 |
| 35:00– 39:59 | 6.00 |
| 40:00– 44:59 | 7.00 |
| 45:00– 49:59 | 8.00 |
| 50:00– 54:59 | 9.00 |
| 55:00– 59:59 | 10.00 |
| 1:00:00–1:04:59 | 11.00 |
| 1:05:00–1:09:59 | 12.00 |
| 1:10:00–1:14:59 | 13.00 |
| 1:15:00–1:19:59 | 14.00 |
| 1:20:00–1:24:59 | 15.00 |
| 1:25:00–1:29:59 | 16.00 |
| 1:30:00–1:34:59 | 17.00 |
| 1:35:00–1:39:59 | 18.00 |
| 1:40:00–1:44:59 | 19.00 |
| 1:45:00–1:49:59 | 20.00 |
| 1:50:00–1:54:59 | 21.00 |
| 1:55:00–1:59:59 | 22.00 |
| over 2:00:00 | 23.00 |

*Note:* For times greater than 2 hours, figure points at rate of 2 points/10 minutes for the time over 2 hours.

* Continuous exercise. Do not count breaks, time-outs, etc.

## STATIONARY RUNNING

| TIME (min:sec) | 60-70 * STEPS/MIN | POINT VALUE | 70-80 * STEPS/MIN | POINT VALUE | 80-90 * STEPS/MIN | POINT VALUE | 90-100 * STEPS/MIN | POINT VALUE | 100-110 * STEPS/MIN | POINT VALUE |
|---|---|---|---|---|---|---|---|---|---|---|
| 2:30 | | | 175-200 | ¾ | 200-225 | 1 | 225-250 | 1¼ | 250-275 | 1½ |
| 5:00 | 300-350 | 1 | 350-400 | 1½ | 400-450 | 2 | 450-500 | 2½ | 500-550 | 3 |
| 7:30 | | 1½ | 525-600 | 2¼ | 600-675 | 3 | 675-750 | 3¾ | 750-825 | 4½ |
| 10:00 | 600-700 | 2 | 700-800 | 3 | 800-900 | 4 | 900-1000 | 5 | 1000-1100 | 6 |
| 12:30 | | | 875-1000 | 3¾ | 1000-1125 | 5 | 1125-1250 | 6¼ | 1250-1375 | 7½ |
| 15:00 | 900-1050 | 4 | 1050-1200 | 5½ | 1200-1350 | 7 | 1350-1500 | 8½ | 1500-1650 | 10 |
| 17:30 | | | 1225-1400 | 6¾ | 1400-1575 | 8½ | 1575-1750 | 10¼ | 1750-1925 | 12 |
| 20:00 | 1200-1400 | 6 | 1400-1600 | 8 | 1600-1800 | 10 | 1800-2000 | 12 | 2000-2200 | 14 |
| 22:30 | | | 1575-1800 | 9¼ | 1800-2025 | 11½ | 2025-2250 | 13¾ | 2250-2475 | 16 |
| 25:00 | 1500-1750 | 8 | 1750-2000 | 10½ | 2000-2250 | 13 | 2250-2500 | 15½ | 2500-2750 | 18 |
| 27:30 | | | 1925-2200 | 11¾ | 2200-2475 | 14½ | 2475-2750 | 17¼ | 2750-3025 | 20 |
| 30:00 | 1800-2100 | 10 | 2100-2400 | 13 | 2400-2700 | 16 | 2700-3000 | 19 | 3000-3300 | 22 |

* Count only when the left foot hits the floor. Knees must be brought up in front, raising the feet at least 8 inches from the floor.

## STATIONARY CYCLING *
### (Using a screw-down resistance)

## POINT VALUE

| TIME (min:sec) | 15 MPH/ 55 RPM | 17½ MPH/ 65 RPM | 20 MPH/ 75 RPM | 25 MPH/ 90 RPM | 30 MPH/ 105 RPM |
|---|---|---|---|---|---|
| 3:00 | —— | —— | | —— | 1 |
| 4:00 | ½ | —— | 1 | —— | —— |
| 5:00 | —— | —— | 1¼ | 2 | 2½ |
| 6:00 | ¾ | —— | 1½ | 2⅛ | 2¾ |
| 7:00 | —— | 1 | 1¾ | 2¼ | 3 |
| 8:00 | 1 | 1¼ | 2 | 2½ | 3⅓ |
| 9:00 | —— | 1⅜ | 2¼ | 2¾ | 3⅔ |
| 10:00 | 1¼ | —— | 2½ | 3 | 4 |
| 11:00 | —— | 1½ | 2⅝ | 3¼ | 4¼ |
| 12:00 | 1⅜ | 1⅝ | 2¾ | 3½ | 4½ |
| 13:00 | 1⅝ | 1⅞ | 2⅞ | 3¾ | 4¾ |
| 14:00 | 1¾ | 2 | 3 | 4 | 5 |
| 15:00 | 1⅞ | 2⅛ | 3⅛ | 4¼ | 5½ |
| 16:00 | 2 | 2¼ | 3¼ | 4½ | 6 |
| 17:00 | 2⅛ | 2⅜ | 3⅜ | 4¾ | 6½ |
| 18:00 | 2¼ | 2⅝ | 3⅝ | 5 | 7 |
| 19:00 | 2⅜ | 2¾ | 3¾ | 5⅓ | 7½ |
| 20:00 | 2½ | 2⅞ | 3⅞ | 5⅔ | 8 |
| 22:30 | 3 | 3⅛ | 4½ | 6⅝ | 9 |
| 25:00 | 3¼ | 3¾ | 5 | 7½ | 10 |
| 27:30 | 3½ | 4½ | 5¾ | 8½ | 11½ |
| 30:00 | 3¾ | 5 | 6½ | 9½ | 12½ |
| 35:00 | 4¾ | 6 | 8 | 11 | 14½ |
| 40:00 | 5¾ | 7¼ | 9½ | 13 | 17 |
| 45:00 | 6¾ | 8½ | 11 | 15 | 19½ |
| 50:00 | 7¾ | 9¾ | 12½ | 17 | 22½ |
| 55:00 | 8¾ | 11 | 14 | 19 | 25 |
| 60:00 | 9¾ | 12½ | 16 | 22 | 28 |

*Note:* Add enough resistance so that the pulse rate counted for 10 seconds immediately after exercise and multiplied by 6 equals or exceeds 140 beats per minute.

* Stationary cycling is awarded approximately half the points for regular cycling.

## STATIONARY CYCLING
### (Adjusted for weight and resistance using the
### Schwinn Calibrated Resistance Ergometer)

| WEIGHT (lbs) | LOAD: 1.0 | 2.0 | 3.0 | 4.0 |
|---|---|---|---|---|

15:00 MINUTES

POINT VALUE

| WEIGHT (lbs) | 1.0 | 2.0 | 3.0 | 4.0 |
|---|---|---|---|---|
| 100 | 3.20 | 8.72 | 18.79 | —— |
| 120 | 2.18 | 5.60 | 12.03 | 20.44 |
| 140 | 1.48 | 4.09 | 8.18 | 14.39 |
| 160 | 1.13 | 3.20 | 5.94 | 8.37 |
| 180 | 0.77 | 2.58 | 4.54 | 7.05 |
| 200 | 0.37 | 2.01 | 3.76 | 6.13 |
| 220 | —— | 1.56 | 3.19 | 4.91 |
| 240 | —— | 1.30 | 2.67 | 4.12 |

30:00 MINUTES

POINT VALUE

| WEIGHT (lbs) | 1.0 | 2.0 | 3.0 | 4.0 |
|---|---|---|---|---|
| 100 | 6.40 | 17.44 | 37.58 | —— |
| 120 | 4.35 | 11.19 | 24.05 | 40.88 |
| 140 | 2.96 | 8.18 | 16.36 | 28.79 |
| 160 | 2.27 | 6.40 | 11.87 | 16.74 |
| 180 | 1.53 | 5.15 | 9.09 | 14.09 |
| 200 | 0.73 | 4.01 | 7.57 | 12.26 |
| 220 | —— | 3.13 | 6.38 | 9.82 |
| 240 | —— | 2.60 | 5.34 | 8.24 |

45:00 MINUTES

POINT VALUE

| WEIGHT (lbs) | 1.0 | 2.0 | 3.0 | 4.0 |
|---|---|---|---|---|
| 100 | 9.60 | 26.16 | 56.36 | —— |
| 120 | 6.53 | 16.79 | 36.08 | 61.31 |
| 140 | 4.43 | 12.26 | 24.54 | 43.18 |
| 160 | 3.40 | 9.60 | 17.81 | 25.10 |
| 180 | 2.30 | 7.73 | 13.63 | 21.14 |
| 200 | 1.10 | 6.02 | 11.27 | 18.38 |
| 220 | —— | 4.69 | 9.56 | 14.72 |
| 240 | —— | 3.89 | 8.01 | 12.36 |

60:00 MINUTES

POINT VALUE

| WEIGHT (lbs) | 1.0 | 2.0 | 3.0 | 4.0 |
|---|---|---|---|---|
| 100 | 12.80 | 34.88 | 75.15 | —— |
| 120 | 8.70 | 22.38 | 48.10 | 81.75 |
| 140 | 5.91 | 16.35 | 32.72 | 57.57 |
| 160 | 4.53 | 12.80 | 23.74 | 33.47 |
| 180 | 3.06 | 10.30 | 18.17 | 28.18 |
| 200 | 1.46 | 8.02 | 15.02 | 24.51 |
| 220 | —— | 6.25 | 12.75 | 19.63 |
| 240 | —— | 5.19 | 10.68 | 16.48 |

*Note:* Resistance is consistent, regardless of speed.

## STAIR CLIMBING
### (10 steps; 6″–7″ in height; 25°–30° incline)

ROUND TRIPS—AVERAGE NUMBER PER MINUTE

| TIME (min:sec) | 5 | 6 | 7 | 8 | 9 | 10 |
|---|---|---|---|---|---|---|
| | | | POINT VALUE | | | |
| 3:00 | — | — | — | — | — | 2½ |
| 3:30 | — | — | — | — | 2 | — |
| 4:00 | — | — | 1½ | 1¾ | — | 3¼ |
| 4:30 | — | — | — | — | 2¾ | — |
| 5:00 | ½ | 1 | 1¾ | — | — | 4 |
| 5:30 | — | 1¼ | — | 2½ | 3½ | — |
| 6:00 | ¾ | — | 2 | — | — | 4¾ |
| 6:30 | — | 1½ | — | 3 | 4¼ | — |
| 7:00 | 1 | — | 2¼ | — | — | 5½ |
| 7:30 | — | 1¾ | — | 3½ | 4½ | — |
| 8:00 | 1¼ | — | 2¾ | — | — | 6½ |
| 8:30 | — | 2 | — | 3¾ | 5½ | — |
| 9:00 | 1½ | — | 3 | 4 | 5¾ | 7¼ |
| 9:30 | — | 2¼ | — | 4¼ | 6 | — |
| 10:00 | 1¾ | — | 3¼ | 4½ | 6½ | 8 |
| 10:30 | — | — | 3½ | 4¾ | 6¾ | — |
| 11:00 | 2 | 2½ | 3¾ | 5 | 7 | 8¾ |
| 11:30 | — | — | — | 5¼ | 7¼ | — |
| 12:00 | 2¼ | 2¾ | 4 | 5½ | 7½ | 9½ |
| 12:30 | — | — | — | 5¾ | 7¾ | — |
| 13:00 | 2½ | 3 | 4¼ | 6 | 8 | 10¼ |
| 13:30 | — | — | — | 6¼ | 8¼ | — |
| 14:00 | 2¾ | 3¼ | 4½ | 6½ | 8½ | 11 |
| 14:30 | — | — | — | 6¾ | 8¾ | — |
| 15:00 | 3 | 3½ | 4¾ | — | — | — |

### Point Value For Using a Single Step
### (approximately 7 inches in height)

| STEPPING RATE (per min) | TIME (min:sec) | POINT VALUE |
|---|---|---|
| 30 | 6:30 | 1½ |
| | 9:45 | 2¼ |
| | 13:00 | 3 |
| 35 | 6:00 | 2 |
| | 9:00 | 3 |
| | 12:00 | 4 |
| 40 | 5:00 | 2½ |
| | 7:30 | 3¾ |
| | 10:00 | 5 |

## ROPE SKIPPING

| TIME (min:sec) | 70–90 STEPS/MIN | 90–110 STEPS/MIN | 110–130 STEPS/MIN |
|---|---|---|---|
| | POINT VALUE | | |
| 5:00 | 1½ | 2 | 2½ |
| 7:30 | 2¼ | 3 | 3¾ |
| 10:00 | 3 | 4 | 5 |
| 12:30 | 3¾ | 5 | 6¼ |
| 15:00 | 4½ | 6 | 7½ |
| 17:30 | 6¾ | 8½ | 10¼ |
| 20:00 | 8 | 10 | 12 |
| 22:30 | 9¼ | 11½ | 13¾ |
| 25:00 | 10½ | 13 | 15½ |
| 27:30 | 11¾ | 14½ | 17¼ |
| 30:00 | 13 | 16 | 19 |

*Note:* Skip with both feet together, or step over the rope, alternating feet.


## GOLF

| HOLES | POINT VALUE |
|---|---|
| under 2 | 0 |
| 3– 5 | 0.5 |
| 6– 8 | 1.0 |
| 9–11 | 1.5 |
| 12–14 | 2.0 |
| 15–17 | 2.5 |
| 18–20 | 3.0 |
| 21–23 | 3.5 |
| 24–26 | 4.0 |
| 27–29 | 4.5 |
| 30–32 | 5.0 |
| 33–35 | 5.5 |
| over 36 | 6.0 |

*Note:* No motorized carts!


## ROWING

| TIME (min) | POINT VALUE |
|---|---|
| 15:00 | 3.5 |
| 30:00 | 7.0 |
| 45:00 | 10.5 |
| 60:00 | 14.0 |

*Note:* 2 oars, 20 strokes a minute, continuous rowing. For times greater than 1 hour, figure points at a rate of 3.5 points/15 minutes.

# TENNIS/BADMINTON/AERIAL TENNIS
## (Doubles)

| TIME (hr:min:sec) | POINT VALUE |
|---|---|
| under 14:59 | 0 |
| 15:00– 29:59 | 0.25 |
| 30:00– 44:59 | 0.50 |
| 45:00– 59:59 | 0.75 |
| 1:00:00–1:14:59 | 1.00 |
| 1:15:00–1:29:59 | 1.25 |
| 1:30:00–1:44:59 | 1.50 |
| 1:45:00–1:59:59 | 1.75 |
| over 2:00:00 | 2.00 |

*Note:* Points are awarded to players of equal ability. For times greater than 2 hours, figure points at a rate of ⅓ point/20 minutes.

## (Singles)

| TIME (min:sec) | POINT VALUE |
|---|---|
| under 4:59 | 0 |
| 5:00– 9:59 | 0.37 |
| 10:00–14:59 | 0.75 |
| 15:00–19:59 | 1.12 |
| 20:00–24:59 | 1.50 |
| 25:00–29:59 | 1.87 |
| 30:00–34:59 | 2.25 |
| 35:00–39:50 | 2.62 |
| 40:00–44:59 | 3.00 |
| 45:00–49:59 | 3.37 |
| 50:00–54:59 | 3.75 |
| 55:00–59:59 | 4.12 |
| over 60:00 | 4.50 |

*Note:* Points are awarded to players of equal ability. For times greater than 1 hour, figure points at a rate of 1½ points/20 minutes.

# DANCING

| | TIME (min) | POINT VALUE |
|---|---|---|
| Square | 30:00 | 2½ |
| Polka | 30:00 | 2½ |
| Waltz | 30:00 | 1½ |
| Hustle, etc. | 30:00 | 2 |

*Note:* Count only the time you are actively dancing.

# SKIING

| TIME (hr:min:sec) | POINT VALUE |
|---|---|
| under 4:59 | 0 |
| 5:00– 9:59 | 0.5 |
| 10:00– 14:59 | 1.0 |
| 15:00– 19:59 | 1.5 |
| 20:00– 24:59 | 2.0 |
| 25:00– 29:59 | 2.5 |
| 30:00– 34:59 | 3.0 |
| 35:00– 39:59 | 3.5 |
| 40:00– 44:59 | 4.0 |
| 45:00– 49:59 | 4.5 |
| 50:00– 54:59 | 5.0 |
| 55:00– 59:59 | 5.5 |
| 1:00:00–1:04:59 | 6.0 |
| 1:05:00–1:09:59 | 6.5 |
| 1:10:00–1:14:59 | 7.0 |
| 1:15:00–1:19:59 | 7.5 |
| 1:20:00–1:24:59 | 8.0 |
| 1:25:00–1:29:59 | 8.5 |
| 1:30:00–1:34:59 | 9.0 |
| 1:35:00–1:39:59 | 9.5 |
| 1:40:00–1:44:59 | 10.0 |
| 1:45:00–1:49:59 | 10.5 |
| 1:50:00–1:54:59 | 11.0 |
| 1:55:00–1:59:59 | 11.5 |
| over 2:00:00 | 12.0 |

*Note:* Water or snow skiing. For cross-country skiing, either triple or quadruple the point value, depending on the severity of the terrain. For times greater than 2 hours, figure points at a rate of 2 points/10 minutes. Remember, for downhill skiing, it requires 4 to 5 hours on the slopes to accumulate 1 hour of actual skiing.

# SKATING

| TIME (hr:min) | POINT VALUE |
|---|---|
| 15:00 | 1 |
| 30:00 | 2 |
| 45:00 | 3 |
| 1:00:00 | 4 |
| 1:15:00 | 5 |
| 1:30:00 | 6 |
| 1:45:00 | 7 |
| 2:00:00 | 8 |

*Note:* Either ice or roller skating. For speed skating, triple the point value. For times greater than 2 hours, figure points at a rate of 1 point/15 minutes.

# VOLLEYBALL

| TIME (min:sec) | POINT VALUE |
|---|---|
| under 4:59 | 0 |
| 5:00– 9:59 | 0.33 |
| 10:00–14:59 | 0.67 |
| 15:00–19:59 | 1.00 |
| 20:00–24:59 | 1.33 |
| 25:00–29:59 | 1.67 |
| 30:00–34:59 | 2.00 |
| 35:00–39:59 | 2.33 |
| 40:00–44:59 | 2.67 |
| 45:00–49:59 | 3.00 |
| 50:00–54:59 | 3.33 |
| 55:00–59:59 | 3.67 |
| over 60:00 | 4.00 |

*Note:* For times greater than 1 hour, figure points at a rate of 1 point/15 minutes.

# CURLING
## (Sweeps only)

| TIME (min) | POINT VALUE |
|---|---|
| 15:00 | 1.5 |
| 30:00 | 3.0 |
| 45:00 | 4.5 |
| 60:00 | 6.0 |

*Note:* For times greater than 1 hour, figure points at a rate of 1½ points/15 minutes.

# FENCING

| TIME (hr:min:sec) | POINT VALUE |
|---|---|
| 10:00 | 1 |
| 20:00 | 2 |
| 30:00 | 3 |
| 40:00 | 4 |
| 50:00 | 5 |
| 1:00:00 | 6 |
| 1:10:00 | 7 |
| 1:20:00 | 8 |
| 1:30:00 | 9 |
| 1:40:00 | 10 |
| 1:50:00 | 11 |
| 2:00:00 | 12 |

*Note:* For times greater than 2 hours, figure points at a rate of 1 point/10 minutes.

## FOOTBALL

| TIME (hr:min:sec) | POINT VALUE |
|---|---|
| under 4:59 | 0 |
| 5:00– 9:59 | 0.5 |
| 10:00– 14:59 | 1.0 |
| 15:00– 19:59 | 1.5 |
| 20:00– 24:59 | 2.0 |
| 25:00– 29:59 | 2.5 |
| 30:00– 34:59 | 3.0 |
| 35:00– 39:59 | 3.5 |
| 40:00– 44:59 | 4.0 |
| 45:00– 49:59 | 4.5 |
| 50:00– 54:59 | 5.0 |
| 55:00– 59:59 | 5.5 |
| 1:00:00–1:04:59 | 6.0 |
| 1:05:00–1:09:59 | 6.5 |
| 1:10:00–1:14:59 | 7.0 |
| 1:15:00–1:19:59 | 7.5 |
| 1:20:00–1:24:59 | 8.0 |
| 1:25:00–1:29:59 | 8.5 |
| 1:30:00–1:34:59 | 9.0 |
| 1:35:00–1:39:59 | 9.5 |
| 1:40:00–1:44:59 | 10.0 |
| 1:45:00–1:49:59 | 10.5 |
| 1:50:00–1:54:59 | 11.0 |
| 1:55:00–1:59:59 | 11.5 |
| over 2:00:00 | 12.0 |

*Note:* Count only the time you are actively participating. For times greater than 2 hours, figure points at a rate of 2 points/10 minutes.

## WRESTLING AND BOXING

| TIME (min:sec) | POINT VALUE |
|---|---|
| under 4:59 | 0 |
| 5:00– 9:59 | 2.0 |
| 10:00–14:59 | 4.0 |
| 15:00–19:59 | 6.0 |
| 20:00–24:59 | 8.0 |
| 25:00–29:59 | 10.0 |
| 30:00–34:59 | 12.0 |
| 35:00–39:59 | 14.0 |
| 40:00–44:59 | 16.0 |
| 45:00–49:59 | 18.0 |
| 50:00–54:59 | 20.0 |
| 55:00–59:59 | 22.0 |
| over 60:00 | 24.0 |

*Note:* For times greater than 1 hour, figure points at a rate of 4 points/10 minutes.

## CALISTHENICS

| TIME (min) | POINT VALUE |
|---|---|
| 10:00 | 0.25 |
| 20:00 | 0.50 |
| 30:00 | 0.75 |
| 40:00 | 1.00 |
| 50:00 | 1.25 |
| 60:00 | 1.50 |

*Note:* These are continuous, repetitive calisthenics that are more stretching than muscle-strengthening.

## WALKING OR RUNNING ONE MILE ON A MOTORIZED TREADMILL
### (No incline)

| TIME (min:sec) | SPEED (mph) | POINT VALUE |
|---|---|---|
| 6:00 | 10 | 6 |
| 6:30 | 9.25 | 6 |
| 7:00 | 8.5 | 5 |
| 7:30 | 8 | 5 |
| 8:00 | 7.5 | 5 |
| 8:30 | 7 | 4 |
| 9:00 | 6.66 | 4 |
| 9:30 | 6.33 | 4 |
| 10:00 | 6 | 4 |
| 12:00 | 5 | 3 |
| 13:30 | 4.5 | 2 |
| 15:00 | 4 | 1 |
| 17:30 | 3.5 | 1 |
| 20:00 | 3 | 1 |

### (Treadmill set at various inclines)

| TIME (min:sec) | SPEED (mph) | 0% | 5% | INCLINE 10% | 15% | 20% |
|---|---|---|---|---|---|---|
| | | | | POINT VALUE | | |
| 6:00 | 10 | 6.00 | 7.33 | 9.33 | 13.33 | 20.00 |
| 8:00 | 7.5 | 5.00 | 5.50 | 7.00 | 10.00 | 15.00 |
| 10:00 | 6 | 4.00 | 4.40 | 5.60 | 8.00 | 12.00 |
| 12:00 | 5 | 3.00 | 3.30 | 4.20 | 6.00 | 9.00 |
| 14:30 | 4.14 | 2.14 | 2.35 | 3.00 | 4.28 | 6.42 |
| 20:00 | 3 | 1.00 | 1.10 | 1.40 | 2.00 | 3.00 |
| 25:00 | 2.4 | 0.40 | 0.44 | 0.56 | 0.80 | 1.20 |

# WALKING OR RUNNING ONE MILE AT VARIOUS ALTITUDES

| TIME (min:sec) | | POINT VALUE |
|---|---|---|
| **Standard** | **5,000 Feet** | |
| 10:59–14:30 | 20:29–15:00 | 1 |
| 14:29–12:00 | 14:59–12:30 | 2 |
| 11:59–10:00 | 12:29–10:30 | 3 |
| 9:59– 8:00 | 10:29– 8:30 | 4 |
| 7:59– 6:30 | 8:29– 7:00 | 5 |
| under  6:30 | under  7:00 | 6 |
| **8,000 Feet** | **12,000 Feet** | |
| 20:59–15:30 | 21:29–16:30 | 1 |
| 15:29–13:00 | 16:29–14:00 | 2 |
| 12:59–11:00 | 13:59–12:00 | 3 |
| 10:59– 9:00 | 11:59–10:00 | 4 |
| 8:59– 7:30 | 9:59– 8:30 | 5 |
| under  7:30 | under  8:30 | 6 |

## PREDICTED MAXIMUM HEART RATES ADJUSTED FOR AGE AND FITNESS

| AGE | VERY POOR AND POOR | FAIR | GOOD AND EXCELLENT | AGE | VERY POOR AND POOR | FAIR | GOOD AND EXCELLENT |
|---|---|---|---|---|---|---|---|
| 20 | 201 | 201 | 196 | 45 | 174 | 183 | 183 |
| 21 | 199 | 200 | 196 | 46 | 173 | 182 | 183 |
| 22 | 198 | 199 | 195 | 47 | 172 | 181 | 182 |
| 23 | 197 | 198 | 195 | 48 | 171 | 181 | 182 |
| 24 | 196 | 198 | 194 | 49 | 170 | 180 | 181 |
| 25 | 195 | 197 | 194 | 50 | 168 | 179 | 180 |
| 26 | 194 | 196 | 193 | 51 | 167 | 179 | 180 |
| 27 | 193 | 196 | 193 | 52 | 166 | 178 | 179 |
| 28 | 192 | 195 | 192 | 53 | 165 | 177 | 179 |
| 29 | 191 | 193 | 192 | 54 | 164 | 176 | 178 |
| 30 | 190 | 193 | 191 | 55 | 163 | 176 | 178 |
| 31 | 189 | 193 | 191 | 56 | 162 | 175 | 177 |
| 32 | 188 | 192 | 190 | 57 | 161 | 174 | 177 |
| 33 | 187 | 191 | 189 | 58 | 160 | 174 | 176 |
| 34 | 186 | 191 | 189 | 59 | 159 | 173 | 176 |
| 35 | 184 | 190 | 188 | 60 | 158 | 172 | 175 |
| 36 | 183 | 189 | 188 | 61 | 157 | 172 | 175 |
| 37 | 182 | 189 | 187 | 62 | 156 | 171 | 174 |
| 38 | 181 | 188 | 187 | 63 | 155 | 170 | 174 |
| 39 | 180 | 187 | 186 | 64 | 154 | 169 | 173 |
| 40 | 179 | 186 | 186 | 65 | 152 | 169 | 173 |
| 41 | 178 | 186 | 185 | 66 | 151 | 168 | 172 |
| 42 | 177 | 185 | 185 | 67 | 150 | 167 | 171 |
| 43 | 176 | 184 | 184 | 68 | 149 | 167 | 171 |
| 44 | 175 | 184 | 184 | 69 | 148 | 166 | 170 |
|  |  |  |  | 70 | 147 | 165 | 170 |

*Note:* If the level of fitness is unknown prior to stress testing, use the "Fair" category.

# POINTS VERSUS METS AS MEASUREMENTS OF PHYSICAL ACTIVITY

Aerobic Points are estimates of the energy cost of various types of physical activity. One aerobic point is the equivalent of an oxygen cost (in excess of the resting oxygen consumption) of approximately 7 ml/kg/min. (milliliters of oxygen per kilogram of body weight per minute). Therefore, running a mile in 6:30 minutes requires an energy expenditure (above resting) of 42.0 ml/kg/min., and a point value of 6 is given. For running a mile between 6:30 and 8:00 minutes, 5 points are awarded, since points are given for the slowest time in an interval, and the energy cost to run a mile in 8:00 minutes is 35.8 ml/kg/min. It is important to note that points are awarded in a stepwise rather than a linear manner. In some instances, fewer points are awarded than the exercise actually deserves, but ultimately, more effort is required to reach the 24–30 point-per-week goal. This assures the achievement of an age-adjusted maximum oxygen consumption of at least 36–42 ml/kg/min.

Aerobic points are not strictly rate measurements, but are dependent upon both the intensity and duration of the activity. METs (an acronym for Multiples of the Resting Energy requirement) are rate measurements only.

At a distance of one mile, METs and points are equally related; i.e., 1 point is worth approximately 3 METs. For example, running a mile in 6:00 minutes is worth 6 points, and this is equivalent to a 17-MET activity. However, running 2 miles in less than 12:00 minutes is worth 13 points, but this is a 17-, not a 39-, MET activity.

If a physician wishes to restrict his patient to a certain MET level of activity, it is still possible to use the Aerobic point system and work up to 30 points per week. For example, if a patient is restricted to physical activity not to exceed 6 METs, he can accumulate 32 points by walking 3 miles in less than 43:30 minutes four times weekly. For a comparison of MET activity versus Aerobic points, the following chart for walking, jogging, and running has been developed.

*Note:* The MET values were taken from *Exercise Testing and Training of Individuals with Heart Disease or at High Risk for Its Development: A Handbook for Physicians* (© 1975). Reprinted with permission of the American Heart Association.

## 3-MET Activity

| WALKING (miles) | TIME (min:sec) | POINT VALUE |
|---|---|---|
| 1 | 20:00 (3 mph) | 1 |
| 2 | 40:00 | 3 |
| 3 | 60:00 | 5 |

## 6-MET Activity

| WALKING (miles) | TIME (min:sec) | POINT VALUE |
|---|---|---|
| 1 | 14:30 (4¼ mph) | 2 |
| 2 | 29:00 | 5 |
| 3 | 43:30 | 8 |

## 8-MET Activity

| WALKING AND JOGGING (miles) | TIME (min) | POINT VALUE |
|---|---|---|
| 1 | 12:00 (5 mph) | 3 |
| 2 | 24:00 | 7 |
| 3 | 36:00 | 11 |

## 10-MET Activity

| JOGGING (miles) | TIME (min) | POINT VALUE |
|---|---|---|
| 1 | 10:00 (6 mph) | 4 |
| 2 | 20:00 | 9 |
| 3 | 30:00 | 14 |

## 17-MET Activity

| RUNNING (miles) | TIME (min) | POINT VALUE |
|---|---|---|
| 1 | 6:00 (10 mph) | 6 |
| 2 | 12:00 | 13 |
| 3 | 18:00 | 20 |

## CORONARY RISK FACTOR CHARTS

To use the following coronary risk factor charts, select the chart according to your age and sex. Review the chart with your physician and together complete the various requirements. Determine the weighting for each factor and place that number in the appropriate box. Total both the horizontal and vertical numbers to determine the overall coronary risk.

*Preliminary* data suggest that a coronary problem (e.g., sudden death, development of angina, heart attack, or need for a coronary bypass procedure) may occur over the next five years with the following frequency:

| | |
|---|---|
| Very low | less than 2% |
| Low | less than 10% |
| Moderate | up to 40% |
| High | up to 70% |
| Very high | over 70% |

Changing the risk increases or decreases the risk accordingly.

*Note:* If underwater weighing or displacement techniques are not available for percent body fat determination, skinfold measurements can be used. This technique is described on page 278.

If either the Bruce or Ellestad treadmill tests are used, estimate the time from the nomogram on page 277. As a general rule, the treadmill time can also be estimated from the 2-mile-run times, as follows:

| TIME FOR 2 MILES (min) | BALKE TREADMILL TIME (min) |
|---|---|
| 24:00 | 12:00 |
| 20:00 | 15:00 |
| 16:00 | 18:00–19:00 |
| 14:30 | 22:00–23:00 |
| <14:00 | 25:00 |

# COOPER CLINIC / Dallas, Texas — Fitness Level and Coronary Risk Profile

Name: _____

## MALES: *UNDER 30 YEARS OF AGE

| PERCENTILE RANKINGS (YOUR VALUES) | BALKE TREADMILL TIME (min.) | CHOLESTEROL (mg. %) | TRIGLYCERIDE (mg. %) | GLUCOSE (mg. %) | URIC ACID (mg. %) | % BODY FAT | RESTING HEART RATE (bpm) | RESTING BLOOD PRESSURE SYSTOLIC (mm Hg) | RESTING BLOOD PRESSURE DIASTOLIC (mm Hg) |
|---|---|---|---|---|---|---|---|---|---|
| 99 | 29:00 | 120.2 | 27.2 | 74.9 | 4.4 | 7.2 | 39.7 | 94.2 | 59.6 |
| 95 | 25:00 | 142.2 | 48.4 | 83.4 | 4.9 | 9.6 | 45.8 | 102.3 | 64.3 |
| 90 | 22:30 | 153.7 | 55.3 | 87.9 | 5.4 | 11.6 | 50.0 | 109.7 | 69.8 |
| 85 | 22:00 | 160.2 | 61.8 | 89.8 | 5.6 | 12.9 | 52.1 | 110.3 | 70.3 |
| 80 | 21:00 | 164.9 | 66.2 | 92.6 | 5.8 | 13.9 | 54.4 | 112.3 | 72.3 |
| 75 | 20:00 | 171.6 | 71.3 | 94.9 | 5.9 | 15.3 | 55.9 | 116.4 | 74.5 |
| 70 | 20:00 | 178.0 | 76.2 | 96.0 | 6.1 | 16.2 | 57.6 | 118.3 | 77.6 |
| 65 | 19:00 | 185.1 | 82.2 | 98.2 | 6.2 | 17.1 | 59.2 | 119.7 | 78.2 |
| 60 | 18:25 | 190.4 | 87.2 | 99.7 | 6.4 | 18.0 | 60.1 | 120.0 | 79.6 |
| 55 | 18:00 | 194.7 | 92.8 | 100.2 | 6.5 | 19.1 | 61.7 | 120.2 | 79.8 |
| 50 | 17:10 | 199.2 | 99.7 | 102.0 | 6.7 | 20.1 | 62.8 | 120.5 | 80.0 |
| 45 | 17:00 | 202.5 | 110.0 | 103.1 | 6.8 | 21.2 | 64.3 | 123.9 | 80.2 |
| 40 | 16:00 | 206.8 | 123.1 | 104.3 | 7.0 | 22.3 | 65.5 | 127.7 | 80.4 |
| 35 | 15:30 | 211.2 | 135.6 | 104.9 | 7.1 | 23.4 | 67.7 | 129.7 | 81.8 |
| 30 | 16:00 | 217.8 | 148.1 | 105.3 | 7.3 | 25.4 | 69.5 | 130.1 | 83.9 |
| 25 | 14:55 | 222.1 | 169.9 | 106.3 | 7.5 | 27.4 | 70.5 | 131.9 | 86.4 |
| 20 | 13:45 | 228.9 | 180.3 | 109.2 | 7.7 | 28.6 | 72.4 | 136.2 | 87.9 |
| 15 | 12:50 | 240.3 | 199.9 | 110.3 | 8.0 | 30.5 | 76.3 | 139.6 | 89.9 |
| 10 | 12:00 | 250.5 | 234.4 | 113.1 | 8.3 | 32.8 | 80.4 | 140.4 | 90.4 |
| 5 | 10:00 | 268.9 | 296.0 | 117.6 | 9.0 | 39.0 | 87.9 | 149.6 | 99.5 |
| 1 | 7:00 | 300.1 | 761.8 | 123.1 | 10.1 | 49.0 | 99.7 | 158.3 | 109.7 |
| POP. SIZE | 371 | 273 | 271 | 271 | 271 | 248 | 358 | 367 | 367 |
| AVERAGE | 17:21 | 200.3 | 132.7 | 100.8 | 6.7 | 21.6 | 64.3 | 124.2 | 80.3 |
| STANDARD DEVIATION | 4:25 | 39.1 | 107.8 | 14.5 | 1.2 | 9.1 | 12.5 | 13.4 | 9.6 |
| NORMAL LIMITS** | 19:00* | (250.0) | (135.0) | (110.0) | (8.0) | (19.0) | (72.0) | (140.0) | (90.0) |

*Data based on first visit only
**Upper limits generally accepted by most physicians

© Institute for Aerobics Research — 1977

---

### PERSONAL HISTORY OF HEART ATTACK
- 0 ☐ NONE
- 2 ☐ OVER 5 YEARS AGO
- 5 ☐ 2 - 5 YEARS AGO
- ☐ 1 - 2 YEARS AGO
- ☐ 0 - 1 YEARS AGO

### FAMILY HISTORY OF HEART ATTACK
- 0 ☐ NONE
- 2 ☐ YES, OVER 50 YEARS
- 4 ☐ YES, 50 YEARS OR UNDER

### SMOKING HABITS
- 0 ☐ NONE
- 1 ☐ PIPE/CIGAR
- 1 ☐ PAST ONLY/QUIT
- 2 ☐ 1 - 10 DAILY
- 3 ☐ 11 - 20 DAILY
- ☐ 20+ DAILY

### TENSION — ANXIETY
- 0 ☐ NO TENSION, VERY RELAXED
- 0 ☐ SLIGHT TENSION
- 1 ☐ MODERATE TENSION
- 2 ☐ HIGH TENSION
- 3 ☐ VERY TENSE, "HIGH STRUNG"

### RESTING ECG / EXERCISE ECG
- 0 ☐ NORMAL (NEGATIVE) ☐ 0
- ☐ EQUIVOCAL (BORDERLINE) ☐ 4
- ☐ ABNORMAL (POSITIVE) ☐ 8

### AGE FACTOR
- 0 ☐ UNDER 30 YEARS OF AGE
- 1 ☐ 30 - 39 YEARS OF AGE
- 2 ☐ 40 - 49 YEARS OF AGE
- 3 ☐ 50 - 59 YEARS OF AGE
- 4 ☐ 60+ YEARS OF AGE

### TOTAL CORONARY RISK
- ☐ VERY LOW ( 0 - 4 )
- ☐ LOW ( 5 - 14 )
- ☐ MODERATE (15 - 24)
- ☐ HIGH (25 - 34)
- ☐ VERY HIGH (35+)

# COOPER CLINIC / Dallas, Texas — Fitness Level and Coronary Risk Profile

Name: _____

## MALES: "30-39 YEARS OF AGE"

| PERCENTILE RANKINGS / VALUE % | BALKE TREADMILL TIME (min) | CHOLESTEROL (mg.%) | TRIGLYCERIDE (mg.%) | GLUCOSE (mg.%) | URIC ACID (mg.%) | % BODY FAT | RESTING HEART RATE (bpm) | BLOOD PRESSURE SYSTOLIC (mm Hg) | BLOOD PRESSURE DIASTOLIC (mm Hg) |
|---|---|---|---|---|---|---|---|---|---|
| 99 | 27:00 | 134.8 | 34.8 | 74.9 | 4.0 | 7.1 | 39.9 | 95.9 | 59.8 |
| 95 | 24:00 | 157.8 | 49.8 | 84.7 | 4.8 | 11.3 | 46.3 | 102.2 | 67.9 |
| 90 | 22:00 | 163.3 | 59.6 | 88.7 | 5.3 | 13.4 | 50.0 | 106.3 | 69.9 |
| 85 | 21:00 | 175.4 | 66.9* | 90.6 | 5.6 | 14.8 | 52.4 | 109.9 | 70.4 |
| 80 | 20:00 | 181.8 | 74.7 | 93.6 | 5.8 | 16.2 | 54.5 | 110.4 | 73.9 |
| 75 | 19:00 | 188.1 | 79.9 | 94.9 | 5.9 | 17.2 | 56.0 | 114.0 | 75.6 |
| 70 | 18:10 | 192.3 | 86.9 | 96.0 | 6.1 | 18.2 | 57.8 | 116.3 | 78.0 |
| 66 | 18:00 | 197.4 | 93.1 | 96.7 | 6.3 | 19.2 | 59.3 | 118.3 | 79.8 |
| 60 | 17:00 | 203.1 | 99.8 | 99.8 | 6.4 | 20.1 | 60.0 | 119.7 | 79.8 |
| 55 | 17:00 | 208.1 | 105.1 | 100.3 | 6.6 | 21.1 | 61.5 | 120.0 | 80.0 |
| 50 | 16:00 | 214.6 | 112.5 | 101.7 | 6.7 | 22.0 | 62.5 | 120.2 | 80.1 |
| 45 | 16:00 | 219.6 | 120.1 | 103.5 | 6.9 | 22.8 | 64.1 | 121.5 | 80.3 |
| 40 | 15:00 | 224.3 | 129.3 | 104.8 | 7.1 | 23.6 | 65.1 | 123.8 | 80.5 |
| 35 | 15:00 | 229.5 | 139.7 | 105.3 | 7.2 | 24.4 | 66.6 | 125.9 | 83.9 |
| 33 | 14:10 | 234.6 | 150.0 | 106.7 | 7.4 | 25.5 | 68.3 | 129.6 | 84.7 |
| 25 | 13:40 | 240.1 | 163.7 | 109.6 | 7.5 | 26.4 | 70.2 | 130.1 | 87.5 |
| 20 | 13:00 | 249.6 | 189.9 | 110.3 | 7.8 | 28.3 | 72.0 | 132.0 | 89.6 |
| 15 | 12:00 | 256.1 | 208.7 | 113.3 | 8.1 | 29.3 | 74.4 | 137.5 | 90.1 |
| 10 | 11:00 | 270.5 | 240.8 | 115.4 | 8.4 | 32.2 | 77.3 | 140.0 | 92.3 |
| 5 | 9:40 | 289.2 | 323.7 | 120.2 | 9.0 | 36.0 | 82.4 | 145.3 | 99.7 |
| 1 | 7:00 | 339.6 | 755.7 | 133.3 | 10.1 | 45.9 | 95.3 | 168.4 | 109.9 |
| POP. SIZE | 1632 | 1387 | 1377 | 1376 | 1375 | 1223 | 1538 | 1615 | 1615 |
| AVERAGE | 16:25 | 216.7 | 143.4 | 102.5 | 6.7 | 22.4 | 63.4 | 122.8 | 61.3 |
| STANDARD DEVIATION | 4:17 | 41.2 | 114.0 | 18.2 | 1.2 | 7.9 | 11.0 | 13.6 | 9.6 |
| "NORMAL"** | 18:00* | (250.0) | (135.0) | (110.0) | (8.0) | (19.0) | (72.0) | (140.0) | (90.0) |

*Data based on first visit only
**Upper limits generally accepted by most physicians

### PERSONAL HISTORY OF HEART ATTACK
- 0 □ NONE
- 0 □ OVER 5 YEARS AGO
- 3 □ 2-5 YEARS AGO
- 5 □ 1-2 YEARS AGO
- 6 □ 0-1 YEARS AGO
- -8 □

### FAMILY HISTORY OF HEART ATTACK
- 0 □ NONE
- 2 □ YES, OVER 50 YEARS
- 4 □ YES, 50 YEARS OR UNDER

### SMOKING HABITS
- 0 □ NONE
- 1 □ PIPE/CIGAR
- 1 □ PAST ONLY/QUIT
- 2 □ 1-10 DAILY
- 3 □ 11-20 DAILY
- 4 □ 20+ DAILY

### TENSION — ANXIETY
- 0 □ NO TENSION, VERY RELAXED
- 0 □ SLIGHT TENSION
- 1 □ MODERATE TENSION
- 2 □ HIGH TENSION
- 3 □ VERY TENSE, "HIGH STRUNG"

### RESTING ECG / EXERCISE ECG
- 0 □ NORMAL / 0 □ NORMAL
- 1 □ EQUIVOCAL (BORDERLINE) / 4 □
- 3 □ ABNORMAL (POSITIVE) / 8 □

### AGE FACTOR
- 0 □ UNDER 30 YEARS OF AGE
- 1 □ 30-39 YEARS OF AGE
- 2 □ 40-49 YEARS OF AGE
- 3 □ 50-59 YEARS OF AGE
- 6 □ 60+ YEARS OF AGE

### TOTAL CORONARY RISK
- □ VERY LOW (0-4)
- □ LOW (5-14)
- □ MODERATE (15-24)
- □ HIGH (25-34)
- □ VERY HIGH (35+)

© Institute for Aerobics Research - 1977

# COOPER CLINIC / Dallas, Texas — Fitness Level and Coronary Risk Profile

**MALES: 40-49 YEARS OF AGE**

| PERCENTILE RANKINGS / YOUR VALUES | BALKE TREADMILL TIME (min.) | CHOLESTEROL (mg. %) | TRIGLYCERIDE (mg. %) | GLUCOSE (mg. %) | URIC ACID (mg. %) | % BODY FAT | RESTING HEART RATE (bpm) | RESTING BLOOD PRESSURE SYSTOLIC (mm Hg) | RESTING BLOOD PRESSURE DIASTOLIC (mm Hg) |
|---|---|---|---|---|---|---|---|---|---|
| 99 | 26:00 | 145.1 | 36.8 | 79.8 | 3.8 | 9.2 | 42.0 | 98.4 | 59.9 |
| 95 | 23:00 | 165.1 | 53.3 | 87.3 | 4.7 | 13.0 | 46.6 | 103.9 | 69.6 |
| 90 | 21:00 | 175.3 | 63.0 | 90.1 | 5.1 | 14.9 | 50.0 | 109.6 | 70.2 |
| 85 | 20:00 | 185.9 | 71.8 | 93.1 | 5.5 | 16.8 | 52.2 | 110.1 | 73.9 |
| 80 | 19:00 | 193.0 | 77.8 | 95.1 | 5.7 | 17.7 | 54.3 | 110.5 | 75.7 |
| 75 | 18:00 | 198.7 | 84.8 | 97.4 | 5.9 | 18.8 | 55.7 | 114.5 | 78.0 |
| 70 | 17:20 | 203.5 | 90.5 | 98.4 | 6.0 | 19.7 | 57.5 | 117.8 | 79.8 |
| 65 | 17:00 | 209.3 | 98.2 | 100.0 | 6.2 | 20.7 | 58.4 | 119.6 | 79.7 |
| 60 | 18:00 | 214.2 | 105.1 | 100.7 | 6.4 | 21.6 | 59.9 | 119.9 | 80.0 |
| 55 | 16:30 | 219.8 | 112.3 | 103.0 | 6.5 | 22.2 | 60.5 | 120.2 | 80.2 |
| 50 | 16:00 | 224.5 | 120.6 | 104.7 | 6.7 | 23.0 | 62.2 | 120.5 | 80.4 |
| 45 | 14:40 | 229.7 | 129.5 | 105.3 | 6.8 | 23.8 | 63.9 | 123.9 | 82.1 |
| 40 | 14:00 | 234.8 | 138.5 | 106.8 | 7.0 | 24.6 | 65.1 | 125.9 | 84.0 |
| 35 | 13:30 | 239.9 | 149.7 | 108.9 | 7.1 | 25.4 | 67.0 | 129.5 | 85.2 |
| 30 | 13:00 | 245.0 | 162.2 | 109.9 | 7.3 | 26.3 | 69.4 | 130.0 | 87.8 |
| 25 | 12:00 | 250.1 | 180.0 | 110.5 | 7.4 | 27.4 | 71.2 | 130.5 | 89.7 |
| 20 | 11:40 | 256.5 | 200.4 | 114.2 | 7.7 | 28.5 | 72.3 | 137.6 | 90.1 |
| 15 | 11:00 | 265.3 | 226.8 | 116.4 | 8.0 | 30.0 | 74.9 | 138.8 | 91.9 |
| 10 | 9:45 | 275.1 | 268.8 | 119.9 | 8.3 | 32.2 | 78.3 | 141.8 | 97.8 |
| 5 | 7:56 | 294.8 | 363.3 | 125.3 | 8.9 | 36.1 | 83.6 | 150.2 | 100.0 |
| 1 | 5:15 | 337.7 | 589.9 | 159.9 | 9.8 | 44.4 | 90.2 | 165.6 | 110.0 |
| POP. SIZE | 1898 | 1881 | 1665 | 1662 | 1663 | 1537 | 1826 | 1880 | 1890 |
| AVERAGE | 15:16 | 226.0 | 191.3 | 105.8 | 6.7 | 23.4 | 63.6 | 124.4 | 83.0 |
| STANDARD DEVIATION | 4:28 | 39.7 | 110.5 | 21.0 | 1.2 | 7.1 | 11.5 | 14.5 | 10.0 |
| WTC VAL** | 17:00* | <250.0 | <135.0 | <110.0 | <9.0 | <19.0 | <72.0 | <140.0 | <90.0 |

*This is not a first or last entry
**Upper limits generally accepted by most physicians

## PERSONAL HISTORY OF HEART ATTACK
- 0 □ NONE
- 2 □ OVER 5 YEARS AGO
- 3 □ 2-5 YEARS AGO
- 5 □ 1-2 YEARS AGO
- 8 □ 1 YEARS AGO

## FAMILY HISTORY OF HEART ATTACK
- 0 □ NONE
- 2 □ YES, OVER 50 YEARS
- 4 □ YES, 50 YEARS OR UNDER

## SMOKING HABITS
- 0 □ NONE
- 1 □ PIPE/CIGAR
- 2 □ PAST ONLY/YOU'T
- 3 □ 1-10 DAILY
- 3 □ 11-20 DAILY
- 3 □ 20+ DAILY

## TENSION — ANXIETY
- 0 □ NO TENSION, VERY RELAXED
- 0 □ SLIGHT TENSION
- 1 □ MODERATE TENSION
- 2 □ HIGH TENSION
- 3 □ VERY TENSE, "HIGH STRUNG"

## RESTING ECG    EXERCISE ECG
- 0 □ NORMAL (NEGATIVE)
- 1 □ EQUIVOCAL (BORDERLINE) □ 4
- 2 □ ABNORMAL (POSITIVE) □ 8

## AGE FACTOR
- 0 □ UNDER 30 YEARS OF AGE
- 1 □ 30-39 YEARS OF AGE
- 2 □ 40-49 YEARS OF AGE
- 3 □ 50-59 YEARS OF AGE
- 4 □ 60+ YEARS OF AGE

## TOTAL CORONARY RISK
- VERY LOW (0-4)
- LOW (5-10)
- MODERATE (11-20)
- HIGH (21-30)
- VERY HIGH (31+)

© Institute for Aerobics Research — 1977

# COOPER CLINIC / Dallas, Texas — Fitness Level and Coronary Risk Profile

Name: _____

## MALES: *50-59 YEARS OF AGE

| PERCENTILE RANKINGS | BALKE TREADMILL TIME (min.) | CHOLESTEROL (mg.%) | TRIGLYCERIDE (mg.%) | GLUCOSE (mg.%) | URIC ACID (mg.%) | % BODY FAT | RESTING HEART RATE (bpm) | RESTING BLOOD PRESSURE SYSTOLIC (mm Hg) | DIASTOLIC (mm Hg) |
|---|---|---|---|---|---|---|---|---|---|
| 99 | 25:05 | 148.7 | 44.2 | 80.4 | 3.7 | 9.0 | 42.1 | 98.2 | 60.2 |
| 95 | 21:15 | 173.0 | 55.1 | 88.1 | 4.6 | 13.1 | 46.7 | 105.2 | 69.8 |
| 90 | 20:00 | 185.0 | 67.4 | 91.5 | 5.0 | 15.8 | 49.8 | 110.1 | 71.6 |
| 85 | 18:00 | 193.3 | 74.7 | 94.7 | 5.4 | 17.4 | 52.4 | 113.6 | 75.1 |
| 80 | 17:00 | 200.5 | 82.5 | 96.0 | 5.8 | 18.4 | 54.7 | 116.3 | 77.7 |
| 75 | 16:00 | 205.4 | 89.0 | 99.2 | 5.8 | 19.6 | 56.0 | 115.5 | 79.6 |
| 70 | 16:15 | 210.6 | 94.7 | 99.9 | 5.9 | 20.4 | 57.7 | 119.9 | 79.8 |
| 65 | 15:00 | 215.4 | 100.2 | 100.5 | 6.1 | 21.4 | 59.3 | 120.2 | 60.0 |
| 60 | 14:10 | 220.3 | 106.7 | 102.7 | 6.2 | 22.1 | 60.1 | 121.9 | 80.2 |
| 55 | 13:45 | 225.3 | 115.9 | 104.8 | 6.4 | 22.9 | 61.7 | 124.6 | 80.4 |
| 50 | 13:00 | 230.1 | 123.5 | 105.4 | 6.6 | 23.8 | 62.5 | 127.9 | 82.2 |
| 45 | 12:30 | 235.0 | 132.5 | 107.8 | 6.7 | 24.8 | 63.8 | 129.6 | 84.2 |
| 40 | 12:00 | 240.0 | 142.3 | 109.7 | 6.9 | 25.4 | 64.8 | 130.2 | 85.5 |
| 35 | 11:30 | 245.0 | 153.2 | 110.3 | 7.0 | 26.1 | 66.4 | 132.4 | 87.9 |
| 30 | 11:00 | 250.0 | 165.4 | 112.5 | 7.2 | 27.0 | 68.2 | 137.8 | 89.6 |
| 25 | 10:10 | 265.4 | 185.2 | 116.3 | 7.6 | 28.0 | 70.1 | 139.8 | 90.0 |
| 20 | 10:00 | 263.9 | 200.3 | 118.2 | 7.8 | 29.1 | 72.1 | 140.3 | 90.4 |
| 15 | 9:00 | 274.1 | 229.6 | 119.9 | 7.9 | 30.9 | 74.6 | 144.2 | 95.3 |
| 10 | 8:00 | 284.8 | 299.7 | 124.4 | 8.2 | 32.8 | 76.9 | 150.2 | 99.6 |
| 5 | 6:00 | 299.9 | 369.6 | 134.6 | 8.8 | 35.9 | 82.1 | 159.8 | 101.9 |
| 1 | 3:30 | 344.1 | 690.1 | 160.2 | 9.9 | 44.8 | 94.6 | 180.3 | 114.1 |
| POP. SIZE | 1087 | 942 | 936 | 935 | 938 | 847 | 1046 | 1073 | 1073 |
| AVERAGE | 13:26 | 233.1 | 156.6 | 103.2 | 6.6 | 24.1 | 63.4 | 129.3 | 84.4 |
| STANDARD DEVIATION | 4:34 | 40.5 | 120.9 | 21.2 | 2.0 | 7.0 | 11.0 | 17.2 | 10.4 |
| **VALUE ** | 16:00* | (250.0) | (135.0) | (110.0) | (8.0) | (19.0) | (72.0) | (140.0) | (90.0) |

Percentile ranking groups (CORONARY RISK): VERY LOW / LOW (99–55), MODERATE (50–35), HIGH (30–15), VERY HIGH (10–1).

*Data based on first visit only
**Upper limits generally accepted by most physicians

---

**PERSONAL HISTORY OF HEART ATTACK**
- 0 □ NONE
- 2 □ OVER 8 YEARS AGO
- 3 □ 2-8 YEARS AGO
- 5 □ 1-2 YEARS AGO
- 8 □ 0-1 YEARS AGO

**FAMILY HISTORY OF HEART ATTACK**
- 0 □ NONE
- 2 □ YES, OVER 60 YEARS
- 4 □ YES, 50 YEARS OR UNDER

**SMOKING HABITS**
- 0 □ NONE
- 1 □ PIPE/CIGAR
- 1 □ PAST ONLY/QUIT
- 2 □ 1-10 DAILY
- 3 □ 11-30 DAILY
- 4 □ 30+ DAILY

**TENSION — ANXIETY**
- 0 □ NO TENSION, VERY RELAXED
- 1 □ SLIGHT TENSION
- 1 □ MODERATE TENSION
- 2 □ HIGH TENSION
- 3 □ VERY TENSE, "HIGH STRUNG"

**RESTING ECG          EXERCISE ECG**
- 0 □ NORMAL/NEGATIVE □ 0
- 1 □ EQUIVOCAL (BORDERLINE) □ 4
- 3 □ ABNORMAL (POSITIVE) □ 8

**AGE FACTOR**
- 0 □ UNDER 30 YEARS OF AGE
- 1 □ 30-39 YEARS OF AGE
- 2 □ 40-49 YEARS OF AGE
- 3 □ 50-59 YEARS OF AGE
- 4 □ 60+ YEARS OF AGE

**TOTAL CORONARY RISK**
- □ VERY LOW ( 0 - 4)
- □ LOW ( 5 - 14)
- □ MODERATE (15 - 24)
- □ HIGH (25 - 34)
- □ VERY HIGH (35+)

© Institute for Aerobics Research — 1977

# COOPER CLINIC / Dallas, Texas

# Fitness Level and Coronary Risk Profile

Name: _____

**MALES: 60+ YEARS OF AGE**

| PERCENTILE RANKINGS | BALKE TREADMILL TIME (min.) | CHOLESTEROL (mg.%) | TRIGLYCERIDE (mg.%) | GLUCOSE (mg.%) | URIC ACID (mg.%) | % BODY FAT | RESTING HEART RATE (bpm) | RESTING BLOOD PRESSURE SYSTOLIC (mm Hg) | RESTING BLOOD PRESSURE DIASTOLIC (mm Hg) |
|---|---|---|---|---|---|---|---|---|---|
| 99 | 24:00 | 151.9 | 42.9 | 82.7 | 4.0 | 10.5 | 38.3 | 98.3 | 59.7 |
| 95 | 20:38 | 172.7 | 54.5 | 89.5 | 4.7 | 12.3 | 48.2 | 108.4 | 67.8 |
| 90 | 18:00 | 180.4 | 65.6 | 91.5 | 5.0 | 14.1 | 51.6 | 112.4 | 70.0 |
| 85 | 15:45 | 189.7 | 73.1 | 94.4 | 5.4 | 16.2 | 54.0 | 117.8 | 72.0 |
| 80 | 15:00 | 196.3 | 76.2 | 96.1 | 5.6 | 17.2 | 55.0 | 119.7 | 75.7 |
| 75 | 14:30 | 200.5 | 81.8 | 99.9 | 5.7 | 18.0 | 55.9 | 120.2 | 78.0 |
| 70 | 13:30 | 205.4 | 88.8 | 101.5 | 5.9 | 18.9 | 57.6 | 124.0 | 79.6 |
| 65 | 12:30 | 209.7 | 94.8 | 103.6 | 6.0 | 19.9 | 58.3 | 127.9 | 79.8 |
| 60 | 11:40 | 214.1 | 100.2 | 104.9 | 6.2 | 20.8 | 59.7 | 129.7 | 80.0 |
| 55 | 11:00 | 217.3 | 108.0 | 106.0 | 6.3 | 21.5 | 60.3 | 130.1 | 80.2 |
| 50 | 10:00 | 224.6 | 114.7 | 108.0 | 6.4 | 22.3 | 62.0 | 130.5 | 80.5 |
| 45 | 10:00 | 228.3 | 122.4 | 109.7 | 6.6 | 23.3 | 63.8 | 135.0 | 83.6 |
| 40 | 9:00 | 234.4 | 129.1 | 110.2 | 6.8 | 24.4 | 65.1 | 139.5 | 84.3 |
| 35 | 8:50 | 240.0 | 142.2 | 112.4 | 7.0 | 25.4 | 66.5 | 140.0 | 86.3 |
| 30 | 8:00 | 249.8 | 150.0 | 115.2 | 7.2 | 26.9 | 68.2 | 140.4 | 88.3 |
| 25 | 7:00 | 255.8 | 150.1 | 117.6 | 7.4 | 28.0 | 70.3 | 144.6 | 89.9 |
| 20 | 6:30 | 263.7 | 170.4 | 119.9 | 7.6 | 28.9 | 71.9 | 149.8 | 90.3 |
| 15 | 5:30 | 288.4 | 195.4 | 123.5 | 8.0 | 30.1 | 74.7 | 152.3 | 94.0 |
| 10 | 4:00 | 279.7 | 233.4 | 129.0 | 8.3 | 32.5 | 76.8 | 160.0 | 97.9 |
| 5 | 3:00 | 300.5 | 290.5 | 139.8 | 8.9 | 35.6 | 80.5 | 167.8 | 100.3 |
| 1 | 2:00 | 345.1 | 652.1 | 170.3 | 10.3 | 42.4 | 93.8 | 183.8 | 117.8 |
| POP. SIZE | 279 | 243 | 241 | 241 | 211 | 240 | 207 | 275 | 275 |
| AVERAGE | 10:52 | 228.4 | 135.5 | 110.4 | 6.6 | 23.1 | 63.4 | 134.6 | 83.31 |
| STANDARD DEVIATION | 5:03 | 39.1 | 99.4 | 23.4 | 1.2 | 7.2 | 10.4 | 18.3 | 11.02 |
| NORMATIVE VALUE** | 12:30† | <250.0 | <135.0 | <115.0 | <9.0 | <19.0 | <72.0 | <140.0 | <90.0 |

Fitness categories (left margin, grouped by percentile): VERY HIGH, HIGH, MODERATE, LOW, VERY LOW — CORONARY RISK

*Data based on first visit only
**Upper limits generally accepted by most physicians

## CORONARY RISK PROFILE

**PERSONAL HISTORY OF HEART ATTACK**
- 0 ☐ NONE
- 2 ☐ OVER 5 YEARS AGO
- 4 ☐ 2-5 YEARS AGO
- 6 ☐ 1-2 YEARS AGO
- 8 ☐ -1 YEARS AGO

**FAMILY HISTORY OF HEART ATTACK**
- 0 ☐ NONE
- 2 ☐ YES, OVER 60 YEARS
- 4 ☐ YES, 60 YEARS OR UNDER

**SMOKING HABITS**
- 0 ☐ NONE
- 1 ☐ PIPE/CIGAR
- 2 ☐ PAST ONLY/QUIT
- 3 ☐ 1-10 DAILY
- ☐ 11-20 DAILY
- ☐ 20+ DAILY

**TENSION — ANXIETY**
- 0 ☐ NO TENSION, VERY RELAXED
- ☐ SLIGHT TENSION
- ☐ MODERATE TENSION
- ☐ HIGH TENSION
- ☐ VERY TENSE, "HIGH STRUNG"

**RESTING ECG / EXERCISE ECG**
- 0 ☐ NORMAL (NEGATIVE) ☐ 0
- 1 ☐ EQUIVOCAL (BORDERLINE) ☐ 4
- 3 ☐ ABNORMAL (POSITIVE) ☐ 8

**AGE FACTOR**
- 0 ☐ UNDER 30 YEARS OF AGE
- 1 ☐ 30-39 YEARS OF AGE
- 2 ☐ 40-49 YEARS OF AGE
- 3 ☐ 50-59 YEARS OF AGE
- 4 ☐ 60+ YEARS OF AGE

**TOTAL CORONARY RISK**
- ☐ VERY LOW (0- 4)
- ☐ LOW (5-10)
- ☐ MODERATE (11-24)
- ☐ HIGH (25-34)
- ☐ VERY HIGH (35+)

© Institute for Aerobics Research — 1977

# COOPER CLINIC / Dallas, Texas  —  Fitness Level and Coronary Risk Profile

Name: _____

## FEMALES: *UNDER 30 YEARS OF AGE

| PERCENTILE RANKINGS / YOUR VALUE | BALKE TREADMILL TIME (min.) | CHOLESTEROL (mg. %) | TRIGLYCERIDE (mg. %) | GLUCOSE (mg. %) | URIC ACID (mg. %) | % BODY FAT | RESTING HEART RATE (bpm) | RESTING BP SYSTOLIC (mm Hg) | RESTING BP DIASTOLIC (mm Hg) |
|---|---|---|---|---|---|---|---|---|---|
| 99 | 21:00 | 135.2 | 30.2 | 56.2 | 2.2 | 4.8 | 47.6 | 90.1 | 55.7 |
| 95 | 18:00 | 143.9 | 42.7 | 74.9 | 2.8 | 6.6 | 52.1 | 95.5 | 60.0 |
| 90 | 16:30 | 150.3 | 46.0 | 81.2 | 3.2 | 11.6 | 55.4 | 99.6 | 63.3 |
| 85 | 16:00 | 159.6 | 47.1 | 85.2 | 3.6 | 14.5 | 57.8 | 100.1 | 64.7 |
| 80 | 15:00 | 164.8 | 49.7 | 86.3 | 3.7 | 15.1 | 59.2 | 100.5 | 67.7 |
| 75 | 14:00 | 169.9 | 51.5 | 87.4 | 3.9 | 16.1 | 59.8 | 104.6 | 69.7 |
| 70 | 13:30 | 170.2 | 57.9 | 90.2 | 4.0 | 19.3 | 60.3 | 105.1 | 70.0 |
| 65 | 13:00 | 174.3 | 60.4 | 91.7 | 4.2 | 20.2 | 61.8 | 109.7 | 70.2 |
| 60 | 12:00 | 181.8 | 65.1 | 93.7 | 4.4 | 23.2 | 62.5 | 108.1 | 71.6 |
| 55 | 11:30 | 185.3 | 72.1 | 84.3 | 4.5 | 24.1 | 64.2 | 110.4 | 73.9 |
| 50 | 11:00 | 190.1 | 76.6 | 95.1 | 4.8 | 24.9 | 65.2 | 112.3 | 74.8 |
| 45 | 10:30 | 194.7 | 80.9 | 97.4 | 4.9 | 25.6 | 67.6 | 115.1 | 75.4 |
| 40 | 10:30 | 196.4 | 97.9 | 98.7 | 5.0 | 26.2 | 69.5 | 117.6 | 77.7 |
| 35 | 10:10 | 199.6 | 100.8 | 99.3 | 5.2 | 27.3 | 70.2 | 118.2 | 78.3 |
| 30 | 10:00 | 203.1 | 109.3 | 99.8 | 5.3 | 28.2 | 71.9 | 119.7 | 79.6 |
| 25 | 9:30 | 214.6 | 120.0 | 100.3 | 5.4 | 30.3 | 73.8 | 120.0 | 79.9 |
| 20 | 8:30 | 219.2 | 125.9 | 101.0 | 5.6 | 33.3 | 75.0 | 120.3 | 80.1 |
| 15 | 7:45 | 224.3 | 138.3 | 102.5 | 6.0 | 36.4 | 79.7 | 121.9 | 80.3 |
| 10 | 6:30 | 251.7 | 157.2 | 104.8 | 6.5 | 38.5 | 84.3 | 130.0 | 81.6 |
| 5 | 5:40 | 265.1 | 235.1 | 115.3 | 7.2 | 45.5 | 89.3 | 139.7 | 87.5 |
| 1 | 5:00 | 379.8 | 634.8 | 199.8 | 8.2 | 62.9 | 100.4 | 140.5 | 90.1 |
| POP. SIZE | 119 | 68 | 68 | 67 | 67 | 61 | 115 | 118 | 118 |
| AVERAGE | 11:37 | 195.4 | 101.5 | 96.0 | 4.6 | 25.0 | 67.4 | 113.5 | 73.8 |
| STANDARD DEVIATION | 3:40 | 41.8 | 89.7 | 20.9 | 1.1 | 11.2 | 12.0 | | 7.9 |
| NORMAL** | 13:00 | (250.0) | (135.0) | (110.0) | (8.0) | (22.0) | (72.0) | (140.0) | (90.0) |

*Data based on first visit only
**Upper limits generally accepted by most physicians

### PERSONAL HISTORY OF HEART ATTACK
- 0 □ NONE
- 2 □ OVER 5 YEARS AGO
- 3 □ 2-5 YEARS AGO
- 5 □ 1-2 YEARS AGO
- 6 □ 0-1 YEARS AGO

### FAMILY HISTORY OF HEART ATTACK
- 0 □ NONE
- 3 □ YES, OVER 60 YEARS
- 4 □ YES, 60 YEARS OR UNDER

### SMOKING HABITS
- 0 □ NONE
- 1 □ PIPE/CIGAR
- 0 □ PAST ONLY/QUIT?
- 2 □ 1-10 DAILY
- 3 □ 11-30 DAILY
- 4 □ 30+ DAILY

### TENSION - ANXIETY
- 0 □ NO TENSION, VERY RELAXED
- 1 □ SLIGHT TENSION
- 2 □ MODERATE TENSION
- 3 □ HIGH TENSION
- 4 □ VERY TENSE, "HIGH STRUNG"

### RESTING ECG / EXERCISE ECG
- 0 □ NORMAL (NEGATIVE)      0 □
- 1 □ EQUIVOCAL (BORDERLINE) 4 □
- 3 □ ABNORMAL (POSITIVE)    8 □

### AGE FACTOR
- 0 □ UNDER 30 YEARS OF AGE
- 1 □ 30-39 YEARS OF AGE
- 2 □ 40-49 YEARS OF AGE
- 3 □ 50-59 YEARS OF AGE
- 4 □ 60+ YEARS OF AGE

### TOTAL CORONARY RISK
- □ VERY LOW ( 0 - 4)
- □ LOW ( 5 - 14)
- □ MODERATE (15 - 24)
- □ HIGH (25 - 34)
- □ VERY HIGH (35+)

© Institute for Aerobics Research - 1977

Name: _____

**FEMALES: *30-39 YEARS OF AGE**

| PERCENTILE RANKINGS / YOUR VALUES | BALKE TREADMILL TIME (min.) | CHOLESTEROL (mg. %) | TRIGLYCERIDE (mg. %) | GLUCOSE (mg. %) | URIC ACID (mg. %) | % BODY FAT | RESTING HEART RATE (bpm) | RESTING BLOOD PRESSURE SYSTOLIC (mm Hg) | RESTING BLOOD PRESSURE DIASTOLIC (mm Hg) |
|---|---|---|---|---|---|---|---|---|---|
| 99 | 20:00 | 123.7 | 26.1 | 69.7 | 2.6 | 5.1 | 47.8 | 89.8 | 69.5 |
| 95 | 17:30 | 141.0 | 38.5 | 78.5 | 3.2 | 10.1 | 52.0 | 97.7 | 60.2 |
| 90 | 16:00 | 157.5 | 43.5 | 82.8 | 3.6 | 13.1 | 54.9 | 99.2 | 65.0 |
| 85 | 15:00 | 164.8 | 47.9 | 85.4 | 3.7 | 14.8 | 57.3 | 100.2 | 69.5 |
| 80 | 14:30 | 167.8 | 50.5 | 87.5 | 3.9 | 16.7 | 58.4 | 103.7 | 69.8 |
| 75 | 13:30 | 171.5 | 55.3 | 89.9 | 4.0 | 18.3 | 60.0 | 108.3 | 70.0 |
| 70 | 13:00 | 176.0 | 59.3 | 90.6 | 4.2 | 19.3 | 61.8 | 109.6 | 70.2 |
| 65 | 12:00 | 183.5 | 62.3 | 92.2 | 4.3 | 20.5 | 62.4 | 109.9 | 70.5 |
| 60 | 12:00 | 187.5 | 68.0 | 94.8 | 4.5 | 21.6 | 64.8 | 110.1 | 73.5 |
| 55 | 11:00 | 191.0 | 73.0 | 94.9 | 4.5 | 22.5 | 65.0 | 110.4 | 75.0 |
| 50 | 11:00 | 195.2 | 76.8 | 95.3 | 4.8 | 23.6 | 67.5 | 113.8 | 76.3 |
| 45 | 10:15 | 200.1 | 80.0 | 96.7 | 4.9 | 24.8 | 69.4 | 116.3 | 79.6 |
| 40 | 10:00 | 203.5 | 84.6 | 98.9 | 5.0 | 25.5 | 70.1 | 118.1 | 79.8 |
| 35 | 9:30 | 206.0 | 88.1 | 99.7 | 5.2 | 26.3 | 71.7 | 119.7 | 80.0 |
| 30 | 9:00 | 211.0 | 93.0 | 100.1 | 5.3 | 27.6 | 73.6 | 120.0 | 80.1 |
| 25 | 8:41 | 218.0 | 99.7 | 100.5 | 5.5 | 29.0 | 74.8 | 120.3 | 80.3 |
| 20 | 8:00 | 223.5 | 107.5 | 103.0 | 5.7 | 31.3 | 75.6 | 121.8 | 81.8 |
| 15 | 7:15 | 230.5 | 119.8 | 105.0 | 6.0 | 34.8 | 79.5 | 124.5 | 84.9 |
| 10 | 6:30 | 240.2 | 131.5 | 106.8 | 6.2 | 38.1 | 81.5 | 129.9 | 89.8 |
| 5 | 6:00 | 254.5 | 156.5 | 110.5 | 6.5 | 42.9 | 85.3 | 139.9 | 90.4 |
| 1 | 3:45 | 300.3 | 420.3 | 116.4 | 6.9 | 68.6 | 107.7 | 160.0 | 110.2 |
| POP. SIZE | 309 | 301 | 220 | 220 | 220 | 192 | 280 | 301 | 301 |
| AVERAGE | 11:07 | 197.0 | 88.6 | 95.2 | 4.8 | 24.8 | 66.1 | 114.7 | 76.6 |
| STANDARD DEVIATION | 3:36 | 38.0 | 68.0 | 14.3 | 1.1 | 11.0 | 11.5 | 13.3 | 9.9 |
| NORMAL LIMITS** | 12:00* | <250.0 | <135.0 | <110.0 | <8.0 | <22.0 | <72.0 | <140.0 | <90.0 |

*Data based on first visit only
**Upper limits generally accepted by most physicians

**PERSONAL HISTORY OF HEART ATTACK**
- 0 □ NONE
- 2 □ OVER 5 YEARS AGO
- 3 □ 2-5 YEARS AGO
- 4 □ 1-2 YEARS AGO
- 5 □ 0-1 YEARS AGO

**FAMILY HISTORY OF HEART ATTACK**
- 0 □ NONE
- 1 □ YES, OVER 60 YEARS
- 2 □ YES, 50-60 YEARS AGO
- 4 □ YES, 50 YEARS OR UNDER

**SMOKING HABITS**
- 0 □ NONE
- 1 □ PIPE/CIGAR
- 1 □ PAST ONLY/QUIT
- 2 □ 1-10 DAILY
- 3 □ 11-30 DAILY
- 4 □ 30+ DAILY

**TENSION - ANXIETY**
- 0 □ NO TENSION, VERY RELAXED
- 1 □ SLIGHT TENSION
- 2 □ MODERATE TENSION
- 0 □ HIGH TENSION
- 3 □ VERY TENSE, "HIGH STRUNG"

**RESTING ECG**
- 0 □ NORMAL (NEGATIVE)
- 1 □ EQUIVOCAL (BORDERLINE)
- 3 □ ABNORMAL (POSITIVE)

**EXERCISE ECG**
- 0 □
- 4 □
- □

**AGE FACTOR**
- 0 □ UNDER 30 YEARS OF AGE
- 1 □ 30-39 YEARS OF AGE
- 2 □ 40-49 YEARS OF AGE
- 3 □ 50-59 YEARS OF AGE
- 4 □ 60+ YEARS OF AGE

**TOTAL CORONARY RISK**
- □ VERY LOW (0-4)
- □ LOW (5-14)
- □ MODERATE (15-24)
- □ HIGH (25-34)
- □ VERY HIGH (35+)

© Institute for Aerobics Research — 1977

Name: _____

**FEMALES: *40-49 YEARS OF AGE**

| PERCENTILE RANKINGS / YOUR VALUES | BALKE TREADMILL TIME (min.) | CHOLESTEROL (mg. %) | TRIGLYCERIDE (mg. %) | GLUCOSE (mg. %) | URIC ACID (mg. %) | % BODY FAT | RESTING HEART RATE (bpm) | RESTING BLOOD PRESSURE SYSTOLIC (mm Hg) | DIASTOLIC (mm Hg) |
|---|---|---|---|---|---|---|---|---|---|
| 99 | 20:00 | 129.7 | 34.7 | 74.6 | 2.5 | 7.3 | 43.3 | 89.8 | 57.7 |
| 95 | 16:00 | 157.5 | 44.8 | 81.9 | 3.1 | 12.0 | 51.8 | 99.5 | 60.4 |
| 90 | 14:30 | 171.0 | 49.3 | 86.0 | 3.6 | 15.8 | 55.3 | 100.2 | 65.2 |
| 85 | 13:00 | 177.9 | 55.8 | 87.9 | 3.7 | 17.9 | 57.8 | 102.0 | 69.8 |
| 80 | 12:00 | 184.1 | 57.9 | 89.7 | 3.9 | 19.5 | 59.7 | 104.9 | 69.8 |
| 75 | 11:20 | 190.2 | 62.5 | 90.6 | 4.1 | 21.0 | 60.2 | 109.7 | 70.1 |
| 70 | 11:00 | 195.0 | 67.3 | 92.2 | 4.3 | 21.8 | 61.8 | 110.0 | 70.4 |
| 65 | 11:00 | 198.0 | 73.0 | 93.9 | 4.5 | 22.7 | 62.9 | 110.3 | 73.6 |
| 60 | 10:00 | 200.8 | 77.4 | 94.9 | 4.6 | 23.9 | 64.0 | 111.8 | 75.0 |
| 55 | 10:00 | 204.9 | 82.1 | 95.4 | 4.7 | 24.9 | 65.1 | 114.3 | 77.9 |
| 50 | 9:10 | 209.9 | 86.0 | 98.6 | 4.8 | 25.9 | 66.4 | 117.5 | 79.6 |
| 45 | 9:00 | 212.5 | 90.9 | 98.3 | 5.0 | 25.7 | 68.2 | 119.5 | 79.7 |
| 40 | 8:30 | 217.3 | 97.8 | 99.1 | 5.1 | 27.6 | 69.9 | 119.8 | 79.9 |
| 35 | 8:00 | 223.4 | 104.6 | 100.1 | 5.2 | 28.2 | 71.6 | 120.1 | 80.1 |
| 30 | 8:00 | 228.1 | 110.3 | 100.5 | 5.3 | 29.1 | 72.3 | 120.4 | 80.2 |
| 25 | 7:10 | 235.1 | 117.5 | 103.5 | 5.5 | 30.2 | 74.4 | 124.4 | 80.4 |
| 20 | 7:00 | 240.9 | 130.4 | 105.0 | 5.7 | 31.4 | 75.8 | 129.5 | 82.4 |
| 15 | 6:00 | 252.2 | 148.1 | 107.4 | 5.9 | 33.7 | 79.5 | 131.6 | 86.2 |
| 10 | 6:00 | 263.6 | 162.2 | 111.0 | 6.2 | 37.4 | 80.4 | 137.8 | 90.0 |
| 5 | 5:00 | 282.6 | 222.7 | 116.3 | 6.4 | 43.1 | 87.2 | 149.7 | 94.0 |
| 1 | 3:00 | 319.3 | 450.3 | 163.4 | 6.4 | 49.7 | 99.7 | 163.7 | 110.0 |
| POP. SIZE | 266 | 218 | 216 | 215 | 215 | 183 | 260 | 282 | 282 |
| AVERAGE | 9:42 | 213.9 | 106.0 | 98.1 | 4.8 | 26.1 | 67.8 | 117.9 | 77.5 |
| STANDARD DEVIATION | 3:30 | 39.4 | 89.9 | 16.6 | 0.8 | 8.6 | 10.7 | 15.7 | 10.2 |
| NORMAL ** | 11:00* | (250.0) | (135.0) | (110.0) | (8.0) | (22.0) | (72.0) | (140.0) | (90.0) |

* Data based on first visit only
** Upper limits generally accepted by most physicians

**PERSONAL HISTORY OF HEART ATTACK**
- 0 ☐ NONE
- 2 ☐ OVER 5 YEARS AGO
- 3 ☐ 2-5 YEARS AGO
- 5 ☐ 1-2 YEARS AGO
- -8 ☐ 0-1 YEARS AGO

**FAMILY HISTORY OF HEART ATTACK**
- 0 ☐ NONE
- 2 ☐ YES, OVER 50 YEARS
- 4 ☐ YES, 50 YEARS OR UNDER

**SMOKING HABITS**
- 0 ☐ NONE
- 1 ☐ PIPE/CIGAR
- 1 ☐ PAST ONLY (QUIT)
- 2 ☐ 1-10 DAILY
- 3 ☐ 11-20 DAILY
- 4 ☐ 20+ DAILY

**TENSION - ANXIETY**
- 0 ☐ NO TENSION, VERY RELAXED
- 0 ☐ SLIGHT TENSION
- 0 ☐ MODERATE TENSION
- 3 ☐ HIGH TENSION
- 3 ☐ VERY TENSE, "HIGH STRUNG"

**RESTING ECG / EXERCISE ECG**
- 0 ☐ NORMAL (NEGATIVE) ☐ 0
- 1 ☐ EQUIVOCAL (BORDERLINE) ☐ 4
- 3 ☐ ABNORMAL (POSITIVE) ☐ 8

**AGE FACTOR**
- 0 ☐ UNDER 30 YEARS OF AGE
- 1 ☐ 30-39 YEARS OF AGE
- 2 ☐ 40-49 YEARS OF AGE
- 3 ☐ 50-59 YEARS OF AGE
- 4 ☐ 60-69 YEARS OF AGE
- 5 ☐ 70+ YEARS OF AGE

**TOTAL CORONARY RISK**
- ☐ VERY LOW (0 - 4)
- ☐ LOW (5 - 14)
- ☐ MODERATE (15 - 24)
- ☐ HIGH (25 - 34)
- ☐ VERY HIGH (35*)

© Institute for Aerobics Research - 1977

# COOPER CLINIC / Dallas, Texas

# Fitness Level and Coronary Risk Profile

Name: _____

## FEMALES: 50-59 YEARS OF AGE

| PERCENTILE RANKINGS | BALKE TREADMILL TIME (min.) | CHOLESTEROL (mg.%) | TRIGLYCERIDES (mg.%) | GLUCOSE (mg.%) | URIC ACID (mg.%) | % BODY FAT | RESTING HEART RATE (bpm) | SYSTOLIC BLOOD PRESSURE (mm Hg) | DIASTOLIC BLOOD PRESSURE (mm Hg) |
|---|---|---|---|---|---|---|---|---|---|
| YOUR VALUES: | | | | | | | | | |
| 99 | 26:00 | 157.7 | 39.9 | 77.9 | 3.2 | 10.8 | 45.1 | 90.3 | 57.7 |
| 95 | 16:00 | 170.4 | 49.7 | 85.1 | 3.6 | 15.9 | 51.6 | 100.2 | 63.7 |
| 90 | 13:00 | 180.4 | 60.1 | 89.2 | 3.8 | 18.2 | 55.2 | 107.9 | 68.5 |
| 85 | 12:00 | 191.8 | 66.7 | 91.3 | 4.0 | 21.0 | 57.9 | 109.9 | 69.9 |
| 80 | 11:00 | 197.6 | 70.3 | 93.0 | 4.2 | 22.3 | 59.5 | 110.3 | 70.3 |
| 75 | 11:00 | 201.8 | 76.8 | 94.6 | 4.4 | 23.9 | 60.0 | 115.4 | 72.7 |
| 70 | 10:00 | 205.6 | 81.9 | 95.4 | 4.6 | 25.1 | 61.1 | 118.4 | 75.2 |
| 65 | 9:30 | 213.5 | 91.1 | 96.8 | 4.8 | 26.1 | 62.4 | 119.8 | 76.4 |
| 60 | 9:00 | 217.9 | 97.9 | 99.4 | 5.0 | 27.0 | 63.6 | 120.1 | 78.5 |
| 55 | 8:30 | 221.3 | 105.2 | 99.9 | 5.1 | 27.7 | 64.7 | 120.4 | 79.8 |
| 50 | 8:00 | 225.3 | 109.8 | 100.3 | 5.3 | 28.4 | 66.5 | 122.4 | 80.0 |
| 45 | 8:00 | 229.6 | 114.9 | 102.0 | 5.5 | 29.6 | 67.8 | 127.8 | 80.3 |
| 40 | 7:30 | 233.6 | 118.3 | 104.6 | 5.6 | 30.4 | 68.7 | 129.7 | 81.5 |
| 35 | 7:00 | 235.6 | 125.1 | 105.3 | 5.8 | 31.4 | 70.2 | 130.2 | 83.9 |
| 30 | 7:00 | 241.4 | 129.9 | 107.7 | 5.9 | 32.5 | 71.9 | 134.4 | 85.3 |
| 25 | 6:30 | 249.3 | 144.5 | 109.6 | 6.1 | 33.4 | 73.6 | 139.7 | 88.0 |
| 20 | 6:00 | 260.3 | 165.3 | 110.0 | 6.3 | 34.7 | 75.1 | 140.2 | 89.6 |
| 15 | 5:38 | 267.3 | 175.1 | 110.5 | 6.4 | 37.1 | 78.0 | 142.1 | 90.1 |
| 10 | 5:00 | 274.8 | 217.9 | 114.9 | 6.8 | 39.2 | 83.3 | 148.3 | 92.2 |
| 5 | 4:07 | 295.1 | 241.7 | 120.1 | 7.2 | 44.4 | 89.4 | 150.7 | 100.0 |
| 1 | 2:15 | 320.3 | 305.1 | 135.1 | 7.5 | 51.2 | 104.7 | 171.8 | 109.9 |
| POP. SIZE | 169 | 137 | 136 | 137 | 136 | 127 | 162 | 167 | 167 |
| AVERAGE | 8:47 | 228.2 | 122.8 | 101.8 | 5.2 | 29.2 | 67.8 | 125.4 | 80.4 |
| STANDARD DEVIATION | 3:38 | 37.3 | 67.1 | 15.1 | 1.0 | 9.5 | 11.7 | 16.8 | 10.6 |
| VALUE** | 9:20* | (250.0) | (135.0) | (110.0) | (1.0) | (22.0) | (72.0) | (140.0) | (90.0) |

*Case based on first visit only
**Upper limits generally accepted by most physicians

### PERSONAL HISTORY OF HEART ATTACK
- 0 ☐ NONE
- 2 ☐ OVER 5 YEARS AGO
- 3 ☐ 3-5 YEARS AGO
- 5 ☐ 2-3 YEARS AGO
- 8 ☐ 0-1 YEARS AGO

### FAMILY HISTORY OF HEART ATTACK
- 0 ☐ NONE
- 2 ☐ YES, OVER 50 YEARS AGO
- 4 ☐ YES, 50 YEARS OR UNDER

### SMOKING HABITS
- 0 ☐ NONE
- 1 ☐ EX/PIPE/CIGAR
- 2 ☐ PAST ONLY/W/OUT
- 3 ☐ 1-10 DAILY
- 3 ☐ 11-30 DAILY
- 4 ☐ 30+ DAILY

### TENSION — ANXIETY
- 0 ☐ NO TENSION, VERY RELAXED
- 1 ☐ SLIGHT TENSION
- 2 ☐ MODERATE TENSION
- 3 ☐ HIGH TENSION
- 3 ☐ VERY TENSE, "HIGH STRUNG"

### RESTING ECG    EXERCISE ECG
- 0 ☐ NORMAL (NEGATIVE) ☐ 0
- 2 ☐ EQUIVOCAL (BORDERLINE) ☐ 4
- 3 ☐ ABNORMAL (POSITIVE) ☐ 8

### AGE FACTOR
- 0 ☐ UNDER 30 YEARS OF AGE
- 1 ☐ 30-39 YEARS OF AGE
- 2 ☐ 40-49 YEARS OF AGE
- 3 ☐ 50-59 YEARS OF AGE
- 4 ☐ 60+ YEARS OF AGE

### TOTAL CORONARY RISK
- ☐ VERY LOW (0 - 4)
- ☐ LOW (5 - 14)
- ☐ MODERATE (15 - 24)
- ☐ HIGH (25 - 39)
- ☐ VERY HIGH (35+)

© Institute for Aerobics Research — 1977

# COOPER CLINIC / Dallas, Texas

Name: _____

## Fitness Level and Coronary Risk Profile

### FEMALES, *60* YEARS OF AGE

| PERCENTILE RANKINGS (YOUR VALUES) | BALKE TREADMILL TIME (min.) | CHOLESTEROL (mg.%) | TRIGLYCERIDE (mg.%) | GLUCOSE (mg.%) | URIC ACID (mg.%) | % BODY FAT | RESTING HEART RATE (bpm) | RESTING BLOOD PRESSURE SYSTOLIC (mm Hg) | RESTING BLOOD PRESSURE DIASTOLIC (mm Hg) |
|---|---|---|---|---|---|---|---|---|---|
| 99 | 16:00 | 126.9 | 41.9 | 74.9 | 2.7 | 6.8 | 45.9 | 109.7 | 66.0 |
| 95 | 12:00 | 179.5 | 45.5 | 79.5 | 3.5 | 13.1 | 50.1 | 117.7 | 69.8 |
| 90 | 11:00 | 184.5 | 62.4 | 88.4 | 3.9 | 17.2 | 52.2 | 119.8 | 70.0 |
| 85 | 11:00 | 187.5 | 72.4 | 89.9 | 4.3 | 19.3 | 55.7 | 120.0 | 70.5 |
| 80 | 9:15 | 209.5 | 80.3 | 91.3 | 4.6 | 22.2 | 56.8 | 120.4 | 74.6 |
| 75 | 8:30 | 219.5 | 87.3 | 94.3 | 4.8 | 24.0 | 59.3 | 122.3 | 75.3 |
| 70 | 8:30 | 222.5 | 90.4 | 97.2 | 5.0 | 25.1 | 59.9 | 124.7 | 76.0 |
| 65 | 8:00 | 234.5 | 92.8 | 98.3 | 5.1 | 26.6 | 60.3 | 125.3 | 77.6 |
| 60 | 8:00 | 235.0 | 97.1 | 99.8 | 5.3 | 27.1 | 61.0 | 128.2 | 78.5 |
| 55 | 7:38 | 237.5 | 105.1 | 100.2 | 5.5 | 27.9 | 63.0 | 129.8 | 79.7 |
| 50 | 6:30 | 240.0 | 110.0 | 102.0 | 5.8 | 29.8 | 63.9 | 130.3 | 79.9 |
| 45 | 6:10 | 244.5 | 124.0 | 103.7 | 5.9 | 30.4 | 64.3 | 132.2 | 80.1 |
| 40 | 6:00 | 245.2 | 128.9 | 104.7 | 6.1 | 30.8 | 66.3 | 136.1 | 80.3 |
| 35 | 5:33 | 246.0 | 133.9 | 106.9 | 6.2 | 31.2 | 70.0 | 138.5 | 80.5 |
| 30 | 5:30 | 261.5 | 139.8 | 109.5 | 6.4 | 31.7 | 71.8 | 139.9 | 83.7 |
| 25 | 5:00 | 264.5 | 163.8 | 109.8 | 6.5 | 32.5 | 72.3 | 140.3 | 86.0 |
| 20 | 4:30 | 268.5 | 182.7 | 110.1 | 6.9 | 34.7 | 74.2 | 141.9 | 88.4 |
| 15 | 4:00 | 274.5 | 203.7 | 110.4 | 7.3 | 35.2 | 75.0 | 150.1 | 90.0 |
| 10 | 3:15 | 275.5 | 227.8 | 114.6 | 8.0 | 38.3 | 79.2 | 159.7 | 97.7 |
| 5 | 3:00 | 310.0 | 276.6 | 119.6 | 9.1 | 39.9 | 80.4 | 165.2 | 99.7 |
| 1 | 1:00 | 335.1 | 400.1 | 130.1 | | 51.2 | 85.1 | 188.0 | 100.4 |
| POP. SIZE | 46 | 40 | 39 | 39 | 32 | 43 | 49 | 46 | |
| AVERAGE | 7:08 | 236.9 | 131.4 | 101.6 | 6.5 | 28.3 | 65.2 | 134.5 | 61.0 |
| STANDARD DEVIATION | 3:05 | 40.9 | 71.6 | 14.9 | 1.2 | 8.5 | 9.6 | 16.2 | 8.8 |
| NORMAL** | 8:00 | (250.0) | (135.0) | (110.0) | (8.0) | (22.0) | (72.0) | (140.0) | (90.0) |

*Data based on first visit only
**Upper limits generally accepted by most physicians

### PERSONAL HISTORY OF HEART ATTACK
- 0 □ NONE
- 2 □ OVER 5 YEARS AGO
- 3 □ 2-5 YEARS AGO
- 5 □ 1-2 YEARS AGO
- 8 □ 0-1 YEARS AGO

### FAMILY HISTORY OF HEART ATTACK
- 0 □ NONE
- 2 □ YES, OVER 60 YEARS
- 4 □ YES, 60 YEARS OR UNDER

### SMOKING HABITS
- 0 □ NONE
- 1 □ PIPE/CIGAR
- 1 □ PAST ONLY/QUIT
- 2 □ 1 — 10 DAILY
- 3 □ 11 — 30 DAILY
- 4 □ 30+ DAILY

### TENSION — ANXIETY
- 0 □ NO TENSION, VERY RELAXED
- 0 □ SLIGHT TENSION
- 2 □ MODERATE TENSION
- 2 □ HIGH TENSION
- 3 □ VERY TENSE, "HIGH STRUNG"

### RESTING ECG / EXERCISE ECG
- 0 □ NORMAL (NEGATIVE) □ 0
- 1 □ EQUIVOCAL (BORDERLINE) □ 4
- 3 □ ABNORMAL (POSITIVE) □ 8

### AGE FACTOR
- 0 □ UNDER 20 YEARS OF AGE
- 1 □ 20-39 YEARS OF AGE
- 2 □ 40-49 YEARS OF AGE
- 3 □ 50-59 YEARS OF AGE
- 4 □ 60 YEARS OF AGE

### TOTAL CORONARY RISK
- □ VERY LOW (0-4)
- □ LOW (5-14)
- □ MODERATE (15-24)
- □ HIGH (25-34)
- □ VERY HIGH (35+)

© Institute for Aerobics Research — 1977

# STRESS TESTING CENTERS

(Reprinted from the January/February 1978 issue of *Jogger*, with the permission of the National Jogging Association, 1910 K St., N.W., No. 202, Washington, D.C. 20006.)

ALABAMA
L. T. Sheffield, M.D.
Cardiology Division
School of Medicine
University of Alabama
University Station
Birmingham, Ala. 35294
(205) 934-2274

T. Dye, M.D.
NASA Medical Center
Marshall Space Flight Center
Building 4249
Huntsville, Ala. 35815
(205) 453-2391

T. R. Figarola
University of Alabama Medical
  School
Ambulatory Care Center
Huntsville, Alabama 35815
(205) 453-2391

ARKANSAS
B. S. Brown, M.D.
Department of Physical
  Education
Human Performance Laboratory
University of Arkansas
Fayetteville, Ark. 72701
(501) 575-2859

H. Olree, Ed.D.
Exercise Physiology Laboratory
Box 765
Harding College
Searcy, Ark. 72143
(501) 268-6161

CALIFORNIA
Director
CPR Center
Arcadia Methodist Hospital
300 West Huntington Drive
Arcadia, Calif. 91006
(213) 445-4441

Director
CPR Center
Mercy Hospital
2215 Truxtun Avenue
Bakersfield, Calif. 93301
(805) 327-3371

P. Schloemp
Central YMCA
2001 Allston Way
Berkeley, Calif. 94707
(415) 848-6800

N. H. Mellor, M.D.
Cardiovascular Stress Test and
  Work Evaluation Unit
Circle City Hospital
730 Old Magnolia Avenue
Corona, Calif. 91720
(714) 735-1211

J. H. Wilmore, Ph.D.
Adult Fitness Program
Department of Physical
  Education
University of California/Davis
Davis, Calif. 95616
(916) 752-0511

Director
CPR Center
433 West Bastanchury Road
Fullerton, Calif. 92635
(714) 870-9577

Director
CPR Center
Memorial Hospital
1420 South Central Avenue
Glendale, Calif. 91204
(213) 246-6711

D. R. Fitch, M.D.
F. E. Gossard, M.D.
J. B. Maryland, M.D.
1808 Verdugo Boulevard
Glendale, Calif. 91208
(213) 790-4631

267

Director
CPR Center
Antelope Valley Hospital
1600 West Avenue "J"
Lancaster, Calif. 93534
(805) 948-4577

Director
CPR Center
Marina Mercy Hospital
4650 Lincoln Boulevard
Marina del Rey, Calif. 90291
(213) 823-8911

Director
CPR Center
Mission Community Hospital
27802 Puerto Real Highway
Mission Viejo, Calif. 92675
(714) 831-2300

Director
CPR Center
Riverside Hospital
12629 Riverside Drive
North Hollywood, Calif. 91607
(213) 980-9200

Director
CPR Center
1215 West LaVeta
Suite 101
Orange, Calif. 92668
(714) 997-1222

W. L. Haskell, Ph.D.
Division of Cardiology
Stanford Medical School
730 Welch Road
Palo Alto, Calif. 94034
(415) 497-6254

J. L. Boyer, M.D.
Adult Physical Fitness Program
Exercise Laboratory
San Diego State University
San Diego, Calif. 92115
(714) 287-2222

F. W. Kasch, Ph.D.
Adult Fitness Program
Physical Education Building
San Diego State University
San Diego, Calif. 92182
(714) 286-5560

R. Martin
Aerobic Fitness Program
Downtown YMCA
1115 Eighth Avenue
San Diego, Calif. 92101
(714) 323-7451

H. D. Peabody, Jr., M.D.
Department of Cardiology
Rees-Stealy Clinic
2001 Fourth Avenue
San Diego, Calif. 92101
(714) 234-6261

B. H. McFadden, M.D.
Santa Barbara Heart and Lung
    Institute
Galeta Valley Hospital
351 Patterson Avenue
Santa Barbara, Calif. 93111
(805) 967-3411

Steven M. Kaye, M.D.
2416 B. Castillo St.
Santa Barbara, Calif. 93205
(805) 964-1582

T. D. Gardiner, M.D.
18740 Ventura Blvd.
Tarzana, Calif. 91356
(213) 881-2232

Director
South Bay CPR Center
22352 Hawthorne Boulevard
Torrance, Calif. 90505
(213) 373-6769

F. P. Cafdello, M.D.
YMCA Exercise Testing Program
4201 Torrance Boulevard
Suite 360
Torrance, Calif. 90503
(213) 540-5522

Director
CPR Center
Whittier Hospital
15151 Janine Drive
Whittier, Calif. 90605
(213) 945-3561

COLORADO
B. Balke, M.D.
Aspen Cardiopulmonary
    Rehabilitation Unit
Box 630
Aspen, Colo. 81611
(303) 925-1992

G. P. Smith, Director
Cardiac Reconditioning
Hilltop House
515 Patterson Avenue
Grand Junction, Colo. 81501
(303) 242-2801

DELAWARE
Director
Cardiac and Pulmonary
104 Hagley Building
Concord Plaza
3411 Silverside Road
Wilmington, Del. 19810
(302) 478-7930

WASHINGTON, D.C.
S. M. Fox, III, M.D.
Cardiology Exercise Laboratory
Georgetown University
3800 Reservoir Road, N.W.
Washington, D.C. 20007
(202) 625-2001

J. R. Snyder, M.D.
Washington Cardiovascular
    Evaluation Center
916 Nineteenth Street, N.W.
Washington, D.C. 20006
(202) 541-4666

FLORIDA
J. Esterson, M.D.
2526 East Hallandale Beach
    Boulevard
Hallandale, Fla. 33009
(305) 456-5115

Director
CPR Center
Mercy Professional Building
Suite 2
3661 South Miami Avenue
Miami, Fla. 33133
(305) 854-0982

H. Gilmore
Pankey Dental Institute
DuPont Plaza Hotel
Miami, Fla. 33131
(305) 371-8711

Director
Cardiac Rehabilitation Unit
Florida Hospital
601 East Rollins Street
Orlando, Fla. 32803
(305) 896-6611

Z. C. Burton, Jr., M.D.
500 East Colonial Drive
Orlando, Fla. 32803
(305) 841-7151

Director
CPR Center
1717 North "E" Street
P.O. Box 19036
Pensacola, Fla. 32503
(904) 434-4666

GEORGIA
J. D. Cantwell, M.D.
Preventive Cardiology Clinic
433 Highland Avenue, N.E.
Atlanta, Ga. 30312
(404) 524-3633

J. D. Cantwell, M.D.
G. F. Fletcher, M.D.
Cardiology Division
Georgia Baptist Hospital
300 Boulevard, N.E.
Atlanta, Ga. 30312
(404) 659-4211

C. A. Gilbert, M.D.
Cardiac Function Laboratory
Grady Memorial Hospital
69 Butler Street, S.E.
Atlanta, Ga. 30303
(404) 588-4449

## HAWAII
J. Scaff, Jr., M.D.
Cardiac Rehabilitation Program
Central YMCA
401 Atkinson Drive
Honolulu, Hawaii 96814
(808) 941-3344

## ILLINOIS
R. G. Knowlton, Ph.D.
Adult Fitness Program
Department of Physical
  Education
Southern Illinois University
Carbondale, Ill. 62801
(618) 453-2575

Director
CPR Center
Galesburg Cottage Hospital
695 North Kellogg Street
Galesburg, Ill. 61401
(309) 343-8131

N. D. Nequin, M.D.
Physiological Performance
  Laboratory
Leaning Tower YMCA
6300 West Touhy Avenue
Niles, Ill. 60648
(312) 647-8222

Director
CPR Center
Rock Island Franciscan Hospital
2701 Seventeenth Street
Rock Island, Ill. 61201
(309) 793-1000

## INDIANA
R. R. Jirka, Ph.D.
Cardiovascular Rehabilitation
  and Prevention
YMCA of Madison County
Twelfth and Jackson

P.O. Box 231
Anderson, Ind. 46015
(317) 644-7796

## IOWA
N. Tremble, Ph.D.
Cardiovascular Fitness Clinic
Department of Physical
  Education
Drake University
Des Moines, Iowa 50311
(515) 271-2866

## KANSAS
Director
CPR Center
Providence-St. Margaret Hospital
759 Vermont Avenue
Kansas City, Kans. 66101
(913) 621-0700

W. H. Osness, Ph.D.
Department of Physical Education
108 Robinson
University of Kansas
Lawrence, Kans. 66044
(913) 864-3371

## KENTUCKY
R. G. McAllister, Jr., M.D.
Cardiology Division
Veterans Administration Hospital
Lexington, Ky. 40507
(606) 233-4511

## MARYLAND
Director
Maryland General Hospital
827 Linden Avenue
Baltimore, Md. 21201
(301) 728-7900

J. P. Segal, M.D.
5530 Wisconsin Avenue
Chevy Chase, Md. 20015
(301) 656-9070

D. L. Santa Maria, Ed.D.
Sports Medicine and Physical
  Fitness Center
University of Maryland
College Park, Md. 20742
(301) 454-4750

Director
CPR Center
Memorial Hospital
Memorial Avenue
Cumberland, Md. 21502

Director
CPR Center
Fallston General Hospital
200 Milton Avenue
Fallston, Md. 21047
(301) 722-2900

K. M. Lindgren, M.D.
Department of Cardiology
Washington Adventist Hospital
7600 Carroll Avenue
Takoma Park, Md. 20012
(301) 891-7672

MASSACHUSETTS
Director
CPR Center
Faulkner Health Care
780 American Legion Highway
Roslindale, Mass. 02131
(617) 325-1000

MICHIGAN
Director
CPR Center
St. Joseph's Hospital
302 Kensington Avenue
Flint, Mich. 48502
(313) 238-2601

Dr. Thomas J. Clay
308 Medical Arts Building
26 Sheldon Ave. S.E.
Grand Rapids, Mich. 49503
(616) 451-3021

G. Schultz, P.E.D.
R. Parr, Ed.D.
J. Roitman, Ed.D.
J. Paulisko
Adult Fitness Program
Central Michigan University
Mount Pleasant, Mich. 48858
(517) 774-3580

R. J. Stewart, D.O.
Macomb Cardiac Rehabilitation
40600 Van Dyke

Sterling Heights, Mich. 48087
(313) 939-1313

J. Arends, M.D.
1551 West Big Beaver Road
Troy, Mich. 48084
(313) 643-7770

MISSOURI
Mark Crooks, Ph.D.
Cardiovascular Rehabilitation
 Institute
6724 Troost—Suite 108
Kansas City, Mo. 64131
(816) 444-6131

NEBRASKA
K. Berg, Ed.D.
W. Gust, M.D.
Department of Physical Education
6100 Dodge
University of Nebraska/Omaha
Omaha, Nebr. 68601
(402) 554-2670

NEVADA
Director
CPR Center
Sunrise Hospital
3186 Maryland Parkway
Las Vegas, Nev. 89109
(702) 735-2789

Stephen Dow, M.D.
Nevada Heart Fitness Inst.
c/o The Athlete's Foot
580 North McCarran Blvd.
Sparkes, Nev. 89431
(702) 331-3145

NEW JERSEY
Joan Carter
Stress Testing
56 Haddon Avenue
Haddonfield, N.J. 08033
(609) 795-2220

I. M. Levitas, M.D.
Bergen County Heart Association
 Program
Hackensack Hospital
22 Hospital Place
Hackensack, N.J. 07601
(201) 487-4000 ext. 383

E. M. Stein, M.D.
Memorial General Hospital
Stress Testing Lab.
1000 Galloping Hill Rd.
Union, N.J. 07083
(201) 487-4000

G. Sheehan, M.D.
Stress Testing Program
Riverview Hospital
Red Bank, N.J. 07701
(201) 741-2700

Director
CPR Center
St. Francis Hospital
601 Hamilton Avenue
Trenton, N.J. 08629
(609) 396-7676

NEW MEXICO
H. A. Atterbom, Ph.D.
Human Performance Laboratory
Johnson Gymnasium
University of New Mexico
Albuquerque, N. Mex. 87131
(505) 277-4441

NEW YORK
Director
Victory Memorial Hospital
Brooklyn, N.Y. 11228
(516) 422-1000

V. N. Smodlaka, M.D.
Rehabilitation Medicine
    Department
Methodist Hospital
506 Sixth Street
Brooklyn, N.Y. 11215
(212) 780-3266

R. M. Kohn, M.D.
50 High Street
Suite 1104
Buffalo, N.Y. 14203
(716) 885-2400

W. J. Tomik, Ph.D.
Physical Fitness and Heart
    Disease Intervention

State University College
Cortland, N.Y. 13045
(607) 753-4944

Director
Central Nassau CPR
1900 Hempstead Turnpike
East Meadow, N.Y. 11756
(516) 794-9797

M. McCain
Cardiovascular Testing and
    Exercise Program
Central Queens YMCA
89-25 Parsons Boulevard
Jamaica, N.Y. 11432
(212) 739-6600

Director
EKG Department
CPR Center
Phelps Memorial Hospital
North Broadway
North Tarrytown, N.Y. 10541
(914) 631-5100

Director
Manhattan CPR Center
211 East Fifty-first Street
New York, N.Y. 10022
(212) 371-6281

David Alderson
West Side YMCA
5 West Sixty-third Street
New York, N.Y. 10023
(212) 787-4400

W. S. Gualtiere, Ph.D.
A. J. Delman, M.D.
Cardio-Metrics Institute
295 Madison Avenue
New York, N.Y. 10017
(212) 889-6123

Director
Staten Island Diagnostic and
    Rehabilitation Center
11 Ralph Place
Staten Island, N.Y. 10304
(212) 727-4900

**NORTH CAROLINA**
P. Ribisl, Ph.D.
Cardiac Rehabilitation Program
Human Performance Laboratory
Department of Physical
  Education
Wake Forest University
Winston-Salem, N.C. 27109
(919) 761-5394

**OHIO**
T. J. White
Downtown Canton YMCA
405 Second Street, N.W.
Canton, Ohio 44702
(216) 455-1536

T. E. Donaldson
Exercise Testing Laboratory
Central YMCA
2200 Prospect Avenue
Cleveland, Ohio 44115
(216) 696-2200

C. Long II, M.D.
Cardiac Evaluation and
  Rehabilitation Program
Highland View Hospital
3901 Ireland Drive
Cleveland, Ohio 44122
(216) 464-9600

Dr. Wayne Sinning
Applied Physiology Research
  Laboratory
Kent State University
Kent, Ohio 44242
(216) 672-2859

R. L. Miller, M.D.
Comprehensive Executive Health
  Evaluations
Executive Health Maintenance
  Programs
5335 Far Hills Avenue
Kettering, Ohio 45459
(513) 435-0220

Director
CPR Center
Lima Memorial Hospital
Linden and Mobel Streets

Lima, Ohio 45804
(419) 225-5967

Director
CPR Center
Mercy Hospital
1248 Kinneys Lane
Portsmouth, Ohio 45662
(614) 353-2131

W. J. Rowe, M.D.
Exercise Stress Testing
St. Vincent's Hospital
2213 Cherry Street
Toledo, Ohio 43608
(419) 259-4167

**OKLAHOMA**
Director
CPR Center
St. John's Hospital
1923 South Utica Avenue
Tulsa, Okla. 74104
(918) 744-2699

**OREGON**
Henry B. Garrison, M.D.
CAPRI
7645 South West Capital Highway
Portland, Ore. 97219
(543) 245-2291

W. A. Ray
Portland YMCA Cardiovascular
  Health Program
2831 S.W. Barbur Blvd.
Portland, Ore. 97201
(503) 223-9622

M. W. Tichy, Ph.D.
Adult Fitness Program
Portland State University
P.O. Box 751
Portland, Oreg. 97207
(503) 229-4989

**PENNSYLVANIA**
Director
CPR Center
Allentown Sacred Heart
  Hospital
1200 South Cedarcrest Boulevard
Allentown, Pa. 18103
(215) 821-2121

S. E. Zeeman, M.D.
901 North Nineteenth Street
Allentown, Pa. 18104
(215) 437-5505

Director
CPR Center
Maple Avenue Hospital
Maple Avenue
DuBois, Pa. 15801
(814) 371-3440

H. Weber, Ph.D.
Adult Fitness and Heart
   Evaluation
Koehler Field House
East Stroudsberg State College
East Stroudsberg, Pa. 18301
(717) 424-3336

Director
CPR Center
2024 Lehigh Street
Easton, Pa. 18042
(215) 252-0301

Director
CPR Center
Hamot Medical Center
201 State Street
Erie, Pa. 16512
(814) 455-6711

Director
CPR Center
Medical Arts Building, Room 208
225 West Twenty-fifth Street
Erie, Pa. 16502
(814) 453-5485

Mr. Keys
Central Branch YMCA
Front and North Streets
Harrisburg, Pa. 17101
(717) 234-6221

Director
CPR Center
Northwestern Building
Suite 1108-1110

Hazelton, Pa. 18201
(717) 455-9070

Ronald Legum, M.D.
CPR Center
St. Joseph's Hospital
250 College Avenue
Lancaster, Pa. 17603
(717) 291-8291

Director
CPR Center
Spencer Hospital
1034 Grove Street
Meadville, Pa. 16335
(814) 724-6622

Director
CPR Center
4950 Wilson Lane
Mechanicsburg, Pa. 17055
(717) 697-8350

Director
CPR Center
JFK Memorial Hospital
Cheltenham Avenue and
   Langdon Street
Philadelphia, Pa. 19124
(215) 289-6000

G. Berger
Physical Fitness Program
Central Branch YMCA
1421 Arch Street
Philadelphia, Pa. 19102
(215) 241-1200

N. Makous, M.D.
Cardiology Department
Pennsylvania Hospital
829 Spruce Street
Philadelphia, Pa. 19107
(215) 829-3000

L. N. Adler, M.D.
Cardiac Rehabilitation Institute
532 South Aiken Avenue,
   No. 108
Pittsburgh, Pa. 15232
(412) 682-6201

B. J. Robertson, Ph.D.
Human Laboratory
Department of Health and
   Physical Education
University of Pittsburgh
242 Trees Hall
Pittsburgh, Pa. 15261
(412) 624-4387

Director
CPR Center
748 Quincey Avenue
Scranton, Pa. 18510
(717) 961-3090

Director
CPR Center
Sharon General Hospital
740 East State Street
Sharon, Pa. 16146
(412) 981-1700

E. R. Buskirk, Ph.D.
Laboratory for Human
   Performance Research
College of Health, Physical
   Education, and Recreation
Pennsylvania State University
University Park, Pa. 16802
(814) 865-3453

Director
CPR Center
Mercy Hospital
196 Hanover Street
Wilkes-Barre, Pa. 18703
(717) 822-8101 Stress Lab

Director
CPR Center
924 C Colonial Avenue
York, Pa. 17403

SOUTH CAROLINA
P. C. Gazes, M.D.
Cardiovascular Division
Medical University Hospital
171 Ashley Ave.
Charleston, S.C. 29403
(803) 792-3355

S. N. Blair, P.E.D.
Human Performance Laboratory

College of Physical Education
University of South Carolina
Columbia, S.C. 29205
(803) 777-3890

TEXAS
K. H. Cooper, M.D.
Institute for Aerobics Research
12100 Preston Road
Dallas, Tex. 75230
(214) 239-7223

J. Quiocho
Physical Conditioning and
   Evaluation
YMCA
701 Montana Avenue
El Paso, Tex. 79902
(915) 533-3941

D. Cardus, M.D.
Cardiac Rehabilitation
Texas Institute for Rehabilitation
   and Research
P.O. Box 20095
Texas Medical Center
Houston, Tex. 77025
(713) 797-1440

A. K. Johnston
Houston Downtown YMCA
1600 Louisiana
Houston, Tex. 77002
(713) 797-1440

UTAH
H. W. Buckner
YMCA
737 East Second South
Salt Lake City, Utah 84102
(801) 322-1291

VIRGINIA
F. Anderson, M.D.
Cardiology Department
Northern Virginia Doctors
   Hospital
601 Carlin Springs Road
Arlington, Va. 22204
(703) 671-1200

R. F. Dietz, Jr., M.D.
Cardiac Laboratory
Arlington Hospital
Arlington, Va. 22205
(703) 558-6267

G. E. Hahn, M.D.
Department of Cardiology
Prince William Hospital
8700 Sudley Road
Manassas, Va. 22110
(703) 368-8121

WASHINGTON
CAPRI
Green River College
So. Seattle, Wash. 98002
(206) 323-7550

W. Mead, M.D.
Universal Testing Services
8118 Greenlake Drive North
Seattle, Wash. 98103
(206) 523-4700

H. R. Pyfer, M.D.
Cardio-Pulmonary Research
    Institute (CAPRI)
914 East Jefferson Street
Seattle, Wash. 98122
(206) 323-7550

D. Ballew, M.D.
Yakima Heart Center
302 South Tenth Avenue
Yakima, Wash. 98901
(509) 248-7715

WISCONSIN
P. K. Wilson, Ed.D.
Cardiac Rehabilitation Program
University of Wisconsin/LaCrosse
Mitchell Hall
1820 Pine Street
LaCrosse, Wis. 54601
(608) 785-8684

R. J. Corliss, M.D.
F. Nagel, Ph.D.
Biodynamics Laboratory
University of Wisconsin
2000 Observatory Drive
Madison, Wis. 53706
(608) 262-9905

Director
CPR Center
Lutheran Hospital
2200 West Kilbourn Avenue
Milwaukee, Wis. 53233
(414) 344-8800

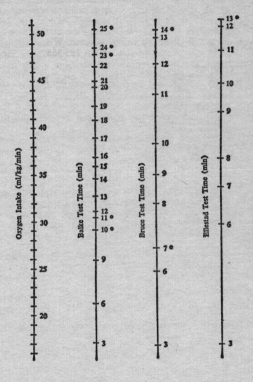

°n < 8, N = 51.

# DETERMINING PERCENT BODY FAT FROM SKINFOLD MEASUREMENT

Approximately one half of the body's total fat content is located in the tissues beneath the skin. The feasibility of measuring this subcutaneous fat was suggested by anthropologists at the end of World War I. By 1930 researchers had developed a special pincer-type caliper that enabled them to measure this fat at representative sites on the body with relative accuracy. The caliper works on the same principle as the micrometer used to measure the distance between two points. The procedure for measuring skinfold thickness is to grasp firmly with the thumb and forefinger a fold of skin and subcutaneous fat away from the underlying muscular tissue, following the natural contour of the skinfold. The pincer arms of the caliper can then exert constant tension at their point of contact with the skin. The thickness of the double layer of skin and subcutaneous tissues can then be read directly from the caliper dial. The procedure for taking the skinfold measurements, as well as the precise location of the skinfold sites, must be standardized if results are to be reliable and used for comparative purposes. Following are locations of skinfold sites for the chest (pectoral muscle), axilla (underarm), triceps, and suprailiac (crest of pelvic girdle):

Chest: Diagonal fold one third of the distance between the anterior axillary line and nipple.

Axilla: Vertical fold on the midaxillary line at approximately the level of the nipple.

Triceps: Vertical fold on the posterior midline of the upper arm (over triceps), halfway between the acromion and olecranon processes, with the elbow extended and relaxed.

Suprailiac: Diagonal fold on the crest of the ilium at the midaxillary line.*

Percent body fat generally increases with age, and also varies between men and women. Standards at the Aerobics Center require males to be 19 percent fat or less and females to be 22 percent fat or less. From an athletic standpoint, men should be 15 percent fat or less and women 18 percent fat or less. Following are classification guidelines for men and women:

|           | MEN     | WOMEN   |
|-----------|---------|---------|
| Very lean | <10%    | <13%    |
| Lean      | 11–15%  | 14–18%  |
| Average   | 16–19%  | 19–22%  |
| Fat       | 20–24%  | 23–27%  |
| Very fat  | >25%    | >28%    |

Percent body fat is calculated from body density according to this formula:

$$\% \text{ Body Fat} = \frac{4.950}{\text{Density}} - 4.500 \times 100$$

* From *Nutrition, Weight Control and Exercise* by F. Katch and W. McArdle. Copyright © 1977 by Houghton Mifflin Company. Reprinted by permission.

Body density for *women* is found according to this formula:

$$X_1 = \text{Suprailiac (crest of pelvic girdle) skinfold (mm)}$$
$$X_2 = \text{Tricep skinfold (mm)}$$

$$\text{Density} = 1.0764 - (.00081X_1) + (.00088X_2)$$

Body density for *men* is found according to this formula:

$$X_1 = \text{Axilla (underarm) skinfold (mm)}$$
$$X_2 = \text{Chest (pectoral muscle) skinfold (mm)}$$
$$X_3 = \text{Tricep skinfold (mm)}$$

$$\text{Density} = 1.088468 - (.0007123X_1) - (.0004834X_2) - (.0005513X_3)$$

*References:*

W. E. Siri, "Gross Composition of the Body," in J. H. Lawrence and C. A. Tobias, eds., *Advance in Biological and Medical Physics* IV (New York: Academic Press, Inc., 1956).

A. W. Sloan, J. J. Burt, and C. S. Blyth, "Estimation of Body Fat in Young Women," *Journal of Applied Physiology* 16 (1962): 967–70.

L. R. Pascale, M. I. Grossman, H. S. Sloane, and T. Frankel, "Correlations between Thickness of Skinfolds and Body Density in 88 Soldiers," *Human Biology* 28 (1956): 165–76.

## MEN'S AEROBICS FITNESS CLASSIFICATION (PREDICTED)

| CATEGORY | MEASURE | AGE (years) | | | | | |
|---|---|---|---|---|---|---|---|
| | | 13–19 | 20–29 | 30–39 | 40–49 | 50–59 | 60+ |
| I. Very poor | O₂ uptake (ml/kg/min) | <35.0 | <33.0 | <31.5 | <30.2 | <26.1 | <20.5 |
| | *T. M. time (min:sec) | <14:30 | <12:50 | <12:00 | <11:00 | <9:00 | <5:30 |
| | 12-min. dist. (ml) | <1.30 | <1.22 | <1.18 | <1.14 | <1.03 | <.87 |
| | 1.5-mile time min:sec | >15:31 | >16:01 | >16:31 | >17:31 | >19:01 | >20:01 |
| II. Poor | O₂ uptake (ml/kg/min) | 35.0–38.3 | 33.0–36.4 | 31.5–35.4 | 30.2–33.5 | 26.1–30.9 | 20.5–26.0 |
| | *T. M. time (min:sec) | 14:30–16:44 | 12:50–15:29 | 12:00–14:59 | 11:00–13:29 | 9:00–11:29 | 5:30–8:49 |
| | 12-min. dist. (ml) | 1.30–1.37 | 1.22–1.31 | 1.18–1.30 | 1.14–1.24 | 1.03–1.16 | .87–1.02 |
| | 1.5-mile time min:sec | 12:11–15:30 | 14:01–16:00 | 14:44–16:30 | 15:36–17:30 | 17:01–19:00 | 19:01–20:00 |
| III. Fair | O₂ uptake (ml/kg/min) | 38.4–45.1 | 36.5–42.4 | 35.5–40.9 | 33.6–38.9 | 31.0–35.7 | 26.1–32.2 |
| | *T. M. time (min:sec) | 16:45–21:07 | 15:30–18:59 | 15:00–17:59 | 13:30–16:59 | 11:30–14:59 | 8:50–12:29 |
| | 12-min. dist. (ml) | 1.38–1.56 | 1.32–1.49 | 1.31–1.45 | 1.25–1.39 | 1.17–1.30 | 1.03–1.20 |
| | 1.5-mile time min:sec | 10:49–12:10 | 12:01–14:00 | 12:31–14:45 | 13:01–15:35 | 14:31–17:00 | 16:16–19:00 |
| IV. Good | O₂ uptake (ml/kg/min) | 45.2–50.9 | 42.5–46.4 | 41.0–44.9 | 39.0–43.7 | 35.8–40.9 | 32.2–36.4 |
| | *T. M. time (min:sec) | 21:08–24:44 | 19:00–21:59 | 18:00–20:59 | 17:00–19:59 | 15:00–17:59 | 12:30–15:44 |
| | 12-min. dist. (ml) | 1.57–1.72 | 1.50–1.64 | 1.46–1.56 | 1.40–1.53 | 1.31–1.44 | 1.21–1.32 |
| | 1.5-mile time min:sec | 9:41–10:48 | 10:46–12:00 | 11:01–12:30 | 11:31–13:00 | 12:31–14:30 | 14:00–16:15 |
| V. Excellent | O₂ uptake (ml/kg/min) | 51.0–55.9 | 46.5–52.4 | 45.0–49.4 | 43.8–48.0 | 41.0–45.3 | 36.5–44.2 |
| | *T. M. time (min:sec) | 24:45–27:47 | 22:00–24:59 | 21:00–23:59 | 20:00–22:59 | 18:00–21:14 | 15:45–20:37 |
| | 12-min. dist. (ml) | 1.73–1.86 | 1.65–1.76 | 1.57–1.69 | 1.54–1.65 | 1.45–1.58 | 1.33–1.55 |
| | 1.5-mile time min:sec | 8:37–9:40 | 9:45–10:45 | 10:00–11:00 | 10:30–11:30 | 11:00–12:30 | 11:15–13:59 |
| VI. Superior | O₂ uptake (ml/kg/min) | >56.0 | >52.5 | >49.5 | >48.1 | >45.4 | >44.3 |
| | *T. M. time (min:sec) | >27:48 | >25:00 | >24:00 | >23:00 | >21:15 | >20:38 |
| | 12-min. dist. (ml) | >1.87 | >1.77 | >1.70 | >1.66 | >1.59 | >1.56 |
| | 1.5-mile time min:sec | <8:37 | <9:45 | <10:00 | <10:30 | <11:00 | <11:15 |

* Treadmill time using Balke-Ware technique.

# WOMEN'S AEROBICS FITNESS CLASSIFICATION (PREDICTED)

| CATEGORY | MEASURE | 13-19 | 20-29 | 30-39 | 40-49 | 50-59 | 60+ |
|---|---|---|---|---|---|---|---|
| I. Very poor | $O_2$ uptake (ml/kg/min) | <25.0 | <23.6 | <22.8 | <21.0 | <20.2 | <17.5 |
| | * T.M. time (min:sec) | <8:30 | <7:46 | <7:15 | <6:00 | <5:38 | <4:00 |
| | 12-min. dist. (mi) | <1.0 | <.96 | <.94 | <.88 | <.84 | <.78 |
| | 1.5-mile time (min:sec) | >18:31 | >19:01 | >19:31 | >20:01 | >20:31 | >21:01 |
| II. Poor | $O_2$ uptake (ml/kg/min) | 25.0-30.9 | 23.6-28.9 | 22.8-26.9 | 21.0-24.4 | 20.2-22.7 | 17.5-20.1 |
| | * T.M. time (min:sec) | 8:30-11:29 | 7:46-10:09 | 7:15-9:29 | 6:00-7:59 | 5:38-6:59 | 4:00-5:32 |
| | 12-min. dist. (mi) | 1.00-1.18 | .96-1.11 | .95-1.05 | .88-98 | .84-93 | .78-86 |
| | 1.5-mile time (min:sec) | 18:30-16:55 | 19:00-18:31 | 19:30-19:01 | 20:00-19:31 | 20:30-20:01 | 21:00-20:31 |
| III. Fair | $O_2$ uptake (ml/kg/min) | 31.0-34.9 | 29.0-32.9 | 27.0-31.4 | 24.5-28.9 | 22.8-26.9 | 20.2-24.4 |
| | * T.M. time (min:sec) | 11:30-13:59 | 10:10-12:59 | 9:30-11:59 | 8:00-10:59 | 7:00-9:29 | 5:33-7:59 |
| | 12-min. dist. (mi) | 1.19-1.29 | 1.12-1.22 | 1.06-1.18 | .99-1.11 | .94-1.05 | .87-98 |
| | 1.5-mile time (min:sec) | 16:54-14:31 | 18:30-15:55 | 19:00-16:31 | 19:30-17:31 | 20:00-19:01 | 20:30-19:31 |
| IV. Good | $O_2$ uptake (ml/kg/min) | 35.0-38.9 | 33.0-36.9 | 31.5-35.6 | 29.0-32.8 | 27.0-31.4 | 24.5-30.2 |
| | * T.M. time (min:sec) | 14:00-17:29 | 13:00-15:59 | 12:00-14:59 | 11:00-12:59 | 9:30-11:59 | 8:00-10:59 |
| | 12-min. dist. (mi) | 1.30-1.43 | 1.23-1.34 | 1.19-1.29 | 1.12-1.24 | 1.06-1.18 | .99-1.09 |
| | 1.5-mile time (min:sec) | 14:30-12:30 | 15:54-13:31 | 16:30-14:31 | 17:30-15:56 | 19:00-16:31 | 19:30-17:31 |
| V. Excellent | $O_2$ uptake (ml/kg/min) | 39.0-41.9 | 37.0-40.9 | 35.7-40.0 | 32.9-36.9 | 31.5-35.7 | 30.3-31.4 |
| | * T.M. time (min:sec) | 17:30-18:59 | 16:00-17:59 | 15:00-16:59 | 13:00-16:59 | 12:00-14:59 | 11:00-11:59 |
| | 12-min. dist. (mi) | 1.44-1.51 | 1.35-1.45 | 1.30-1.39 | 1.25-1.34 | 1.19-1.30 | 1.10-1.18 |
| | 1.5-mile time (min:sec) | 12:29-11:50 | 13:30-12:30 | 14:30-13:00 | 15:55-13:45 | 16:30-14:30 | 17:30-16:30 |
| VI. Superior | $O_2$ uptake (ml/kg/min) | >42.0 | >41.0 | >40.1 | >37.0 | >35.8 | >31.5 |
| | * T.M. time (min:sec) | >19:00 | >18:00 | >17:00 | >16:00 | >15:00 | >12:00 |
| | 12-min. dist. (mi) | >1.52 | >1.46 | >1.40 | >1.35 | >1.31 | >1.19 |
| | 1.5-mile time (min:sec) | <11:50 | <12:30 | <13:00 | <13:45 | <14:30 | <16:30 |

* Treadmill time using Balke-Ware technique.

# 12-MINUTE TEST/1.5-MILE RUN TEST

In the Exercise Physiology Laboratory, cardiovascular fitness—the maximum amount of oxygen the body can process during intense effort—can be measured directly. Analysis of expired air shows the amount of oxygen one's body can process. The aerobic capacity is measured in ml/kg/min—milliliters of oxygen per kilogram of body weight per minute. This type of testing is necessary for research, but impractical on a large scale, due to cost of equipment, personnel, and time. Thus for application to the general population, simpler field tests have been developed. The 12-minute test/1.5-mile run test correlates well with one's maximum oxygen consumption established from laboratory results.

## Test Administration

This test requires a nearly exhaustive effort and for this reason it is important to point out that it is not recommended for use until after at least six weeks of training. This should allow adequate time for the important physiological adaptations to take place. It should also be stressed that individuals should not necessarily run to complete exhaustion when taking this test but should use some caution in how hard they will push themselves—it should certainly not be much harder than the higher intensities at which they are training. Again, it is assumed that the subject has had the proper medical exam and clearance prior to this time, and that he or she has been progressing satisfactorily in the exercise program.

## Equipment

1. A stopwatch or clock with a sweep second hand.
2. An indoor or outdoor track or another suitable running area measured to 1.5 miles.
3. Testing forms to record data.

## Procedure

1. Utilize an indoor or outdoor track or another suitable running area measured so that exact distances are indicated.
2. If possible, each subject should have experienced some practice in pacing prior to the test. Often subjects will attempt to run at too fast a pace early in the run and become fatigued too early. A trained pacer might accompany the participants around the track during the actual test.
3. On the day of testing, the participant should refrain from any physical exertion and should abstain from smoking or eating for 2 hours preceding the test.
4. It is advisable to allow adequate time prior to the test for stretching and warm-up exercises.
5. During the administration of the tests the participants can be informed of their lap times. If several participants run at once, their individual times at the finish can be called out and recorded later.
6. An important consideration at the end of the run is the "cool-down" period. The participants should be cautioned about standing around immediately after the run, to prevent venous pooling (i.e., pooling of blood in the lower extremities, which reduces the return of blood to

282

the heart). Instead they should be instructed to walk for an additional 5 minutes in order to enhance venous return and aid in recovery.

7. The distance covered in 12 minutes or time for 1.5 miles can be compared to the norm tables listed on pages 280 and 281.

8. For indoor testing, dividing into two or more groups and using a buddy system for accurately counting laps has considerable merit.

ALTITUDE ADJUSTMENTS FOR THE
1.5-MILE FITNESS CATEGORIZATION TEST

| Altitude in Feet at Which Acclimatized | Times to be Added to the Age Requirements for Running 1.5 Miles † |
|---|---|
| 5,000 * | 30 seconds |
| 6,000 | 40 seconds |
| 7,000 | 50 seconds |
| 8,000 | 1 minute |
| 9,000 | 1 min 15 sec |
| 10,000 | 1 min 30 sec |
| 11,000 | 1 min 45 sec |
| 12,000 | 2 minutes |

* Up to 5,000 feet, use the 1.5-Mile Run Test chart without altitude correction (page 89).
† 1.5-Mile Test for Men.

## GOOD SHOES FOR BAD FEET

A. One of the best shoes available for the problem.
B. May help relieve the problem, assuming other positive factors.
C. Not recommended for this area of pain.
D. This shoe may aggravate the problem.

| POPULAR TRAINING SHOES (Alphabetically) | Achilles Tendonitis | Ankle Sprains, Instability | Arch Problems, Flat Feet | Calluses (Bottom of Foot) | Corns (Top of Foot) | Fatigue (Heaviness) | Heel Problems, Back | Heel Problems, Bottom | Forefoot pain | Shin Splints | Width |
|---|---|---|---|---|---|---|---|---|---|---|---|
| Adidas Country | B | A | B | B | B | B | B | B | B | B | C |
| Adidas SL 72/76 | B | B | A | B | C | B | B | B | B | B | C |
| Brooks Villanova II | ? | B | B | B | B | B | C | B | B | B | A |
| E. B. (Lydiard) Roadrunner | C | A | A | B | A | A | A | B | A | B | A |
| Etonic | B | B | A | B | B | B | B | B | B | B | B |
| Karhu 2323 | A | B | B | C | B | B | B | C | A | B | B |
| New Balance Interval 320 | B | B | B | B | C | B | ? | B | B | B | A |
| New Balance Trackster III | B | B | B | A | C | C | B | A | A | C | A |
| Nike Cortez, Road Runner | D | B | C | B | B | C | C | A | C | D | B |
| Nike LD-1000 | ? | A | B | B | B | D | ? | B | B | B | B |
| Nike Waffle Trainer | C | A | B | B | B | B | B | A | B | B | B |
| Puma 9190S | B | B | A | B | B | B | B | C | C | B | B |
| Tiger Montreal | C | B | B | C | B | B | B | B | C | C | B |

Courtesy of Dr. H. F. Hlavac, author of *The Foot Book: Advice for Athletes.* P.O. Box 3964, San Rafael, California 94902.

## RUNNER'S WORLD RANKING OF TRAINING SHOES *

| NAME | (MEN'S) SIZES | APPROXIMATE COST ($) |
|---|---|---|
| 1. New Balance 320 | 3½ AA–15 EEE | 26.95 |
| 2. Brooks Villanova | 4–13 | 19.95 |
| 3. New Balance 305 | 3½ AA–15 EEE | 24.95 |
| 4. Etonic | —— | 24.95 |
| 5. Nike LD-1000 | 3–13 | 39.95 |
| 6. Nike Waffle Trainer | 3–13 | 28.95 |
| 7. New Balance 220 | 3½ AA–15 EEE | 23.95 |
| 8. Brooks 271-B | 4–13 | 18.50 |
| 9. Karhu 2322–2323 | 3–13 | 23.95–25.95 |
| 10. Nike Nylon Cortez | 3–13 | 25.95 |
| 11. Adidas SL 72/76 | 3–15 | 30.95 |
| 12. Puma 9190–9190S | 4–13 | 30.00 |
| 13. Nike Road Runner | 3–13 | 23.95 |
| 14. Spotbilt 850 | 6–13 | (Unknown) |
| 15. E. B. (Lydiard) Roadrunner | 3½–13 | 34.95 |

* Reprinted by permission of *Runner's World Magazine* (Box 366, Mountain View, California 94042), from the October 1976 shoe issue.

## CHECKLIST FOR CONDUCTING A COMPETITIVE PROGRAM

FOR CONTESTANTS OVER 35
- Has physician clearance
- Has had stress test
- Has been exercising regularly
- Has exercise log
- Has signed release

FOR CONTESTANTS OF ALL AGES
- Mandatory warm-up
- Mandatory cool-down

FOR RACE OFFICIALS
- Physician on hand
- Course supervised
- Adequate equipment
  Portable defibrillator, oxygen,
  means of resuscitation
- Proper fluids on hand

# CALORIE EQUIVALENTS FOR POPULAR FOODS AND BEVERAGES

| FOOD | SIZE/SERVING | APPROXIMATE CALORIES |
|---|---|---|
| **Alcohol** | | |
| gin, rum, vodka, whiskey | | |
| 80 proof | 1½ ounces | 100 |
| 100 proof | 1½ ounces | 125 |
| **Almonds** | 9–10 whole | 70 |
| **Apple** | 2½" diameter | 70 |
| **Apple, baked with sugar** | 1 large | 200 |
| **Applesauce, sweetened** | ½ cup | 115 |
| **Apricots** | | |
| canned in water | ½ cup | 45 |
| canned in syrup | ½ cup | 110 |
| **Apricots, dried** | ½ cup, 20 small halves | 120 |
| **Asparagus** | 6 spears | 20 |
| **Avocado** | ½ average | 185 |
| **Bacon, fried** | 2 slices | 90 |
| **Banana** | 1 average, 6" x 1½" | 80 |
| **Beans, baked with pork** | | |
| in tomato sauce | ½ cup | 160 |
| **Beans (green, wax,** | | |
| or yellow) | ½ cup | 15 |
| **Beans, lima** | ½ cup | 130 |
| **Beef** | | |
| corned, canned | 3 ounces | 185 |
| hamburger, reg. | 3 ounces | 245 |
| oven roast | 3 ounces, lean | 200 |
| pot roast | 3 ounces, lean | 165 |
| steak | 3 ounces, lean | 175 |
| **Beer** | 12 ounces | 150 |
| **Blueberries** | ½ cup, fresh | 45 |
| **Bologna** | 2 ounces, all meat | 170 |
| **Bread** | | |
| white | 1 slice, 16 slices per loaf | 75 |
| whole-wheat | 1 slice, 16 slices per loaf | 70 |
| rye | 1 slice, 16 slices per loaf | 70 |
| **Broccoli** | ½ cup | 30 |
| **Butter** | 1 pat, 16 per ¼ pound | 50 |
| **Cabbage** | 1 cup, raw, shredded | 24 |
| | 1 cup, cooked | 40 |
| **Cake** | | |
| chocolate with chocolate | | |
| icing | 2" wedge of 10" layer cake | 345 |
| plain cake without icing | 3" x 2" x 1½" slice | 155 |
| pound cake | 2¾" x 3" x ⅝" slice | 140 |
| **Candies** | | |
| caramels | 3 medium | 115 |
| chocolate creams | 2 or 3 small | 110 |
| fudge, milk chocolate | 1 ounce | 120 |
| hard candy | 1 ounce | 110 |
| milk chocolate | 1-ounce bar | 150 |

| FOOD | SIZE/SERVING | APPROXIMATE CALORIES |
|---|---|---|
| Cantaloupe | ½ melon, 5" diameter | 60 |
| Carrot | 5½" x 1" | 20 |
| Celery | Two 8" stalks | 10 |
| Cereal | | |
| corn flakes | 1 cup | 95 |
| oatmeal | 1 cup | 130 |
| wheat flakes | 1 cup | 105 |
| Cheese | | |
| American, processed | 1 ounce | 105 |
| Cheddar, natural | 1 ounce | 115 |
| cottage, creamed | 1 ounce | 30 |
| Swiss | 1 ounce | 105 |
| Cherries | | |
| sweet, fresh | ½ cup | 40 |
| sweet, canned with syrup | ½ cup | 105 |
| Chicken | ¼ small, broiled | 185 |
| Cookies | 1 average | 30 |
| Corn | ½ cup | 70 |
| Crab | ½ cup, canned | 85 |
| Crackers | | |
| graham | 4 squares | 55 |
| rye wafers | 2 | 45 |
| saltines | Two, 2" square | 35 |
| Cucumber | ¾" slice | 5 |
| Custard, baked | ½ cup | 140 |
| Egg | 1 large | 80 |
| Frankfurter | 1 average | 155 |
| | 1 with roll | 245 |
| Fruit cocktail | ½ cup with syrup | 100 |
| Gelatin dessert | ½ cup | 70 |
| Grapefruit | Half of 4¼" fruit | 55 |
| | ½ cup, canned with water | 35 |
| | ½ cup, canned with syrup | 90 |
| Gum, chewing | 1 stick | 10 |
| Ham | 3 ounces lean | 160 |
| Honeydew melon | ½ fresh | 50 |
| Ice cream | ½ cup | 145 |
| soda | large | 455 |
| Ice milk | ½ cup | 110 |
| Jams, jellies | 1 tablespoon | 55 |
| Lamb | 3 ounces, lean | 160 |
| Lemonade | 8-ounce glass | 110 |
| Lettuce | 2 large leaves | 10 |
| Liver, beef | 3 ounces | 195 |
| Macaroni | ¾ cup, plain | 115 |
| | ¾ cup, with cheese | 360 |
| Margarine | 1 pat, 16 per ¼ pound | 50 |

# CALORIE EQUIVALENTS FOR POPULAR FOODS AND BEVERAGES (CONTINUED)

| FOOD | SIZE/SERVING | APPROXIMATE CALORIES |
|---|---|---|
| **Milk** | | |
| whole | 1 cup | 160 |
| buttermilk | 1 cup | 90 |
| half-and-half | 1 tablespoon | 20 |
| skim | 1 cup | 90 |
| chocolate | 1 cup | 210 |
| chocolate milkshake | 12 ounces | 500 |
| **Muffin** | | |
| corn | 2¾" diameter | 150 |
| English | 3½" diameter | 135 |
| **Noodles** | ¾ cup | 150 |
| **Oil, salad** | 1 tablespoon | 125 |
| **Orange** | 3" fruit | 75 |
| **Orange juice** | ½ cup | 55 |
| **Pancake** | 4" cake | 55 |
| **Peach** | 2" fruit, fresh | 35 |
| | ½ cup, canned in syrup | 100 |
| **Peanut butter** | 1 tablespoon | 95 |
| **Peanuts** | 2 tablespoons | 105 |
| **Pear** | 3" x 2½" fruit | 100 |
| **Peas** | ½ cup | 60 |
| **Pickle** | | |
| dill | 1¾" x 4" | 15 |
| sweet | ¾" x 1¾" | 30 |
| **Pie** | | |
| fruit | ⅛ of 9" pie | 300 |
| lemon meringue | ⅛ of 9" pie | 270 |
| pecan | ⅛ of 9" pie | 430 |
| **Pineapple** | ½ cup, fresh | 40 |
| | ½ cup, canned | 100 |
| **Plum** | 2" fruit, fresh | 25 |
| | ½ cup, canned | 100 |
| **Popcorn** | 1 cup | 40 |
| **Pork** | 3 ounces, lean | 230 |
| **Potato** | | |
| baked | 2½", 5 ounces | 90 |
| French-fried | Ten 2"-long pieces | 155 |
| mashed | ½ cup | 90 |
| sweet | 5" x 2", 6 ounces | 155 |
| **Potato chips** | 10 medium | 115 |
| **Pretzels** | 5 small sticks | 20 |
| **Prunes** | ½ cup, unsweetened | 150 |
| **Radishes** | 4 small | 5 |
| **Raisins** | ½ cup | 230 |

| FOOD | SIZE/SERVING | APPROXIMATE CALORIES |
|---|---|---|
| Rice, cooked | ¾ cup | 140 |
| Salad dressing | | |
| blue-cheese | 1 tablespoon | 75 |
| French | 1 tablespoon | 65 |
| low-calorie | 1 tablespoon | 15 |
| mayonnaise | 1 tablespoon | 100 |
| Thousand Island | 1 tablespoon | 125 |
| Salmon | 3 ounces, canned | 120 |
| Sausage, pork | 2 ounces | 270 |
| Sherbet | ½ cup | 130 |
| Shrimps | 3 ounces, 17 medium, canned | 100 |
| Soft drink | | |
| cola-type | 12-ounce can | 145 |
| fruit flavors | 12-ounce can | 170 |
| ginger ale | 12-ounce can | 115 |
| root beer | 12-ounce can | 150 |
| Soup | | |
| bouillon | 1 cup | 30 |
| chicken noodle | 1 cup | 60 |
| cream of mushroom | 1 cup | 135 |
| minestrone | 1 cup | 105 |
| tomato | 1 cup, made with water | 90 |
| | 1 cup, made with milk | 170 |
| Spaghetti | | |
| plain | ¾ cup | 115 |
| with tomato sauce | ¾ cup | 195 |
| with meatballs | ¾ cup | 250 |
| Spinach | ½ cup | 20 |
| Strawberries | ½ cup, fresh | 30 |
| | ½ cup, frozen | 140 |
| Sugar | 1 teaspoon | 15 |
| Tomato juice | ½ cup | 20 |
| Tomatoes | ½ cup | 25 |
| Tuna | 3 ounces, canned | 170 |
| Turkey | 3 ounces, light meat | 150 |
| | 3 ounces, dark meat | 175 |
| Veal | 3 ounces, lean | 185 |
| Waffle | 1 average | 210 |
| Watermelon | one 2-pound wedge | 115 |
| Wines | | |
| dessert | 3½ ounces | 140 |
| table | 3½ ounces | 85 |
| Yogurt | 1 cup, plain | 120 |
| | 1 cup, with fruit | 260 |

## AEROBICS INTERNATIONAL RESEARCH SOCIETY (AIRS)

In an effort to follow a large group of people for several years, correlating their physical activity with their state of health, the Aerobics International Research Society (AIRS) is being established. People from all over the world who are exercising regularly are encouraged to join this society so that the results of regular exercise can be more extensively and objectively evaluated. Members will receive a blank exercise log that they can fill out daily (for a sample of a filled-out exercise log, see next page). AIRS will determine the number of points they earn each month, and that information will be stored in the AIRS data bank. Each member will receive a summary of his or her monthly activity (see example, pages 292–293) for personal files, along with a research report and newsletter from the Aerobics Activities Center. In other words, AIRS can enable you to become a correspondent member of the Aerobics Activities Center. Periodically, you will be asked to complete a health questionnaire, so that the effect of your exercise program can be documented. If you are interested in becoming a member of AIRS (for which there is a nominal yearly fee), write to the Aerobics International Research Society, P.O. Box 22359, Dallas, Texas 75222, and more detailed information will be sent to you. I hope you will join, since it will be motivational for you and will provide our research institute with an invaluable source of data.

# AEROBICS EXERCISE LOG

The Aerobics Center / 12100 Preston Rd. / Dallas, Tx. 75230

NAME: (LAST NAME, FIRST NAME)
[B,R,O,W,N,_,_,_] [R,O,B,E,R,T,_,_]

Identification Number
[_,2,8,6,3,1,0]

SEX  Male [X]  Female [ ]

## ACTIVITY CODES:

| | | ALLOWABLE UNITS: |
|---|---|---|
| 01 = JOGGING/RUNNING | | MI, YD |
| 02 = WALKING | | MI, YD |
| 03 = STATIONARY RUNNING | | SM (steps/min) |
| 04 = CYCLING | | MI |
| 05 = STATIONARY CYCLING | | (reps/min or mi/hr) |
| 06 = SWIMMING | | MI, YD |
| 07 = TENNIS (SINGLES) | | SE, GM |
| 08 = TENNIS (DOUBLES) | | SE, GM |
| 09 = AERIAL TENNIS (SINGLES) | | SE, GM |
| 10 = AERIAL TENNIS (DOUBLES) | | SE, GM |

CODES:
11 = BADMINTON (SINGLES)
12 = BADMINTON (DOUBLES)
13 = STAIR CLIMBING
14 = WALK/JOG
15 = TREADMILL
16 = GOLF
17 = CALISTHENICS
18 = ROPE SKIPPING
19 = HOCKEY
20 = SOCCER

UNITS:
SE, GM
SE, GM
RTT (time)
MI, YD
(# of times around)
NO

CODES:
21 = LACROSSE
22 = FOOTBALL
23 = SKIING
24 = VOLLEYBALL
25 = HANDBALL
26 = BASKETBALL
27 = SQUASH
28 = WRESTLING

ACTIVITY CODES:
17 - 28
REQUIRE
DURATION
ONLY

**CURRENT MONTH: (JAN, = 01 ... DEC, = 12** [0,1]   **CURRENT YEAR: 19** [7,5] **   CURRENT WEIGHT** [1,6,5] **

| Month | Day | Activity | Distance | Units | Duration (hrs : min : sec) |
|---|---|---|---|---|---|
| [0,1] | [0,1] | [0,1] | [_,_,2,_,_,5,0] | [M,I] | [_,_,1,_,2,:,3,:,3,_,0] |
| [0,1] | [0,2] | [0,2] | [_,_,_,_,2,5] | [M,I] | [_,_,_,2,:,3,:,1,_,5] |
| [0,1] | [0,5] | [0,3] | [_,_,8,0,_,_] | [S,M] | [_,_,_,7,:,2,:,3,_,0] |
| [0,1] | [0,6] | [0,4] | [_,_,_,1,_,5,0] | [M,I] | [_,_,1,6,:,1,:,1,_,5] |
| [0,1] | [0,7] | [0,5] | [1,6,5,0,_,_] | [2,5] | [_,_,1,:,2,:,0,_,0] |
| [0,1] | [0,8] | [0,6] | [_,4,0,0,_,_] | [Y,D] | [_,_,1,:,1,:,3,_,7] |
| [0,1] | [1,0] | [0,7] | [_,_,3,_,_,_] | [S,E] | [2,:,0,0,:,0,:,0,_,0] |
| [0,1] | [1,1] | [1,2] | [_,_,1,2,_,_] | [G,M] | [1,:,1,:,1,8,:,1,0,_,0] |
| [0,1] | [1,1] | [1,3] | [_,_,6,_,_,_] | [R,T] | [_,1,:,1,0,:,1,:,1,_,3] |
| [0,1] | [1,2] | [1,4] | [_,_,2,_,0,0] | [M,I] | [_,1,:,2,0,:,4,_,2] |

| Month | Day | Activity | Distance | Units | Duration (hrs : min : sec) |
|---|---|---|---|---|---|
| [0,1] | [1,5] | [1,6] | [_,_,1,8,_,_,0,0] | [H,O] | [4,:,1,:,0,0,:,1,0,_,0] |
| [0,1] | [1,9] | [1,5] | [_,_,_,7,:,_,0,0] | [0,5] | [_,_,_,_,6,:,3,_,0] |
| [0,1] | [2,3] | [1,7] | | | [_,_,2,:,0,:,0,_,0] |
| [0,1] | [2,3] | [2,0] | | | [1,:,_,3,:,0,:,0,_,0] |
| [0,1] | [2,4] | [2,3] | | | [3,:,1,4,:,5,:,1,_,0,0] |
| [0,1] | [2,5] | [0,1] | [_,_,_,3,_,:,2,5] | [M,I] | [_,5,:,8,0,:,3,_,7,] |
| [0,1] | [2,8] | [1,5] | [_,_,_,3,_,:,3,0,0] | [0,9] | [_,_,1,:,1,8,:,1,0,_,0] |
| [0,1] | [2,9] | [0,5] | [1,6,5,_,:,0,0,0] | [1,0] | [1,:,0,:,0,:,0,_,8] |
| [0,1] | [3,0] | [1,4] | [_,_,_,_,_,7,5] | [M,I] | [_,1,_,:,7,:,2,:,3] |
| [0,1] | [3,1] | [0,1] | [_,_,1,:,0,:,0,0] | [M,I] | [M,I,:,1,:,3,:,3,:,2,_,1] |

291

Your printout gives a
day by day listing of
your exercise.

It gives distances in
miles and yards. Also
quantities.

Everything is converted
into Aerobic Points.

| DATE | ACTIVITY | DISTANCE/QUANTITY | DURATION | AEROBIC POINTS | ERROR CODES |
|------|----------|-------------------|----------|----------------|-------------|
| Mar 1 | Jogging/Running | 2.00 MI | 16:00 | 11.00 | |
| Mar 2 | Jogging/Running | 3.00 MI | 25:00 | 16.40 | |
| Mar 3 | Rope Skipping | 90.00 SM | 20:00 | 9.00 | |
| Mar 5 | Jogging/Running | 5.00 MI | 43:00 | 27.26 | |
| Mar 7 | Walking | 2.00 MI | 30:00 | 5.00 | |
| Mar 8 | Treadmill | 3.30 10 | 30:00 | 3.91 | |
| Mar 9 | Jogging/Running | 2.00 MI | 15:35 | 11.27 | |
| Mar 10 | Calisthenics | | 30:00 | .75 | |
| Mar 11 | Handball | | 1:30:00 | 13.50 | |
| Mar 12 | Rope Skipping | 90.00 SM | 15:00 | 6.25 | |
| Mar 14 | Treadmill | 3.30 10 | 30:00 | 3.91 | |
| Mar 15 | Calisthenics | | 30:00 | .75 | |
| Mar 16 | Jogging/Running | 6.00 MI | 50:00 | 33.80 | |
| Mar 17 | Swimming | 600.00 YD | 12:00 | 6.25 | |
| Mar 18 | Tennis (Singles) | 2.00 SE | 1:00:00 | 4.00 | |
| Mar 20 | Treadmill | 3.30 10 | 30:00 | 3.91 | |
| Mar 21 | Tennis (Doubles) | 3.00 SE | 1:20:00 | 2.00 | |
| Mar 22 | Treadmill | 3.30 10 | 30:00 | 3.91 | |
| Mar 24 | Jogging/Running | 3.00 MI | 23:00 | 17.65 | |
| Mar 25 | Walking | 2.00 MI | 31:00 | 4.74 | |
| Mar 26 | Stationary Cycling | 170.00 35 | 20:00 | 9.25 | |
| Mar 28 | Volleyball | | 1:00:00 | 4.00 | |
| Mar 29 | Skiing | | 1:00:00 | 6.00 | |
| Mar 30 | Jogging/Running | 5.00 MI | 43:00 | 27.26 | |

## MONTHLY and ACCUMULATIVE TOTALS

| | A.Pts | Mileage | Cycling | Swim | St Run | St Cyc | Ten.S |
|---|-------|---------|---------|------|--------|--------|-------|
| Start Mar. '77 | 512.8 | 257.3 60.0 | 82.8 5.0 | 1.3 .7 | 1:00: | 1:30: | 1:00: |
| Totals | 115.8/w | 317.3 | 87.8 | 2.0 | | | |

This bar lists your
weekly Aerobic Points
as well as your
overall points.

292

Times are shown so you can watch your improvement.

| DATE | ACTIVITY | DISTANCE/ QUANTITY | DURATION | AEROBIC POINTS | ERROR CODES |
|------|----------|-------------------|----------|----------------|-------------|
| Mar  1 | Calisthenics | | 30:00 | .75 | |
| Mar  2 | Rope Skipping | 90.00 SM | 15:00 | 6.25 | |
| Mar  4 | Swimming | 600.00 YD | 11:00 | 6.82 | |
| Mar  6 | Stationary Running | 100.00 SM | 15:00 | 10.00 | |
| Mar  7 | Cycling | 5.00 MI | 17:00 | 7.32 | |
| Mar  8 | Stationary Cycling | 170.00 35 | 25:00 | 11.56 | |
| Mar  9 | Tennis (Doubles) | 3.00 SE | 1:20:00 | 2.00 | |
| Mar 10 | Jogging/Running | 4.00 MI | 33:00 | 22.39 | |
| Mar 12 | Stationary Running | 100.00 SM | 15:00 | 10.00 | |
| Mar 13 | Jogging/Running | 3.00 MI | 23:30 | 17.32 | |
| Mar 14 | Basketball | | 1:45:00 | 15.75 | |
| Mar 15 | Jogging/Running | 3.00 MI | 24:00 | 17.00 | |
| Mar 17 | Stationary Running | 100.00 SM | 15:00 | 10.00 | |
| Mar 18 | Calisthenics | | 30:00 | .75 | |
| Mar 19 | Jogging/Running | 4.00 MI | 32:30 | 22.69 | |
| Mar 21 | Walking | 2.00 MI | 29:00 | 5.28 | |
| Mar 22 | Stationary Running | 100.00 SM | 15:00 | 10.00 | |
| Mar 23 | Jogging/Running | 5.00 MI | 42:00 | 27.81 | |
| Mar 24 | Volleyball | | 1:00:00 | 4.00 | |
| Mar 25 | Stationary Cycling | 170.00 30 | 45:00 | 15.42 | |
| Mar 27 | Jogging/Running | 6.00 MI | 50:00 | 33.80 | |
| Mar 28 | Jogging/Running | 3.00 MI | 23:30 | 17.32 | |
| Mar 29 | Skiing | | 1:00:00 | 6.00 | |
| Mar 30 | Calisthenics | | 30:00 | .75 | |

| Ten.D | Treadml | Calisth | Rope Sk | Skiing | Volleyb | Handbal | Basketb |
|-------|---------|---------|---------|--------|---------|---------|---------|
| 2:40: | 2:00: | 2:30: | 50: | 2:00: | 2:00: | 1:30: | 1:45: |

Your printout can chart fourteen of the 28 activities.

AEROBICS
EXERCISE
LOG

293

# Selected References

## CHAPTER 1

Aronow, W. S., and Stemmer, E. A. "Two-year follow-up of angina pectoris: Medical or surgical therapy." *Annals of Internal Medicine,* Vol. 82 (No. 2): 208–12, Feb. 1975.

Bucher, C. A. "Exercise is 'plain good business.'" *Reader's Digest,* Feb. 1976, p. 127.

Corday, E. "Status of coronary bypass surgery." *Journal of the AMA,* Vol. 231 (No. 12): 1245–47, Mar. 24, 1975.

"Coronary arteriography and coronary artery surgery." *Medical Letter on Drugs and Therapeutics,* Vol. 18 (No. 14) (Issue 456): 57–59, July 2, 1976.

"Deaths from heart ills show decline in nation." *Dallas Times Herald,* June 6, 1976.

"Heart attack fatalities rose by 14% since 1950 for men aged 25 to 44." *New York Times,* Apr. 4, 1972, p. 28:3.

*Heart Facts.* New York: American Heart Association, 1972.

Klaw, Spencer. *The Great American Medical Show: The Unhealthy State of U.S. Medical Care and What Can Be Done About It.* New York: Viking Press, 1975.

Mundth, E. D., and Austen, W. G. "Surgical measures for coronary heart disease." *New England Journal of Medicine,* Vol. 293 (No. 1): 13–19, July 3, 1975.

———. (No. 2): 75–80, July 10, 1975.

———. (No. 3): 124–30, July 17, 1975.

Statistics from National Center for Health Statistics. Rockville, Md., 1974.

Oberman, A.; Kouchoukos, N. T.; Harrell, R. R.; Holt, J. H., Jr.; Russell, R. O., Jr.; and Rackley, C. E. "Surgical versus medical treatment in disease of the left main coronary artery." *Lancet,* Vol. II (No. 7986): 591–94, Sept. 18, 1976.

Overbeke, J. E. "Can health care costs be tamed?" *Industry Week,* May 3, 1976, p. 49.

"Record low death rate attained by U.S. in 1974." *Dallas Times Herald,* Feb. 4, 1976, p. 14.

Rhein, R. W., Jr. "The unhealthy state of U.S. medical care." *Business Week,* Feb. 2, 1976, p. 6.

Rimm, A. A.; Barboriak, J. J.; and Anderson, A. J. "Changes in occupation after aortocoronary vein-bypass operation." *Journal of the AMA,* Vol. 236 (No. 4): 361–64, July 26, 1976.

Selden, R.; Neill, W. A.; Ritzmann, L. W.; Okies, J. E.; and Anderson, R. P. "Medical versus surgical therapy for acute coronary insufficiency." *New England Journal of Medicine*, Vol. 293 (No. 26): 1329–33, Dec. 25, 1975.

Takaro, T.; Hultgren, H. N.; and Lipton, M. J. "The VA cooperative randomized study of surgery for coronary arterial occlusive disease. II Subgroup with significant left main lesions." *Circulation*, Suppl. No. 3, Vol. 54 (No. 6): III-107—III-117, Dec. 1976.

Turner, R., and Ball, K. "The cardiologist's responsibility for preventing coronary heart disease." *American Heart Journal*, Vol. 91 (No. 2): 139–47, Feb. 1976.

Walker, W. J. "Success story: The program against major cardiovascular risk factors." *Geriatrics*, Vol. 31 (No. 3): 97–100, 104, Mar. 1976.

Weaver, P. "$70 billion bill for poor health." *Dallas Times Herald*, Aug. 23, 1972, p. 13.

## CHAPTER 2

Balke, B., and Ware, R. W. "An experimental study of 'physical fitness' of Air Force personnel." *U.S. Armed Forces Medical Journal*, Vol. X (No. 6): 675–88, June 1959.

Cooper, K. H.; Purdy, J. G.; White, S. R.; Pollock, M. L.; and Linnerud, A. C. "Age-fitness adjusted maximal heart rates." In Jokl, E. and Hebbelinck, H., eds. *Medicine and Sport*, Vol. 10: *The Role of Exercise in Internal Medicine*. Basel, Switzerland: S. Karger AG, 1977.

Cumming, G. R. "Yield of ischaemic exercise electrocardiograms in relation to exercise intensity in a normal population." *British Heart Journal*, Vol. 34 (No. 9): 919–23, Sept. 1972.

Ellestad, M. H.; Allen, W.; Wan, M. C. K.; and Kemp, G. L. "Maximal treadmill stress testing for cardiovascular evaluation." *Circulation*. Vol. 39 (No. 4): 517–21, April 1969.

Margolis, J. R.; Kisslo, J. A.; Peter, R. H.; Kong, Y.; Behar, V. S.; Rosati, R.; and Wallace, A. G. "Treadmill exercise capacity: Its diagnostic, prognostic, and therapeutic implications in the context of coronary artery disease." Presented to North Carolina Heart Association, May 27, 1976.

Montagu, A. "Rehumanizing Medicine." *New York Times*, Dec. 1, 1975, p. 13.

Pollock, M. L.; Bohannon, R. L.; Cooper, K. H.; Ayres, J. J.; Ward, A.; White, S. R.; and Linnerud, A. C. "A comparative analysis of four protocols for maximal treadmill stress testing." *American Heart Journal*, Vol. 92 (No. 1): 39–46, July 1976.

Robertson, D.; Kostuk, W. J.; and Ahuja, S. P. "The localization of coronary artery stenoses by 12-lead ECG response to graded exercise test: Support for intercoronary steal." *American Heart Journal*, Vol. 91 (No. 4): 437–44, Apr. 1976.

Seidman, H.; Silverberg, E.; and Holleb, A. I. "Cancer statistics, 1976: A comparison of white and black populations." *CA–A Cancer Journal for Clinicians*. Vol. 26 (No. 1): 17, Jan./Feb. 1976.

*Statistical Abstracts of the United States*. Washington: U.S. Government Printing Office, 1976.

Tabershaw, I. "Facts in the future of preventive medicine." *ACPM Newsletter*, Vol. XVI (No. 4): 2, 1975.

## CHAPTER 3

Aronow, W. S. "Tobacco and the heart." *Journal of the AMA*, Vol. 229 (No. 13): 1799–1800, Sept. 23, 1974.

Benditt, E. P. "The origin of atherosclerosis." *Scientific American*, Vol. 236 (2): 74–85, Feb. 1977.

Berkson, D. M.; Stamler, L. J.; Lindberg, H. A.; Miller, W. A.; Stevens, E. L.; Soyugenc, R.; Tokich, T. J.; and Stamler, R. "Heart rate, an important risk factor for coronary mortality—ten-year experience of the Peoples Gas Co. epidemiologic study (1958–1968)." In Jones, R. J., ed., *Atherosclerosis Proceedings of the Second International Symposium*. New York: Springer-Verlag, 1970.

Brunner, D. "The influence of physical activity on incidence and prognosis of ischemic heart disease." In Raab, Wilhelm, ed., *Prevention of Ischemic Heart Disease, Principles and Practice*. Springfield, Ill.: Charles C. Thomas, 1966, pp. 236–43.

———, and Manelis, G. "Myocardial infarction among members of communal settlements in Israel." *Lancet*, Vol. II (No. 7159): 1049–50, Nov. 12, 1960.

Cooper, K. H.; Meyer, B. U.; Blide, R.; Pollock, M.; and Gibbons, L. "The important role of fitness determination and stress testing in predicting coronary incidence." Presented to New York Academy of Science meeting, Oct. 1976 (in press).

Cooper, K. H.; Pollock, M. L.; Martin, R. P.; White, S. R.; Linnerud, A. C.; and Jackson, A. "Physical fitness levels vs. selected coronary risk factors." *Journal of the AMA*, Vol. 236 (No. 2): 166–69, July 12, 1976.

Frank, C. W.; Shapiro, S.; and Sager, R. V. "Physical inactivity as a lethal factor in myocardial infarction among men." *Circulation*, Vol. 34 (No. 6): 1022–33, Dec. 1966.

Friedman, M., and Rosenman, R. H. *Type A Behavior and Your Heart.* New York: Alfred A. Knopf, 1974.

Golding, L. A. "Effects of physical training upon total serum cholesterol levels." *Research Quarterly,* Vol. 32 (No. 4): 499–506, 1961.

Haskell, W., et al. "Plasma lipids and lipoproteins in women runners." Presented to American Heart Association, Nov. 1975.

Holme, I.; Hjermann, I.; Helgeland, A.; Lund-Larsen, P. G.; and Leren, P. "Coronary risk factors and socioeconomic status: The Oslo Study." *Lancet,* Vol. II (No. 8000): 1396–98, Dec. 25, 1976.

Kannel, W. B.; Dawber, T. R.; Friedman, G. D.; Glennon, W. E.; and McNamara, P. M. "Risk factors in coronary heart disease: An evaluation of several serum lipids as predictors of coronary heart disease: The Framingham Study." *Annals of Internal Medicine,* Vol. 61 (No. 5, Pt. 1): 888–99, Nov. 1964.

Kannel, W. B., and Gordon, T., eds. *The Framingham Study: An Epidemiological Investigation of Cardiovascular Disease.* Sections 1–3, Washington: DHEW (NIH), 1968–1975.

Kannel, W. B., and Gordon, T., eds. *The Framingham Study: An Epidemiological Investigation of Cardiovascular Disease.* Section 30: Some Characteristics Related to the Incidence of Cardiovascular Disease and Death: Framingham Study, 18 Year Follow-up. Washington: DHEW (NIH) 74–599, Feb. 1974.

Kannel, W. B.; Gordon, T.; Sorlie, P.; and McNamara, P. M. "Physical activity and coronary vulnerability: The Framingham Study." *Cardiology Digest,* Vol. 6: 28–40, June 1971.

Lopez, A. "Heart Disease." *Mainliner,* Oct. 1975, p. 57.

Lopez, S.; Vial, R.; Balart, L.; and Arroyave, G. "Effect of exercise and physical fitness on serum lipids and lipoproteins." *Atherosclerosis,* Vol. 20: 1–9, 1974.

McGregor, M. "The coronary collateral circulation." *Circulation,* Vol. 52 (4): 529–30, Oct. 1975.

Miller, G. J., and Miller, N. E. "Plasma-high-density-lipoprotein concentration and development of ischaemic heart-disease." *Lancet,* Vol. I (No. 7897): 16–9, Jan. 4, 1975.

Morris, J. N.; Adam, C.; Epstein, L.; Chave, S. P. W.; Sirey, C.; and Sheehan, D. J. "Vigorous exercise in leisure-time and the incidence of coronary heart-disease." *Lancet,* Vol. I (No. 7799): 333–39, Feb. 17, 1973.

Morris, J. N.; Heady, J. A.; Raffle, P. A. B.; Roberts, C. G.; and Parks, J. W. "Coronary heart-disease and physical activity of work." *Lancet,* Vol. II (No. 6795) 1053–57,

Nov. 21, 1953 and Vol. II (No. 1503): 1111–20, Nov. 28, 1953.

Paffenberger, R. S., Jr., and Hale, W. E. "Work activity and coronary heart mortality." *New England Journal of Medicine,* Vol. 292 (No. 11): 545–50, Mar. 13, 1975.

*Planning Fat-Controlled Meals for 1200 and 1800 Calories.* New York: American Heart Association, 1966.

Prout, C. "Life expectancy of college oarsmen." *Journal of the AMA,* Vol. 220 (No. 13): 1709–11, June 26, 1972.

Richard, J. L.; Ducimetiere, P.; Elgrishi, I.; et al. "Quelques résultats concernant les facteurs de risque des cardiopathies ischémiques dans l'étude prospective Parisienne." *Giornale Italiano di Cardiologia,* Vol. 4: 350–65, 1974.

*Risk Factors and Coronary Disease; A Statement for Physicians.* New York: American Heart Association, 1968.

Stanton, G. A. "Diet and exercise in coronary heart disease." Letter to the Editor, *Lancet,* Vol. II (No. 7876): 351–52, Aug. 10, 1974.

Wilhelmsson, C.; Elmfeldt, D.; Vedin, J. A.; Tibblin, G.; and Wilhelmsen L. "Smoking and myocardial infarction." *Lancet,* Vol. I (No. 7904): 415–20, Feb. 22, 1975.

## CHAPTER 4

Cooper, K. H. "Guidelines in the management of the exercising patient." *Journal of the AMA,* Vol. 211 (No. 10): 1663–67, Mar. 9, 1970.

Dodge, R. E., Jr. "Instantaneous and sudden deaths." Letters to the Editor, *Journal of the AMA,* Vol. 226 (No. 10): 1229, Dec. 3, 1973.

Doyle, J. T. Personal letter received Nov. 3, 1975.

Friedman, M.; Manwaring, J. H.; Rosenman, R. H.; Donlon, G.; Ortega, P.; and Grube, S. M. "Instantaneous and sudden deaths." *Journal of the AMA,* Vol. 225 (No. 11): 1319–28, Sept. 10, 1973.

Haskell, W. "Cardiovascular complications during medically supervised exercise training of cardiacs." Presented to American Heart Association, Nov. 1975.

Kannel, W. B.; Doyle, J. T.; McNamara, P. M.; Quickenton, P.; and Gordon, T. "Precursors of sudden coronary death; Factors related to the incidence of sudden death." *Circulation,* Vol. 51 (No. 4): 606–13, Apr. 1975.

Mead, W. F.; Pyfer, H. R.; Trombold, J. C.; and Frederick, R. C. "Successful resuscitation of two near simultaneous cases of cardiac arrest with a review of fifteen cases occurring during supervised exercise." *Circulation,* Vol. 53 (No. 1): 187–89, Jan. 1976.

Pollock, M. L.; Dawson, G. A.; Miller, Jr., H. S.; Ward, A.; Cooper, D.; Headley, W.; Linnerud, A. C.; and Nomeir, M. M. "Physiologic responses of men 49 to 65 years of age to endurance training." *Journal of the American Geriatrics Society*, Vol. XXIV (No. 3): 97–104, Mar. 1976.

Pollock, M. L.; Miller, H.; and Wilmore, J. "Physiological characteristics of champion American track athletes 40–75 years of age." Proceedings Scientific Congress held in conjunction with XX Olympiad, Munich, Germany, 1972.

Puranen, J.; Ala-Ketola, L.; Peltokallio, P.; and Saarela, J. "Running and primary osteoarthritis of the hip." *British Medical Journal*, Vol. 2 (No. 5968): 424–25, May 24, 1975.

Schmidt, J. E. "Jogging can kill you . . . and that's not the half of it." *Playboy*, Vol. 23 (No. 3): 87, 152, 153, Mar. 1976.

Shepard, R. J. "Sudden Death—a significant hazard of exercise?" *British Journal of Sports Medicine*, Vol. 8 (No. 2): 101–10, Aug. 1974.

## CHAPTER 5

Bassler, T. J. "Marathon running and immunity to heart disease." *Physician and Sports Medicine*, Vol. 3 (No. 4): 77–80, Apr. 1975.

Cooper, K. H. "A means of assessing maximal oxygen intake." *Journal of the AMA*, Vol. 203 (No. 3): 201–4, Jan. 15, 1968.

———; Pollock, M. L.; Martin, R. P.; White, S. R.; Linnerud, A. C.; and Jackson, A. "Physical fitness levels vs. selected coronary risk factors." *Journal of the AMA*, Vol. 236 (No. 2): 166–69, July 12, 1976.

Epstein, F. H. "Coronary heart disease prevention." Letters to the Editor, *Circulation*, Vol. XLIX (No. 3): 595, Mar. 1974.

Morehouse, L. E., and Gross, L. *Total Fitness in 30 Minutes a Week*. New York: Simon and Schuster, 1975.

Wilmore, J. H., and Barnard, R. J. "Total fitness in 30 minutes a week." *Medicine and Science in Sports*, Vol. 8 (No. 1): ix, Spring, 1976.

## CHAPTER 6

Allen, T. H. "Measurement of human body fat: A quantitative method suited for use by aviation medical officers." *Aerospace Medicine*, Vol. 34 (No. 10): 907–9, Oct. 1963.

Anderson, T. W.; Reid, D. B. W.; and Beaton, G. H. "Vitamin C and the common cold: a double blind trial." *Canadian Medical Association Journal*, Vol. 107 (No. 6): 503–8, Sept. 23, 1972.

Anderson, T. W.; Suranyi, G.; and Beaton, G. H. "The effect on winter illness of large doses of vitamin C." *Canadian Medical Association Journal*, Vol. III: 31–6, July 6, 1974.

Atkins, R. C. *Dr. Atkins's Diet Revolution: The High Calorie Way to Stay Thin Forever*. New York: David McKay, 1972.

Ayres, S., Jr., and Mihan, R. "Nocturnal leg cramps (systremma): A progress report on response to vitamin E." *Southern Medical Journal*, Vol. 67 (No. 11), Nov. 1974.

"Balanced diet, recommended daily dietary allowances (RDA)." *The Health Letter*, Vol. IV (No. 6), 1974.

Ball, M. F.; Canary, J. J.; and Kyle, L. H. "Tissue changes during intermittent starvation and caloric restriction as treatment for severe obesity." *Archives of Internal Medicine*, Vol. 25 (No. 1): 62–68, Jan. 1970.

Bennett, I., and Simon, M. *The Prudent Diet*. New York: David White Co., 1973.

Brozek, J.; Grande, F.; Anderson, J. T.; and Keys, A. "Densitometric analysis of body composition: Revision of some quantitative assumptions." *Annals of the New York Academy of Sciences*, Vol. 110 (Pt. I): 113–40, Sept. 1963.

"Coffee and heart attacks." *Health Letter*, Vol. VII (No. 9), May 14, 1976.

Consolazio, C. F.; Nelson, R. A.; Johnson, H. L.; Matoush, L. O.; Krzywicki, H. J.; and Isaac, G. J. "Metabolic aspects of acute starvation in normal humans: Performance and cardiovascular evaluation." *American Journal of Clinical Nutrition*, Vol. 20 (No. 7): 684–93, July 1967.

Cowan, D. W. and Diehl, H. S. "Antihistaminic agents and ascorbic acid in the early treatment of the common cold." *Journal of the AMA*, Vol. 143 (No. 5): 421–24, June 3, 1950.

Dykes, M. H. M., and Meier, P. "Ascorbic acid and the common cold." *Journal of the AMA*, Vol. 231 (No. 10): 1073–79, Mar. 10, 1975.

Fessier, M., Jr. "Transcendental running." *Human Behavior*, Vol. 5 (No. 7): 16–20, July 1976.

Gilder, H.; Cornell, G. N.; Grafe, W. R.; MacFarlane, J. R.; Asaph, J. W.; Studenbord, W. T.; Watkins, G. M.; Rees, J. R.; and Thorbjarnarson. "Components of weight loss in obese patients subjected to prolonged starvation." *Journal of Applied Physiology*, Vol. 23 (No. 3): 304–10, Sept. 1967.

Herbert, V., and Jacob, E. "Destruction of vitamin $B_{12}$ by ascorbic acid." *Journal of the AMA*, Vol. 230 (No. 2): 241–42, Oct. 14, 1974.

Hofeldt, F. D.; Adler, R. A.; and Herman, R. H. "Postprandial hypoglycemia—fact or fiction?" *Journal of the AMA*, Vol. 233 (No. 12): 1309, Sept. 22, 1975.

Karlowski, T. R.; Chalmers, T. C.; Frenkel, L. D.; Kapikian, A. Z.; Lewis, T. L.; and Lynch, J. M. "Ascorbic acid for the common cold—a prophylactic and therapeutic trial." *Journal of the AMA*, Vol. 23 (No. 10): 1039–42, Mar. 10, 1975.

Keys, A. (Chairman). "Recommendations concerning body measurements for the characterization of nutritional status." *Human Biology*, Vol. 28: 111–23, 1956.

Lindner, P. "Doctors explain pros, cons of protein-sparing modified fast." *Internist Reporter*, Vol. III (No. 2), Feb. 1977.

Mayer, J. "Some aspects of the problem of regulation of food intake and obesity." *New England Journal of Medicine*, Vol. 274 (No. 13): 722–31, Mar. 31, 1966.

Maugh, T. H. "Coffee and myocardial infarction." *American Heart Journal*, Vol. 88 (No. 5): 672–73, Nov. 1974.

"New link between vitamin E and aging." *Executive Fitness Newsletter*, Vol. 6 (No. 1), Jan. 4, 1975.

Packer, Lester, and Smith, J. R. "Extension of the lifespan of cultured normal human diploid cells by vitamin E." *Proceedings of the National Academy of Sciences of the United States of America*, Vol. 71 (No. 12): 4763–67, Dec. 1974.

Pritikin, N.; Kaye, S. M.; and Pritikin, R. "Diet and exercise as a total therapeutic regimen for the rehabilitation of patients with severe peripheral vascular disease." Presented to American Congress of Rehabilitation Medicine, Nov. 19, 1975.

"Relaxation formula: jogger, sí! jigger, no!" *Physician and Sports Medicine*, Vol. 3 (No. 10): 16, Oct. 1975.

Ryan, A. J. (Moderator); Dempsey, J. A.; Gordon, E. S.; Foss, M. L.; and Oscai, L. D. "Charting the factors of fatness: A round table." *Physician and Sports Medicine*, Vol. 3 (No. 7): 57–70, July 1975.

Salmon, P. A. "The results of small intestine bypass operations for the treatment of obesity." *Surgery, Gynecology, and Obstetrics*, Vol. 132 (No. 6): 965–79, June 1971.

Sharman, I. M.; Down, M. G.; and Norgan, N. G. "The effects of vitamin E on physiological function and athletic performance of trained swimmers." *Journal of Sports Medicine and Physical Fitness*, Vol. 16 (No. 3): 215–25, Sept. 1976.

Stillman, I., and Baker, S. S. *The Doctor's Quick Weight Loss Diet*. Englewood Cliffs, N.J.: Prentice-Hall, 1967.

"Vitamin E: Miracle or myth." *Health Letter*, Vol. IV (No. 12), Dec. 27, 1974.

"Vitamins and mineral storage." *Health Letter*, Vol. VII (No. 8), Apr. 1976.

Whelan, E. M., and Stare, F. J. *Panic in the Pantry.* New York: Atheneum, 1975.

Williams, R. J. "The nutritional approach: How not to become an alcoholic!" *Executive Health,* Vol. III (No. 10) (no date).

Worthington, B. S., and Taylor, L. E. "Balanced low-calorie vs. high-protein–low-carbohydrate reducing diets. I. Weight loss, nutrient intake, and subjective evaluation." *Journal of the American Dietetic Association,* Vol. 64: 47–51, Jan. 1974.

Young, R, L.; Fuchs, R. J.; and Woltjen, M. J. "Chorionic gonadotrophin in weight control; a double-blind crossover study." *Journal of the AMA,* Vol. 236 (No. 22): 2495–97, Nov. 29, 1976.

Yudkin, J. "The low carbohydrate diet in the treatment of obesity." *Postgraduate Medical Journal,* Vol. 51: 151–54, May 1972.

Zuti, W. B., and Golding, L. A. "Comparing diet and exercise as weight reduction tools." *Physician and Sports Medicine,* Vol. 4 (No. 1): 49–53, Jan. 1976.

## CHAPTER 7

Boice, J. D., and Monson, R. R. "X-ray exposure and breast cancer." *American Journal of Epidemiology,* Vol. 104 (No. 3): 349–50, Sept. 1976.

Burkitt, D. P.; Walker, A. R. P.; and Painter, N. S. "Dietary fiber and disease." *Journal of the AMA,* Vol. 229 (No. 8): 1068–74, Aug. 19, 1974.

Christopherson, W. M.; Mendez, W. M.; Ludin, F. E.; and Parker, J. E. "A ten year study of endometrial carcinoma in Louisville, Ky." *Cancer,* Vol. 18: 554–58, May 1965.

Collaborative group for the study of stroke in young women. "Oral contraceptives and stroke in young women: Associated risk factors." *Journal of the AMA,* Vol. 231 (No. 7): 718–22, 1975.

"Estrogens and endometrial cancer." *FDA Drug Bulletin,* Feb.-Mar. 1976.

Gilbertson, V. A. "Proctosigmoidoscopy and polypectomy in reducing the incidence of rectal cancer." *Cancer,* Vol. 34 (Suppl.): 936–39, Sept. 1974.

Heinonen, O. P.; Slone, D.; Monson, R. R.; Hook, E. B.; and Shapiro, S. "Cardiovascular birth defects and antenatal exposure to female sex hormones." *New England Journal of Medicine,* Vol. 296 (No. 2): 67–70, Jan. 13, 1977.

Hoover, R.; Gray, L. A.; Cole, P.; and MacMahon, B. "Menopausal estrogens and breast cancer." *New England*

*Journal of Medicine,* Vol. 295 (No. 8): 401–5, Aug. 19, 1976.

McQuade, W. "Those annual physicals are worth the trouble." *Fortune:* 164–73, Jan. 1977.

"Mammography." *Medical Letter,* Vol. 17 (No. 16), (Iss. 432), Aug. 1, 1975.

Montagu, A. "Rehumanizing medicine." *New York Times,* Dec. 1, 1975, p. 13.

Moore, C. "Smoking and cancer of the mouth, pharynx, and larynx." *Journal of the AMA,* Vol. 191 (No. 4): 283–86, Jan. 25, 1965.

"Multiple fluoroscopies and breast cancer." *FDA Drug Bulletin,* Nov.-Dec. 1976.

*A New Voice for Preventive Medicine.* New York: American Health Foundation.

*1973 Cancer Facts and Figures.* New York: American Cancer Society, 1973.

Powers, J. H. "Prostosigmoidoscopy in private practice." *Journal of the AMA,* Vol. 231 (No. 7): 750–51, Feb. 17, 1975.

Reuben, D. *The Save Your Life Diet: High Fiber Protection from Six of the Most Serious Diseases of Civilization.* New York: Random House, 1975.

Scott, W. G. "Preventable and avoidable cancers and cancers arising from a personal indifference." Presented Annual Meeting of the Medical Association of the State of Alabama, Apr. 22, 1966.

"Serious adverse effects of oral contraceptives and estrogen." *Medical Letter,* Vol. 18 (No. 5): Feb. 27, 1976.

Smith, D. C.; Prentice, R.; Thompson, D. J.; and Herrmann, W. L. "Association of exogenous estrogen and endometrial carcinoma," *New England Journal of Medicine,* Vol. 293 (No. 23): 1164–67, Dec. 4, 1975.

Spark, R. "The case against regular physicals." *New York Times Magazine,* July 25, 1976, p. 10.

Sparks, J. *The Works of Benjamin Franklin.* Vol. 8, p. 12, Boston, 1839.

Spector, R.; Lightfoote, J. B.; Cohen, P.; and Chylack, L. T., Jr. "Should tonometry screening be done by technicians instead of physicians?" *Archives of Internal Medicine,* Vol. 135 (No. 9): 1260–62, Sept. 1975.

Stecker, R. H.; Devine, K. D.; and Harrison, E. G., Jr. "Verrucose 'snuff dipper's' carcinoma of the oral cavity." *Journal of the AMA,* Vol. 189 (No. 11): 838–40, Sept. 14, 1964.

Tabershaw, I. R. "Faith in the future of preventive medicine."

*American College of Preventive Medicine Newsletter*, Vol. 16 (No. 4), Dec. 1975.

Vickery, D. M., and Fries, J. F. *Take Care of Yourself: A Consumer's Guide to Medical Care.* Reading, Mass.: Addison-Wesley, 1976.

Vincent, R. G., and Marchetta, F. "The relationship of the use of tobacco and alcohol to cancer of the oral cavity, pharynx, or larynx." *American Journal of Surgery*, Vol. 106 (No. 3): 501–5, Sept. 1963.

*Vital Statistics of the United States.* Washington: DHEW PHS, 1973.

Wynder, E. L. "Overview: Nutrition and cancer." *Preventive Medicine*, Vol. 4 (No. 3): 322–27, Sept. 1975.

————, and Peacock, P. "The practice of disease prevention." *Journal of the AMA*, Vol. 229 (No. 13): 1743, Sept. 23, 1973.

Wynder, E. L.; Onderdonk, J.; and Mantel, N. "An epidemiological investigation of cancer of the bladder." *Cancer*, Vol. 16 (No. 11): 1388–1407, Nov. 1963.

Ziel, H. K., and Finkle, W. D. "Increased risk of endometrial carcinoma among users of conjugated estrogens." *New England Journal of Medicine*, Vol. 293 (No. 23): 1167–70, Dec. 4, 1975.

## CHAPTER 8

Alvarez, E., Jr. quoted in *President's Council on Physical Fitness and Sports Newsletter*, July 6, 1973.

Andrews, V. "The joy of jogging." *New York Magazine*, Vol. 10 (No. 1), Dec. 27, 1976/Jan. 3, 1977.

"Athletes: Their academic achievement and personal-social status." *Physical Fitness Research Digest*, Ser. 5 (No. 3): 6, July 1975.

Brown, R. S., and Smith, A. "A good sweat can lift your spirits." *Virginia-Pilot* (Norfolk), Oct. 3, 1975.

Cooper, K. H.; Purdy, J. G.; Friedman, A.; Bohannon, R. L.; Harris, R. A.; and Arends, J. A. "An aerobics conditioning program for the Fort Worth, Texas, School District." *Research Quarterly*, Vol. 46 (No. 3): 345–50, Oct. 1975.

Furlong, W. B. "The fun in fun." *Psychology Today*, Vol. 10: 35–38, 80, June 1976.

Glasser, W. *Positive Addiction.* New York: Harper and Row, 1976.

"Health practices and physical health status." *Physical Fitness Research Digest*, Ser. 6 (No. 2): 1–11, Apr. 1976.

Ismail, A. H., and Trachtman, L. E. "Jogging the imagination." *Psychology Today*, Mar. 1973, pp. 79–82.

Kennedy, C. C.; Spiekerman, R. E.; Lindsay, M. I.; Mankin, H. T.; Frye, R. L.; and McCallister, B. D. "One-year graduated exercise program for men with angina pectoris; evaluation by physiologic studies and coronary arteriography." *Mayo Clinic Proceedings,* Vol. 51 (No. 4): 231–36, Apr. 1976.

Killinger, R. Personal letter.

McQuaid, J. Personal letter, June 19, 1975.

Mitchell, C. "Billy Graham's amazing physical fitness program." *Reader's Digest,* July 1965.

Moran, Sheila. "Jogging: how to run after good health." *Harper's Bazaar,* Vol. 109 (No. 75): 75, 124, May 1976.

Proxmire, W. Preface in Cooper, K. H., *Aerobics.* New York: M. Evans and Co., 1968, pp. vii–viii.

Sheehan, G. "How to handle your enemy, the doctor." *NJA Newsletter,* Spring 1976.

"Thin executives." *Parade Magazine,* Nov. 23, 1969.

"Unsuspected reasons why exercise is your best investment in personal performance." *Executive Fitness Newsletter,* Vol. 7 (No. 4), Feb. 14, 1976.

## CHAPTER 9

Adams, G. M., and deVries, H. A. "Physiological effects of an exercise training regimen upon women aged 52 to 79." *Journal of Gerontology,* Vol. 28 (No. 1): 50–55, 1973.

Butler, N. R., and Alberman, E. D., eds. *Prenatal Problems. The Report of the 1958 British Prenatal Mortality Survey.* London: E. and S. Livingstone, 1969.

Charney, E.; Goodman, H. C.; McBride, M.; Lyon, B.; and Pratt, R. "Childhood antecedents of adult obesity: Do chubby infants become obese adults?" *New England Journal of Medicine,* Vol. 295 (No. 1): 6–9, July 1, 1976.

Christen, A., and Cooper, K. H. "Strategic withdrawal from cigarette smoking." (To be published in *Dental Clinics of North America,* Summer 1978.)

Cooper, K. H.; Gey, G. O.; and Bottenberg, R. A. "Effects of cigarette smoking on endurance performance." *Journal of the AMA,* Vol. 203 (No. 3): 189–92, Jan. 15, 1968.

Cooper, K. H.; Purdy, J. G.; Friedman, A.; Bohannon, R. L.; Harris, R. A.; and Arends, J. A. "An aerobics conditioning program for the Fort Worth, Texas, School District." *Research Quarterly,* Vol. 46 (No. 3): 345–50, Oct. 1975.

Cooper, K. H., and Zechner, A. "Physical fitness in U.S. and Austrian military personnel." *Journal of the AMA,* Vol. 215 (No. 6): 931–34, Feb. 8, 1971.

deVries, H. A. "Physiological effects of an exercise training regimen upon men aged 52–88." *Journal of Gerontology,* Vol. 25 (No. 4): 325–36, 1970.

Enos, W. F.; Holmes, R. H.; and Beyer, J. "Coronary disease among U.S. soldiers killed in action in Korea." *Journal of the AMA,* Vol. 152 (No. 12): 1090–93, July 18, 1953.

Gettman, L. R.; Pollock, M. L.; Durstine, J. L.; Ward, A.; Ayres, J.; and Linnerud, A. C. "Physiological responses of men to 1, 3, and 5 day per week training programs." *Research Quarterly,* Vol. 47 (No. 4): 638–46, Dec. 1976.

Graham, M. F. "Preventing coronary heart disease: The pediatrician's role." *Texas Medicine,* Vol. 70 (No. 6): 47–56, June 1974.

Heinzelmann, F., and Bagley, R. W. "Response to physical activity programs and their effects on health behavior." *Public Health Reports,* Vol. 85 (No. 10): 905–11, Oct. 1970.

Hennekins, C. H.; Jesse, M. J.; Klein, B. E.; Gourley, J. E.; and Blumenthal, S. "Cholesterol among children of men with myocardial infarction." *Pediatrics,* Vol. 58 (No. 2): 211–17, Aug. 1976.

Hershkowitz, M. "Penile frostbite, an unforseen hazard of jogging." Correspondence to *New England Journal of Medicine,* Vol. 296 (No. 3): 178, Jan. 20, 1977.

Holleb, A. I. "Cigarettes and teenage girls." *CA-A Cancer Journal for Clinicians,* Vol. 26 (No. 3): 191–2, May/June 1976.

Holman, R. L.; McGill, H. C., Jr.; Strong, J. P.; and Geer, J. C. "The natural history of atherosclerosis: the early aortic lesions as seen in New Orleans in the middle of the 20th century." *American Journal of Pathology,* Vol. 34 (No. 2): 209–35, Mar./Apr. 1958.

McNamara, J. J.; Molot, M. A.; Stremple, J. F.; and Cutting, R. T. "Coronary artery disease in combat casualties in Vietnam." *Journal of the AMA,* Vol. 216 (No. 7): 1185–87, May 17, 1971.

Pollock, M. L.; Dawson, G. A.; Miller, H.; Ward, A.; Cooper, D.; Headley, W.; Linnerud, A.; and Nomeir, A. "Physiologic responses of men 49 to 65 years of age to endurance training." *American Geriatrics Society Journal,* Vol. 24: 97–104, 1976.

Pollock, M. L.; Jackson, A.; Ayres, J.; Ward, A.; Linnerud, A. C.; and Gettman, L. R. "Body composition of elite class distance runners." *Annals of the New York Academy of Sciences.* (In press.)

Slovic, P. "Eating away precious minutes." *Runner's World* magazine, Vol. 9 (No. 11); 34–35, Nov. 1974.

Strong, J. P.; Eggen, D. A.; Oalmann, M. C.; et al. "Pathology and epidemiology of atherosclerosis." *Journal of the American Dietetic Association*, Vol. 62: 262–68, Mar. 1973.

Strong, J. P.; McGill, H. C.; Tejada, C.; and Holman, R. L. "The natural history of atherosclerosis; comparison of the early aortic lesions in New Orleans, Guatemala, and Costa Rica." *American Journal of Pathology*, Vol. 34 (Pt. 2) (No. 4): 731–44, July/Aug. 1958.

## CHAPTER 10

Dutton, R. E. "The executive and physical fitness." *Personnel Administration*, Vol. XXIX (No. 2): 13–18, Mar.-Apr. 1966.

"Fitness movement seen curbing high cost of illness to U.S. industry." *Commerce Today*, Vol. 5 (No. 9): 11–14, Feb. 3, 1975.

Humphrey, Hubert H. Bicentennial speech presented July 4, 1976.

"Keeping fit in the company gym." *Fortune*, Vol. 92 (No. 4): 136–43, Oct. 1975.

Knowles, J. "Wiser way of living, not dramatic cures seen as key to health. Preventive care to become more important." *Wall Street Journal*, Mar. 23, 1976.

"Staying in shape for the rigors of management '75: 2. . . . a sound body." An interview with Glenn Swengros. *Management Review*, Vol. 64: 12–17, Jan. 1975.

"Staying trim, productive . . . and alive." *Nation's Business*, Vol. 62: 26–8, Dec. 1974.

Stone, Florence. "Staying in shape for the rigors of management '75: 1. A sound mind . . ." *Management Review*, Vol. 64: 4–11, Jan. 1975.

"Will exercise improve *your* production?" *Pilot's Log* (New England Mutual Life Insurance Company): 1–10, Sept. 1976.

# Index

# ABOUT THE AUTHOR

DR. KENNETH H. COOPER, a former lieutenant colonel in the medical corps of the United States Air Force and senior flight surgeon, is the author of many books, including *Aerobics* and *The Aerobics Program for Total Well-Being,* which have sold thirteen million copies in twenty-two languages. The exercise program developed by Dr. Cooper has been featured in practically every major magazine; is the basis for the conditioning programs for many professional football teams and a number of NCAA colleges such as Nebraska; it is used in over 200 schools throughout the country as their basic physical education program; and is the official fitness program for both the U.S. Navy and Air Force. Dr. Cooper graduated from the University of Oklahoma in 1952, received his M.D. at the University of Oklahoma School of Medicine in 1956 and his M.P.H. from Harvard School of Public Health in 1962. He served his residency in aerospace medicine at the USAF School of Aerospace Medicine, Brooks Air Force Base, Texas; is a diplomate of the American Board of Preventive Medicine; and is a member of the following organizations:

* Fellow, American College of Preventive Medicine
* Fellow, American Geriatrics Society
* Fellow, American College of Sports Medicine
* Academy Member and North American Representative of the International Military Sports Council
* Member, American Federation of Clinical Research
* Director, National Jogging Association
* Advisor, Texas Chapter, American Physical Therapy Association

In 1974 Dr. Cooper received the Presidential Citation from the American Association for Health, Physical Education and Recreation. That same year he also received an honorary doctoral degree in science from Oral Roberts University. In 1968 Dr. Cooper received the National Jaycee Award for Leadership in Physical Fitness and in 1977 received the Lecturer of the Year Award from the International Platform Association. He now serves on the Governor's Committee for Physical Fitness for the State of Texas. After 13 years in the air force, Dr. Cooper left the service and set up the Aerobics Center, a preventive medicine center on 11½ acres in Dallas, Texas. He is considered by many to be the leading advocate of physical fitness in America today.